The European Monetary Union in a Public Choice Perspective

The Locke Institute

Founded in 1989, The Locke Institute is an independent, non-partisan, educational and research organization. The Institute is named for John Locke (1632–1704), philosopher and political theorist, who based his theory of society on natural law which required that the ultimate source of political sovereignty was with the individual. Individuals are possessed of inalienable rights variously defined by Locke as 'life, health, liberty and possession', or, more directly, 'life, liberty and property'. It is the function of the state to uphold these rights since individuals would not enter into a political society unless they believed that it would protect their lives, liberties and properties.

The Locke Institute seeks to engender a greater understanding of the concept of natural rights, its implications for constitutional democracy and for economic organization in modern society. The Institute encourages high-quality research utilizing in particular modern theories of property rights, public choice, law and economics and the new institutional economics as a basis for a more profound understanding of important and controversial issues in political economy. To this end, it commissions books, monographs and shorter studies involving substantive scholarship written for a wide audience, organizes major conferences on fundamental topics in political economy and supports independent research. The Institute maintains a publishing relationship with Edward Elgar Publishing. It also publishes its own monograph series.

In order to maintain independence, The Locke Institute accepts no government funding. Funding for the Institute is solicited from private foundations, corporations and individuals. In addition, the Institute raises funds from the sale of publications and from conference fees. The Institute is incorporated in the State of Virginia, USA, and enjoys non-profit, tax-exempt status under Section 501(c)3 of the United States Internal Revenue Code.

Officers of the Institute are listed above. Please direct all enquiries to the address given below.

4084 University Drive, Suite 103, Fairfax, Virginia 22030, USA
Tel: (703) 383 6952 Fax: (703) 352 9747
email: locke@thelockeinstitute.org
http://www.TheLockeInstitute.org

The European Monetary Union in a Public Choice Perspective

Jennifer C. Martin-Das

Earned her doctorate in economics from George Mason University, USA and is currently a Research Analyst at the Institute for Women's Leadership at Rutgers, The State University of New Jersey, USA.

THE LOCKE INSTITUTE

Edward Elgar

Cheltenham, UK • Northampton, MA, USA

Published by
Edward Elgar Publishing Limited
Glensanda House
Montpellier Parade
Cheltenham
Glos GL50 1UA
UK

Edward Elgar Publishing, Inc.
136 West Street
Suite 202
Northampton
Massachusetts 01060
USA

A catalogue record for this book is available from the British Library

Library of Congress Cataloguing in Publication Data
Martin-Das, Jennifer C., 1971–
The European Monetary Union in a public choice perspective / Jennifer C. Martin-Das.
p. cm. — (The Locke Institute series)
Includes index.
1. Economic and Monetary Union. 2. Monetary unions—European Union countries. Europe—Economic integration. I. Title II. Series.

HG925 .M376 2002
332.4'566'094—dc21

2001051072

ISBN 1 84064 561 X
Printed and bound in Great Britain by Biddles Ltd, *www.biddles.co.uk*

Contents

List of figures

List of tables

List of abbreviations

ADA	Americans for Democratic Action
OE	Austria
B	Belgium
BTO	Brussels Treaty Organization
CEEC	Committee for European Economic Cooperation
CAP	Common Agricultural Policy
CFSP	Common Foreign and Security Policy
CLM	Community Loan Mechanism
ECOFIN	Council of Economics and Finance Ministers
CM	Council of Ministers
COPA	European Farmers' Union
COREPER	Council of Permanent Representatives
DK	Denmark
ECA	Economic Cooperation Administration
EAEC	European Atomic Energy Community
ECB	European Central Bank
ECSC	European Coal and Steel Community
EC	European Community
ECU	European Currency Unit
EEA	European Economic Area
EEC	European Economic Community
EFTA	European Free Trade Association
EMA	European Monetary Agreement
EMCF	European Monetary Cooperative Fund
EMI	European Monetary Institute
EMS	European Monetary System
EMU	European Monetary Union
EPU	European Payments Union
EPU	European Political Union
ERM	Exchange Rate Mechanism
ERP	European Recovery Program
ESCB	European System of Central Banks
EU	European Union
EUA	European Unit of Account

EDP	Excessive Deficit Procedure
FOMC	Federal Open Market Committee
FRS	Federal Reserve System
FI	Finland
F	France
GMU	German Monetary Union
G	Germany
H	Greece
GDP	Gross Domestic Product
GNP	Gross National Product
GSP	Growth and Stability Pact
HICP	Harmonized Index of Consumer Prices
IGC	Inter-governmental Conference
IEPA	Intra-European Payments Association
EI	Ireland
IT	Italy
JHA	Justice and Home Affairs
LMU	Latin Monetary Union
L	Luxembourg
MTFA	Medium-term Financial Assistance system
MEP	Member of European Parliament
NATO	North Atlantic Treaty Organization
NL	Netherlands
OCA	Optimum Currency Area
OECD	Organization for Economic Cooperation and Development
OEEC	Organization for European Economic Cooperation
PO	Portugal
PR	Proportional Representation
QMV	Qualified Majority Vote
RoP	Rules of Procedure
SCU	Scandinavian Currency Union
STMS	Short-term Monetary Support system
SEA	Single European Act
ES	Spain
SW	Sweden
TEU	Treaty on European Union
UK	United Kingdom
VAT	Value Added Tax
VSTF	Very Short-term Financing

Preface

This book provides an analysis of the European Union institutions that participate in the policy-making process of the European monetary union. It employs concepts from the public choice literature to model the political marketplace of the EMU at the EU level. It examines the interaction between the European Council, Council of Ministers, European Commission, European Parliament and the European Central Bank. It notes the principal–agent relationship between the EU governing institutions and the supranational monetary authority, the ECB.

Following a review of optimum currency area theory, this book presents the empirical evidence on the suitability of EU countries for membership in a single currency arrangement. Economic heterogeneities and limited adjustment mechanisms shed strong doubt on the suitability of a common monetary policy. Fiscal limits on national debt constitute a further constraint on regional adjustment policy.

Differences in national monetary and fiscal policy preferences following economic shocks may lead to divergent policy demands within EU institutions. The win-set framework demonstrates how one or more countries may become disaffected by policy decisions along these dimensions in the presence of less than unanimous decision rules. Subsequent pressures upon representatives of disaffected national constituencies may lead to the withdrawal of such countries from the single currency arrangement and a return to sovereign currency systems.

This book is an outgrowth from my dissertation at George Mason University. I would like to thank my dissertation advisor, Dr. Charles K. Rowley, for his encouragement, support and guidance throughout the preparation of this book. I would also like to thank the members of my dissertation committee, Dr. Willem Thorbecke of the Economics Department at George Mason and Dr. Francesco Parisi of the George Mason School of Law. I owe a special debt of gratitude to Dr. Walter E. Williams, Professor and Chairman of the Department of Economics at George Mason, who kindly arranged financial support throughout my graduate study and encouraged me throughout the program. Generous financial support throughout my graduate study was provided by the Lynde and Harry Bradley Foundation and the George Mason Economics Department. Finally, I would like to express my gratitude to The Locke Institute for its invaluable assistance in the preparation of this book.

Acknowledgments

I wish to express my appreciation to the respective authors and/or publishers for their permission to reprint material from the following articles:

Kenen, Peter (1995), *Economic and Monetary Union in Europe: Moving Beyond Maastricht*, Cambridge, UK: Cambridge (Table 3. 1, p. 62).
Von Hagen, Jürgen and Manfred J.M. Neumann (1994), 'Real Exchange Rates Within and Between Currency Areas: How Far Away is EMU?', *The Review of Economics and Statistics*, **76** (2), 236–44 (Table 1, p. 238).

1. Introduction

The European Monetary Union (EMU) stands as one of the most important economic issues of the new millennium. For many European policy-makers, this project marks the pinnacle of the move towards European economic and political integration since the end of World War II. The success of this monetary arrangement depends upon the ability of European Union (EU)-level institutions to satisfy the monetary and fiscal policy demands of sufficient numbers of national constituents, interest groups and multinational corporations.

This book provides an analysis of the EU institutions that participate in the policy-making process of the EMU. Using concepts from the public choice literature, it examines the European Council, Council of Ministers, European Commission, European Parliament and the European Central Bank (ECB). It notes the potential principal–agent relationship between the EU-governing institutions and the supranational monetary authority, the European Central Bank.

Following a review of optimum currency area theory, the book presents the empirical evidence on the suitability of EU countries for membership in a single currency arrangement. Economic heterogeneities and limited adjustment mechanisms shed strong doubt on the suitability of a common monetary policy. Fiscal limits on national debt constitute a further constraint on regional adjustment policy.

Economic shocks may lead to divergent monetary and fiscal policy preferences among EU constituents. In response, domestic demanders of policy call on their national representatives to promote and secure policies favorable to their interests within the decision framework of the EU. Spatial models demonstrate how one or more country may become disaffected by policy decisions along these dimensions in the presence of less than unanimous decision rules. Subsequent pressures upon representatives of disaffected domestic constituencies may lead to the withdrawal of such countries from the single currency arrangement and a return to sovereign currency systems.

Chapter 2 provides a brief survey of Western European efforts at economic and political integration since the beginning of the nineteenth century. During this period, a number of customs and monetary unions formed and subsequently disbanded. The disintegration of these unions resulted from economic circumstances that drove national governments to undertake divergent policies.

Chapter 3 provides a brief survey of Western European efforts at economic and political integration since the end of World War II. The chapter concentrates on the affiliations and institutions that serve as the predecessors of the EU. The motivations for the integration that took place over this period were twofold: participating countries first sought to promote economic development and growth in the war-torn economies of the region; second, they sought to promote political cooperation in order to prevent further violent conflicts. The EMU evolved from the continued efforts at economic and political integration after the war.

Chapter 4 provides a theoretical overview of issues relevant to the creation and operation of currency unions drawing from the optimum currency area theory literature. Foremost among the criteria that define an optimum currency area is the suitability of a single monetary policy response to economic disturbances for the participating regions, particularly following economic disturbances. Whether or not a single monetary policy is suitable for one or more regional economies depends upon the similarity of economic disturbances and the operation of sufficient adjustment mechanisms. Adjustment mechanisms include, but are not limited to, real exchange rate flexibility, factor and output market flexibility, wage and price flexibility, industrial and portfolio diversification, economic openness and fiscal policy.

The institutional framework of a currency union also plays an important role in determining the success of single currency areas. The introduction of a currency union may include the transfer of monetary policy to a new central institution. This transfer implies that individual regions no longer retain authority over monetary and exchange rate policy. Fiscal policy may also be subject to constraints because of participation in a currency union.

Chapter 5 presents an overview of the issues relevant to the proposed EMU from optimum currency area theory and related empirical results. The consensus in the literature holds that the EU does not comprise an optimum currency area. In comparison with the US and Canadian currency unions, the EU does not possess the available adjustment mechanisms to respond sufficiently to economic disturbances.

The chapter also considers the motivations for and costs of participation in EMU, as well as the three-stage transition to EMU. Motivations are economic and political. Economic motivations include the goal of price stability, reduced exchange rate uncertainty and cost savings from a reduction in intra-EU currency conversions. Political motivations include the advancement of a political union within Western Europe, access to wider credit markets in a single currency and pecuniary transfers from the EU. The costs of participation in EMU stem from the constraints that participation in the currency union places on national monetary, exchange rate and fiscal policy.

Chapter 6 examines the implications of EMU for monetary and fiscal policy and institutions. Participation in the EMU implies that countries surrender monetary and exchange rate policy to the ECB. The latter directs the European System of Central Banks (ESCB), which includes the central banks of the participating countries. These banks serve as the national agents of the ECB. The EU possesses no central fiscal authority. Countries retain fiscal powers but face limits on the size of domestic debt levels and possible penalties for violation of these levels in accordance with the Growth and Stability Pact (GSP).

Chapter 7 introduces the rational choice approach to institutional analysis of actors within the political marketplace. These actors consist of policy brokers, demanders, and suppliers. These actors interact with each other in the political marketplace in a manner analogous to the consumers and producers of the commercial marketplace. Policy brokers differ from the producers of the commercial marketplace because they do not necessarily create new wealth by producing goods and services from various factor inputs. Rather, they affect transfers of existing wealth among different constituencies. The Council of Ministers, European Commission and European Parliament act as policy brokers at the EU level. Voters and interest groups act as policy demanders and suppliers. Members of the European Commission may also demand policies from the Council and Parliament.

Chapter 8 examines the role of the Council of Ministers, Commission and Parliament in monetary policy determination. Agenda power and decision rules play a limited role in the determination of monetary policy. The European Council, in particular, plays a decisive role in major policy matters. This body consists of national representatives that are responsible to domestic constituencies at the ballot box. The Treaty on European Union (TEU) holds the Commission and ECB accountable to the Council. The Parliament plays a very limited role in actual policy-making. For these reasons, the European Council may direct monetary policy within the EU.

Chapter 9 discusses economic shocks in the context of the EMU. A number of studies attempt to empirically determine whether regions of the EU are subject to asymmetric shocks. Differences in factor market regulations and industrial diversity affect the extent to which regions face asymmetric disturbances. Empirical evidence illustrates the existence of economic heterogeneity within the EU. Rigidities in national labor markets may increase the costs of adjustment to shocks to regional economies.

Chapter 10 presents a win-set model of the possible political implications of asymmetric macroeconomic shocks to the EMU. Empirical evidence indicates that national constituent support for elected politicians and for EU participation depends positively on the performance of the domestic economy. Based on majority rule, this model suggests that two or more countries may introduce changes in monetary and fiscal policy away from the *status quo*. Countries disaffected by such a European Council policy response, particularly in the face of a shock, but also alternatively because of an exogenous shift in tastes, may withdraw from the arrangement. Such withdrawal highlights the fact that no regime of fixed exchange rates is irrevocable.

2. European economic and monetary integration, prior to the creation of the European Communities

2.1 INTRODUCTION

The historical path to a European monetary union stretches back in time to early efforts at integration long before World Wars I and II. In the face of economic and technological development, as well as recurrent political and territorial conflicts, the integration of countries appeared as an alternative that would enable greater wealth creation and accumulation to participating countries. Advocates of integration boasted such potential benefits as access to larger markets, reduced barriers to trade, the avoidance of internal armed conflict, the provision of a stronger defense against common external enemies and greater negotiating power *vis-à-vis* other polities.

This chapter provides a historical overview of early efforts at European economic and monetary integration prior to the creation of the European Communities during the 1950s. Section 2 briefly reviews early attempts at integration in Europe prior to 1870. Section 3 reviews early attempts at monetary integration in Europe during the nineteenth century. Section 4 reviews European economic and political relations from 1870–1914. Section 5 reviews the economic and political situation in Western Europe from the beginning of World War I through the end of World War 11. Section 6 reviews the economic and political situation in Western Europe from 1945–52. The final section concludes with a review of the trends in European economic and monetary integration from a political economy perspective.

2.2 EARLY ATTEMPTS AT ECONOMIC INTEGRATION: 1800–1870

Calls for integration dot the history of the European continent. The Greeks (600–200 BC) raised perhaps the earliest suggestion of European integration. In the thirteenth century, the merchants of the Hanseatic League called for an enlarged economic sphere to realize greater returns from exchange from access to larger and more diverse markets and to eliminate profit-reducing barriers to trade. Religious thinkers of the Middle Ages (11–13th centuries) called for the integration of the states of Europe under the common bond of Christianity. Similarly thinkers of the Enlightenment (14–15th centuries) advanced the case for an integrated Europe on the basis of shared humanitarian ideals.

2.2.1 Economic Thought and Integration

Until the 1700s, mercantilist thought dominated international policy and economic affairs. Mercantilism saw nation states as competitors with each other in a struggle to amass wealth. The goal of national policy was to attain economic self-sufficiency. Countries sought to acquire gold in order to finance national defense and domestic expenditures. Trade barriers sought to promote exports and discourage imports. Protectionism, as advocated by mercantilists, was the order of the day.

Calls for integration began to challenge the mercantilist orthodoxy from the late eighteenth century. Pollard (1981, 12–14) identifies two approaches that characterize these renewed discussions of European integration. The first approach illustrates the case of integration motivated by economic interests. This economic approach emphasizes the potential for increased material wealth through the exploitation of advances in communications (postal and telegraph services), production (factory machines) and transportation (steam engines) technologies, newly built domestic infrastructure (railroads, roads and ports), and recently introduced standardized units of measurement (the Imperial and Metric systems) and timetables (Overturf 1986, 5). Integration would promote the dispersion and exchange of technical knowledge, widen the spectrum. of exchange, and lead to increased specialization.

The second approach illustrates the case of integration motivated by shared cultural heritage and common political concerns. Cultural motivations include a shared religious experience (Christianity) and common social and intellectual traditions. Political motivations include integrated transportation and infrastructure networks, prevention of military conflict in order to avoid the destructive effects of war and defense against common external enemies in order to retain existing sovereign arrangements. In 1693, William Penn prepared an essay providing for an assembly of representatives from across Europe to promote political cooperation and prevent further military conflict. Penn wrote this essay in light of the destructive effects of the Thirty Years' War (1618–48). Advocates of this approach included Abbé de Saint Pierre, Jean-Jacques Rousseau and Jeremy Bentham. The latter thinkers specifically promoted the creation of a European assembly and suggested a standing army.

Increasing developments in economic activities and relationships during the nineteenth century provided the motivation and opportunity for European integration. These advances enabled Europe to aspire to new heights of wealth accumulation. A brief look at the political geography of the continent reveals the direction integration has taken over the past 200 years.

2.2.2 The German Zollverein: An Example of European Integration

Germany provides an illustrative example. At the beginning of the 1800s, the present-day German State consisted of a large number of relatively small political units, in some cases corresponding to the size of contemporary US towns or counties. Such polities derived their jurisdiction from local or regional sovereigns or diocesan leaders. Many of these polities levied taxes on passers-by who were transporting goods through their lands, over their roads or along their waterways. These duties derived from long-standing privileges, exclusive rights or hereditary patents (Pollard 1981, 19).

This system of localized customs collection did not endure. In 1815, the various German states organized together in a Confederation and called for the reduction of barriers to trade. Between 1816 and 1818, the Prussian government introduced the Zollverein or German customs union of the small German states. The objective of the Zollverein was to replace the system of local customs duties with a uniform tariff on exports from outside of the union.[1] The Prussian-created Zollverein served as the foundation for the German Empire, which was formed in 1871.[2]

2.2.3 The Growth of European Trade Arrangements

At least a dozen additional states joined customs unions during the nineteenth century. In 1847, Moldavia and Wallachia formed their own customs union. The Swiss cantons formed a customs union in 1848. In 1849 two Italian provinces, Parma and Modena, acceded to the customs union between the Austrian provinces of the Habsburg Empire and Bohemia, which began in 1775. Hungary joined this union in 1850, followed by Croatia, Slavonia and Transylvania in 1857. In the same year, Russia and Poland formed a customs union of their own. The growth of customs unions attests to the expectations of positive returns to economic integration among European states in the 1800s.

Trade-liberalizing treaties emerged in addition to customs unions as a means of reducing the costs of intra-European trade. One school of thought behind freer trade originated in the UK. Manchesterism suggested that closer economic integration would increase the wealth of European countries, as well as eliminate the likelihood of destructive conflicts between them. The UK entered into the first trade treaty providing for a bilateral lowering of tariffs and the extension of most favored nation status to each member with France in 1860.[3] This treaty, known as the Cobden–Chevalier Treaty, was the first of a number of such treaties between European states. Subsequently, France signed such treaties with Prussia, Belgium, Italy, Switzerland, Sweden–Norway, the Hanse towns, Spain–Holland, Austria and Portugal.

2.3 EARLY ATTEMPTS AT MONETARY INTEGRATION: 1800–1914

Monetary integration efforts accompanied the growth of customs unions and bilateral trade treaties. Three major monetary unions formed during the nineteenth century in Western Europe. The first union represented the monetary integration of the German states. The second union, the Latin Monetary Union (LMU), grew out of the French monetary system. The third union, the Northern or Scandinavian Currency Union (SCU), developed among three of the Scandinavian states. A fourth major monetary arrangement, the international gold standard system, also developed in the 1800s.

2.3.1 The German Monetary Union

The first major monetary union to form in the nineteenth century was that of the German states. This union followed the formation of the Confederation of German States in 1815 and the Zollverein in 1834. The multitude of independent German states had previously employed a variety of different local coins. Growing economic and political relations motivated the move towards monetary integration in order to reduce the costs of exchange associated with currency conversions and exchange rate uncertainty.

Regional monetary integration marked the beginning of the path to a unified monetary system for the German states. In 1837, the German states south of the River Main signed the Munich Coin Treaty providing for a system of common coinage. A year later in 1838, the entire Zollverein partook in the Dresden Coin Convention, which granted full legal tender to the thaler and the florin in their respective regions of domination and union-wide legal tender of a hybrid money based on the two regional coins (Del Mar 1895). Silver provided the base for all of these coins.

The monetary union of German states met with success. In 1857, the Treaty of Vienna provided for the accession of Austria and a number of additional German states to the system. The Treaty also enabled local currencies to circulate beyond their issuing states as long as they held sufficient silver reserves to back them. In 1859, Austria withdrew from the German Monetary Union (GMU) having failed to adhere to the convertibility criteria for its own currency. The German states decided in 1866 to move from a silver to a gold standard. This shift was motivated in part by the change in relative prices of gold and silver due to recent silver discoveries. In 1876, the newly unified German State created its own central bank, the Reichsbank, and its own currency, the mark. Both institutions evolved from the monetary union of the German states and the Zollverein.[4]

2.3.2 The Latin Monetary Union

The Latin Monetary Union (LMU) developed from the French monetary system based on a bimetallic standard since 1803. Four countries signed the agreement formally establishing the LMU in 1865: France, Belgium, Switzerland and Italy. Members of the LMU accepted each other's coins at par and printed coins according to a specified weight and metal content. The 1865 meeting legally formalized the LMU and attempted to address the problem of fluctuating silver content in the coins of the members.[5]

In 1867, the French invited Great Britain and the United States, among other states, to the Paris International Exhibition to invite them to join the LMU in order to create a universal currency.[6] The UK and the USA declined to participate in the arrangement out of fears of the erosion of the bimetallic standard and a preference for the imposition of a gold standard. The LMU did not lead to a universal currency as hoped by France in spite of the expansion of membership in 1867 to Greece and the later alignment of the Spanish and Portuguese currencies to the Union's standard.

The LMU met with two major obstacles. The first obstacle arose in the 1850s with the discovery of gold in California, Russia and Australia. The price of gold dropped and led to massive hoarding of silver within the Union.[7] The second obstacle arose during the 1860s and 1870s. Large discoveries of silver in Nevada and Mexico, aided by improvements in silver extracting and processing techniques, as well as sales of silver in the LMU by Holland and Germany, which were moving to a gold standard, led to a major silver influx into the Union. Following this shift in supply, gold became relatively more valuable and the gold content of coinage declined for the same reason as in the earlier case of silver.[8] Excessive volatility plagued the bimetallic system of the LMU. For this reason, the union eventually adopted the gold standard de facto.[9]

2.3.3 The Scandinavian Currency Union

The Scandinavian Currency Union (SCU), also known as the Northern Monetary Union, was formed in the 1870s. Three countries, Denmark, Norway and Sweden, signed the treaty creating the SCU in 1872. However, due to the treaty's rejection by the Norwegian Parliament, only Denmark and Sweden undertook the creation of the arrangement. Three years later in 1875, the Norwegian Parliament rescinded its earlier decision and Norway entered the SCU.

The SCU exemplified a successfully operating currency union (De Cecco 1992). The union employed a gold standard as the base and introduced the krona as the unit of account. Participants accepted each other's coins and currency at par. By the mid-1880s, the central banks of the SCU extended non-discounted drawing rights to each other.

The SCU began to decline in the early years of the twentieth century (Bergman et al. 1993). The first step in this direction occurred in 1905 with the breakdown of Norway and Sweden's political union. Following this event, central banks stopped extending drawing rights at par to each other. The second step in this direction occurred in 1914 when the three states left the gold standard. From this period, money growth rates began to vary between countries and real exchange rates diverged from pre-war parities (Bergman et al. 1993). The final step occurred in 1921 after Denmark and Norway undertook a policy of exporting small coinage for redemption in large quantities to Sweden. Sweden responded to this policy by returning the coins to their countries of origin and eliminating the fixed rate of exchange between the currencies of the three states.

2.3.4 The International Gold Standard

The fourth monetary arrangement, which occupied a central role in world financial markets, was the international gold standard centered on the British pound sterling. Great Britain first legally adopted the gold reserve standard in 1821.[10] The gold standard operated with the exception of the years surrounding the Napoleonic Wars, 1797–1819, when convertibility was suspended. As the UK expanded into a global power with the growth of its colonial and imperial holdings, the pound sterling played an increasing role in international transactions and quickly became the predominant currency in the world monetary system.

The adoption of the gold standard by Germany in 1871 and the SCU bolstered the central role of the British gold standard. In the 1870s, the countries of the LMU gradually turned effectively to the gold standard. Russia, Japan and the United States also turned to the gold standard from 1879. The gold standard took on a central role in world financial markets, which lasted until the beginning of World War I.[11]

2.4 EUROPEAN ECONOMIC AND POLITICAL RELATIONS: 1870–1914

The last quarter of the nineteenth century marked a fundamental shift in European economic and political relations. This shift resulted from several real shocks that adversely affected the economies of the states of Western Europe. These shocks led to a shift away from economic integration and a movement towards domestic protectionism.

Simultaneously, national rivalries also began springing up between European states. These rivalries stemmed from strategic territorial concerns within Europe as well competition for colonial territories around the globe. These circumstances provided fertile ground for the growth of nationalistic pressures and the erection of barriers to trade.

2.4.1 Political Situation

The political situation of Europe became one of increasing national rivalries from 1870. The nation states of Europe had taken form by this time and countries were attempting to exert their independence within Europe and beyond.[12] The Franco–Prussian War of 1870–71 evidenced the growing rivalries between the French and German states. The initial motivation behind the war was the proposal of the accession of a member of the Prussian Hohenzollern family to the Spanish throne. France objected to this suggestion. Prussian Kaiser Wilhelm I permitted the withdrawal of this proposal. Nevertheless, subsequent antagonisms between the two countries led to war on July 19, 1870. The war came quickly to an end with the defeat of France in 1871 and the settlement contained in the Treaty of Frankfurt.

Rivalries continued to develop among European countries. In 1882, Germany, Austro-Hungary and Italy formed the Triple Alliance to support its members against their opposition in France and Russia. France, Great Britain and Russia later formed the Triple Entente as a counterpart to the Triple Alliance. Both groups stood effectively in opposition of each other during the period leading up to World War I and undertook the accumulation of vast stockpiles of armaments in anticipation of further military conflict.

External rivalries among European countries also grew during this period. Competition arose for the construction of vast colonial empires in Africa, especially. These empires represented sources of primary inputs to production and markets for European manufactures. Conflicts between France and Germany occurred in 1905–6 and 1911 over French attempts to colonize Morocco. Competition also arose between these countries and the UK, as the three attempted to carve out their claims to territories in Africa.

2.4.2 Economic Situation and Trade Relations

Following the Franco–Prussian War, a recession overcame much of Europe in 1873. Both industrial and agricultural sectors experienced real negative shocks. France, in particular, was vulnerable to these shocks due to its recent defeat in the Franco–Prussian War. France faced the burden of reparations payments to the German Empire and endured the loss of the regions of Alsace and Lorraine.

The first real shock to strike Europe affected the industrial sector. Vast quantities of manufactures from the United States challenged industrial products in Europe. US producers enjoyed superior production technologies, which enabled them to produce larger quantities of items at lower cost (Pollard 1981, 42–5). These costs were sufficiently low that, transportation costs notwithstanding, American imports were available at more competitive prices. Declining transportation costs accelerated this trend. Profit margins and revenues fell in the European industrial sector. In response to these events, industrial interests lobbied their governments for assistance and protection of their markets.

The second real shock that struck Europe affected the agricultural sector. Increasing grain imports from North America and India led to falling agricultural prices. Successive seasons of poor harvests reduced the crops and subsequently the revenues of European farmers (Pollard 1981, 42–5). Both events placed pressures on European farmers struggling to cover their costs of operation. Agricultural interests, like industrial interests, turned to their governments for assistance in the form of domestic subsidies and import barriers.

The industrial and agricultural shocks led to the migration of capital and labor. Capital flowed to regions where it could earn greater returns and labor flowed to regions where it could find employment. Although capital was the more fluid of the two factors, labor migration also took place on a large scale.[13] Eventually, these labor movements gave rise to national pressures for restrictions on labor migration. Restrictions on capital migration followed in the early years of the twentieth century.

Tariff increases marked the years surrounding the turn of the century. From 1878 until 1902, Germany implemented four rounds of increasing tariffs. Manufacturing and agricultural interests, in particular, collaborated in pressuring the German government for barriers to imports. Tariffs were seen as a method to satisfy domestic demands for protection, as well as a means to collect revenues for the state. France implemented its first tariff on grain imports in 1881. Tariff increases followed in 1885 and 1887. The Meline tariff of 1892 represented the response of the French government to continued agricultural and industrial pressures for protection.

A succession of tariff wars followed the rise of protectionist policies. Among these tariff wars were the Franco–Italian (1887–99), the Franco–Swiss (1893–95) and the Franco–Spanish (1882–85) (Pollard 1981, 58–9). The United Kingdom and the Netherlands were the only European states not increasing barriers to imports (Overturf 1986, 6).

2.4.3 Calls for Integration

Calls for economic integration persisted in spite of growing protectionist pressures. These calls focused on intra-European unions to the exclusion of non-European countries. Interestingly, proposals for economic integration arose from countries that were experiencing strong pressures for protection and were actively engaged in tariff wars. In 1879, Guido de Molinari of France launched the suggestion of a customs union of central European countries. His proposed union was to include Austria Belgium, Denmark, France, Germany, Holland and Sweden.

German Chancellor Bismarck resisted repeated proposals brought before him for central European economic integration. Hungarian Guido von Baussern proposed the creation of an Austro–German customs union to Bismarck. Subsequently, German economist Lujo Brentano advanced von Baussern's idea. In 1904, another German economist, Julius Wolff, organized the Mitteleuropaeische Wirtschaftsverein that promoted the idea of a central European customs union (Stirk 1996, 10). The Zollverein served as an exemplary model for customs unions and thus was an example others in Europe sought to imitate.

Growing nationalism accompanied rising protectionism. Countries increasingly pitted themselves in bitter conflict against each other for access to and control of productive resources and markets for their output. Interests organized not only along sectoral lines, but also increasingly along national lines. By the beginning of World War I military conflict replaced the political conflict and economic competition of the preceding century.

2.5 ECONOMIC AND POLITICAL SITUATION OF WESTERN EUROPE: 1914–45

From the beginning of World War I through the end of World War II, Western Europe endured a sequence of major economic, military and political conflicts. World War I marked the beginning of these troubles. By virtue of the advances that accompanied the Industrial Revolution, European economies found a host of new policy tools at their disposal and a myriad of economic and political hurdles to overcome. Failures in their endeavors to cross these hurdles resulted in the conditions, which led to World War II. Yet, in spite of these conflicts, calls for European integration continued to ring out.

2.5.1 World War I

The first of the major European military conflicts of the twentieth century, World War 1, began on July 28, 1914. The conflict originated between two countries, Austria and Serbia, but quickly expanded to incorporate the rest of Europe. The roots of the war lay in the growing economic and political rivalries of the preceding 50 years. Increased trade protection, successive trade wars, growing colonial rivalries, enlarged military arsenals, tensions between the Triple Alliance and the Triple Entente, and the rise of nationalism marked the European situation prior to the war. Recent conflicts in the Balkans (1908 and 1912–13) further exacerbated relations between the European countries.

World War I was the first global war of its kind. The European continent, as well as regions within Africa, Asia and the Middle East, was embroiled in the conflict. Battles waged between opposing sides within Europe and around the world in various colonial outposts. The United States entered the war in 1917 on the side of the Allied forces within Europe. The war, which was the first conflict to make use of technological advances in air, tank and submarine warfare, finally ended on November 11, 1918.

The Treaty of Versailles marked the final settlement after the end of World War I in 1918. The four Allied powers, Great Britain, France, Italy, and the USA, developed the Treaty at the Paris Peace Conference in January 1919. Six months later they signed the treaty that set up the Reparations Commission to determine the amount of reparations to be paid by the Germans, and provided for the cessation of all trade and production of war-related commodities in Germany and the demilitarization of the Rhineland. The Treaty also transferred the areas of Alsace and Lorraine from Germany to France and placed the Saar valley under the jurisdiction of the League of Nations for the next 15 years.

In addition, the Treaty of Versailles provided for the creation of the League of Nations. The League was to be the first global organization with the purpose of maintaining world peace. The idea for the League originated in Woodrow Wilson's Fourteen Points Plan (1918). The organization, however, met with limited success. One major factor behind this fate was the failure of the United States to ratify the Treaty of Versailles. Another factor was the exclusion of Germany. The Allies had barred the Germans from attending and participating in the Paris Peace Conference.

2.5.2 The Inter-war Years: Economic Situation

World War I served as a major shock to Western Europe. From the beginning of the War, the countries of Western Europe suspended the convertibility of currencies into gold.[14] The movement away from gold and the imposition of exchange controls were necessary to allow countries freedom from the requirements associated with the parities of their currencies against gold. Free from these restrictions, countries could protect gold and foreign exchange reserves and resort to the printing presses and short- and long-term debt markets to generate funds with which to pay for wartime expenses. The suspension of convertibility prevented the correct adjustment of exchange rates to reflect economic conditions.

The economies of Europe experienced significant fluctuations in the period immediately after the war. Following a short-lived boom driven by productive capacity that peaked during the war (1919–20), a major recession set in. Pressures for protectionist policies sprung up as countries sought to protect their domestic markets.[15]

After the war's end, the countries of Europe adopted floating exchange rates. Major depreciations ensued reflecting the effects of wartime inflationary finance and credit and inadequate fiscal revenues. Two further factors contributed to post-war currency valuations below their pre-war levels. First, countries needed high levels of imports, especially food and physical inputs to production in order to reconstruct their economies. The United States was an important source of grain and other foods, cotton and textiles, factory equipment and manufacturing inputs. Demand for foreign exchange with which to purchase these commodities placed further downward pressures on domestic currencies. Second, in the cases of Germany and Italy, the need to make reparations payments placed additional downward pressure on the mark and lira, respectively, *vis-à-vis* the other currencies of Europe.

The League of Nations called a conference to address the economic circumstances after the war in Brussels in September 1920. This conference had two objectives. The first goal was to convince countries to cease inflationary financing that characterized the period during the war. The second goal was to convince countries to cease deficit spending in order to bring down national debts. The League chose these goals in the hope that, if followed, they would end successive currency depreciations (Strakosch 1937, 155). The conference concluded without concrete proposals for the future.

The League of Nations undertook another attempt to assist in the post-war adjustment in 1922 with the Genoa Conference. The purpose of this conference was to plan a return to the gold standard. In an effort to secure a return to the relatively stable currency markets of the pre-war period, countries were eager to re-implement the earlier system. Most countries sought to return to the gold standard at their pre-war parities. This desire prolonged the time at which they could return to gold. The attendees of the Genoa Conference did not adopt the plan developed. However, the European countries later incorporated many of the outlined proposals in their post-war monetary regimes, including the institution of a gold exchange standard instead of the gold reserve standard of the pre-war period.

Another conference was held in 1924 to address the issues of German reparations payments and European reconstruction loans. The Treaty of Versailles had not identified the amount of payments due by the Germans and this matter quickly became a matter of contention. As a result of German failures to meet reparations obligations during the German hyperinflation, France and Belgium invaded the Ruhr valley in 1923.

The USA intervened by sending a representative, Charles Dawes, to convene a conference to resolve the matter. The Dawes Conference of 1924 devised a plan for German reparations payments, provided a loan to the German government to assist with these payments and with the post-war reconstruction of Germany, and arranged for the French and Belgian withdrawal from the Ruhr valley by 1925.

The Germans faced the greatest difficulties following the war as a major hyperinflation took over in the early 1920s.[16] Inflation reached over 200 percent (Dornbusch and Fischer 1988, 414). The German government eventually brought the hyperinflation under control through a comprehensive program of stabilization policies (Dornbusch and Fischer 1988). In August 1924, the Reichsmark replaced the Rentenmark at an exchange rate of one to one trillion. A loan from the Dawes Plan assisted the Reichsbank in its stabilization of the German monetary system and mandated the independence of the Reichsbank from the German government.[17,18]

Other European countries suffered from instability in their currencies. Italy endured two major crises. In 1921 and 1926, the Italian stock market experienced major declines. The first crisis occurred when a bubble in securities prices burst. The second crisis resulted from the overvaluation of the lira following its return to gold. France and Great Britain both experienced high inflation. French inflation exceeded 300 percent. The inflationary experience of Great Britain, where prices more than doubled, paled in comparison (Dornbusch 1988, 414). The French franc endured a major speculative attack in the winter of 1923–24. A large loan in March 1924 by JP Morgan prevented the franc from having to revalue (Kindleberger 1986, 33).

Gradually countries followed up on their individual desires to return to the gold standard. Great Britain returned to the gold standard in 1925, followed by Finland, the Netherlands and Sweden. The British returned at their pre-war parity, which represented an overvaluation given the country's post-war situation. Between 1926 and 1927, Belgium, Denmark and Poland returned to gold. Italy, France, Norway and Greece returned to gold in 1928, and Portugal followed in 1929.

Domestic concerns played a prominent role in post-war exchange rate policy and the return to the gold standard. Parities and changes in parities, meaning devaluations and revaluations, evolved from domestic pressures relating to concerns by agricultural and industrial producers, as well as labor interests (Simmons 1994). Exchange rate policy was a tool to affect the price competitiveness of domestic products on international markets, as well as a way to affect foreign currency and gold reserves. The stabilization of the franc in 1926 represented a compromise between the incumbent conservative leadership and the moderate left. The former focused on the goal of attaining currency stabilization that would promote the repatriation of capital while the latter focused on adopting a program of domestic stability that would promote social programs and domestic financial interests (Schmid 1974). The revaluation of the lira in 1927 also stemmed from the political desire of the leadership to advance policies favorable to large domestic interest groups (Cohen 1972).

The desired economic stability, however, did not materialize for a number of reasons. First, countries undertook plans to reintroduce and manage their currencies without sufficient cooperation with each other (Strakosch 1937, 157). Such cooperation might have facilitated the introduction of a stable currency system wherein central banks pursued shared policy goals.[19] Countries focused on attempting to relieve domestic concerns related to inflation and unemployment. Second, incorrect alignments to gold, meaning over- or undervaluations, resulted in speculative capital movements. The overvaluation of the British pound sterling in 1925 and the undervaluation of the French franc in 1926 both led to disequilibrium in the currency markets characterized by speculative flows.[20]

A second round of rising tariffs took place from the mid-1920s. Falling wheat prices sparked off these increases. Italy was the first country to raise its tariffs in 1925, followed by Germany and France in 1926. France also imposed a local content requirement on wheat by-products. The League of Nations responded to these tariffs with the World Economic Conference in 1927 (Kindleberger 1986, 64). The League's calls for the reduction of trade barriers failed to bring about a change in trade policies primarily because of domestic pressures for protection in Europe and the USA.

Domestic producers raised pressures for further protection at the end of the 1920s. One factor behind these pressures was continuing balance-of-payments difficulties and misaligned currencies. A second factor behind these pressures was the onset of the Depression. Falling prices and decreasing demand led to reduced revenues. Additional domestic subsidies, tariffs, quotas clearing arrangements and import restrictions followed (Strakosch 1937, 164).

Renewed monetary troubles sprung up around Europe towards the end of the 1920s. French monetary policy played a critical role in the franc's decline. A law of June 25, 1928 prevented the Bank of France from purchasing foreign exchange. Henceforth, the Bank could only purchase and retain reserves in gold. Gold subsequently flooded France from repatriated holdings abroad, as well as from speculators attracted by its below-market price. As gold left London for Paris, the overvalued British pound sterling underwent renewed pressures to devalue in 1929. In May 1931, the Austrian Kredit-Anstalt Bank collapsed. The Reichsbank experienced a large-scale capital flight in the following month. Bank runs also occurred in Czechoslovakia, Hungary, Poland

and Romania. On September 21, 1931, the UK suspended convertibility of sterling in response to a massive speculative attack.

Sweden followed the UK off gold on September 29, 1931. Norway, Denmark and Finland left in October 1931.

In June 1933, the League of Nations sponsored the World Monetary and Economic Conference to discuss the world's weak economies and the instability of world currencies. The conference was unable to propose a plan to remedy the situation. Gradually, however, the world economic situation began to improve from 1934. The prices of manufactures increased and trade expanded again. From 1934, Great Britain experienced growth in its automobile, chemical, electrical and housing industries (Kindleberger 1986, 240). During the early to mid-1930s, Germany and Italy began the manufacture of armaments to build up the arsenals for their respective war machines. France and Belgium undertook deflationary policies and allowed their currencies to revalue at rates closer to their market values from 1936. The Netherlands and Switzerland followed France and Belgium with deflations.

In October 1936, the USA, France and Great Britain signed the Tripartite Agreement. Although the Agreement provided no specific plan for the direction of policy, it indicated renewed international faith in the gold exchange standard at the new valuations and demonstrated a willingness on the part of these countries to engage in international cooperation on monetary matters. Renewed faith in the international economy brought an economic boom in the winter of 1936–37. A subsequent recession in 1937 caused further pressure for the erection of trade barriers. By 1938, however, the economies of Western Europe began to gear up for war again as Hitler began to pursue German expansion within Europe.

2.5.3 The Inter-war Years: Political Situation

World War I left deep scars in the political landscape of Europe. Four continental empires met with their demise in the course of the conflict: Austro–Hungary, Imperial Germany, the Ottoman Empire and Tsarist Russia. The Treaty of Versailles provided in part for new national boundaries illustrating the shifts in power and the birth of a number of countries in the North and East. The ambiguity remaining in the new demarcations, however, later served as a major point of contention.

Significant political shifts marked the two decades following the war in some parts of Europe. The National Socialist Party began its rise to power in Germany in the early 1920s. Founded in 1919, Hitler gained control over the party in 1921. The Party grew rapidly in popularity, largely because of the dire economic circumstances in the country. In October 1922, Benito Mussolini and his Fascist Party took power of the Italian government in Rome. France also endured domestic political upheaval during the inter-war years as a succession of governments entered and left office. The country underwent more than ten changes of regime during this period.

2.5.4 The Inter-war Years: Calls for Integration

In spite of the economic and political experiences of the European countries, proposals for integration began to reappear as early as 1922. Several factors motivated these proposals. First, destruction of wealth caused by the war gave rise to desires to prevent the reoccurrence of such an event. By binding together in a close economic and political system, it was thought that a repeat of the war could be avoided. Both the Allies and the aggressors faced enormous costs in terms of financial capital, property, productive capacity, human life and political strength.

Second, remaining ill-will between France and Germany represented a threat to peaceful relations on the continent. French displeasure with Germany due to its failure to deliver timely reparations payments was only one factor behind this discord (Kindleberger 1986). Similarly, Germany resented the French invasion of the Ruhr in 1923 and French demands for reparations payments which it felt excessive and which inhibited German efforts at rebuilding its economy.

The third factor stemmed from security concerns. Northern France and Belgium were the sites of the majority of the ground war in Western Europe and these countries harbored deep-seated resentment towards Germany. Both countries feared future aggressions by Germany into their respective territories.[21]

Two additional factors originating outside of Western Europe further fueled the integration fire. The first factor was the growing economic and political strength of the USA. Europeans worried about the USA becoming a major global power and thereby ascending to a dominant position in world trade and power politics. The second factor giving rise to concerns was the Bolshevik Revolution in Russia. Europeans worried over the recent internal instability within Europe and were apprehensive about security threats from the East.

Proponents of European integration stemmed from all over the continent. One of the first advocates was Austrian Count Coudenhove-Kalergi. In 1922, he founded the Pan-European Union to promote European unification. Coudenhove-Kalergi was dissatisfied with the League of Nations' efforts at the creation of a global order and worried about the stability of post-war Europe. In his 1923 pamphlet 'Pan-Europa', he called for a convention of European governments, the development of a protocol for negotiations and the creation of a customs union.

Additional proponents followed in the tradition of Coudenhove-Kalergi. In 1924, Leon Trotsky publicized his plan for a United Socialist States of Europe.

In the same year, integration advocates established the International Committee for a European Customs Union. In January 1925, Edouard Herriot, Prime Minister of France, publicly stated his wish for a United States of Europe (Pegg 1962). In May of the same year, the German Reichstag responded favorably to Herriot's proposal. No action, however, by the French or the Germans followed Herriot's suggestion. In 1929, French Foreign Minister Aristide Briande, launched the idea of a United Europe before the League of Nations. French security concerns in part motivated this idea. Briande's plan, which resulted in the formation of a study group on European Union at the League of Nations, however, fell by the wayside with the onset of the Depression.

The idea of European integration continued to occupy European intellectual discourse throughout the 1930s. Two schools of thought characterized the debate over European integration: the first advocated the functionalist approach; the second advocated the federalist approach.

Functionalism suggested that countries gradually integrate themselves sector-by-sector or policy area-by-policy area. Vested interests and cultural diversity might necessitate the continuation of national as opposed to supranational power leading to an inter-governmental approach (Curtis 1965, 14). In the 1950s and 1960s, noted integration scholar Ernst Haas suggested the gradual functionalist approach.[22] According to this view, integration would lead to spillover effects, which would extend from existing sectors or policy areas to additional sectors or areas.[23]

The second approach, federalism, called for a Western European federation with its own democratic structure. Federalists believed that a democratic European government would be able to transcend national rivalries. Federalists proposed the creation of a European constitution and European institutions with powers that superceded those of the individual.[24]

The efforts of these advocates of integration failed due to the economic and political realities of the period. First, the economies of the European powers were still suffering from the burden of World War I and the ensuing tumultuous behavior of domestic and international economic and monetary systems. Second, reparations remained a matter of contention between France and Germany. Third, no European country was prepared to undertake a customs union with its neighbors that might jeopardize its trading relationship with the United States.[25] Fourth, continental countries, especially France and Germany, realized that a European customs union might force Great Britain to choose between closer relations with Europe or with the British Commonwealth. Fifth, the early 1930s saw the arrival of a major recession. Agriculture suffered serious losses during this recession due to falling prices in the dairy, grain and sugar markets.

A number of efforts at the creation of customs unions during the inter-war period took place. Those efforts between small countries mostly succeeded, while those between larger countries failed. Small countries depended upon trade in order to obtain needed resources and to gain access to wider markets. In the 1920s, two customs unions between the smaller countries were formed. These unions were between Belgium and Luxembourg (1922) and Switzerland and Liechtenstein (1924). In 1939, an additional customs union formed between Italy, San Marino and Albania.

Efforts at the creation of larger unions in Europe met with failure. In 1930, the Scandinavian countries sought to create their own customs union, the Northern Customs Union. Two years later, the Benelux countries also attempted to form their own customs union. In both cases, objections by Great Britain led the countries to withdraw their plans for integration. Similarly, French objections to the proposed German–Austrian customs union of 1931 bore partial responsibility for its abandonment. Six months after Germany and Austria concluded this agreement, the Permanent Court of International Justice of the League of Nations decided against the plan (Stirk 1996, 39).

The larger countries were less reliant on relations with each other. The UK, for example, had close relations with the countries of its vast empire. The Ottawa Agreement of 1932 provided for a preferential trading arrangement among the members of the Commonwealth. Such relations led to a diversion of British trade away from continental Europe (Pollard 1981, 70). Germany also was less concerned with enhanced trading relations with its Western European neighbors. Growing nationalistic aspirations, combined with the ambiguous boundary demarcations to the East, led Germany to look increasingly to the East for trading. Germany entered a number of clearing arrangements with Eastern countries, for example with Hungary (February 1934), Yugoslavia (May 1934) and Romania (March 1935), to affect a bartering of goods in order to preserve foreign exchange (Stirk 1996, 43).[26]

2.5.5 World War II

The second of the major European military conflicts of the twentieth century, World War II, began in the fall of 1939. The conflict originated with German aggressions under Adolf Hitler's Nazi regime. Following his rise to the position of German Chancellor in 1933, Hitler quickly moved to assert German power in Europe. The roots of the war in Europe lay primarily in the unchecked growth of nationalism in Germany during the inter-war period. This growth resulted from the dire economic circumstances in which the country found itself from the end of World War I. The inability of Western European countries to resolve their domestic difficulties during the inter-war period bore partial responsibility for the rise of Nazism in Germany and Fascism in Italy. Expansionist desires by Stalin's government in the Soviet Union contributed further to the development of the conflict.

World War II was the second global war of its kind. The European continent was embroiled in the conflict, along with regions in northern Africa and Asia. The Germans and Russians were the dominant forces within the Axis powers.[27] The Germans led most of the aggressions by Axis powers within Europe. The German–Soviet alliance ended in June 1941 with the German invasion of the Soviet Union. The British and the Americans were the dominant forces within the Allied powers. Following the German invasion of the Benelux countries and France, the task of defending the last vestiges of free Europe fell to the British, aided by the Americans and the members of the Resistance throughout the occupied areas. The UK and the USA rapidly mobilized their economies to support the war effort. Armaments manufacture and the production of food and textiles increased dramatically.

The German drive for expansion met with a major setback with the German defeat by the Soviets in early 1943 in Stalingrad. Soviet troops forced the German forces back to the West. Over the course of the next two years, the German war machine met with its demise. Years of pursuing Hitler's expansionary dreams wore down the country, economically, morally and politically. Hitler's efforts at eastward expansion left the western front vulnerable to the attacks of the Allies, strengthened by the assistance of the Americans. The Allies finally ended the conflict in 1945.

The leaders of the USA, USSR and the UK convened two meetings during 1945 to discuss plans to end German aggressions in Europe. The Yalta Conference was the first of these meetings and took place from February 4–11, 1945.[28] The second meeting took place from July 17 until August 2, 1945 in Potsdam following the German surrender in May 1945. This meeting planned for the division of Germany into three zones of occupation and for a central administrative authority in charge of the German state after the war. The Allies, in fact, divided Germany into four zones that the Americans, British, French and Soviets controlled, respectively.

World War II brought destruction on a scale unseen before in Europe. German destruction stemmed not only from Allied offenses, but also from several factors peculiar to its own policy. First, its limited resources at the beginning of the war caused it to depend heavily on acquired territories for food, armaments and other supplies. Second, Hitler's limited economic foresight and his haste for power resulted in a gross neglect of the preservation and promotion of the gainful industry necessary to sustain his war machine and the regions under his domination. Likewise, the Nazi practice of looting reduced the productive capabilities of conquered regions. Third, Hitler rejected proposals for the creation of customs unions and currency unions among the territories under German control.[29,30] Fourth, the clearing arrangements devised by Germany with its eastern territories quickly became a means of acquiring tribute (Stirk 1996, 59).

Allied suffering resulted from austere economic policies and the concentration of production on armaments for war, as well as German air, land and sea attacks. The Germans targeted military and commercial infrastructure on the continent and on the isle of Great Britain. These attacks leveled much of Europe and left the bulk of its productive capacity in heaps of rubble. At the war's end, the countries of Western Europe were left to reconstruct their economies with limited resources, reduced gold reserves and little foreign exchange.[31]

The ruin that accompanied this conflict, however, would not have been possible without the technological advances that occurred in the inter-war period. Improved transportation facilitated the rapid deployment of troops and improved aeronautical technologies enabled the extensive use of air strikes (Lieberman 1992, 1). Targets of attack included communication and transportation lines, bridges, ports, industrial centers and seats of power. The Allies and Axis powers, alike, destroyed these structures in efforts to weaken each other. The results of the campaign of destruction in Europe were catastrophic.

2.5.6 Calls for Integration

Calls for European integration arose both during and after the war. Two notions motivated these calls. The first notion advocated integration as a way to promote the growth of European economies that had struggled since World War I and had endured growing protectionism since the last quarter of the previous century. The second notion advocated integration as a way to avoid further armed conflict on the continent (Lieberman 1992, 2).

These calls stemmed from all parts of Europe. One of the earliest calls for integration came from the UK. In September 1939, Lord Davies urged the British to advocate a United States of Europe (Stirk 1996, 51). Two years later, a group of Italian federalists set forth their Ventotene Manifesto that suggested a federal government for the European states. In the same year, German Helmuth von Moltke proposed an inter-governmental arrangement for Europe consisting of a council and a democratically elected legislative assembly (Stirk 1996, 60–61). Members of the Resistance also put forward calls for integration. These calls were driven by a desire to prevent future armed conflict. These thinkers also acknowledged the possibility of explosive consequences of united nation-states in a binding federation. To some extent, however, these calls were overshadowed by the tainted image of European integration as advanced by the Nazis (Stirk 1996, 60).

The years from 1914 to 1945 marked a tumultuous period in European history. Economic and political conflict was rampant during these years. Nationalistic policies in which countries attempted to enrich and empower themselves at the expense of other countries ultimately led to the second major conflict within

30 years. This conflict and the policies that led to it served as major motivating forces behind the drive for European economic and political integration.

2.6 ECONOMIC AND POLITICAL SITUATION OF WESTERN EUROPE: 1945–52

Following the end of World War II, the countries of Western Europe focused their energies on the reconstruction and re-establishment of their respective economies and polities. Economic and political affiliations among Western European countries began to form in the second half of the 1940s. These organizations sought to promote the reconstruction of the economies of Western Europe and to form a basis for peaceful political relations within the region.

2.6.1 Political Realities

The political situation of Western Europe at the war's end reflected the events of the preceding war years. The UK emerged as the sole undefeated country and the only country to remain unoccupied. The British government under Winston Churchill led the country to victory in Europe on May 8, 1945. The Labour Party defeated the Conservative Party in a General Election on July 26, 1945 and Churchill relinquished the Prime Ministership. Clement Attlee took over as Prime Minister and led the country into the post-war period.

Germany divided France into two zones during the war: the Germans occupied the northern zone and placed their own administrative government in office led by Marshall Petain; the southern zone retained its own government in the form of the collaborationist Vichy regime. Following the war, the country was left to install a new government for the entire country. General Charles de Gaulle was elected French President on a platform of re-establishing French political leadership and separating the Rhineland from Germany.

German-administered governments ruled the Benelux countries, Denmark and Norway, until the Allies' victory. These countries faced the need to re-elect national governments. The governments of Ireland, Sweden and Switzerland maintained their sovereignty throughout the conflict. However, all three countries attempted to cooperate with Nazi Germany. Irish desires to collaborate with the Nazis were preempted by British threats of invasion. Sweden served as a supplier of inputs to the manufacture of war material. Switzerland operated as banker to Hitler's Germany. These governments faced the task of operating in a Europe hostile to the Nazi movement, but eager to get back on its feet. Portugal and Spain also received gold stolen by the Nazis, but likewise retained their sovereignty.[32]

The Allied victors permitted the re-establishment of a sovereign German State, the Federal Republic of Germany (FRG), on May 24, 1949. This country consisted of the western parts of Germany that the British, French and Americans had occupied. The eastern part of Germany remained under Soviet occupation and governance. The Allied powers forbade the development of an armed force by the new German State.

2.6.2 Economic Realities

The immediate priorities facing European governments following the war included the provision of food, the purchase of fuel and fertilizer, the repair and reconstruction of factories, housing and infrastructure, the re-establishment of their currencies and the reintroduction of international trade. As a result of the destruction of the war, the economies of Western Europe lacked the necessary funds with which to finance their reconstruction. The USA and the Soviet Union appeared as the possible sources for the needed support. The USA took up the task of providing aid to the region. Its motivation was rooted in self-interest: Europe provided markets for its exports. Weak demand abroad would adversely affect its domestic industries. More importantly, Europe would not be able to move forward without outside assistance. Similarly, the expansion of Soviet hegemony westward posed the threat of further Communist encroachment. In the interests of maintaining the emerging balance of power, the USA stepped forward to take on the role of European benefactor.

Successive harsh winters threatened the recovery in the agricultural sector from 1946. The bad weather led to poor crop harvests. Adverse effects were felt in at least two areas: food supplies for humans and livestock, and crops for sale. Mass starvation loomed as a grave threat (Lieberman 1992, 1).

A growing dollar shortage threatened the overall economic recovery, particularly in the industrial sector, from the war's end. Western European countries imported machines and raw materials in large quantities from the USA. These imports required payments in dollars. Scarce European exports to the USA implied the accumulation of few dollar reserves with which to pay for purchases of US goods. Exchange controls sought to preserve dollar reserves, but were unable to round up sufficient amounts to cover imports.

Two proposals arose in 1941 to provide for the institution of international clearing arrangements in order to promote the settlement of international payments obligations. Although neither of these plans was adopted, they contributed to the provisions that established the Bretton Woods monetary system, along with the International Monetary Fund and the International Bank for Reconstruction and Development (Lieberman 1992, 19–20). The Bretton Woods plan provided for a system of fixed but adjustable exchange rates based upon the US dollar that undertook a fixed parity with gold. Countries deemed a fixed, but adjustable, exchange rate preferable to a floating arrangement because of their experience with floating rates during the 1930s that was marked by instability.

The USA endeavored to assist the countries of Western Europe in their reconstruction via the Marshall Plan. US Secretary of State, General George C. Marshall, first proposed the assistance provided by the Marshall Funds on June 5, 1947. These funds were made available on the condition that the European countries undertake a cooperative plan to reconstruct their economies (Lieberman 1992, 16).

The first endeavor to this end was a conference held in Paris from July 12 through September 22, 1947. The countries of Western Europe, with the exception of Spain, created the Committee of European Economic Cooperation (CEEC) to manage the proposed European Recovery Program (ERP). In light of this progress, the US Congress voted in favor of the Foreign Assistance Act that provided for the Marshall Plan on April 3, 1948. The Congress also passed the Economic Cooperation Act that established the Economic Cooperation Administration (ECA) to monitor the disbursement of US Marshall Funds in Europe. Over four years, the OEEC handled the disbursement of $12 billion of funds for reconstruction from the Marshall Fund.

In April 1948, the CEEC also decided to continue operation after the Marshall Plan funds ended and thereby developed the treaty creating the Organization for European Economic Cooperation (OEEC). The goals of the OEEC included European economic cooperation, increased agricultural and industrial output, resolution of the dollar shortage and elimination of inflation. Germany became a member of the OEEC in October 1949. In 1960, the OEEC changed its name to the Organization for Economic Cooperation and Development (OECD) and expanded its membership to include non-European countries.

2.6.3 Post-war Integration

The motivations for European integration following World War II fan into two categories: economic and political. Economic motivations centered on the need to rebuild European industries, maintain access to markets, prevent rising unemployment and ensure access to productive inputs, especially raw materials. During the war, European countries directed productive resources to the manufacture and development of armaments to the exclusion of products unrelated to the support of the war effort. This practice held for both the Allies and the aggressors.

Political motivations behind integration following the war centered on fears of security and political threats from within and security threats from without. Internal security fears stemmed from concerns over renewed German aggressions in the future. Internal political fears stemmed from the rise of the Left in post-war elections and the associated fears of a Communist takeover. Following the war, Leftist parties entered office in Belgium, France, the UK, Italy, the Netherlands and Norway (Lieberman 1992, 5). The success of these parties resulted in part from their active role in the Resistance, as well as the performance of the Right-wing governments that ruled during the war. Internal concerns also included the prevention of the large-scale nationalism characteristic of the 1930s. Many Europeans held nationalism and its associated protectionist and beggar-thy-neighbor policies responsible for the circumstances that led to World War II.

External fears stemmed from concerns over Soviet advances from the East. Fears of Communist and Soviet aggressions grew from 1948 following the Communist takeover of Prague in March and the Soviet blockade of Berlin in April. Furthermore, the inability of the globally oriented League of Nations to prevent or contain the aggressions that led to World War II provided grounds for skepticism about the efficacy of this organization to maintain peace. For this reason, a regional solution held appeal.

The federalist–functionalist debate occupied center stage in the discussions about European integration. Advocates of the federalist approach came mostly from those countries that the Germans had occupied during the war. These states included France, Italy and the Benelux countries (Kitzinger 1964, 4). The federalists saw an integrative political approach as the path to follow. This approach included the creation of European institutions that assumed supranational powers. Federalists thought that such a framework would prevent the rise of nationalistic tendencies in order to prevent future conflicts and would present a single regional stance to the rest of the world in matters of foreign policy.

The UK and the countries of Scandinavia adhered to the less inclusive functionalist approach (Kitzinger 1964, 4). The functionalists were reluctant to transfer sovereign power to a central supranational authority. Rather, they saw European integration as a process where cooperation took place on a sectoral or policy issue-by-policy issue basis. Inter-governmental meetings and institutions would be responsible for directing regional cooperation.

The UK represented the most ardent opposition to European integration. The reasons for this position are several. First, Great Britain was the only country to remain unoccupied and undefeated in the recent conflict. Second, Great Britain felt little endearment to either of the other major European countries that would belong to an integrated association: France and Germany. Third, Great Britain sought to preserve its close commercial and political relations with the USA. Uncertainty existed regarding whether or not British affiliation with a European regional associated would be perceived unfavorably.[33] Fourth, Great Britain played a central role *vis-à-vis* its Empire and the Commonwealth. These countries offered supplies of inputs to production and markets for its products. British trade with Europe represented less than one-third of its international trade. Of this amount, British trade with the Scandinavian countries constituted a significant part (Wallace 1990, 74).

To promote economic reconstruction and political cooperation, and to dispel fears of aggression from the East, the countries of Europe undertook the creation of a number of affiliations. One of the first cooperative endeavors following the war was between Great Britain and France. The primary motivation behind this agreement was European security. On March 4, 1947, the two countries signed the Dunkirk Treaty, which provided for either country to support the other in the event of future German aggressions. In part, British concerns about a weak French government following de Gaulle's resignation on January 20, 1946 and the rise of Communism in France motivated this Treaty.

The first cooperative economic endeavor was between the Benelux countries. The smaller countries of Europe hoped to gain access to raw materials, additional markets and needed foreign exchange through economic integration. In 1946, Belgium and the Netherlands stated their desire to participate in a customs union agreement. Finally, on October 29, 1947, the Benelux countries signed the treaty creating the Benelux Economic Union. The Benelux customs union eliminated tariffs between the three member countries and imposed a common external tariff on non-member imports.

A year later, on March 17, 1948, the Benelux countries, France and the UK signed the Brussels Pact, creating the Brussels Treaty Organization (BTO), which would serve as a regional defense organization. This body represented an expansion of the earlier Dunkirk Treaty between Great Britain and France. The BTO was an inter-governmental body led by a council of foreign ministers from each of the member countries. In addition, the BTO also created a standing military force known as UNIFORCE (Curtis 1965,13).

The BTO reorganized to include the United States, Canada, Denmark, Iceland, Italy, Norway and Portugal to become the Atlantic Alliance on April 4, 1949. This body operated to promote cooperation in defense matters among its members. Members of the Atlantic Alliance, notably the UK, had insisted on this reorganization in light of the re-establishment of Germany. Great Britain saw the BTO as a potential counterweight to Germany. A year later, in 1950, the Atlantic Alliance revised its statutes and changed its name to the North Atlantic Treaty Organization (NATO).

In December 1947, the International Committee for the Coordination of Movements for European Unity announced its intention to convene a meeting in The Hague from May 7–10, 1948. This Congress, headed by Winston Churchill, prepared the plan for the Council of Europe. This body would promote political cooperation and negotiation among its members.[34]

In 1949, ten countries signed the statute creating the Council of Europe, known as the Treaty of London. These countries included the signatories to the Brussels Pact (1948) and Denmark, Ireland, Italy, Norway and Sweden. The Council of

Europe was an inter-governmental body among European countries that would serve as a parliamentary assembly that would make decisions according to majority rule. The unanimity rule took effect instead of majority rule and the body never attained the amount of decision-making power its members initially hoped for (Salmon and Nicolle 1997, 38). Since its inception, the Council has expanded to include 24 additional European and Mediterranean countries.

The next decade brought the inception of several additional Western European affiliations. These organizations included the European Coal and Steel, Economic and Atomic Communities. These organizations served as the institutional foundation for the European Union which would later strive to implement an economic and monetary union among the countries of Western Europe.

2.7 CONCLUSION

This review of European economic and monetary history of the past century and a half reveals some important patterns. The first pattern is the tendency for sovereign countries to pursue economic policy that reflects the preferences of domestic constituents. International agreements notwithstanding, governments succumb to pressures by domestic groups to adjust policy. In times of economic weakness, countries resort to various forms of economic intervention including monetary policy, trade policy and price and wage controls. The second pattern is the tendency for countries to raise calls for European integration in order to gain access to resources and markets and to enjoy economies of scale. The third pattern is the tendency for intellectuals to advocate integration as a potential remedy for repeated conflicts. These calls tend to ignore contemporary economic interests. Yet, precisely these economic interests drive the political process and the forces that enable or disable integrative measures. The fourth pattern is for European countries to resort to military conflict following a succession of economic, political and territorial disputes.

NOTES

1. Observers have suggested opposing motivations for the creation of the Zollverein. One approach asserts that the Prussians instituted the union in order to reduce the costs of customs collections in order to increase net revenues and to promote internal trade. Another approach asserts that the Zollverein represented an attempt on the part of the states themselves to reduce the costs of trade between them and to encourage the movement of goods. A third approach posits that the Prussians intended the Zollverein to assist them in consolidating their power over the German states.
2. For more on the Zollverein and nineteenth-century European trading arrangements, please see: (1) William Otto Henderson (1959), *The Zollverein*, London: Frank Cass (1st edn 1933); and, (2) William Otto Hendersen (1962), *The Genesis of the Common Market*, London: Frank Cass.

3. Interestingly, Overturf (1986) writes that the UK lowered its tariffs to zero on all French imports except for wine. France reduced its tariffs on British imports to a maximum remaining tariff of 25 percent.
4. Holtfrerich (1993) notes that the Reichsbank was but a transformation of the already existing Prussian Bank created in 1847.
5. The LMU had in fact been gathering adherents since 1832. In this year, Belgium first accepted French coins as legal tender. Switzerland entered into an arrangement with France for the use of its silver coins in 1850, two years after the Swiss cantons created a monetary union among themselves. Italy then joined the French currency-based monetary system in 1862 and agreed to accept Belgian and Swiss coinage as well.
6. Attendees of the convention debated two fundamental matters (Perlman 1993, 21–3). The first issue concerned the choice of monetary standard. The options under consideration were a gold, silver or bimetallic standard. The convention decided that the bimetallic standard would eventually be replaced by a gold standard. The concerned states never made any plans for the transition, so the bimetallic standard of the French system remained. The second issue concerned the choice of legal tender across countries, as well as the ability of such a currency to serve as a universal unit of account. The latter issue was a matter of contention because of the reigning coinage arrangement in the UK, which was based on a duodecimal system. No change from the *status quo* ensued.
7. The silver content of coinage declined as individuals attempted to retain the relatively more valuable metal in accord with Gresham's Law.
8. So much silver continued arriving that the states of the LMU finally decided in 1874 to limit the right of coin issuance to governments themselves. This decision led to massive exports of silver coinage by the Italian government in an attempt to garner returns from seigniorage at the expense of the other states. The central banks of the LMU eventually decided to redeem foreign coins only up to what they considered reasonable limits. Subsequent to this decision, excessive coinage exports ceased out of fear of the direct return of these issues to the originating country and the resulting inflationary pressures that would follow (Flandreau 1993, 505).
9. For a closer examination of the LMU, please see: Henry Parker Willis (1902), *A History of the Latin Union*, Chicago: University of Chicago Press.
10. Prior to this time, the UK had effectively employed a gold standard since 1717. Eichengreen (1992b, 4) notes that the gold standard took over the UK's bimetallic monetary system as a result of the overpricing of gold in terms of silver.
11. Gradually, a dominant relationship sprung up between the central countries of the international gold system that promoted the smooth operation of the system, The central countries included the UK, France and Germany. The Bank of England undertook the task of setting parities and maintaining convertibility, while the central banks of France and Germany stood willing to supply reserves to the Bank of England when it needed them. A relationship developed between these countries and the other countries adhering to the gold standard that Eichengreen (1992b) terms a core-periphery or leader–follower relationship.
12. In 1830, Belgium became independent of the Netherlands. In 1861, the Italian states unified. And, in 1815, the German Confederation formed, marking the beginning of the organization of the German Empire that was formed in 1871.
13. The first wave of labor migration targeted North America. Successive waves of migration moved within Europe. The majority of intra-European migration was temporary in nature, with workers returning to their native countries within a number of years (Pollard 1981, 47–8).
14. The UK's abandonment of the gold standard was perhaps the most far-reaching event in this regard given its central role in international currency markets
15. Kindleberger (1986, 61) offers three motivations for these post-war pressures. First, industries, which had developed during the war years in the absence of international trade, sought barriers to competing imports. Second, the countries carved out from the former Austro–Hungarian Empire demanded protection from competitors in more established states. Third, industry and agriculture desired protection from exports that were facilitated by competitive currency devaluations.
16. Two theories attempt to explain the hyperinflation. The first theory asserts that the Reichsbank ran the printing presses to supply the needs of the German government as it engaged in war.

Increasing amounts of money led to strong inflationary pressures. High inflation led to current account deficits and ultimately a massive depreciation of the mark (Bresciano-Turroni 1931). The second theory asserts that enormous fiscal burdens after the war to cover reparations and imports necessary to rebuild the country resulted in rising balance-of-payments deficits. The ensuing depreciation of the mark further raised the cost of imports and led to rising prices. The Reichsbank responded to these price rises by turning to the printing presses with the goal of preventing the growth of unemployment (Laursen and Pedersen 1964).

17. The commitment of the German central bank to low inflation originated in the aftermath of this hyperinflation. As a result of the German stabilization program, interest rates rose and foreign funds flowed into Germany in large amounts. Borrowed funds contributed to the reconstruction of German industry and state and local facilities and infrastructure (Kindleberger 1986, 27).
18. German reparations payments came up for renewed debate in 1929. Germany refused to make scheduled increases in payments out of concern for destabilizing the already fragile Reichsmark. US intervention again led to the convention of an international conference to resolve the matter. Owen Young led the conference that replaced the Dawes Plan and provided for a reduction in German obligations. Two years later, President Hoover called for a one-year moratorium on reparations payments in response to the Great Depression. A year later, the Lausanne Conference reduced the remaining payments to negligible amounts in light of the German monetary situation.
19. The cooperative relationship between the UK, France and Germany, which had enabled the pre-war system to generate the satisfactory results it did, was not re-created (Eichengreen 1992b).
20. These misalignments also affected the countries' respective balance of payments. France, for example, saw an improvement in its balance of payments as French capital returned from overseas. This flow of capital into France included French holdings of gold from London, thus leading to a decline in the gold supplies in the UK. The British balance of payments deteriorated as a result of these capital movements.
21. In 1925, the Locarno Pact reiterated the French and Belgian borders with Germany as stated in the Treaty of Vienna. France, Belgium, German, the UK and Italy were all signatories to this treaty. One matter that the treaty neglected, however, was the demarcation of Germany's borders to the East.
22. Haas's 1958 *The Uniting of Europe* (Stanford, 1958) has become a classic in the field of European integration studies. Another classic in the field is Leon Lindberg's *The Political Dynamics of European Economic Integration* (Stanford, 1963).
23. Jean Monnet and Robert Schuman largely adhered to this school of thought as can be seen by their advocacy of the coal and steel, economic and atomic communities that were created in the 1950s.
24. Altiero Spinelli belonged to this school of thought, which had less of an impact on the European Communities until the 1980s.
25. European states feared US retaliation to any efforts at economic integration. The 1922 Fordney–McCumber Tariff Act and the 1930 Smoot–Hawley Tariff Act evidenced the strength of US producer interests. The weak markets of Europe wanted to provide no cause for further restrictions.
26. Eastern Europe appeared to be a natural trade partner for Germany given the complementarity of the two regions' economies. Germany was primarily a producer of manufactured goods and Eastern Europe a producer of agricultural commodities (Stirk 1996, 44).
27. Italy also belonged to the Axis powers. However, it entered the war belatedly in June 1940. Italy's only successful aggressions preceded World War II and were limited to the takeover of Ethiopia (1935–36) and the occupation of Albania (1939).
28. An earlier conference took place between the three leaders in April 1944 in Teheran. During this session, Churchill and Stalin advocated the creation of a supranational European body following the war in order to prevent further military conflicts in Western Europe in the future. Roosevelt opposed their idea of a regional authority out of fear it might weaken any global authority.

29. Germany was to subordinate its possessions, not to enter cooperative exchange arrangements. The exceptions to this practice were the customs unions between Germany and Luxembourg, the Netherlands, Bohemia and Moravia. Later efforts at customs unions with Denmark and Slovakia failed (Stirk 1996, 57–8).
30. Walther Funk, German Minister of Economics, opposed a European currency or customs union including the southeastern parts of Europe due to the dissimilarity between Germany and the countries of that region. (Quoted in Stirk 1996, 57–8 from W. Lipgens (ed.) (1984), *Documents on the History of European Integration*, Volume 1, Berlin. 63.)
31. The UK, in particular, found itself with major balance-of-payments difficulties as the war's end brought the end of the US Lend–Lease Agreement and the beginning of its payments on the huge debt it owed the USA.
32. Spanish dictator, Francisco Franco, had earlier received support from the German National Socialists and the Italian Fascists during his struggle to gain power in the Spanish Civil War of the mid-1930s.
33. Former US President Franklin Roosevelt preferred the establishment of a global political order to regional orders and the British did not want to provide cause for American upset.
34. France and Britain were instrumental to the development of the bodies of the Council of Europe. The French proposed a legislative assembly for the Council. The British responded with a proposal for a Council of Ministers accompanied by an assembly comprised of government-appointed delegates who voted as a single group representing their respective country. The British were reluctant to sacrifice any sovereignty to an inter-governmental or supranational body (Stirk 1996, 104). The British were also mistrustful of the French, who had turned down their offer of assistance via an Anglo–French union prior to the German invasion of France during World War II (Schlaim 1940, quoted in Stirk 1996, 79). The structure of the Council included a Council of Ministers and an assembly of representatives from the member states. However, the members of the assembly voted individually and received appointments as decided by each state on its own.

3. European economic and monetary integration: the creation and development of the European Communities

3.1 INTRODUCTION

The post-World War II period saw the creation of a number of Western European economic and political associations. Three major organizations established in the 1950s formed the basis of economic and political integration in the region for the succeeding decades. These organizations were the European Coal and Steel Community (ECSC), the European Economic Community (EEC) and the European Atomic Energy Community (EAEC), which later merged and became the European Union (EU). The proposed European Monetary Union (EMU) represents the culmination of the efforts of the European Communities to integrate the economies of their countries.

This chapter provides a historical overview of the creation and development of the European Communities from 1950 until the present. Section 2 reviews the formation of the European Coal and Steel, Economic and Atomic Communities during the 1950s. Section 3 reviews the major developments within the Communities, along with the first calls for monetary integration among Community member countries, during the 1960s. Section 4 reviews monetary integration attempts, in the form of the snake-in-the-tunnel and the European Monetary System (EMS), during the 1970s. Section 5 reviews the progression towards economic and monetary integration during the 1980s. Section 6 reviews the development of the Treaty on European Union (TEU), which provides for the EMU, and the progress made towards this goal during the 1990s. The final section concludes with a review of the trends in European monetary integration.

3.2 THE FORMATION OF THE EUROPEAN COMMUNITIES: 1950–59

The 1950s brought the formation of a number of Western European economic and political affiliations. Economic integration began with the creation of the European Payments Union (EPU), which extended the regional clearing arrangements formed after World War II. Economic integration proceeded, first, along sectoral lines in the form of the ECSC, and later extended to other areas in the forms of the European Economic and Atomic Communities. These associations incorporated an institutional framework, which drew from other Western European associations, and later merged into the institutions of the EU.

3.2.1 Motivations to Integration

Two primary concerns motivated the establishment of these affiliations. These concerns were economic recovery and growth, and the prevention of future armed conflict between Western European countries, particularly arising from Germany. Through regional integration, the countries of Western Europe sought to reduce intra-European barriers to trade, facilitate access to neighboring markets, diminish their need for American economic assistance, reduce their use of the dollar in transactions and prevent the growth of nationalistic rivalries and aggressions.[1]

The task of rebuilding domestic economies continued into the 1950s. By 1952, the Marshall funds ceased to flow into Western Europe, and the countries faced the need to sustain themselves economically. Two matters hampered economic development in Western Europe. These matters served as the motivating forces for the integration of Western European economies.

The first matter consisted of the various trade barriers that impeded intra-European exchange. Tariffs and quantitative restrictions remained in place from the inter-war and World War II periods. These barriers served to maintain artificially high prices, limit foreign imports and preserve international reserves. Capital controls also remained in place in order to prevent capital movements that might place pressure on fixed exchange rates.

The second matter consisted of the shortage of dollars experienced by these countries. Following the war's end, many countries owed debts to the USA for loans extended during the war, assistance provided after the war, and for the payment of purchases of US exports needed following the war. The demand for dollars with which to repay or purchase American exports of goods and/or capital placed downward pressure on Western European currencies. Western European dollar reserves diminished and countries were unable to purchase European exports with convertible currency. The countries of Western Europe possessed insufficient reserves with which to pay for their American imports. This shortage of dollars became known as the dollar gap. Balance-of-payments deficits grew in Western Europe.

3.2.2 The European Payments Union

Payments arrangements between the countries of Western Europe began springing up as early as 1947. In part these arrangements developed in response to the shortage of dollars in Western Europe. These arrangements also served to assist Western European economies in the face of devaluations and balance-of-payments difficulties. In 1947, the UK was the first country to attempt to return its currency to convertibility. This effort failed miserably, meeting with massive losses of foreign reserves at the Bank of England. The UK devalued the pound sterling and kept it at this rate until 1967. The UK did not allow convertibility of the pound sterling until 1958.

In December 1947, the Benelux countries signed the First Agreement on Multilateral Monetary Compensation. This agreement provided for a clearing system between the states, which would reduce foreign exchange transactions in settlement of trade between each other. The British and American-controlled zones of Germany later joined in the agreement. The Intra-European Payments Agreement (IEPA) replaced the earlier agreement in September 1948. All members of the Organization for European Economic Cooperation (OEEC) participated in the IEPA. A second IEPA replaced the first upon its expiration in June 1949.

The EPU supplanted the Intra-European Payments Agreements in 1950. The OEEC and the USA together devised the EPU to facilitate intra-European transactions in order to reduce the deployment of restrictive trade measures. The USA assisted in the development of the EPU in the face of the dollar shortage. The dollar gap closed in 1952 (Wallace 1990, 42). The OEEC developed the EPU to be a more permanent arrangement than its predecessors. Members would settle their net obligations on a monthly basis with the EPU instead of on a bilateral basis with their trading partners. When members faced severe payments difficulties, the EPU would assist through a system of temporary credits (Ungerer 1997, 27). The EPU was the first post-war affiliation to include the Federal Republic of Germany.

The EPU operated until December 1958 when the European Monetary Agreement (EMA) succeeded it. The return to convertibility of the currencies of the United Kingdom and the members of the ECSC precipitated the abolition of the EPU according to the conditions for its operations from the Treaty creating it (Lieberman 1992, 38). The EMA codified signatories' intentions to maintain exchange rates within ±0.75 percent of their par values.

3.2.3 The European Coal and Steel Community

The European Coal and Steel Community (ECSC) was the next major step towards economic integration. The French proposal for the ECSC followed American and British calls for increases in the quotas of German steel production.[2,3] At Jean Monnet's suggestion, French Prime Minister Robert Schuman developed and presented the Schuman Plan, which called for the creation of a European association with supranational authority over coal and steel. Monnet desired the creation of an affiliation between France and Germany, which would be able to attract the participation of the United Kingdom (Wallace 1990, 20). The Schuman Plan served as the basis for the treaty providing for the ECSC.

An Inter-governmental Conference (IGC) convened in Paris from June 20–27, 1950 to finalize the details of the plan. France, Germany, Italy and the Benelux countries signed the Joint Declaration establishing the ECSC on April 18, 1951. The ECSC regulated the extraction, production, pricing and distribution of coal and steel commodities in its member states. These commodities included coal, coke, iron ore, pig iron, crude steel and finished rolled products (Keesing's Research Report 1975, 7). The Treaty took effect on July 25, 1952 and on August 10, 1952 the High Authority of the ECSC assumed power.[4]

The ECSC introduced four institutions: the Council of Ministers, the High Authority, the European Assembly and the Court of Justice. The Council of Ministers consisted of the ministers of the various government divisions from each of the respective countries. The Council of Foreign Ministers oversaw the overall development of Community policies and relations, whereas specific ministers attended to issues within their individual policy spheres. The High Authority consisted of nine members appointed from the member countries. These members were to act independently of the interests of their country of origin and, rather, to focus on Community interests. The European Assembly consisted of representatives from each of the member countries placed in office according to national procedures. The number of representatives of each country roughly corresponded to its population size. The Common Assembly of the Council of Europe served as the model on which this body was designed. The Court of Justice served to observe the accordance of Community policy and the operation of the Community's institutions with the ECSC Treaty.

Varying motivations drove the countries to participate in the ECSC. French motivation stemmed from a desire to limit German industrial expansion, particularly in heavy manufacturing, in order to restrict the growth of its economic and political strength. Coal and steel were essential to the heavy industries, which had developed at the core of manufacturing in Europe and had been integral to both of the major war efforts of the twentieth century. Since the inter-war period, the locations of these industries were matters of dispute. Following both wars, the French had sought to gain control of the German Ruhr and Saar valleys. French coal and steel producers, eager to handicap their competitors in Germany, were quick to avail themselves of France's relative political strength at the time (Kirschen et al. 1969, 2). The Benelux countries' participation sprung from the importance of the coal and steel industries to their economies, as well as the need for access to French and German markets in these industries. Italian participation resulted from its desire to demonstrate its commitment to economic and political cooperation with Western Europe

(Wallace 1990, 21). German participation resulted from the limited options available for the development of these industries given the existing political economic circumstances in Western Europe.

Great Britain decided against joining the new organization. The British refused to affiliate such key industries as coal and steel in an organization that would have the power to dictate policy in these sectors. The British government had nationalized the coal and steel industries after the war's end. Membership in the ECSC would have placed an important element of British industrial policy under the control of a European supranational authority. British labor unions also stood against this possibility (Kitzinger 1964, 18).

The UK offered an alternative plan for closer Western European relations in the coal and steel industries. Their plan minimized the extent of supranational authority granted to the association by subordinating it to the existing Council of Europe. The French, however, especially Jean Monnet, opposed this plan (Stirk 1996, 130–31).

Nevertheless, the UK sought to initiate closer relations with the association in order to retain its economic and political ties with the member countries. In addition, the British coal and steel industry desired access to the relevant European markets. On December 21, 1954, the British government entered into an arrangement with the ECSC that would allow trade barriers between British coal and steel industries and the ECSC to fall, if not cease to exist. This arrangement began operation on September 23, 1955 (Keesing's Research Report 1975, 8). In May 1955, Switzerland entered a similar bilateral arrangement with the ECSC.

3.2.4 The European Economic and Atomic Communities

Plans for further integration among the members of the ECSC proceeded in the mid-1950s. First, these plans were motivated in part by the faltering of the ECSC. A recession in the coal and steel industries overcame the ECSC in 1954. Second, OEEC efforts to reduce Western European trade barriers during the first half of the 1950s did not satisfy all of the countries of Western Europe. The Netherlands complained that the OEEC measures neglected tariff reductions and exempted government acquisitions (Stirk 1996, 36–7; Kitzinger 1964, 17). However, the UK and France opposed further liberalization measures within the OEEC. Both countries had imperial holdings around the globe and feared that trade liberalization in Western Europe would adversely affect their trading relationships overseas. The UK in particular, was also concerned about its extensive trading relationship with the USA, which it did not wish to endanger as a result of preferential trading arrangements within Europe. France and Germany undertook a number of bilateral agreements in the coal and steel areas with each other (Archer and Butler 1996, 24–5). The other members of the ECSC worried about the potential dissolution of the association.

Jean Monnet again advanced the drive for Western European integration in November 1954. Monnet called upon the members of the ECSC to develop proposals for integration in additional sectors (Archer and Butler 1996, 24–5). The foreign ministers of the six ECSC members meeting in Messina in June 1955 appointed the Inter-governmental Committee on European Integration to devise a plan for Western European cooperation in atomic research and development and for a customs union (Kitzinger 1964, 18). Belgian Foreign Minister, Henri Spaak, led this committee. The committee's proposal appeared on April 21, 1956. The Spaak Report served as the basis for the economic and atomic communities formed by the Treaty of Rome.

The Treaty of Rome created the European Economic Community (EEC) and Atomic Energy Community (EAEC), respectively. The membership of these communities was the same as that of the ECSC, namely, France, Germany, Italy and the Benelux countries. The EEC was to be a customs union among member countries. The EEC would reduce intra-Community tariffs on industrial goods and erect a common external tariff on such commodities.[5] Euratom was to be an association that promoted research and development of atomic energy and regulated inputs into the production of nuclear energy.

The objectives of the EEC were to be accomplished in several phases. The customs union would be phased in over a 12-year transitional period, starting on January 1, 1958. Tariff reductions would occur in three phases, each lasting four years. In 1959, the EEC implemented its first round of tariff reductions among member countries. The Common External Tariff would also be implemented in a series of three phases starting on January 1, 1962. Both of these measures were to be completed by the end of the transitional phase in 1970 (Kitzinger 1964, 29).

Several factors motivated the creation of the EEC. First, members expected that a European customs union would expand trade between members and enable them to gain access to wider markets. Trade would expand as a result of the reduction of trade barriers, in particular, tariffs. EEC members expected that trade expansion would promote economies of scale and scope in production, as well as increased knowledge spillover. Second, EEC members sought to reduce their economic dependence on the USA. Third, the EEC sought to contain the growth of Germany within a larger Western European framework (Dedman 1996, 59, 61–2, 67).

Several factors motivated the creation of the EAEC (Wallace 1990, 46). First, the advances in nuclear energy development expected to result from the EAEC would enable member countries to shift energy demand away from coal, which was diminishing in supply, toward atomic energy. Second, these expected advances would lead to the availability of a less costly energy source. Community producers would benefit from this cheaper production input. Third, France, especially, wanted to control the development of nuclear energy for military purposes within Western Europe (Stirk 1996, 143).

The motivations behind the establishment of the EEC and EAEC varied across members. As a result of these varying motivations, the two communities became linked together, in spite of their individual origins. France, in particular, sought the creation of the Atomic Community in order to control the development of nuclear energy.

Germany also had an interest in Euratom that stemmed from its perception of the need for Western European cooperation in defense matters, given US priorities beyond Europe and around the globe (Stirk 1996, 142). French Foreign Minister Christian Pineau proposed the advancement of the Euratom Treaty before the EEC Treaty. German concerns over French abandonment of the EEC Treaty after acceptance of the Euratom Treaty led to an agreement on May 9, 1956 to link the two treaties (Stirk 1996, 142). The Netherlands also favored economic integration. Given the importance of economic integration to the Benelux countries and the need for German support, France had little choice but to agree to link the two treaties in order to gain support for its preferred association.

French support for the EEC depended on two additional points of national interest. First, France wanted social costs harmonized (Stirk 1996, 143). France had begun domestic programs to equalize men's and women's wages and to limit the work week, as well as increasing the number of paid holidays per annum (Stirk 1996, 140). These programs increased the relative cost of labor in France, thereby placing it at a competitive disadvantage to other Western European countries. Second, France wanted financial assistance to develop her overseas territories. In February 1957, France negotiated a special provision for its overseas territories in order to obtain funding from the new Community (Stirk 1996,145).

The EEC and Euratom possessed a similar institutional structure to the ECSC. Each organization had its own institutions, which included a Council of Ministers, a Commission, an Assembly and a Court of Justice. Their Commissions assumed similar, although more limited, duties to the High Authority of the ECSC.

The United Kingdom decided against joining the EEC and EAEC for two primary reasons. First, the UK opposed the supranational aspects of the associations. Second, the UK did not want to jeopardize its existing trade relations with the USA, as well as with the members of the Commonwealth. The UK however, worried over the possibility of a protectionist Western European bloc of which it was not a member, and to which it was unable to provide formative input.

The countries of Northern, Eastern and Southern Europe did not join the EEC and EAEC for a number of reasons (Ungerer 1997, 34). The Scandinavian countries – Denmark, Norway and Sweden – had begun undertaking cooperative economic measures with each other following the war.[6] Their trade centered in the region, as well as with the UK. Finland and the countries of Eastern Europe were unable to participate in the arrangement due to their affiliation with the Soviet Union. Spain and Portugal were ineligible to join because of their form of government: dictatorship. Greece's economic development was insufficient to enable its association. Ireland depended too extensively on trade with the UK to join in its absence. Austria was prevented from joining by the treaty granting its independence in 1955 that required its neutrality.

3.3 THE DEVELOPMENT OF THE EUROPEAN COMMUNITIES AND THE BEGINNINGS OF MONETARY INTEGRATION: 1960–69

The 1960s saw the development of economic and political relations between the members of the European Communities, as well as the creation of an alternative economic association, the European Free Trade Area (EFTA). During this decade, EFTA undertook the creation of secondary institutions in the economic and monetary spheres. These institutions were responsible for facilitating member cooperation in monetary and economic policy matters.

3.3.1 The UK, EFTA and the European Communities

The United Kingdom responded to the developments leading to the creation of the European Economic and Atomic Communities with its own proposal for Western European integration. The UK was interested in extending its market-oriented philosophy to the continent. Reginald Maudling of the UK headed an Inter-governmental Committee under the auspices of the OEEC in 1957 with the task of examining the possibility of the conception of a Western European free trade area (Ungerer 1997, 37). A Western European free trade area offered the possibility of the continuation of existing British trade relations with the Commonwealth and the USA. The proposed alternative was also an effort to avoid the exclusion of the British economy from continental preferred trading arrangements, along with the implications of these arrangements for economic policy-making. The French responded with opposition to the Maudling Committee proposal in February 1958. Unlike the European Communities of six countries, the proposed free trade area provided purely for an enlarged trade area and permitted participants to retain their domestic economic institutions and their right to determine national external trade barriers.

The plan developed by the Maudling Committee served as the foundation for the plan for the European Free Trade Area (EFTA). Negotiations on the EFTA Treaty began in 1959. The organization entered operation on May 3, 1960. EFTA originally consisted of seven members: Austria, Denmark, Norway, Portugal, Sweden, Switzerland and the UK. The UK was the largest economy within the association. These members were attracted by the access to wider markets and the ability to retain full domestic sovereignty provided by the EFTA Treaty. The new arrangement provided for the reduction of trade barriers in industrial goods. The EFTA Treaty made no provisions in the areas of agriculture, fishing, economic and monetary policy. Member countries erected no common external tariff.

In July 1961, the UK decided to apply for membership to the European Communities. Their formal application followed in August 1961. Several factors motivated the British application. The first factor was the desire for greater access to EEC markets. As the continental economies of the EEC rebuilt and strengthened themselves, the UK realized the cost it bore by not being more closely affiliated in the exchange process. The growth rate within the EEC quickly outstripped that of the EFTA (Pollard 1981, 88). The second factor was pressure from the USA for the UK to take a more active role in Western Europe (Wallace 1990, 78). The third factor was encouragement from West Germany and the Netherlands. Both countries thought that the Community would benefit from the UK's favorable relations with the USA (Wallace 1990, 78).

French President Charles de Gaulle single-handedly rejected the British application at a press conference in early 1963. French opposition to British membership was partly due to concerns of French agricultural interests regarding competition from the British agriculture sector. The French also feared that Britain would attempt to reduce subsidies to agricultural producers. Agriculture represented a large percentage of French output.

The UK re-applied for Community membership on May 11, 1967. This application was also unsuccessful. On November 27, 1967, de Gaulle announced his rejection of the British application, again at a press conference, based on his perception of weaknesses within the British economy. De Gaulle took this decision without consultation with either other EEC Heads of Government or State or EEC institutions.

3.3.2 The Common Agricultural Policy

The Common Agricultural Policy (CAP) developed from discussions between EEC member country, Commission and agricultural interest group representatives at the Stresa Conference in 1958. Agriculture constituted a major component of the French and Italian economies. The purpose of a Community-level policy was to maintain internal agricultural prices and to facilitate intra-Community exchange in agricultural products. As a result of the CAP, the Council of Agricultural Ministers in association with national representatives took over management of agricultural policy within the European Communities. The CAP represents approximately one-half of the Communities' budget expenditures.

National motivations provided the impetus for the creation of the CAP. A large portion of French GDP derived from agricultural production. French farming practices, however, were inefficient because of limited-scale production due to the multitude of small farm holdings that characterized the industry and because of technological limitations due to the cost and size of this production structure. Germany needed access to the agricultural products of its fellow EC members. The German economy was largely industrial in nature and enjoyed a comparative advantage in such production. Germany desired to enter into a complementary exchange relationship with the rest of the Community. The northern Community members desired Italian membership in order to obtain those products, which could not be produced in their climates.

3.3.3 Economic and Monetary Cooperation in the EEC

Calls for further economic coordination within the European Communities sprang up shortly after the establishment of the EEC. In 1959, the Economic and Financial Committee of the European Parliament raised the notion of a European central banking system along the lines of the Federal Reserve System of the USA (Tsoukalis 1977, 53 in Lieberman 1992, 50–51). Belgian Foreign Minister Pierre Winy also suggested the creation of a common unit of account within the EEC. The motivation for this idea was to increase the role of the EEC in world financial markets. On March 10, 1960, the EEC established the Conjunctural or Short-term Economic Policy Committee to monitor economic developments in the member countries in the short run in order to facilitate policy coordination.

The EEC created several additional bodies to address economic policy matters on April 13, 1964. These bodies monitored specific aspects of the economy more closely than the Short-term Economic Policy Committee. At this time, EEC decision-makers felt that it was necessary for more than one body to consider these areas. The Committee of Governors of Central Banks would discuss interest rate, inflation, money growth and exchange rate matters. The Medium-term Policy Committee would discuss economic policy plans over a horizon of several years that extended beyond the focus of the Short-term Economic Policy Committee. The Budget Policy Committee would discuss fiscal matters, such as taxation, government spending and domestic transfer programs.

3.3.4 The Luxembourg Compromise

The precedent for unanimity in European Council decision-making was set on January 29, 1966. This precedent, known as the Luxembourg Compromise, prevented the operation of majority rule within decision-making proceedings of the Council of Ministers, as provided by the Treaty of Rome. President de Gaulle insisted that unanimity be required for a Commission proposal concerning agriculture and Community financing issues, as well as the Assembly's budgetary powers (Nicoll 1984, 35). Unsatisfied with the direction that the discussion was taking, the French prevented a vote on the proposal by withdrawing its representatives from Community institutions. Their absence forestalled any vote from taking place due to the rule of unanimous attendance in the Council. For this reason, the French strategy became known as its empty-chair policy. Upon its return, the French delegation opposed the proposal and called for replacement of the majority rule with a unanimous rule for issues of vital national importance.

The United Kingdom later unsuccessfully attempted to invoke the Luxembourg Compromise in 1982. The Council of Ministers was considering a Commission proposal to increase agricultural prices. Britain argued that it opposed this proposal because of the costs that it would impose on the Community's budget. At the time, the UK was trying to secure a rebate for its contributions to the Community's budget, which exceeded the transfers it received in return. The Chair of the Council overrode the British attempt to prevent a vote on the proposal.[7] On March 23, 1984, the French President of the Council stated that the Luxembourg Compromise can only be invoked in instances where the specific national interest of concern is explicitly included in the relevant proposal (Nicoll 1984, 41).

3.3.5 Institutional Developments in the European Communities

The first meeting of European heads of government, later known as summits of the European Council, took place in Paris from February 10–11, 1961. De Gaulle arranged this summit to promote his notion of political cooperation among EEC countries. In part, de Gaulle called this summit outside of the framework of the European Communities due to his desire to circumvent the authority of the Commission. None of the original European Community treaties of the 1950s provided for or legitimated European Council summits. This Paris Summit was the first of a long succession of meetings of the European Council.[8]

The primary bodies of the ECSC, EEC and Euratom, that is, the High Commission of the ECSC and the Commissions of the EEC and Euratom, along with the Councils of Ministers and Assemblies of all three affiliations, merged with each other in 1967 (Merger Treaty). The High Authority of the ECSC and the Commissions of the EEC and Euratom combined to form the new Commission of the European Communities. A single Council of Ministers replaced the hierarchy of individual Councils of each Community, although specialized Councils retained authority within their respective policy areas. The Common Assembly incorporated members from all three communities. It was not until 1986 that the Assembly changed its name to the European Parliament as a part of the Single European Act.

3.3.6 Introduction of Monetary Integration to the Community Agenda

In 1969, the first and second Barre Reports led the way toward monetary integration. These Reports arrived in the wake of French balance-of-payments difficulties and the institution of the Common Agricultural Policy. The Commission aspired to develop a proposal for further economic and monetary integration that would benefit other sectors as well. The first Barre Report, named after Commission Vice President Raymond Barre, who chaired the relevant committee, went to the Council of Ministers on February 12, 1969. It offered provisions for improving economic and monetary coordination between members and greater financial assistance to members suffering from balance-of-payments difficulties. The second Barre Report appeared in December 1969 and provided the impetus for the creation of a committee to consider its proposals.

Both Barre Reports followed the rise of European debates on the relationship between economic and monetary integration. Two schools of thought characterized these debates: that of the Economists and that of the Monetarists. The former viewed monetary union as the crowning achievement of a gradual progression toward complete economic integration. The latter viewed monetary integration as a parallel process to be undertaken in tandem with economic integration as quickly as possible. The Germans and the Dutch were the predominant advocates of the Economist approach. The French acted as the leading proponents of the Monetarist approach (Rosenthal 1975).

3.4 THE GROWING MONETARY AGENDA AND NEW MEMBERS: 1970–79

The 1970s were a period of economic turbulence. Significant developments took place in international monetary arrangements. First, the Bretton Woods system of fixed but adjustable exchange rates ended following the abandonment of gold convertibility of the US dollar. Second, the European Communities undertook their first efforts at coordinated exchange rate systems in the form of the snake-in-the-tunnel and the European Monetary System (EMS).

3.4.1 The Werner Report and the Snake-in-the-Tunnel

In March 1970, the Council of Ministers created a committee to undertake a plan for monetary union in light of the Barre Reports. The Council appointed Pierre Werner, Prime Minister of Luxembourg, to chair this committee, which included the chairmen of the Monetary Committee, the Committee of Central Bank Governors, the Short- and Medium-term Economic Policy Committees, the Budgetary Policy Committee and representatives from the Commission. The resultant Werner Plan provided for the creation of a single West European economy using a common currency via a three-stage plan for economic and monetary union. The plan outlined steps to reduce intra-EC exchange rate fluctuations and to increase fiscal policy cooperation among member countries. It also led to the adoption of the European Unit of Account (EUA), which served as a common unit of account within the EC. The EUA originally was pegged directly to the US dollar but later came to be based on a basket of EEC currencies.

The Werner Plan, which sought to reach the middle ground between the Economists and the Monetarists, led to the institution of the so-called snake-in-the-tunnel as the mechanism for limiting exchange rate fluctuations. The purpose of the snake was to institute a fixed exchange rate system among EEC members in order to reduce the volatility arising in international currency markets due to the failure of the USA to defend the parity of the dollar to sustain the Bretton Woods gold exchange standard. Exchange rate stability was desirable in order to enable long-term economic planning between EEC members, for example price setting within the CAP, and to retain greater certainty in the intra-Community exchange process.

The snake, which entered operation in March 1972, consisted of the parities of each member's currency to the other members' currencies. These parities adhered to a specified parity grid that restricted their bilateral fluctuations. This snake operated within the tunnel, which consisted of the currencies' parities to the US dollar. The operation of the snake-in-the-tunnel resulted in part from the French desire to maintain relative exchange rate stability in spite of the wide fluctuations of the US dollar in the face of US President Nixon's policy of benign neglect. This desire on the part of France derived from its concerns regarding fluctuations in agricultural prices which the EEC had determined for given fixed exchange rate parities. By permitting limited fluctuations between member exchange rates, the plan aspired to reduce disparities in monetary policies. In June 1970, EC members chose 1980 as their target year for

European economic and monetary union. The European Council approved this plan in February 1971.

European Economic Community decision-makers attempted to promote exchange rate stability through the creation of various credit facilities (Ungerer 1997, 90–92). In February 1970 the heads of the central banks of the EEC set up the Short-term Monetary Support system (STMS). On March 22, 1971, the Council of Ministers set up the Medium-term Financial Assistance system (MTFA). Neither of these facilities experienced much usage. Following the collapse of Bretton Woods and the first crisis the EEC established the European Monetary Cooperation Fund (EMCF). The European Council devised the EMCF at its Paris Summit in April 1973. This fund sought to promote stabilization within the European currency system by reducing fluctuations among member country currencies through cooperation and providing short-term financial support to member states during adjustment periods. The Community Loan Mechanism (CLM) entered operation in February 1975. The CLM first provided assistance to Community members Ireland and Italy in 1976. In June 1988, the MFTA and the CLM consolidated into a single lending institution.

A number of unforeseen circumstances arose, which threatened the EEC's efforts to maintain a monetary arrangement in the early 1970s. The USA experienced a rising balance-of-payments deficit from the late 1960s due to expenditures on the Vietnam War and President Johnson's War on Poverty (Wood and Yesilada 1996, 58). In addition, the USA undertook a policy of benign neglect of the dollar's value. This policy led to large and frequent fluctuations in its value. In response, European countries allowed their currencies to appreciate against the US dollar (Smithsonian Agreement by the Group of 10, December 18, 1971). In March 1973 the Bretton Woods system finally collapsed.

The snake-in-the-tunnel began operation in 1972. On April 24, the original six EC members placed their currencies within the snake. The UK, Ireland and Denmark began participation on May 1. Norway and Sweden entered agreements with the EC in March 1973, which effectively provided them with full membership in the arrangement.

The members implemented the snake in an effort to reduce intra-Community exchange rate fluctuations. To this end, the Council restricted currency fluctuations within the snake to ±2.5 percent of their par values with respect to the other EEC currencies. However, a speculative attack on the pound sterling demonstrated the difficulty states would face in adhering to the arrangement. The UK withdrew the pound from the snake within two months of entering the arrangement in June 1972 because of this attack and allowed the pound to float. The lira faced a similar crisis in February 1973 and also withdrew from the snake. When the USA closed the gold window in February 1973 the dollar devalued and prompted the decision of West Germany, France, Denmark and the Benelux countries to undertake a joint float of their currencies. By January 1974, the French decided to float the franc independently of the others' currencies.

The oil price shocks of 1973–74 exerted additional pressure upon exchange rate systems by pushing up inflation, leading to rising unemployment, and causing recessions. These events introduced further challenges to the snake-in-the-tunnel. Over time several member states, for example, Ireland, Italy, Switzerland and the United Kingdom, left the snake and resorted to managed floats outside of the specified parities. Denmark left the snake only to return later. France withdrew from the snake in 1973, returned in 1974, and finally withdrew in 1976. Belgium, Germany, Luxembourg and the Netherlands endured the slithering of the snake within and beyond the tunnel. The snake-in-the-tunnel became a *de facto* Deutschmark zone.

Exchange rate fluctuations of Western European currencies continued during the following years and the snake was unable to reduce intra-EEC exchange rate fluctuations. Three factors affected the failure of the snake (Lieberman 1992, 84). The first factor was the predominant efforts of countries to manipulate economic policies, in particular monetary and exchange rate policies, to satisfy domestic interests. The second factor was the inability for members to coordinate economic and monetary policies in order to promote exchange rate stability among the currencies of the snake. The third factor was the US policy of benign neglect, which precipitated the end of the Bretton Woods system.

3.4.2 The First Enlargement

The European Community underwent its first enlargement at the beginning of 1973. Four countries had applied for admission to the European Communities: Denmark, Ireland, Norway and the UK. Denmark, Ireland and Norway submitted applications for membership in 1967. These applications along with the UK's 1967 application remained open for official EC consideration. Prior to joining the EC, these countries participated in the European Free Trade Area (EFTA). These countries and Community leaders signed the Accession Treaties on January 22, 1972. The number of members increased from six to nine. Three of the applicants accepted membership: Denmark, Ireland and the UK. In July 1972 the European Communities signed bilateral agreements with the following EFTA countries: Sweden, Switzerland, Austria, Portugal and Iceland. Simultaneous accession of these three countries can in part be attributed to their close trading relationships. Ireland, for example, had participated in a currency union with the UK since 1826. A referendum in Norway in September 1972 rejected its earlier decision to join if accepted. This change of heart derived from Norwegian agricultural and fishing interests (Stirk 1996, 180).

3.4.3 Institutional Developments in the European Communities

One of the first institutional developments of the 1970s took place in 1970. In April 1970 the members of the European Communities signed the Luxembourg Treaty, which amended the Treaty of Rome. The Luxembourg Treaty called for the creation of a fund to finance Community expenditures by 1975. The Treaty also called for the expansion of the powers of the European Assembly.

In December 1974 at the Paris Summit, the European Council developed a communiqué that provided for the operation of the European Council as a legitimate EC decision-maker. Until 1974, European Council summits periodically convened to discuss and plot the future course of Community affairs. These meetings took place outside of the provisions of the framework of the Community treaties. The extra-treaty nature of this body raised concerns among member countries and particularly among two other Community-level institutions, the Commission and the European Parliament. These latter institutions felt their power reduced in the face of this self-appointed body.

Although the European Council continued to operate outside of the auspices of the Treaties, it was able to formalize its position within the existing institutional framework. By remaining an extra-treaty body the European Council effectively retained greater political latitude than any of the other Community institutions, including the Council of Ministers, whose duties and powers are specified by the Treaties. To assuage fears of a growing democratic deficit within the Community, the European Council agreed to the introduction of direct elections to the European Parliament after 1978.

During the mid-1970s, several committees prepared reports proposing institutional and policy development. The European Council appointed one of the first such committees in December 1974. Belgian Foreign Minister Leo Tindemans led this committee, which advocated greater Community monetary policy coordination, a common Community foreign policy and institutional reforms to increase the decision-making powers of the Council of Ministers and the Commission. The Tindemans Committee introduced the possibility of countries proceeding towards economic integration at different speeds (Stirk 1996, 188). The McDougall Report appeared in April 1977. A committee led by Sir Donald McDougall prepared this report, which emphasized the need for increases in the Community budget. In December 1978 the Marjolin report, also known as the Report of the Three Wise Men, appeared. French President Valéry Giscard d'Estaing appointed the three members of the committee who prepared this report: Barend Bisheuvel of the Netherlands, Edmund Dell of the UK and Robert Marjolin of France. The Report suggested that the EC needed to place greater attention on the relationship between monetary and economic policies and that economic integration represented a means to attain political integration.

The first direct election of members of the European Parliament took place in 1979. Direct election of members stood as an attempt to redress the democratic deficit within the institutions of the EC. Prior to 1979 national parliaments selected members to attend the European Parliament.

3.4.4 The European Monetary System

The pursuit of monetary integration continued in the second half of the 1970s following the appointment of Roy Jenkins as President of the Commission on October 27, 1977. Jenkins perceived a need for a new monetary arrangement within the EEC in order to facilitate the exchange process between the countries to replace the faltering snake and improve the economic conditions within the EC. Fluctuations between member exchange rates resulted in the erection of increased non-tariff barriers to trade, as well as greater uncertainty in long-term exchange agreements such as the CAP. Inflation and high interest rates continued to plague the countries of the EC. The second oil shock in 1979 prolonged these difficulties.

Jenkins' calls for advancing an alternate system, the European Monetary System (EMS), to the snake met with disinterest on the part of EC leaders until December 1977. At this time, German Chancellor Helmut Schmidt advocated Jenkins' calls for a new EC monetary system, additional regional funds and increased credit facilities at the Brussels European Council meeting. German interest in a new system resulted from the relative strength of its currency *vis-à-vis* the rest of the EC currencies, along with the fact that over half of its trade occurred within the Community (Lieberman 1992, 97). Chancellor Schmidt was also in the throes of an election campaign in which the opposition's standing was close to his. Schmidt required a policy stance favorable to German producers and laborers. French President Giscard d'Estaing also supported the proposed EMS because of the stability offered by the Deutschmark which the French franc needed (Oatley 1997, 180). The EMS attracted Italy as a means to secure domestic economic stability. However, both Italy and Ireland were initially hesitant about joining the EMS. Ireland's long-time currency union with the UK heightened its concerns. Both countries overcame their hesitations as a result of commitments by the economically stronger participants to provide subsequent resource transfers (Wood and Yesilada 1996, 60).

The EMS replaced the snake-in-the-tunnel as the coordinating mechanism for EC members' exchange rates on March 13, 1979. All of the EC members, with the exception of the UK, participated in the EMS from its inception. The EMS operated through the Exchange Rate Mechanism (ERM), which employed an index unit known as the European Currency Unit (ECU), which consisted of specified amounts of the currencies of member countries. Conversion rates between each pair of currencies were derived from this unit and related a range of fluctuation permitted between these two currencies before intervention to maintain the defined parities was necessary. This system of paired exchange rates was known as the Exchange Rate Mechanism (ERM). Exchange rates were permitted to fluctuate by up to ±2.25 percent with the exception of the Italian lira, which had wider bands of ±6 percent. The EMS also provided expanded credit facilities to member central banks and required a pooling of some national reserve assets. The German mark dominated this system and the other member countries found their currencies pegged to it *de facto* (Colchester and Buchan 1990, 160–62).

The UK did not enter the EMS at its inception. During the 1970s, the UK had experienced high inflation, rising unemployment and diminished growth rates. The government led by Callaghan wanted to retain the exchange rate as an adjustment mechanism (Oatley 1997, 181). British industry feared that a fixed rate against the German mark would reduce the competitiveness of British industrial production *vis-à-vis* German industrial production. On July 6, 1979, however, the UK did place 20 percent of its gold and dollar reserves in the EMCF (Lieberman 1992, 120). The pound sterling entered the ERM in October 1990.

3.5 FURTHER ENLARGEMENT AND INCREASING ECONOMIC AND MONETARY INTEGRATION: 1980–89

A renewed interest in European economic, monetary and political integration marked the 1980s. The first step toward further integration took place with the formulation of the Single European Act (SEA). The discourse preceding the ratification of the treaty reflected continuing EC concerns over the democratic deficit within the community and desires to rectify this situation through institutional reform. The SEA also provided for the creation of a single market in which goods, services, capital and people might freely move, along with universal legislative requirements which applied to these and other areas of the economic and legal structures of EC member countries. The final years of the decade saw the extension of economic integration plans to the monetary sphere.

3.5.1 Institutional Reform, the Internal Market and the Single European Act

Efforts to renew the pursuit of EC integration, which had slowed during the 1970s due to adverse economic circumstances, accelerated in the next decade. In 1983, German Foreign Minister Hans-Dietrich Genscher and Italian Foreign Minister Emilio Colombo's Solemn Declaration on European Union ignited the drive for further European integration. Their plan emphasized the roles of the European Council, the Council of Ministers and the European Parliament, as well as a new secretariat to handle European political cooperation. The European Parliament's Spinelli Report of September 1983 provided the basis for the Draft Treaty on European Union.

The Draft Treaty introduced proposals for institutional reform. These reforms included the introduction of the subsidiarity principle, the legitimation of the European Council, the decision rules of the European Council, additional legislation on the freedom of movement of goods, services, capital and people, the reduction of fiscal, physical and technical barriers and the addition of social and health policy to the Union's agenda. The subsidiarity principle stated that issues were to be handled at the most appropriate government level. Local authorities would handle issues with limited regional effects. Regional, national or EU-level authorities would handle issues with more widespread effects. The Parliament adopted the Draft Treaty in February 1984.

These plans foretold the progress that followed in the mid-80s. In 1984 French President François Mitterand, who was also President of the European Council at the time, embraced the Draft Treaty and commenced proceedings to provide for the progress and reforms called for by the plans. At the Fontainebleau Summit in June 1984, Mitterand's Presidency arranged for a committee led by former Irish Foreign Minister Jim Dooge to develop a proposal for institutional reforms. At the end of his Council Presidency, Mitterand put forth the name of Jacques Delors for the position of European Commission President. The Commission Presidency of Jacques Delors commenced in January 1985.

Two important reports appeared before the European Council in Milan in June 1985. The first report was the Dooge Report. It provided part of the basis on which the European Council decided to convene an Inter-governmental Conference (IGC) for amending the constituting treaties to accommodate institutional reforms.

The second report, which also bore partial responsibility for motivating the European Council to call an IGC, was the Commission's White Paper, *Completing the Internal Market*. A committee led by Commission Vice President Lord Cockfield prepared this White Paper following the publication of the Cechinni Report. The latter report highlighted the benefits of an integrated European market. In addition to discussing the integration of EC capital markets and promoting financial market liberalization, the White Paper proposed additional integration of factor markets in goods, services and labor. Over the next six months IGC proceedings developed a proposal to amend the Treaties.

The Luxembourg European Council in December 1985 received the drafts of the treaty amendments prepared by the IGC. Three months later in February 1986 the European Council signed the Single European Act (SEA) as prepared by the IGC. The SEA consisted of three pillars. The first pillar pertained to the Single Market Program that provided for the realization of a single European market by 1992. The second pillar created the Common Foreign and Security Policy (CFSP). The third pillar consisted of policies relating to Justice and Home Affairs (JHA). The treaty provided for the liberalization of factor markets, as well as the harmonization of many national regulations. The SEA also returned majority voting to prominence within the Council on matters relating to the internal market. Depending on the issue at hand the decision rule is absolute majority, qualified majority or unanimity, with member countries allotted votes based on population. Majority voting encouraged coalition building and vote trading among Council members (Hayes-Renshaw in Andersen and Eliassen 1996, 157). The SEA took effect in July 1987.

Two additional community reports addressed the issues of capital market integration and monetary union. The first of these reports, the Padoa-Schioppa Report of 1986, highlighted the incompatibility of three of the EU's goals in these spheres. The EU could not simultaneously enjoy high capital mobility, fixed exchange rates and independent monetary policies. Two of these goals could coexist but not three (Colchester and Buchan 1990, 166). The second report, the Basle-Nyborg Agreement of 1987, sought to bolster the ERM by allowing voluntary inframarginal exchange rate adjustments and expanding the availability of short-term financing assistance to EMS members (Masson and Taylor 1993a, 36).

3.5.2 Further Enlargements of the European Communities

Three new member countries acceded to the EC in the 1980s. The first of the three, Greece, joined the EC in 1981. Greece first obtained an Association Agreement with the EC in July 1961. The EC suspended this agreement from April 1967 to July 1974 when a military regime ruled the country. In June 1975, Greece applied for full membership. Although the Greek drachma never entered the ERM on June 10, 1985 Greece placed 20 percent of its gold and dollar reserves in the EMCF (Lieberman 1992, 120).

Five years later, the second and third countries, Spain and Portugal, acceded to the EC, bringing the total number of members to 12. Spanish and Portuguese membership applications arrived in 1977 following the decline of dictatorial regimes in both countries. On January 1, 1986, Spain and Portugal officially became full EC members. The Spanish peseta entered the ERM in July 1989. The Portuguese escudo entered the ERM in April 1992. Both countries' currencies received fluctuation margins of ±6 percent.

3.5.3 The Delors Report

The drive for monetary union received renewed interest shortly after the passage of the SEA. In December 1986 former French and German heads of government, Valery Giscard d'Estaing and Helmut Schmidt, organized the

Committee for the Monetary Union of Europe. Their Committee sought to revive the push for European monetary union. In April 1987 the Committee published its plan, 'A Program for Action', which included provisions for a European central bank, private sector use of the European Currency Unit (ECU) and economic convergence among member countries (Padoa-Schioppa 1994, 143). The realignment of current parities within the ERM in 1987 also played a role in renewed interest in monetary integration.

The European Council responded to the Committee's plan and other suggestions for progress on the economic and monetary union issue in 1988. At the Hanover Summit in June 1988, the European Council created the Committee for the Study of Economic and Monetary Union to develop a proposal for monetary union. Commission President Jacques Delors led this Committee which included the 12 central bank governors of the EC member countries and five other appointees. The so-called Delors Committee put forward its 'Report on Economic and Monetary Union in the European Community' in April 1989. The Report outlined a three-stage plan for achieving monetary union. The Report's approach resembled the approach of the Economists of the 1960s and incorporated the French preference for a speedy transition to monetary union (Giovannini 1995).

Later negotiations prior to and during the economic and monetary union IGC would, however, temper this approach with the concerns of the Germans, in particular, who touted the importance of strict economic convergence criteria prior to monetary union. These convergence criteria addressed domestic monetary stability and outlined stringent requirements necessary for participation in the final stage.[9] These criteria reflected the EU's ultimate goal of a monetary union. According to the plan for EMU, the single, common currency would replace the respective national currencies in 2002.

The European Council considered the report of the Delors Committee at its summit in Madrid in June. The Council was receptive to the ideas contained therein. After six months of additional deliberation on the proposals for EMU, the European Council decided to convene an IGC to amend the constituting treaties. Eleven of the 12 countries favored the development of an amendment proposal on monetary union. The lone dissenting country was the United Kingdom.

3.6 THE TREATY OF MAASTRICHT AND PROGRESS TOWARDS AN ECONOMIC AND MONETARY UNION: 1990–PRESENT

Monetary integration topped the agenda of the European Communities from the beginning of the 1990s. The Treaty on European Union, also known as the Treaty of Maastricht, contained the plan for the creation of a European economic and monetary union. The plan represented the final step in the progression toward the realization of a single European economic and monetary area without internal barriers.

3.6.1 The European Economic Area

The countries of the EU and the EFTA formed the European Economic Area (EEA) in January 1994 to increase each association's members' access to the other association's markets.[10] The purpose of the EEA was to create a free trade area in goods, services, capital and labor. The EEA, however, did not create a single market in the sense of the EC. Border controls between the associations remained and no common external tariff arose. The EFTA countries also did not agree to participate in the EC's Common Commercial and Agricultural Policies, respectively. The EEA possesses several institutions, which include representatives from each of the member countries, as well as representatives from the European Commission and the Economic and Social Committee of the EU.

3.6.2 The Treaty on European Union

During the first half of 1990, proposals for a second IGC on European Political Union (EPU) met with approval by the European Council. Pre-negotiations and preparations for both IGCs took place throughout 1990. Both IGCs met in Rome in December. The following year saw numerous meetings and discussions of the EMU and EPU issues. The European Council in Maastricht in December 1991 finally settled the remaining debates from the IGCs and set forth the Treaty of Maastricht, which incorporated the resolutions on economic, monetary and political integration issues.

Individual national ratification of the Maastricht Treaty on European Union necessarily followed the Treaty's approval by the European Council. Ratification, however, proved more difficult and less clear-cut than Heads of Government expected. One member, the UK, only ratified the Treaty after they received an individual opt-out clause from the monetary integration process. The British Parliament's approval came in July 1993. France and Denmark attained narrow majorities in favor of the Treaty in national referenda. The latter only attained a majority in a second referendum following the negotiation of an additional opt-out clause. A fourth member, Germany, faced resistance in the form of a suit that alleged that the Treaty violated the German Constitution, the Grundgesetz. The German Constitutional Court determined that the Treaty did not violate the Grundgesetz. Finally, the Treaty obtained the necessary ratification and took effect in November 1993.

The Maastricht Treaty introduced a three-stage plan for European monetary union. Stage I lasted from July 1, 1990 to December 31, 1993. During this stage, all member countries would enter the EMS and their economies would attain further convergence in accordance with the SEA. Stage II took place from January 1, 1994 to June 30, 1998. During Stage II, economic convergence would continue. Participating countries would retain monetary sovereignty, although the European Monetary Institute (EMI) would enter operation to facilitate monetary cooperation and lay the groundwork for the European Central Bank. At the end of Stage II, the ECB took over monetary affairs by replacing the EMI. Stage III would begin when the EU determined that at least a core group of countries had sufficiently satisfied the convergence criteria for monetary union. At the beginning of May 1998, the EU decided that 11 states would advance toward the first round of monetary union. These countries were Austria, Belgium, Germany, Finland, France, Ireland, Italy, Luxembourg, the Netherlands, Portugal and Spain. Stage III began on July 1, 1998. At this time, the ECB replaced the EMI. On January 1, 1999 the exchange rates of the first round of participants were irrevocably fixed. The next phase of Stage III began on January 1, 2002 when the EU introduced the new currency, the euro, into circulation. From January 1, 2000 to July 1, 2002, the euro would circulate side-by-side with national currencies. From July 1, members will withdraw national notes and coins from circulation.

3.6.3 Enlargement of the European Union

The European Communities experienced two enlargements in the first half of the 1990s. The first enlargement stemmed from the reunification of Germany on October 3, 1990. The monetary unification between the former East and West Germany on July 1, 1990 provides an indication of possible consequences of a European monetary union. Following reunification inflationary pressures arose in Germany, which the Bundesbank staved off through increased interest rates. The overall German unemployment rate increased dramatically and the fiscal burden faced by the Western region and the federal government skyrocketed.

The second enlargement of the EU took place in 1995 with the accession of Austria, Sweden and Finland. The number of EU members increased to 15. Austrian membership was motivated by the fall of Communism in the countries of Eastern Europe, which created a desire for it to associate itself more closely with the EU in order to enjoy the relative protectionism membership offered. Swedish membership derived from internal difficulties it faced due to its socialist economic policies. Finland joined in response to Swedish application because of the close trading relations between the two countries. The collapse of the hegemonic Soviet Union enabled Finland to undertake this affiliation. Norway, Sweden and Finland tied their currencies to the ECU in October 1990,

May 1991 and July 199 1, respectively. Austria entered the ERM on January 9, 1995. Finland entered the ERM on October 14, 1996.

3.6.4 1992–93 Speculative Attacks

The EMS underwent a series of speculative attacks during 1992–93. Several factors brought on these crises. First, the ERM had not permitted a realignment of its currencies since 1987. Second, tight German monetary policies battling domestic inflationary pressures following the German reunification led to increased interest rates, which placed upward pressure on the exchange rate of the Deutschmark. Third, increased capital mobility resulting from the Single Market Program led to greater capital movements within the EU. Fourth, the Danish referendum's rejection of the Treaty on European Union (TEU) created uncertainty regarding the future of the EU and its economic and monetary plans. Additional factors include the declining value of the US dollar and excessive fiscal spending within the UK in response to a domestic recession.

The series of attacks began in September 1992. The British pound was the first currency to suffer. Following growing pressure from August the pound sterling endured a major attack on September 16, 1992, known as Black Wednesday. As a result of this attack, the pound withdrew from the ERM. The Italian lira experienced pressures within the ERM during the same month in spite of official attempts to stave off an attack by devaluation. On September 17, 1992, the lira withdrew from the ERM unable to remain within its fluctuation margins, which were narrowed to 2.25 percent on January 8, 1990. The lira did not reenter the ERM until November 1996. Finland, Sweden and Norway abandoned their currencies' associations with the ERM on September 8, 1992, November 19, 1992 and December 10, 1992, respectively.

Pressures on ERM currencies continued in the following months. The Irish punt depreciated by 10 percent in January 1993. The Spanish peseta and Portuguese escudo devalued twice between November 1992 and May 1993. The French franc faced speculative attacks in July 1993. To forestall the withdrawal of the franc the EU expanded the permitted fluctuation margins for all currencies within the ERM except the German mark and the Dutch gilder to ±15 percent on August 2, 1993.

3.6.5 The 1996 Inter-governmental Conference, the Treaty of Amsterdam and the Growth and Stability Pact

The TEU provided for an Inter-governmental Conference to meet in 1996 to further address a number of unresolved issues. These issues related to monetary integration and institutional reform. Attention to monetary integration was necessary to further decide on monetary union participation criteria, as well as other details related to the transition and the final system. Attention to institutional reform was necessary to improve the operation of EU institutions and to increase institutional accountability to the European populace.

The IGC met in Turin in March 1996. The IGC discussed measures to increase the efficiency of EU institutions, as well as to reduce the democratic deficit of EU institutions. Resolution on the Growth and Stability Pact remained to be reached following the IGC. The Treaty of Amsterdam finally gathered the required national approvals on October 2, 1997.

On June 16, 1997, the European finance ministers accepted the Growth and Stability Pact initiated by German Finance Minister Theo Waigel in November 1995. The purpose of the Growth and Stability Pact was to delineate further fiscal policy criteria for entrance to the monetary union specifically with respect to domestic budget deficits. The Pact defines excessive budget deficits, outlines a timetable for deficit reduction and delineates the sanctions for excessive budget deficits. The issue of budget deficits had been a matter of contention between France and Germany. The former feared that strict limitations and stringent punishments would adversely affect unemployment.

3.6.6 The Introduction of the Euro: January 1, 1999

The euro officially entered operation on January 1, 1999. EMU participants officially locked their currencies' exchange rates to the euro at rates decided by the European Council on December 31, 1998. Table 3.1 presents the conversion rates employed.

Table 3.1 Euro conversion rates

Member Country	Currency	Value of 1 euro
Austria	ATS	13.7603
Belgium	BEF	40.3399
Finland	FIM	5.94573
France	FRF	6.55957
Germany	DEM	1.95583
Ireland	IEP	0.787564
Italy	ITL	1936.27
Luxembourg	LUF	40.3399
Netherlands	NLG	2.20371
Portugal	PTE	200.482
Spain	ESP	166.386

Since its introduction in January 1999, the euro has followed a downward trend *vis-à-vis* the US dollar (see Figure 3.1). This relative weakness has helped to spur on the booming economies at the fringes of the euro-zone in Ireland, Spain, Portugal and Finland. It has also encouraged euro-zone exports to the rest of the world. However, speculation fears surrounding the transition proved to be unfounded.

Figure 3.1 *US dollar–euro average weekly exchange rates (January 6, 1999 to July 6, 2000)*

3.6.7 Latest Admission to the EMU

On January 1, 2001, Greece officially joined the euro-zone. Its entry follows a June 2000 decision by Ecofin to accept its application for admission to the EMU. Its entry stems from reductions in government debt, economic growth and an inflation rate near 2 percent. This improvement in Greece's fiscal position follows a major reform of its tax collection system that began in 1993. This reform has brought significant increases in government revenue.

3.6.8 Remaining Admissions to the EMU

Three EU member currencies have yet to join the EMU. The three remaining countries are Denmark, Sweden and the UK. Of these countries, Denmark decided in September 2000 not to join. The Danish decision centered on sovereignty concerns. In October 2000, Sweden decided to postpone its vote on whether or not to seek admission. Meanwhile, the UK continues to dance around the touchy issue of whether to apply.

3.6.9 Potential Expansions of the EU and EMU

Myriad Eastern European countries and Mediterranean countries are clamoring for admission to the EU. Along with this interest, these countries harbor long-term wishes to join the euro-zone. Eastern European would-be members include Poland, the Czech Republic, Slovenia, Slovakia, Bulgaria, Hungary, Romania and the Baltic republics of Estonia, Latvia and Lithuania. Would-be members from the shores of the Mediterranean include Cyprus, Malta and Turkey.

Thus far, the EU has neither laid down criteria nor devised a timeline for admission. Among the obstacles that are hindering the EU's decision process are unresolved issues about the institutional reforms that will accompany an expansion in membership. Institutional concerns focus on the size of the Commission and Parliament, as well as the use of the unanimity rule in decision-making. Political concerns center on the issues of labor movement, agricultural subsidies and environmental policy. An optimistic guess suggests that enlargement will begin after 2003.

3.6.10 Upcoming Inter-governmental Conference

At its meeting in Cologne in June 1999, the European Council decided to hold an Inter-governmental Conference in 2000 to address the issue of procedural rules. The IGC began meetings in February 2000. Specific issues under examination included the number and origin of members within the Commission, the system of weighted votes within the Council and the extension of qualified voting in the Council. A related issue that the Council addressed was the institution of a two-speed EU. Such an arrangement would venture from the current situation by allowing groups of members in favor of increased integration of EU governance into national territory to go ahead with such a policy. Dissenting countries, such as those who fear surrendering national policy domain to the EU, remain behind in a second, less integrated group. Advocates of this acceleration of integration include the European Commission, France and Germany. The UK opposes such a measure.

3.7 CONCLUSION

This review of European economic and monetary history of the past 40 years reveals some important patterns. The first pattern is the tendency for policy initiatives to come from a single individual within the political élite. The second pattern is the primary position of national concerns in matters of monetary policy. From the decision of the French to float the franc in January 1974 independently of the currencies of other snake participants' currencies to the recent French insistence upon further EU attention to unemployment problems in light of the Growth and Stability Pact, this pattern is clear. The third pattern is for speculative capital flows to disable the operation of European monetary arrangements as in the cases of the snake-in-the-tunnel and the ERM prior to the expansion of the fluctuation margins in 1993. The fourth pattern is for EU monetary policy to be subject to political intervention. The fifth pattern is the gradual regularization of institutional operations. For example, the European Council has met at least once every six months since 1974. Similarly, the European Parliament now holds regular elections. The sixth pattern is for the EU to follow a gradual pattern of increasingly imprinting itself on the bureaucratic and administrative roadmap that is winding its way into sovereign political territory.

NOTES

1. Western Europe addressed these concerns in a contest different than that of the years preceding World War II. A new balance of power between the USA in the West and the Soviet Union in the East emerged in the post-World War II world. The Soviet Union first drew the Iron Curtain in 1946 and in 1955 established the Warsaw Pact. Western Europe lay in the middle of these two opposing world powers. For fear of the expansionist tendencies of the Soviet Communists and due to alliances in the World Wars and in the interest of trade and economic interests, Western Europe affiliated itself more closely with the United States.
2. The American and British representatives at the Foreign Ministers' Conference in London on May 10, 1950 urged for German steel quotas to be raised (Stirk 1996, 121).
3. In 1949, the International Ruhr Authority (IRA) was set up to monitor the reconstruction of the industrial areas in the German Rhineland in order to prevent the stockpiling of weapons for future German aggressions. The IRA maintained limits on German coal and steel production in this region. The UK, France, Germany, the Benelux countries and the USA administered the IRA (Archer and Butler 1996, 21).
4. The provisions of the ECSC agreement took effect at different dates for the various commodities (Keesing's Research Report 1975, 7). The common market in coal, scrap and iron ore began on February 10, 1953; the common market in steel began on May 1, 1953; and the common market for special steels began on August 1, 1954. February 10, 1953 marked the completion of the initial transition period of five years. Following the creation of the common market, production of all of these commodities both among the member countries and with the rest of the world increased. Coal production declined from 1957, however, due to the rise in natural gas and oil production. Steel production, in contrast, continued to increase (Keesing's Research Report 1975, 4, 7).

5. For a discussion of early EU advocates' preference for a common market instead of a customs union or free trade area, see Dedman (1996, 97–104).
6. For more on the development of Scandinavian relations following World War II, see Michael Pollard (1981, 88).
7. For more on this instance, see William Nicoll (1994), 'The Luxembourg Compromise', *Journal of Common Market Studies*, **23** (1), 42.
8. Troy Johnston (1994, 5) points out that the Paris Summit marks the beginning of a trend in which French plans for a summit looked to German support to bring the meeting to fruition.
9. The four convergence criteria follow: (1) price stability characterized by an inflation rate within 1.5 percentage points of the average of the three best performing countries' inflation rates; (2) low long-term interest rates characterized by rates within 2 percentage points of the average of the three countries with the lowest rates; (3) stable exchange rates characterized by exchange rate movements within the allowable range of the ERM for the past two years; and (4) a budget deficit which is less than 3 percent of the country's annual GDP and public debt which is less than 60 percent of annual GDP. (*The Economist* October 17, 1997, 22–3.)
10. One exception to the membership exists. Switzerland, a member of the EFTA, decided not to participate in the EEA based on the outcome of a referendum in December 1992.

4. The theory of currency unions

4.1 INTRODUCTION

Currency unions represent one form of monetary arrangement between different regions. The use of a single currency as the predominant medium of exchange characterizes this type of arrangement. Currency unions are a type of fixed exchange rate arrangement in which countries share a common currency and relinquish domestic monetary and exchange rate policy.

This chapter provides a theoretical overview of issues relevant to the creation and operation of currency unions. Section 2 provides a brief explanation of currency unions as a form of economic integration. Section 3 discusses the theory of optimum currency areas. Section 4 considers the implications of currency unions for monetary and exchange policy. Section 5 considers the implications of currency unions for fiscal policy. Section 6 examines the role of monetary authorities within a currency union. Section 7 examines the role of fiscal authorities within a currency union. Section 8 discusses the motivations for the creation of a currency union. Section 9 considers the costs of participation in a currency union. Section 10 reflects on issues related to the transition to a currency union. The final section concludes.

4.2 FROM MARKET INTEGRATION TO CURRENCY INTEGRATION

Economic (and political) integration has appealed to peoples across time as a means to promote and protect wealth expansion.[1] Several forms of market integration exist. Increasing degrees of factor and product market integration distinguish these types of arrangements. These arrangements include customs unions, free trade areas and common markets. Customs unions are trading arrangements in which participating countries impose reduced (if any) trade barriers within the relevant area and common trade barriers to non-participants. Free trade areas are trading arrangements in which participating countries eliminate trade barriers between each other; each country reserves the right to impose trade barriers according to its own preferences towards non-participants. Common markets are customs unions in which participating countries allow the free movement of factors between each other.

Advocates of currency unions have put forth a number of arguments that a fixed exchange rate system, that is, monetary or currency union, may facilitate the operation of integrated markets.[2] Currency unions represent one form of fixed exchange rate arrangement[3] in which participating countries cease to maintain sovereign currencies. Currency unions represent a greater degree of integration than monetary unions due to the elimination of separate national currencies which typically, although not necessarily, accompanies the former.[4]

Currency unions differ from monetary unions and other fixed exchange rate unions in the following manner. Sovereign countries may affect the relative nominal valuation of their domestic currency as long as it exists. However, once this currency ceases to exist the sovereign country no longer possesses the option of utilizing the tools of monetary policy to affect this valuation. A currency union therefore shifts the burden of adjustment to economic shocks to fiscal institutions, real (as opposed to nominal) internal prices and factor and output movements.

The institution of a common currency in a region already characterized by relatively extensive market integration raises a major long-term concern particularly when the relevant regions constitute sovereign countries. Krugman (1993, 243–8) suggests that market integration alone will affect the economic structures of the regions such that regions become highly specialized in their production. This assertion depends upon the existence of increasing returns to scale in production. High factor mobility may lead to the geographical concentration of productive factors and technologies where potential increasing returns to scale exist. Geographical concentration may result in a divergence of regional growth rates and increase the vulnerability of these regions to asymmetric shocks. Such shocks may lead to factor movements and further divergences in regional rates of growth. The existence of a single currency and monetary policy will limit the ability of national authorities to respond to regional disturbances due to the absence of at least two policy instruments, monetary and exchange rate policy, and possibly a third instrument, fiscal policy. These limitations may inhibit the ability of the affected regions to satisfactorily recover and result in centrifugal forces within the region.

4.3 OPTIMUM CURRENCY AREA THEORY

The theory of currency unions derives in large part from the theory of optimum currency areas (OCA) as presented in articles by Mundell (1961), McKinnon (1963) and Kenen (1969). Mundell presented the following logic for the creation of a currency union. Consider, for example, four regions: A, B, C and D. Regions A and B belong to country First and regions C and D belong to country Second. First operates as a currency union and so does Second. These countries experience shocks to their respective economies. Regions A–C and B–D, respectively, behave similarly in response to shocks. These pairs of regions from First and Second could benefit by correspondingly adopting single currencies because of the ability of similar policy responses to assist in their respective adjustment processes. Such combinations would enable the monetary authorities to cater to more homogeneous constituencies in terms of responses to economic disturbances and monetary policy reactions. Although these currency areas would not coincide with existing currency unions, these new currency areas constitute regions better suited to common monetary policies (Bayoumi and Eichengreen 1993, 195).

According to OCA theory, two factors determine the viability of a currency union. These factors are the disturbances that affect the relevant economies and the adjustment mechanisms available to these regions to respond to these shocks. The following subsections examine these factors in detail.

4.3.1 Shocks

Shocks are any of a variety of disturbances that disrupt the normal functioning of the production and exchange process. Any economy is subject to a wide range of shocks. The structure of the relevant economy and private and public sector responses thereto will determine the effects of any shock.

Economic shocks can be distinguished along at least six lines. The first distinction lies in the source of the shock. Sources may lie within the domestic economy or stem from abroad. Sources may also lie within a particular region or industry.

The second distinction is the nature of the shock, that is, whether real or nominal. The following examples illustrate this distinction. A real shock causes a shift in either or both of the supply and demand curves. The oil shocks of 1973 and 1979 are examples of negative real supply shocks. A nominal shock causes a redenomination of prices and may or may not lead to a shift of either or both of the supply and demand curves. Unexpected inflation represents a nominal shock. Shocks that equally affect the supply and demand curves may have neutral effects. Shocks that differentially affect the supply and demand curves may have non-neutral effects. Non-neutral effects may result from shocks due to the existence of imperfect information and nominal rigidities, for example, long-term contracts, menu costs (Mankiw 1985) and staggered pricing schemes (Taylor 1979; Taylor 1980; Blanchard 1983; Ball and Cecchetti 1988).

The third distinction is the temporal nature of the shock. Shocks may be temporary or permanent occurrences. Similarly, they may persist for short-, medium- or long-term horizons. The effects of shocks depend upon their temporal nature and the speed with which the affected economies respond. Temporary shocks may result in limited adjustments if their expected duration is short. For example, countries may respond to temporary shocks with short-term financing arrangements. Permanent shocks may lead to more extensive adjustments, particularly if they are expected to recur or have long-term effects. In such situations, the expected benefits may justify costly adjustments. Countries may respond to shocks with more permanent medium- and long-term effects with policies for structural adjustments.

The fourth distinction relates to the prior awareness of the affected areas. As with many occurrences in the economy, shocks may be expected or unexpected. Sufficient anticipation of a shock may enable the affected areas to undertake preparations to accommodate the expected disturbance. Such preparations may lessen the impact of the shock. Unexpected shocks, however, may only be prepared for by contingent contracts or automatic mechanisms that respond to relative price changes. The possibility of unexpected shocks constitutes an important element of uncertainty in planning.

The fifth distinction concerns the areas affected by the shock. This distinction relates to the symmetry or asymmetry of the effects of the shock. Symmetry refers to the equality of distribution of the effects of the shock across regions, industries or factor markets. Symmetric shocks affect regions, industries and/or factor markets similarly. Asymmetric shocks affect regions, industries and/or factor markets differentially.

In the case of currency unions, the areas affected by a shock may transcend political jurisdictions at any of a number of levels, such as national, regional and local. Shocks that affect areas differentially, meaning asymmetric shocks, may lead to pressures for assistance from unaffected or positively affected regions. Such assistance may take the form of pecuniary and resource transfers. Kenen (1969, 195) noted the increased possibility of asymmetric shocks in regions characterized by industrial diversification. To the extent that market integration promotes industrial diversification, as Krugman (1993, 243–8) points out, currency unions that possess a high degree of market integration may be especially vulnerable to asymmetric shocks.

The sixth distinction concerns the cause of the shock. Three possible causes of shocks are cyclical, political and structural features of the relevant economy or economies. Cyclical shocks occur at intervals that correspond to regular occurrences within the economy. For example, cyclical shocks may accompany the seasonal cycle of the calendar year (Barsky and Miron 1989) or the electoral cycle (Rogoff 1990). Political instability relates to the strength of the incumbent regime, as well as the interaction between the domestic institutions. Political instability in particular may increase the amount of uncertainty within the economy. Sudden regime changes may cause agents to revise their expectations regarding the economy. Structural shocks include natural disasters, resource discoveries and technological advances. Unanticipated structural shocks will also contribute to uncertainty and similarly cause agents to revise their expectations.

4.3.2 Adjustment Mechanisms

Adjustment mechanisms are conventions that facilitate economic stabilization in response to disturbances to the economy.[5] Those adjustment mechanisms that are available to a country with its own sovereign currency differ from those available to a country participating in a currency union. As discussed earlier, participation in a currency union precludes countries from undertaking independent monetary and exchange rate policies. Fiscal policies may also be subject to budget or market-imposed constraints. For this reason, OCA theory suggests other means by which countries participating in a currency union may adjust to economic shocks.

The first type of adjustment occurs through changes in the real exchange rate. The following equation depicts the real exchange rate:

$$R = E\ (p_f/p_h)$$

where R = the real exchange rate of the domestic currency in terms of foreign currency, E = the nominal exchange rate of the domestic currency in terms of foreign currency, p_f = price of goods in terms of the foreign currency and p_h = price of goods in terms of the domestic currency (Vaubel 1994b, 31). The real exchange rate may change as a result of changes in any of its determinants.[6] Such price changes may result from real shocks to either the foreign or the domestic economy. Barriers to capital movement, as well as expectations, may also affect the real exchange rate (Frankel et al. 1993, 279–81). Real exchange rate changes take place when commodity prices move across regions even within a single currency area where there is no fluctuation in nominal currency values.

The second type of adjustment involves fiscal policy. Fiscal policy measures may be either automatic or discretionary. Automatic measures occur as a result of changes in economic conditions. Automatic stabilizers respond to changes in economic conditions in order to increase or decrease the economic burden faced by relevant constituencies. Discretionary measures result from decisions by the fiscal authority, whether the executive or legislative branch, as statutorily defined, in response to particular circumstances.

Several mechanisms exist by which fiscal policy may facilitate adjustment to an economic shock. These measures include transfer programs that redistribute income from regions unaffected or positively affected to regions negatively affected by a disturbance and insurance programs that collect funds for distribution in case of adverse shocks. The fiscal authority may also undertake counter-cyclical spending policies to assist in the process of adjustment to negative events. These mechanisms may operate in addition to automatic stabilizers that are built in to transfer programs and the tax code.[7,8]

Studies of the United States indicate the role of fiscal policy in alleviating negative asymmetric shocks. Sala-i-Martin and Sachs (1991) suggest the possibility of transfers from prosperous to stagnant regions to assist with regional differences. In particular, they find that for a one-dollar fall in regional income due to an asymmetric shock the effective net reduction in income is 60 cents. The offsetting 40 cents represents the combination of a tax reduction of 34 cents and an inflow of federal transfer payments of 6 cents.

Flexibility in factor and output markets may also serve as an adjustment mechanism. Factor and output flexibility refers to the ease with which factors respond to disturbances. Factors of production include labor, financial capital and physical capital. Output includes intermediate and final products. Flexibility refers to the ease with which factors and output adjust to shocks that affect relative prices through the supply and demand functions.

Factor movements result from changes in relative prices in different regions. Factors move until their marginal products and unit wages are equal across locations, *ceteris paribus*.[9] However, certain barriers may reduce the propensity of factors to move.

Output mobility can serve as a substitute for factor mobility. Output mobility refers to the ability of products to move in response to price changes. Output movements may serve to re-equilibrate supply and demand in response to changes in price and thereby eliminate the need for factor mobility. Only those products that are tradable represent viable substitutes to factor movements.[10]

Two aspects of flexibility apply to labor as a factor of production. The first aspect is the ability to move across geographic regions in search of opportunity. Relocation, transportation, start-up costs, immigration policy, language and cultural differences, union presence, recognition of training and skills, system compatibility, standardized measures and welfare policies affect the ability and willingness of workers to relocate. The second aspect of flexibility is the possibility for factors to increase or reduce their participation rate. For example, in response to a negative demand shock for laborers, workers may accept reduced hours, early retirement packages or decide to leave the labor force. Similarly, physical capital, such as buildings and real estate, may lay idle; owners may retain such property rather than offer it for sale or change its usage to an alternative application.

Wage and price flexibility serves as another adjustment mechanism to macroeconomic shocks. Wage and price flexibility refers to the ease with which real wages and prices move in response to positive or negative demand or supply shocks. Wages tend to be relatively rigid in a downward direction, thus limiting wage changes as an adjustment mechanism. However, flexibility depends upon the time horizon under consideration. Long-term contracts may preclude the rapid adjustment of wages or prices to unexpected events. The cost of adjusting in the short run typically exceeds the cost of adjusting over the long-run. Over time factors and producers are able to renegotiate contracts and seek out substitute sources or activities.

Openness refers to the amount of exchange undertaken by the domestic economy with the rest of the world relative to national output. The extent to which a country's economy is open to the rest of the world affects the potential benefits from and costs of monetary integration, as well as its vulnerability to external shocks. For example, a closed economy is less susceptible to negative shocks from the rest of the world than an open economy. The more dependent or interdependent an economy is on the external economy, the more vulnerable it is to shocks affecting its trading partners. In other words, the larger its tradable versus non-tradable sector, the more vulnerable the country is to external shocks.[11] Participants in a single currency area tend to have a relatively large amount of trade with each other.

Similarly, the openness of regional economies affects regions' ability to adjust to domestic shocks. Countries that are more integrated into external economies may experience greater capital, labor and goods flows in response to disturbances. Factor and output flows will cost relatively less in regions participating in a preferential trading arrangement than in regions characterized by high barriers to external trade.

Industrial and portfolio diversification affects the ability of regions to accommodate disturbances. Industrial diversification is the extent to which the domestic economy consists of a variety of productive activities, no one or single group of which constitutes a major portion of the domestic economy. A more diversified country produces a wider range of products than does a less diversified or specialized country. Industrial diversification affects the extent to which shocks may affect a country. Although a diversified economy is more susceptible to asymmetric shocks, it may be less costly for such an economy to undertake a program of internal transfers or operate an insurance program for domestic shocks. Industrial diversification may also increase the opportunity set facing displaced factors of production.

Individual countries, however, may or may not be individually industrially diversified. Countries may be specialized in specific industries. Alternatively, countries may engage in various industries. In the former case, an optimum currency area may facilitate additional inter-industry exchange. In the latter case, an optimum currency area may facilitate additional intra-industry exchange. Countries may specialize in narrow aspects of the production processes of various industries.

Portfolio diversification is the extent to which holders of financial capital have distributed their wealth across a variety of investment instruments. Such diversification may take the form of international holdings, risky versus safe assets, for example, government securities versus commercial securities, or forward or futures investments. Financial holdings enable individuals and organizations to own claims to a larger variety of undertakings than they could typically undertake on their own. By increasing the variety of claims they own, investors may protect their wealth against diversifiable adverse events. Portfolio diversification operates as an insurance mechanism, which may strengthen the ability of individuals and organizations to endure and survive various shocks. Interestingly, Atkeson and Bayoumi (1991, 198) find that capital holders undertake portfolio diversification to cushion against economic disturbances to a significantly greater extent than non-capital holders who obtain their income from labor alone. Portfolio and industrial diversification may be relatively more valuable in the short run in response to temporary shocks. Permanent shocks may require structural changes.

Adjustment mechanisms play an important role in responding to economic shocks. These mechanisms obtain greater relevance within a currency union where regions are unable to adjust their nominal exchange rates. Some mechanisms may effectively substitute for others. The extent to which these mechanisms promote economic stabilization and growth will affect the long-term success of the monetary regime.

4.4 IMPLICATIONS OF A CURRENCY UNION FOR MONETARY POLICY

Monetary policy consists of the decisions and actions taken by the government and/or monetary authority to affect the supply of money and credit within its/their jurisdiction. The government and/or monetary authority may pursue one or more policy goals. The monetary authority has four tools at its disposal to affect the domestic supply of money and credit. These tools are open market operations, discount rates, reserve requirements and exchange rate policy. The following sections examine these aspects of monetary policy in the context of a currency union.

4.4.1 Goals of Monetary Policy

The monetary authority may choose from a number of policy goals. Hubbard (1995, 526–8) identifies six goals. Three of these goals relate to the stability of variables within the monetary sector. These variables include the price level, interest rates and foreign exchange rates. The monetary authority may target stable prices, as characterized by a fixed rate of increase of inflation or as characterized by zero inflation. In the latter case nominal prices do not move due to changes in the money supply.

The monetary authority may also strive to maintain stability within the financial system. Financial stability is important in order to maintain stability within the overall economy. To this end the monetary authority may observe and regulate financial institutions. The monetary authority may conduct studies of economic conditions in order to keep policy-makers and market participants abreast of the domestic economic situation. It may also monitor the balance sheets of financial institutions. These efforts assist in alerting the monetary authority to potential crises within the financial system.

The monetary authority may also strive to maintain low domestic unemployment. The monetary authority may target the unemployment level or its growth rate. Such factors as unemployment insurance, the minimum wage and labor unions also affect the level of domestic unemployment (Barro 1990, 264–7).

Finally, the monetary authority may choose economic growth as a goal. Economic growth concerns the use of policies conducive to increased production and real wealth within the economy. The monetary authority may facilitate growth by pursuing other goals such as economic stability, for example price, interest rate and exchange rate stability. Reducing the instability of such factors may promote long-term planning and investment decisions by reducing uncertainty.

4.4.1.1 Role of monetary policy in adjusting to shocks

Monetary policy is one means by which the monetary authority and/or government may respond to shocks to its economy. The monetary authority may expand or contract the money supply and/or credit supply in order to accommodate shocks. Such efforts may aim to achieve any of the above-mentioned goals.

Whether or not monetary policy has real effects on the domestic economy has been a matter of theoretical and empirical debate among economists. This debate revolves around two assumptions. First, the appearance of real effects depends upon whether or not markets clear perfectly and instantaneously. Imperfect information,[12] nominal rigidities and regulation may affect the impact such policies have on the domestic economy. Second, it depends upon whether policy is anticipated or unanticipated. The rational expectations approach asserts that agents utilize all available information and do not make systematic errors in forming their expectations regarding government policy, in particular monetary policy. To the extent that agents possess rational expectations they are able to anticipate monetary policy actions based upon the previous record of the monetary authority. Agents may undertake contingent contracts with provisions for known monetary policy decision functions. To the extent that agents are not fully informed or make systematic errors, agents may be unable to fully anticipate monetary policy actions. In this case, monetary policy may have real effects.

Monetary policy enables the government and/or monetary authority to respond directly or indirectly to constituent concerns in the face of economic disturbances. The extent to which these bodies so do depends upon the region's monetary constitution. In particular the types of rules or amount of discretion contained within the constitution will affect these bodies' ability to intervene.

The monetary authority controls monetary policy within its monetary jurisdiction. In the case of the creation of a currency union, sovereign monetary authorities must surrender their policy-making power to the authority of the union. Countries lose their ability to independently affect domestic money and credit supplies through monetary policy. Similarly, they lose their ability to affect the domestic nominal exchange rate. The union's monetary authority dictates policy which affects the single common currency. The loss of monetary and exchange rate policy removes two mechanisms of economic intervention from sovereign governments. Rather the union authority acquires these mechanisms on behalf of the entire currency area.

4.4.2 Tools of Monetary Policy

In order to achieve its long-run monetary goals, the monetary authority makes use of intermediate and operating targets. Intermediate targets are economic variables, which approximate the long-term goals and are more easily attained and observed in the medium-term. Examples of intermediate targets include the money supply and interest rates.[13]

Operating targets are those economic variables that the monetary authority can affect in the short run and is able to use to approximate the intermediate targets. Examples of operating targets are the overnight, inter-bank borrowing rate, meaning the fed funds rate and non-borrowed reserves. In order to be useful operating targets, variables must be measurable, controllable and predictable (Hubbard 1995, 533–5). Monetary policy actions may exert additional affects on economic variables due to imperfect information and nominal rigidities within the economy.

The monetary authority uses four instruments to affect its operating targets. These instruments affect domestic money and credit supplies. These instruments include open market operations, the discount rate, reserve requirements and exchange rate policy. The first three instruments affect the supply and demand for the country's currency and domestic credit, The final instrument affects the country's nominal exchange rate relative to other countries' exchange rates in international currency markets.

Open market operations consist of the purchases and sales of government securities by the monetary authority on behalf of the fiscal authority. The monetary authority may conduct open market operations in order to expand or reduce the domestic money supply.

Open market operations determine the risk-free interest rate in money and capital markets. The risk-free rate serves as a baseline in the determination of all other interest rates in the domestic market. The monetary authority of a currency union may buy or sell centrally issued securities on behalf of the supranational political authority or regional securities issued by regional governments.

The discount rate is the price depository institutions pay to borrow funds from the monetary authority. The monetary authority may raise or lower the discount rate in order to expand or reduce the domestic money supply. This discount rate will affect any institution that borrows funds from the currency union's monetary authority.

Reserve requirements are the amount of funds depository institutions must hold on account at the monetary authority as a fraction of their total deposits. Reserve requirements constitute a tax on the holdings of depository institutions. The monetary authority may raise or lower reserve requirements in order to expand or reduce the domestic money supply.

Exchange rate policy is the monetary authority's behavior surrounding the determination and support of the nominal valuation of the domestic currency *vis-à-vis* foreign currencies. Within the currency union, all regions share the same nominal exchange rate with the rest of the world. However, a currency union may undertake a fixed, floating or combination exchange rate arrangement with respect to the rest of the world. In determining or leaving the market to determine the currency union's exchange rate *vis-à-vis* foreign currencies, the currency's exchange rate is set. If the monetary authority permits this rate to fluctuate against other currencies, the arrangement constitutes some version of a floating exchange rate system. If the monetary authority endeavors to utilize its tools to prevent the exchange rate from appreciating or depreciating in international currency markets, the arrangement constitutes some version of fixed exchange rate system. Under either of these systems the monetary authority may sell or purchase reserves of foreign currency. These decisions may affect the domestic money supply. Similarly, foreign sales or purchases of the domestic currency may affect the money supply. The domestic monetary authority may attempt to prevent such sales or purchases from affecting the money supply through sterilized intervention.

4.4.3 Political Economy of Monetary Policy

The political economy of monetary policy concerns the interaction between political institutions and the monetary authority. If monetary policy has real effects, it may be a powerful tool for affecting wealth accumulation. Whether or not monetary policy has real effects depends upon agents' expectations, nominal rigidities, information quality and availability and the various lags associated with its implementation (for more on lags please see endnote 8). To the extent that monetary policy has real effects, it is valuable to politicians whose continued power depends upon constituent support. For this reason, politicians may seek to utilize monetary policy-making in order to benefit their interests and those of their benefactors.

Three political variables may play a role in monetary policy-making: (1) the electoral cycle; (2) the incumbent political party; and (3) the behavior of interest groups (Goodman 1992, 5). The electoral cycle may have several effects on monetary policy. First, incumbent politicians may undertake expansive monetary policies in order to create the appearance of a strong economy immediately prior to an election (Nordhaus 1975). The inflationary impact of such a policy will be felt only after the election.[14] Second, partisan effects may lead to monetary policies that target either inflation or unemployment. For the case of the United States, Alesina (1987) finds that conservative governments tend to pursue more restrictive monetary policies to limit inflation; liberal governments tend to pursue less expansionary monetary policies to reduce unemployment.[15] Interest groups may affect monetary policy-making by successful lobbying of the government for policies that best suit their interests. For example, debt-laden interests prefer inflationary policies that reduce the real burden of their debt.

The monetary authority plays an important role not only in affecting the domestic economy, but also as a source of revenue creation for the government. The monetary authority's role of selling and purchasing government securities determines the government's access to credit. Similarly, the monetary authority's willingness to monetize the debt affects the government's ability to engage in deficit finance. The monetary authority's ability to increase or decrease the money supply affects inflation and the real value of debts.

Money creation raises two kinds of revenue for the domestic government. First, money creation generates seigniorage, which is the difference between the cost of producing the money in real terms and its purchasing power. Within a currency union the generation and distribution of seigniorage may become a matter of political debate (Buiter and Kletzer 1991, 233). The second kind of revenue money creation generates is implicit in the reduction of real debt due to inflation. Nominal government obligations that are not fully indexed decrease in value with inflation. Money creation enables more government expenditure than justified by claims on real assets alone. The likelihood of money creation to satisfy governmental demands depends upon the degree of monetary authority independence and the willingness of the monetary authority to finance government expenditures.

4.5 IMPLICATIONS OF A CURRENCY UNION FOR FISCAL POLICY

Fiscal policy is undertaken through government taxation, expenditure and debt issuance policies. Taxation policy concerns the collection of revenue from individuals and productive enterprises within the relevant jurisdiction. Government expenditures consist of the purchase of goods and services by the governing body. Debt issuance concerns the practice of government borrowing through financial markets. Fiscal policy serves as the primary means to obtain and distribute revenue in order to finance government expenditures.

4.5.1 Goals of Fiscal Policy

Fiscal policy may have several goals. The first goal is public goods provision. Public goods are those goods and services that are non-rival and non-excludable. The second goal of fiscal policy is wealth redistribution. Through the tax system, the fiscal authority collects funds, which the government then distributes. Recipients of revenue distribution need not coincide with those who made the original contributions. The third goal of fiscal policy is to affect private sector decisions. For example, tax rates may be increased or decreased in order to create incentives or disincentives, respectively, for particular types of behavior. Similarly, government purchases may stimulate regional economies or particular industrial sectors.

4.5.1.1 Role of fiscal policy in adjusting to shocks

Fiscal policy may play an important role in adjusting to shocks to the economy. As discussed in the context of OCA theory, it offers several mechanisms that may facilitate adjustment to economic disturbances. These mechanisms include inter-regional transfers, tax policy, insurance programs and government expenditures. These mechanisms may inject adversely affected regions with funds for revitalization.

4.5.2 Tools of Fiscal Policy

The fiscal authority possesses several tools for carrying out fiscal policy. These tools include taxation, expenditure and debt issuance policies. The fiscal authority employs these tools to achieve government fiscal policy objectives. The ability of fiscal policy, like monetary policy, to affect the domestic economy depends on whether or not agents possess rational expectations.

Taxation policy may be of several forms. The first type of taxation is based on percentages. One form of taxation is based on a fixed percentage. Such taxes are known as proportional or flat taxes. A second form of taxation is based on a variable percentage which corresponds with income level. Progressive taxes place a higher absolute burden on individuals and entities with relatively high income. Regressive taxes place a higher absolute burden on individuals and entities with relatively low income. A second type of taxation is lump sum. Such taxes consist of a fixed sum. The fiscal authority may levy these taxes on a variety of wealth sources. These sources include labor, capital and corporate income.

Taxation policies may affect the economy in one of several ways. First, taxes may serve as incentives or disincentives for different activities. For example, so-called sin taxes serve to discourage consumption of certain products. Second, unexpected taxes may affect domestic consumption where agents make spending decisions according to the permanent income hypothesis and possess rational expectations (Hall 1978). Unexpected taxes induce agents to change their spending behavior in order to smooth their income. Third, taxes may serve to gather funds from one or more segments of the population in order to transfer them to another segment of the population. Such transfers may result from existing wealth differentials or in response to adverse shocks to the regional economies. Fourth, taxes may act as an automatic adjustment mechanism to adverse events by smoothing domestic income.[16]

Expenditure policies may also affect the economy in several ways. First, expenditures on goods and services may serve to provide items to constituents which the private market might not offer, such as public goods. Second, expenditures may serve to support a particular geographical region or industry because of narrow interest group pressures. Expenditure policies may serve to distribute funds, goods or services to one segment of the population after collection from a different segment. The type of government purchases, for example consumption versus investment, may have different effects on regional economies.

Debt issuance policies consist of the sale and purchase of government securities. Such issues serve to provide the government with funds to undertake expenditures. Government debt instruments may have short-, medium- or long-term duration. They may or may not be directly tied to specific expenditures.

Government debt issues may affect the economy in several ways. First, government debt may raise the cost of borrowing in financial markets. Crowding-out is said to occur when government debt displaces private investment. Second, government debt may affect the amount of private domestic saving. The Ricardian equivalence debate revolves around the effects of government debt on individual saving decisions.[17]

4.5.3 Political Economy of Fiscal Policy

The political economy of fiscal policy considers the effects of political incentives on the process of fiscal policy-making. Fiscal policy is a powerful tool for affecting wealth distribution. Politicians value fiscal policy as a means to satisfy constituent demands for income redistribution and public goods provision. The theory of the political economy of fiscal policy includes two major issues: budget deficits and political budget cycles. In the context of currency unions, additional issues arise.

Theories of political budget cycles correlate budgetary behavior with the electoral cycle. Nordhaus (1975) finds a statistically significant relationship between fiscal expenditures and the timing of elections. Incumbent politicians pursue expansionary fiscal and monetary policy immediately prior to elections. Corsetti and Roubini (1993, 71) present similar results. They observe that: (1) budget deficits increase during election years; and (2) countries with unstable coalition governments experience higher deficits than more stable countries. Alesina and Tabellini (1993) find that two factors motivate incumbent governments to incur large deficits. The first factor is a low probability of re-election. The second factor is the difference in ideologies between the incumbent party and its opposition. Rogoff (1990) suggests that incumbents utilize the budget as a signal to demonstrate their administrative competence.

Additional theories seek to explain the existence of budget deficits external to the electoral cycle. First, budget deficits may constitute an attempt to transfer the burden of payment over generations. Second, counter-cyclical deficits may enable the government to assist the domestic economy during economic downturns. Such downturns include unanticipated shocks.

Several means exist to limit deficit finance within a currency union. First, a fiscal constitution or set of rules may place thresholds on jurisdictional spending limits. Exceptions to these rules may accommodate deviations from the thresholds. These rules require a binding enforcement mechanism to be successful. The constitution may levy penalties on countries or regions that violate their limits. Discipline imposed by financial markets may eliminate the need for statutory limits. The market may limit the size of deficits by requiring interest rates which exceed the amount the borrowing government is willing to pay for additional debt issuance. Such conventions may prevent individual countries from issuing debt instruments that lead to *excessive* deficits. Goldstein and Woglom (1992, 229 and 232) observe the existence of a risk premium on US state bonds that is positively correlated with the indebtedness of states. Budgetary rules, however, must be carefully crafted in order to leave governments with enough flexibility to accommodate shocks.

4.6 MONETARY AUTHORITY OF A CURRENCY UNION

The primary responsibility of the monetary authority of a currency union is to conduct monetary operations within the union. The monetary authority of a currency union faces a different set of concerns and constraints than that of a country with its own sovereign currency. A central monetary authority carries the interests of a much larger geographical area in deciding and conducting its policy. It may be unable or unwilling to cater to the interests of all regions especially those that are politically weaker. This section examines the responsibilities of a monetary authority in general and within a currency union, the organization and distribution of power of the central monetary authority, and the political economy of central banking.

4.6.1 Responsibilities of the Monetary Authority

The monetary authority of a country with its own currency carries a variety of responsibilities. In the context of a currency union these responsibilities remain. Several alternative arrangements exist to carry out the operation of a currency union. A central monetary authority or other institutions must carry out these duties.

The operations of the monetary sector fall into three general categories. The first category concerns the maintenance of the money supply. This category includes the size and growth of the internal money and credit supplies, as well as the size and growth of foreign exchange reserves. This category may also include the provision of credit or money to the government for financing its purchases.

The second category of responsibility concerns the maintenance of the internal financial and payments system. Within this category are a number of specific tasks. First, the monetary authority may provide liquidity to the financial system in order to prevent the realization of system-wide financial crises. Second, the monetary authority may provide funds to institutions in order to prevent their insolvency even where the effects may not be system-wide; the monetary authority acts as the lender of last resort. Third, the monetary authority may undertake audits and prepare studies of the financial institutions and the industry as a whole in order to inform decision-makers within the monetary authority and the government. Fourth, the monetary authority may regulate aspects of the financial industry in order to promote a stable system.

The third category of responsibility concerns the operation of the internal payments system. In this role, the monetary authority provides for the clearing and settlements process. The monetary authority also plays a central role in the international payments system.

4.6.2 Organization and Distribution of Power of the Central Monetary Authority

The monetary arrangement represented by the currency union will require an institutional arrangement to administer its operation. This institutional arrangement will replace the system of national monetary authorities which were responsible for domestic monetary policy-making. Several considerations regarding central monetary authorities deserve attention in the context of the creation of this new institution. These considerations include organizational structure, internal decision-making hierarchy, regional representation and decision procedures.

Two alternative organizational structures exist for delegating the responsibility of the currency union's monetary policy. Both alternatives make use of the existing framework of monetary authorities within the participating states. The first alternative consists of granting control over the union's monetary policy to the central bank of the dominant country's central bank. The dominant country is the country with the best currency and economic performance record in terms of domestic monetary measures, such as inflation and exchange rate stability. One benefit of this alternative is the opportunity to carry over the credibility of the dominant country's monetary authority to the new arrangement.

The second alternative consists of the creation of a new supranational institution, which will bear responsibility for the union's monetary policy. This institution may direct and coordinate the actions of the national monetary authorities. These banks will serve as the regional outposts of the central monetary authority. One concern with this alternative is uncertainty surrounding the commitment of the new institution to its objectives. Speculators may endeavor to test this commitment through speculative attacks. By sticking to its guns, the new institution may develop a reputation of resolve.

If the first alternative is chosen the decision structure of the monetary authority may remain unchanged. However, currency union participants not already within the jurisdiction of the dominant central bank will likely demand the opportunity to provide input into the decision-making procedure of the body. These participants will seek to send representatives to protect their interests. To the extent that the dominant central bank accepts such missions its power will diminish and its reputation may soften.

If the second alternative is chosen, a new organizational structure and decision-making procedure is required. The monetary authority requires leadership. This leadership may take one of a number of forms. One form consists of a governor or president supported by a committee of representatives from the regions under the monetary control of the authority. Another form consists of a committee of representatives from the various regions. Sovereign countries will likely demand the membership of representatives to any such body in order to ensure attention to their respective interests.

A monetary constitution may depict the organizational structure and operating procedures of the monetary authority. The executive and/or legislative branches of the central government of the currency area may decide on this constitution. The constitution may provide for the appointment of top-level officials, the organizational structure, regional jurisdictions and decision-making procedures. The constitution will also express the degree of goal and instrument independence of the monetary authority.

The decision-making structure within either organizational framework must incorporate the input of representatives from the formerly sovereign monetary jurisdictions. These jurisdictions may or may not have coincided with national boundaries. Decision rules may assign one vote per representative or may employ a weighted voting system based on the size of each jurisdiction as a proportion of the whole area. Decisions may require a simple, qualified or larger majority to act. The decision rules determine the behavior of the monetary authority.

4.6.3 The Federal Reserve System: An Example

The US Federal Reserve System (FRS) provides an insightful example of the organization and operation of a central banking system. The FRS consists of central decision-making bodies comprised of a variety of representatives, along with regional banks representing each of the 12 Federal Reserve districts. These districts correspond to FRS jurisdictions and each includes a number of states and industrial sectors. The intention behind the inclusion of multiple political units and a variety of producer interests was to prevent the domination of regional banks by a single or small group of interests.

Each district possesses its own Federal Reserve Bank, which serves as the representative of the FRS in that region. These regional banks provide discount lending to their members. National banks must join the FRS as a condition of operation, while state banks retain the right to decide whether to join. Membership of the FRS requires the deposit of some funds with the respective district Federal Reserve Bank.

Four bodies comprise the decision-making units within the FRS. These bodies are the regional Federal Reserve Banks, the member banks, the Board of Governors and the Federal Open Market Committee. These bodies each play a role in the process of monetary policy determination.

A board of directors heads each of the regional Federal Reserve Banks. Nine members comprise each board. Member banks participate in the selection of the members to the board. Three criteria determine the composition of the Board. First, three members hail from the banking industry. Second, three members hail from agriculture, commerce and industry. The member banks vote to elect these six board members. Finally, the Federal Reserve Board of Governors appoints three members to represent the public interest. The nine members of the regional board elect the president of the district bank. This method of selection seeks to ensure the representation of a variety of interests on the Board and to prevent the domination of the Board by any single interest group.

The Board of Governors of the FRS consists of seven members. The President of the USA nominates these members; their appointment is subject to approval by the US Senate. Governors serve nonrenewable 14-year terms. Gubernatorial appointments are staggered in order to prevent a single President from nominating the entire Board. These terms expire in alternating Januarys.

A chairman leads the Board of Governors. The President appoints the chairman subject to Senate approval. The chairman serves a renewable four-year term.

The Federal Open Market Committee (FOMC) consists of 12 members from the Board of Governors, the president of the New York district Federal Reserve Bank, and the presidents of the other district Federal Reserve Banks. All of the members of the Board of Governors belong to the FOMC. Only four of the 12 regional Reserve Bank presidents serve as voting members of the FOMC at a time. However, the remaining seven members attend FOMC meetings, which occur eight times per year. The FOMC decides on the FRS' open market operations. The trading desk of the New York Federal Reserve Bank carries out the decisions of the FOMC by buying and selling government securities.

4.6.4 Political Economy of Monetary Policy-making

The political economy of monetary policy-making concerns the interaction between political institutions and the monetary authority. This theory centers on the location of responsibility for monetary policy decision-making. Responsibility for monetary policy decision-making may lie with the executive branch, the legislative branch, the monetary authority or any combination of the three.

Institutional responsibility for monetary policy decision-making depends upon the relationship between the government, meaning the executive and/or legislative branch(es), and the monetary authority. Where the government plays a very limited role in monetary policy determination, the monetary authority enjoys relative independence. This independence precludes government intervention and may be beneficial to the avoidance of short-term political manipulations of the money supply for political benefit and for the prevention of the establishment of a political business cycle (Hubbard 1995). Where the government plays an interventionist role in monetary determination the monetary authority enjoys little or no independence.

Central bank independence denotes the ability of the monetary authority to decide on the objectives and/or tools of monetary policy free from political influence. Arguments in favor of central bank independence stem from concerns that political actors and/or institutions may attempt to utilize the monetary authority to achieve short-term goals for political reasons. These goals may be counter to medium- and long-run stability and/or growth. Arguments against central bank independence stem from concerns that democratically elected officials should be able to utilize monetary policy in order to achieve objectives desired by the electorate (Mankiw 1994, 491). Central bank independence breaks the link between electorate and public official.[18] However, central bank independence enables the monetary authority to undertake policies which, although politically unpopular in the short run, may promote long-run economic growth and stability.

Two types of central bank independence exist: goal independence and instrument independence. Goal independence refers to the ability of the central bank to determine its policy goal or goals. This goal will dictate the objective(s) the monetary authority strives to achieve. Examples of goals include zero or low inflation and specific growth rates for a particular monetary aggregate. Instrument independence refers to the ability of the central bank to determine the tools it uses to conduct policy. Examples of instruments include the discount rate, reserve requirements and open market operations.

Politicians may seek to influence the monetary authority for several purposes. The first reason for such influence stems from electoral considerations. The second reason is that politicians may seek to monetize the government's debt through money creation. Third, politicians may seek access to credit on preferred terms from the monetary authority. Fourth, politicians may seek to satisfy interest group pressures regarding monetary policy or through the use of monetary policy.

Political influence of monetary policy may take place irrespective of the statutory independence of the monetary authority. The opportunity for such influence will depend upon the interrelations between the monetary authority and the political institutions, such as the executive and legislative branches of the government. A monetary constitution may reduce the ability of political actors to influence monetary policy. Tight rules may further reduce the influence of political actors upon the monetary authority. Yet, in spite of the existence of a monetary constitution careful provisions may fail to eliminate possibilities for political influence over the monetary authority.[19]

A number of avenues exist which may enable the exertion of political influence upon the monetary authority. These avenues result from incentives that affect individual officials within the monetary authority. Two major avenues are personnel and budget policies.

Personnel policies include hiring and firing procedures as well as official compensation packages. First, political appointees may respond to pressures from their erstwhile supporters to whom they owe their position. Similarly, where reappointment is contingent upon political support, officials may succumb to current period political pressures in an effort to obtain political support in later periods. Long-term appointments may reduce the vulnerability of monetary officials to political factors particularly related to electoral cycles. Non-renewable appointments may eliminate this possibility. However, non-renewable appointments prevent the benefits from the continued employment of experienced officials within the bank. Where employment after tenure at the central bank is contingent upon future political support, officials may also advocate politically desired policies in an effort to increase their future professional opportunity set. Similarly, political appointees may respond to various pressures in order to increase their employment opportunities after their tenure. Monetary authority officials may also be subject to political influence if the executive and/or legislative branches possess discretionary powers over officials' compensation packages.

Budget policies concern the sources of revenues for financing the operation of the monetary authority. Political institutions may exert control over the monetary authority's budget in at least two ways. First, political institutions may appropriate funds to the monetary authority as a part of the government's annual budget proceedings. Second, political institutions may design or alter the constitution of the monetary authority and thereby affect the budgetary autonomy of the institution. To the extent that political institutions possess discretion over the monetary authority's budget, the latter is vulnerable to pressures from the former.

4.7 FISCAL AUTHORITY OF A CURRENCY UNION

The fiscal authority of a currency union is that body responsible for conducting fiscal operations within the regions of the union. The fiscal authority may consist of a central institution responsible for the entire currency union or separate regional authorities. The structure of the fiscal authority affects the concerns and constraints it faces. This section examines the responsibilities of a fiscal authority in general and within a currency union, the organization and distribution of power of the central fiscal authority, and the political economy of fiscal policy-making.

4.7.1 Responsibilities

The fiscal authority possesses responsibilities in three areas of fiscal policy-making: taxation, expenditure and debt issuance. Whether the fiscal authority serves a country with its own sovereign currency, a state or region within a currency union or an entire currency union, these tasks arise. However, fiscal authorities differ in one key respect from monetary authorities. Fiscal authorities depend upon the executive and legislative branches of their own countries for revenue collection and expenditure policy. The structure of the fiscal authority may affect the success of the currency union.

4.7.2 Organization and Distribution of Power

A number of different arrangements may characterize the fiscal authority of a currency union. These arrangements differ according to the location of fiscal decision-making and the proximity of the fiscal decision-makers to their relevant constituencies. The fiscal authority handles taxation, expenditures and debt insurance policies. The scale at which the fiscal authority carries out these responsibilities depends upon the fiscal arrangement, that is whether local, regional or national.

The first possible arrangement consists of the continuation of the *status quo*. For many countries, this may mean the continued operation of national fiscal authorities. In this case, countries retain the right and the power to determine national fiscal policy. The implications of independent fiscal policies include the external effects of deficit finance on union-wide interest rates and the spillover of public goods across fiscal boundaries. In addition, market integration may enable mobile tax bases to flock to lower tax regions.

The second possible arrangement consists of the union-wide replacement of the *status quo* according to the principle of fiscal equivalence. Fiscal equivalence, also known as reciprocity, stresses the need for the coincidence of geographical costs and benefits in terms of public goods provision.[20] Fiscal equivalence provides a unique correspondence between the benefits and costs of public programs. It may thereby avoid imposing externalities on neighboring fiscal jurisdictions (Von Hagen 1993b, 266–7). One benefit of fiscal equivalence is the inhibition of the growth of a central Leviathan (Brennan and Buchanan 1977). However, the problem of how to get the government to impose its own binding constraints remains.

The third type of arrangement is the fiscal counterpart to the concept of subsidiarity: fiscal federalism. According to fiscal federalism, fiscal decisions are made at the governmental level closest to the individuals and groups affected. A fiscal federation consists of multiple levels of government responsible for fiscal policy decision-making, each with their own powers in certain areas of taxation and expenditures.

Several benefits exist for jurisdictions belonging to a fiscal federation. The first benefit is the relative proximity between the decision-makers and their constituents. This proximity facilitates the conveyance of preferences by constituents to political decision-makers. Fiscal federalism may promote the satisfaction of heterogeneous preferences. The second benefit, due to the existence of multiple jurisdictions at each governmental level, is the possibility for competition among jurisdictions. Jurisdictions compete to provide public goods to their residents at the least cost. The possibility of residential exit will drive jurisdictional competition. The third benefit is the inhibition of the growth of a central Leviathan (Brennan and Buchanan 1977).

Several potential disadvantages exist for jurisdictions belonging to a fiscal federation. The first possible disadvantage is the inefficient scale of public goods provision. The second possible disadvantage is the possibility of spillovers to other jurisdictions. Such spillovers may be positive or negative. In either case, the responsible jurisdiction is either not receiving the full benefit or paying the full cost of its decisions. The third possible disadvantage is the lack of coordination across jurisdictions in response to multi-jurisdictional shocks whether symmetric or asymmetric.

A fiscal union is the fiscal counterpart to a monetary union. Participants in a fiscal union surrender taxing and spending decisions to a central fiscal authority. This authority determines fiscal policy for all regions of the polity.

Several possible benefits exist with fiscal unions. The first benefit is the ability for the decision-making authority to command enough resources to attain economies of scale. The second benefit is the ability to make transfers across jurisdictions in case of asymmetric shocks. The third benefit is the ability to facilitate fiscal policy coordination across jurisdictions.

Several possible disadvantages exist with fiscal unions. The first possible disadvantage is the elimination of the exit option for residents. Where a central authority determines fiscal policy residents lose the option to relocate to a nearby jurisdiction that follows a different fiscal policy. The second possible disadvantage is the absence of choice of fiscal environments for individuals and enterprises with heterogeneous preferences. Fiscal competition among jurisdictions may lead to the optimal provision of public goods. The absence of this competition may lead to reduced individual utility. The third possible disadvantage is that the concerns of all jurisdictions may not be given the attention that is satisfactory to their respective constituents. A single group or groups of interests may capture the central authority to the detriment of the other interests. To the extent that these interests correspond to political jurisdictions dissatisfaction of excluded constituents will grow.

4.7.3 Political Economy of Fiscal Authority

The close institutional relationship between fiscal authorities and government institutions precludes the need for an analysis of the interaction between the two bodies. The fiscal authority is typically an agent directed by and directly responsible to the government. The interaction between these two bodies is therefore analogous to a principal–agent relationship. The fiscal authority is the bureaucratic agent of the government. In this respect, the relationship between the fiscal authority and the government, and the monetary authority and the government, may differ.

The fiscal incentives facing national governments may change under a currency union regime. Individual countries may undertake budgetary policies which lead to deficits in excess of their ability to repay. Such actions may exert negative externalities on other members of the currency union. For example, central interest rates may increase depending upon market expectations about a bailout by the union's monetary authority. Similarly, interest rates on other governments' debts may rise if markets fear the appearance of additional government deficits.

4.8 MOTIVATIONS FOR THE CREATION OF A CURRENCY UNION

Two closely related motivations lead to the creation of a currency union. These motivations are political and economic in nature. Political motivations are those factors from which politicians expect to gain relative strength because of the preparation for, transition to and operation of a currency union. These motivations may incorporate economic motivations. Economic motivations consist of all of the expected benefits to the economy from the creation and operation of a currency union.

Economic motivations revolve around the creation and accumulation of wealth as a result of the elimination of trade barriers associated with the existence of multiple exchange rates. Goodman (1992, 203) identifies three motivations related to the three uses of money. First, the reduction of transactions costs attributable to currency conversions within the currency union enhances the role of money as a medium of exchange. Second, pricing in the common currency facilitates internal price comparisons and thereby enhances the role of money as a unit of account. Third, the common currency abolishes exchange rate risk within the union. By eliminating uncertainty regarding movements in internal, relative currency valuations, the need for forward and futures markets disappears with the replacement of sovereign currencies. As a result, money's role as a store of value strengthens.

The creation of a currency union may lead to savings in several other respects as well. First, participating national monetary authorities need no longer acquire and hold foreign exchange reserves of the currencies of participating countries in the currency union. Seigniorage gains will follow. Second, participants in and providers of services in internal foreign exchange transactions will save on costs associated with multi-currency accounting, payments and planning. These resources may be devoted to other productive activities. Increased production and trade may follow allowing producers to enjoy new economies of scale and scope. Third, a currency union may introduce the opportunity for inflation-prone countries to enjoy lower inflation strategies. The average rate of inflation may fall between the historical inflation rates of the most and least inflation-prone countries. Those countries with historical inflation above this average will gain. Those countries with historical inflation below this average will lose. To the extent that financial markets accept the former countries! lower inflation policies as credible, financial markets may demand lesser risk premia on the purchases of national debt issues.[21] However, markets may demand higher risk premia from historically low-inflation governments.[22] Participation alone may serve as a signal of national governments! resolve to follow the monetary policy of the currency union. This resolve may benefit governments with a reputation of exchange rate manipulation. A currency union may also introduce the opportunity for low-inflation countries to undertake relatively more inflationary policies. Although such a policy will impose costs on certain sectors of the formerly low-inflation country, other sectors may enjoy the opportunity to indulge their preferences in a less restricted monetary environment.

4.9 COSTS OF PARTICIPATION IN A CURRENCY UNION

Two major costs accompany participation in a currency union. These costs include policy and microeconomic costs. The first costs relate to macroeconomic losses in the form of monetary, exchange rate and fiscal policy. These costs arise in the period prior to participation in and during the operation of the arrangement. The second costs relate to additional microeconomic costs associated with the transition from an existing arrangement of sovereign currencies.

4.9.1 Policy Costs

Policy costs from participation in a currency union may occur in three areas: monetary, exchange rate and fiscal policies. These costs result from the inability of currency union members to indulge national preferences regarding monetary and exchange rate policy, and, possibly, to some extent, fiscal policy. The success of the currency union will depend on participants' ability to promote their economies in a manner satisfactory to the constituents of the currency union.

The first policy loss that countries experience by joining a currency union is monetary policy. Monetary policy is important for economic growth, as well as for domestic stabilization policy. The latter includes adjustment to shocks to the domestic economy. The government and/or the monetary authority may use the money and credit supply to boost or dampen aggregate demand and supply. The resulting effects of these actions may be to increase or decrease national output. The money supply and expectations regarding the money supply also affect domestic interest rates and inflation. Interest rates and inflation are important for long-term planning and investment decisions.

Two major concerns for governments are inflation and unemployment. Both issues are also major concerns to domestic constituencies. Different groups perceive these issues differently depending upon how each affects their existing wealth and their ability to create additional wealth.[23] To the extent that currency union membership limits countries' abilities to affect these variables in the interests of their constituents, a currency union may or may not enjoy long-term durability.

When sovereign countries join a currency union, they also surrender their ability to print national currency. The government loses its ability to generate revenue by the creation of money, seigniorage. The effects of the loss of seigniorage may be most strongly felt in those countries with large underground economies and pervasive tax evasion where seigniorage serves as an effective inflation tax.

The second loss that countries experience by joining a currency union is exchange rate policy. Exchange rates may be useful instruments for countries to affect their balance on current account (Destler and Henning 1989, 10). By accepting an irrevocable, fixed exchange rate during the transition to monetary union the respective participants in the monetary union first relinquish their access to exchange rate policy changes. Then by surrendering their domestic currency in favor of a common currency that is subject to a new monetary authority, the sovereign currency ceases to exist. The country may no longer use the exchange rate to insulate domestic prices from price changes on the world market and to improve the current account balance.

The third loss that countries experience by participation in a currency union is fiscal policy. Fiscal policy may be useful for collecting revenue, distributing income and financing government purchases. Unlike monetary and exchange rate policy, fiscal policy need not necessarily be lost as a tool of sovereign governments. Governments may continue to collect taxes, issue debt and make purchases. These policies will encounter limitations if a monetary constitution restricts fiscal policy. Such restrictions would address debt issues. Mobility of the tax base may further limit taxation policy.

4.9.2 Additional Costs of Transition

Additional costs arise during the transition from individual national currencies to a single, common currency. These costs are of three varieties. The first variety of cost relates to speculation in financial markets. First, speculators may endeavor to test the commitment of the participating countries to the fixed rates of exchange adopted prior to the replacement of national currencies with the common currency. Second, speculators may test the resolve of the new and existing monetary authorities to defend the value of the new currency once it replaces the national currencies.

The second variety of cost relates to microeconomic matters. First, the changeover from multiple national currencies to a single currency will affect not only the medium of exchange but also the unit of account. Information management and service provision software and equipment will require conversion to accommodate the new unit of account and the new currency and coinage. For example, vending machines will require redenomination. Second, long-term nominal contracts may need to be redenominated and/or renegotiated depending upon the basis on which payment is made. For example, financial contracts which render a fixed nominal payout will need to be renegotiated in order to account for the new currency system (Crawford 1996, 184–5). Other nominal pricing arrangements will also require redenomination. Such arrangements include price labels, catalogs, menus and salaries.

In addition to these tangible costs, one important intangible cost arises (Dowd 1993, 267). This cost stems from people's psychological resistance or willingness to accept this new currency arrangement. People's preferences regarding the existing currency system also may affect their ability to adapt to the new money.

4.10 TRANSITION TO CURRENCY UNION

The transition to a currency union requires the setting of exchange rate parities between currency union participants and the replacement of national currencies with the common currency. Several considerations arise in the context of this transitional period. First, economic convergence relates the similarity of economic structures and performance between prospective participants. Second, the speed of transition expresses the length of time the transitional period will last. Third, sources of instability suggest possible destabilizing elements during the transition.

4.10.1 Economic Convergence

Optimum Currency Area (OCA) theory is silent on economic convergence as an element of currency union operation. Economic convergence is absent from these elements because it is neither a prerequisite nor an unavoidable consequence from the creation of a currency union. The law of comparative advantage suggests the benefits of trade among heterogeneous regions. Measures of convergence include industry structures, services versus manufacturing as a proportion of GDP, domestic infrastructure networks, organized labor unions, public spending as a proportion of GDP, methods of public finance, market regulation, inflation rates, per capita GNP and the natural rate of unemployment.

Two general types of convergence exist: nominal convergence and real convergence. Nominal convergence refers to the reduction of differences in nominal economic variables. An example of nominal convergence is the elimination of national inflation rate differentials. Real convergence refers to the reduction of differences in real aspects of the economy. The structure of a country's economy represents one area in which real convergence may take place. Structural convergence may occur in factor market and production regulations. For example, countries may agree to impose common regulations across the region in order to reduce or eliminate the competitive advantage of relatively less costly producers *vis-à-vis* more costly producers. National production requirements, such as environmental protection mandates concerning production techniques and waste disposal, lead to higher production costs in certain political jurisdictions. By eliminating differential regional regulations and instituting common requirements producers across the region face more similar costs of production. Regulatory convergence serves to reduce artificial, political barriers to the creation and exchange of products and services across countries.

Convergence may or may not increase the likelihood of success of a new currency union. Policy convergence may serve as a signaling mechanism. For example, convergence of monetary and fiscal policy may demonstrate a commitment to money creation, money management and taxing and spending policies that accord with the monetary goals of the currency union. Convergence may demonstrate a commitment by countries to conform to common policies within the currency area. However, different domestic economic situations may justify heterogeneous policies. In addition increasing geographical concentration of productive enterprises may lead to divergences between regional economies. Such divergences may demand heterogeneous responses. The ability of such responses to meet the needs of their constituents will determine the long-run success of any such arrangement.

4.10.2 Speed of Transition

The transition from national monetary arrangements to a currency union may follow one of two paths. These paths of transition are the rapidly implemented, one-off move and the slow, gradual move. The former occurs on a single date with limited preliminary stages preceding the elimination of national monetary systems. The latter occurs through a series of stages over a period of some length, each one bringing the given countries' monetary systems closer to union.

Each path presents its own advantages and disadvantages. There are several advantages to a rapid transition. First, a rapid transition avoids the possibility of speculative attacks on intermediate exchange rate valuations. Second, a rapid transition precludes the possibility of prospective participants undertaking unauthorized devaluations or revaluations during the transitional period. Third, a rapid transition reduces the exchange rate uncertainty among participating countries more quickly. A disadvantage of the rapid move may include insufficient time to accommodate valuation changes.

There are several advantages to a gradual transition. The first advantage is the availability of time to accommodate changes in fundamental economic conditions. This additional time reduces the cost of adjustment (Cobham 1989, 205). The second advantage is the availability of time to familiarize the private and public sectors with the new system while continuing to rely on the existing system. Similarly, additional time eases the transition by providing the market with time to monitor the behavior of the new monetary authority (Currie and Whitley 1994, 182). The third advantage is the time to replace software and equipment which accommodated the old currency, to software and equipment that accommodates the new currency. The disadvantages of the gradual transition may include the risk of speculative attacks and the possibility of countries undertaking discretionary policy during the transition phase, which reduces the credibility of the proposed arrangement. The advantages and disadvantages of either approach will depend on the specifics of the individual transition scheme.

4.10.3 Sources of Instability during Transition

The period of transition from individual national currencies to single, common currency introduces two sources of potential instability.[24] Currency substitution represents the first source of instability. Currency substitution occurs when currency holders (primarily investors) switch their holdings out of currencies they expect to lose value as a result of the monetary union and into currencies they expect to gain value. The changes in relative currency demand associated with currency substitution may impose unexpected pressures on the relevant currencies and thereby necessitate a revaluation of currencies.

Speculative attacks represent the second source of instability. Speculative attacks occur when investors believe a currency to be over- or undervalued. Speculators purchase currencies which they believe to be undervalued and sell currencies they believe to be overvalued in order to obtain profits equal to the difference between the current value and the expected equilibrium value less transactions costs. Monetary authorities may attempt to stave off speculators by selling foreign reserves in favor of a particular currency or by purchasing foreign reserves. These efforts serve to place upward and downward pressure on the currency at issue in order to repel the attacks. Speculative attacks may occur during the transitional phases before monetary union or after the single currency has replaced the national currencies. In either case, speculators may be testing the resolve of monetary authorities to maintain the existing parities. Changes in the underlying economic fundamentals may, however, justify parity adjustments during the transitional period.

4.11 CONCLUSION

The theory of optimum currency areas provides a general description of the economic characteristics of regions that might succeed as single currency areas. These characteristics relate the ability of these areas to adjust to economic disturbances. These adjustment mechanisms include but are not limited to real exchange rate flexibility, factor and output market flexibility, wage and price flexibility, industrial and portfolio diversification, economic openness and fiscal policy. The ability of these mechanisms to contribute to the stabilization process in response to disturbances will affect the viability of a currency union.

The institutional framework of a currency area will also play an important role in determining the success of single currency areas. A currency union introduces serious policy limitations for sovereign countries in the areas of monetary, exchange rate and to some extent fiscal policy. The institutional framework incorporates the structure, organization and distribution of power between the political, monetary and fiscal institutions. Institutional features will determine the assignment of different constituencies to different decision-makers and the extent to which they are able to respond to and satisfy the demands of their respective populations. These factors affect the incentives facing the relevant decision-makers.

NOTES

1. See Chapters 2 and 3 for examples in Europe.
2. Section 8 of this chapter discusses possible benefits associated with participation in a currency union. Section 4 of Chapter 5 discusses particular motivations for the creation of a currency union following the institution of an open market in labor, capital, goods and services, in the European Union.
3. A fixed exchange rate system stands in contrast to a floating exchange rate system. The latter system is characterized by the absence of any fixed relationship between domestic and foreign currencies and by the movement of exchange rates in response to domestic and international developments and/or expectations. Countries undertaking a floating exchange rate retain the ability to use the exchange rate, as well as monetary and fiscal policy, to affect their economics domestically and internationally. Various intermediate regimes that draw from each of these extreme arrangements also exist.
4. Regional currencies may continue to operate in a currency union; however, a single common currency occupies the dominant position as medium of exchange in such arrangements.
5. Adjustment mechanisms may also exist which seek to reduce or eliminate economic differences between countries participating in a currency union. Such efforts may be motivated by a desire on the part of relatively less wealthy countries to acquire some of the wealth and/or

wealth-creation abilities of the more wealthy countries. Calls for such adjustment fall under the rubric of leveling-the-playing-field economic arguments. This chapter avoids discussion of these types of adjustment mechanisms in the interests of relevance and space.

6. Vaubel (1994b, 34) writes that: 'There is broad agreement among Keynesian and modern classical economists that such relative price adjustments are most easily effected through nominal exchange rate adjustments.'
7. However, Martino (1990, 528, footnote 17) notes that: 'It is not enough to say that empirical evidence does not support the view that stabilization policies have had a stabilizing effect on the economy (Romer 1986). The problem is that empirical evidence suggests that they may have had a *de*stabilizing effect [italics in original]. See Friedman (1984, 33–4).'
8. Hubbard (1995, 684–5) points out the difficulty of activist policies due to lags between the event and the policy response. These lags include the following: (1) data lag; (2) recognition lag; (3) legislation lag; (4) implementation lag; and (5) impact lag.
9. Atkeson and Bayoumi (1991, 196) find that mobility of financial capital may preclude the need for physical capital movements, if this capital generates its returns from investments that are uncorrelated with regional shocks to labor and capital. However, Blanchard and Katz (1992) find that capital does not move from economically booming areas to economically disadvantaged areas.
10. Tradable products as opposed to non-tradable products are those commodities which producers may package, store, and transport. Tradables include non-perishable items, such as electronics and consumer durable items, as well as perishable items that retain their consumptive utility upon reaching the point of sale, such as fruits transported within a sufficiently short time period. Non-tradables include services such as restaurant meals and haircuts. Producers may not package, store and transport these commodities.
11. This assertion assumes that the country's non-tradable sector is relatively less dependent on traded than non-traded factor inputs. If the non-tradable sector is highly dependent on traded factor inputs, the effect of shocks to the economy will be even greater.
12. See Robert E. Lucas (1972), 'Expectations and the Neutrality of Money', *Journal of Economic Theory*, **4**, 103–24.
13. Several definitions of the monetary supply exist. These definitions represent different categories of money according to increasingly inclusive (or decreasingly inclusive, depending upon the perspective taken) definitions. The degree of liquidity of each aggregate distinguishes the categories. Interest rates include short-, medium- and long-run rates. The monetary authority can affect these rates through open market operations, as well as through the discount rate and adjusting reserve requirements.
14. The postponed effects of expansionary policy preceding elections depend on shortsightedness on the part of the electorate. If agents possess rational expectations, the electoral effect on monetary policy cannot persist.
15. Partisan effects result from the efforts of the incumbent party to cater to the preferences of their base of political support.
16. Mobility of the tax base particularly within an economically integrated region may limit taxation. Individuals and productive enterprises may move to avoid relatively high tax rates. Positive spillover effects may enable certain jurisdictions to free-ride on public goods provided by neighboring jurisdictions.
17. The debate centers on the question of whether or not individuals perceive government debt instruments as net wealth. If individuals do not perceive government debt instruments as net wealth and they expect that future taxes will rise in order to generate revenue with which to retire government debt, private saving will increase. If individuals perceive government debt as net wealth and they do not expect to bear the burden of the future taxes corresponding to this debt, private saving will not increase. (For a more precise elucidation of the Ricardian equivalence theorem, see Robert Barro (1974), 'Are Government Bonds Net Wealth?', *Journal of Political Economy*, **82**, 1095–1118.)
18. Elected officials within the executive and legislative branches of the government may be instrumental in the creation of the monetary authority. In particular, they may provide input to the development of the authority's constitution.

19. Goodman (1992, 7–8) notes that central banks may have to consciously strive to retain their independence from political institutions: 'Once the central bank has become independent, however, Its ability to maintain that independence reflects both the resources it possesses and the strategies it chooses to pursue ... by making the central bank independent, governments add a new actor to the political system, one that surely seeks to preserve its own autonomy ...'. The latter portion of Goodman's quote suggests the use of valuable resources by the central bank to pursue its own interests within the policy process.
20. For more on fiscal equivalence please see: Mancur Olson (1969), 'The Principle of "Fiscal Equivalence": The Division of Responsibilities among Different Levels of Government., *American Economic Association, Papers and Proceedings*, **59**, 479–87.
21. This potential benefit of currency integration will depend on a number of factors. These factors include the degree of monetary authority independence from outside influence, as well as the relative political strength of the inflation-prone countries and the fiscal policies and status of such countries. Fiscal concerns stem from the possibility of excessive budget deficits, which may lead to pressures for debt monetization.
22. The benefits of participation in a currency union due to reduced inflation are therefore limited to states whose inflation rates historically exceed the union rate. Only such high inflation countries may experience a strengthening of their reputations on inflation. Similarly, the lower-inflation countries suffer. De Grauwe (1996, 1094) writes: 'When two countries with different reputations concerning inflation (say Germany and Italy) decide to form a monetary union the high inflation country is likely to profit from the reputation of the low inflation country. The converse, is also true: the low inflation country will be "infected" by the bad reputation of the high inflation country and will experience a welfare loss.'
23. For many years policy-makers attempted to exploit the Philips curve, which proposed a tradeoff between these two aspects of the economy. By increasing the amount of money in circulation central banks sought to increase output and thereby reduce unemployment. The increased money supply resulted in an increase in prices and therefore inflation.
24. These sources are in addition to any instability introduced by shocks external to the transition. Section 3 discusses the types of shocks that may arise at any time.

5. Economic background to the European Monetary Union

5.1 INTRODUCTION

The European Monetary Union (EMU) represents a contemporary attempt at the creation of a currency union between European Union (EU) members. The primary goal of this currency union is price stability. This chapter presents an overview of the theoretical issues relevant to the proposed EMU and related empirical results. This chapter follows a similar organization to Chapter 3 in order to highlight the consistencies and inconsistencies between the theoretical aspects of currency unions and the empirical aspects of the EMU. (Chapter 6 discusses the monetary and fiscal aspects of EU policy and institutions.)

This chapter is organized as follows. Section 2 provides a brief history of economic integration in the EU. Section 3 examines the characteristics and performance of the EU in light of the criteria set forth by the theory of optimum currency areas. Section 4 discusses the motivations for the creation of a currency union between European Monetary System (EMS) participants. Section 5 considers the costs of participation in the EMU. Section 6 examines issues related to the transition to EMU. The final section concludes.

5.2 EUROPEAN ECONOMIC INTEGRATION TO CURRENCY INTEGRATION

The countries of Europe have undertaken a variety of fixed exchange rate arrangements in recent history. Chapter 2 highlights the development of the arrangements from the nineteenth century, including the LMU, GMU, SCU and the gold standard system centered on the pound sterling. Chapter 3 highlights the development of European monetary arrangements following World War II.

From this time, the countries of Western Europe have sought to promote both economic and political integration. Monetary integration within Europe followed a progression of legislative efforts at market and political integration. These efforts began with the establishment of the European Communities in response to concerns surrounding national security and economic development in the aftermath of World War II. The creation of a customs union in 1957 was the first major step in this process of market integration. The development of European Community institutions accompanied this process in the political arena. The move toward market integration continued with the Single Market Program (1987), which provided for the elimination of barriers to factor movement within the region.

The collapse of the Bretton Woods system in 1973 provided the opportunity for the institution of a Western European currency arrangement. The countries of the European Community along with some members of the European Free Trade Association sought to develop a fixed exchange rate system against the US dollar. This system was known as the snake-in-the-tunnel. In the ensuing years, the system met with failure.

Only in 1979 did the EC make another effort at fixed exchange rates. This arrangement, known as the EMS, revolved around a system of bilateral parities: the Exchange Rate Mechanism. The EMU replaced the EMS. This replacement marks the gradual displacement of the national currencies of the participating countries with the euro and the taking over of responsibility for participants' monetary policies by the European System of Central Banks. The plan for complete monetary integration finally approached realization with the ratification of the Treaty on European Union (1991).

A European currency union has a number of implications for economic policy within the EU. Perhaps foremost among these implications is its affect on national monetary, exchange rate and fiscal policies. By accepting a single monetary system and currency participating countries agree to maintain fixed, relative nominal currency valuations. Once exchange rates become locked in preparation for the arrival of the single currency the possibility of currency realignments disappears. This process effectively removes the possibility of independent policy actions that would affect the relative nominal valuation of national currencies. Participating countries thereby surrender a significant instrument of economic policy-making.

5.3 THE EUROPEAN CURRENCY UNION: AN OPTIMUM CURRENCY AREA?

Optimum Currency Area (OCA) theory suggests criteria for the successful operation of currency unions.[1] These criteria consist of the similarity of economic shocks that affect the participating regions and the ability of these regional economies to respond to economic shocks. Various adjustment mechanisms facilitate regional adjustments to shocks.

The proposed European currency union will initially include 12 member countries of the EU which have been participants in the ERM. These countries are: Austria, Belgium, Finland, France, Germany, Greece, Ireland, Italy, Luxembourg, the Netherlands, Portugal and Spain. The viability of this currency union will ultimately depend upon the ability of the EMU monetary authorities and individual countries to respond to regional shocks.

The general consensus in the economic literature is that the proposed European currency union does not constitute an optimum currency area.[2] This consensus follows comparative analyses of the economic performance of regions in the USA and Canada with the countries and regions of the EU. However, these analyses suggest that certain regions within the EU may represent potential members of a more narrowly defined currency area.[3]

The following two subsections consider the two factors that determine the viability of a currency union for the case of Western Europe. The first section looks at the types of shocks that have affected the EU in recent years. The second section looks at the adjustment mechanisms of these regions. Both sections draw from the literature on the prospects for the operation of an EMU.

5.3.1 Shocks

The economies of the EU countries of the are subject to a variety of exogenous shocks. These shocks may affect the regions of the EU differentially according to the specific nature of the shocks. The economic structures of the respective regions also affect their vulnerability to and ability to respond to such shocks.

OCA theory asserts that the regions of a viable currency union will be subject to similar shocks. The effects of these shocks may be remedied by common policies with similar effects throughout the EU. The central monetary authority may conduct a single policy suitable for the entire region under its direct jurisdiction. For this reason, pressures for differential policy responses do not arise. Regions that are prone to differential shocks and therefore in need of alternative responses belong outside of the currency area.

Eichengreen (1997c, 104–15) studies the effects of shocks to countries within the area of the proposed EMU. He examines the effects of both supply and demand shocks. His analysis supports the existence of two distinct regional groupings within the EU: a core group consisting of Belgium, Denmark, France, Germany and the Netherlands, and a peripheral group consisting of Greece, Ireland, Italy, Portugal, Spain and the UK. These groupings hold for both supply and demand shocks with slightly stronger relative correlations between core countries in the presence of supply shocks. His analysis also indicates that the distinction between these groupings is not disappearing.

Eichengreen (1997c, 104–105) also undertakes a comparison between the responses of US regions and EU countries in the face of shocks. These comparisons result in two major findings. First, more rapid adjustments take place between US regions than EU countries. Second, EU countries experience greater asymmetric shocks than US regions. These findings suggest that the USA more closely approximates an OCA by virtue of its relatively faster adjustments and the relatively greater symmetry of shocks.

Empirical studies have also found evidence indicative of the differential effects of shocks across regions and countries within the EU. This evidence suggests that: (1) regions may be more susceptible to asymmetric shocks than countries (De Grauwe and Vanhaverbeke 1991, 124–5); and (2) EU countries experience shocks differentially (Bayoumi and Eichengreen 1993, 223). Bayoumi and Eichengreen (ibid., 223) determine that both supply and demand shocks affect two distinct country groupings within the EU differentially. The first country grouping consists of Belgium, Denmark, France, Germany and the Netherlands. The second country grouping consists of Greece, Ireland, Italy, Portugal, Spain and the UK. Supply shocks affect the two groupings most differentially, while the difference between the effects of demand shocks is less. If regional specialization accompanies the integration of EU economies, the effects of demand shocks may become increasingly asymmetric (ibid., 224). These findings provide evidence favorable to the notion of a European currency union of a more homogeneous group of countries.

The EU may or may not develop attributes more conducive to the operation of a currency union as economic integration progresses. On the one hand, further integration, as characterized by the full realization of the Single Market Program, may yield increasingly similar economic structures particularly from a regulatory perspective. Similarly increased factor mobility may reduce factor and output price differentials across the region. On the other hand, increased integration may lead to further regional specialization and therefore accentuate the vulnerability of EU regions to asymmetric shocks (Krugman 1993, 105). If the latter effect dominates, the demand for regional policy responses will preclude common policy responses.

Over the past 30 years, several major shocks affected the countries of the EU. The first shocks consisted of the negative supply shocks in the oil market in 1973 and 1979. These shocks led to increased oil prices. The oil shocks have been partly blamed for the failure of the snake-in-the-tunnel. However, Vaubel (1978) asserts that these shocks in and of themselves did not bring the snake to its end. Rather, 'the choice of an unworkable strategy' may be to blame. He argues that a better strategy may have succeeded where the Werner Plan failed.

The second shock consisted of the economic and monetary unification of Germany in 1990. This shock sent ripples across the EU in large part due to the decision of the German government to exchange East German marks on a one-for-one basis with West German marks. This decision coupled with the sudden accession of a large amount of skilled labor and land to the EC led to strong inflationary pressures within Germany. The Bundesbank responded to these pressures by tightening monetary policy. The increase in German interest rates led to a real appreciation of the mark. ERM countries faced the possibility of large capital outflows and had to raise domestic interest rates in order to retain this capital. This appreciation of the mark, combined with the need for a revaluation within the ERM due to persistent differential inflation rates within the EU, necessitated a revaluation of currencies within the ERM. The failure of ERM participants to undertake this revaluation of their own accord led in part to a series of speculative attacks in 1992–93 which finally forced the revaluation of a number of EU currencies. The response of EU countries to these shocks is suggestive of future policy responses to similar events.

5.3.2 Adjustment Mechanisms

OCA theory suggests the need for a number of adjustment mechanisms to ensure the viability of a currency union. These mechanisms determine the ability of regions to respond to exogenous shocks. This ability to accommodate shocks will affect the long-run viability of the currency union.

These adjustment mechanisms may operate to a varying extent in different regions. Under such conditions, one or a few devices may satisfy a region's need for adjustment. However, where no mechanism or group of mechanisms satisfy regional demands for adjustment, particularly to asymmetric disturbances, pressures will arise for new policy responses or defection from the monetary arrangement will occur. For example, Von Hagen and Fratianni (1991 and 1992 in Masson and Taylor 1993a, 279) note that: 'Trade and capital–market integration alleviates the tension from asymmetric shocks and reduces the importance of transfer payments to keep the members in the union.' Bovenberg, et al. (1991, 390) go on to point out that: 'Monetary unions would not survive in the absence of transfers or other policy tools to cushion shocks, since severe shocks would lead to defections' (Sachs and Sala-i-Martin 1989).

5.3.2.1 Real exchange rate flexibility

The first adjustment mechanism suggested by OCA theory is real exchange rate flexibility. This mechanism consists of the relationship between real prices in different regions. Changes in relative prices may represent responses to economic disturbances affecting the local economy(ies).

Several studies have examined the flexibility of real exchange rates within Europe. These studies provide conflicting results regarding the ability of real exchange rates to serve as an adjustment mechanism. These results may be explained by the existence of alternative adjustment mechanisms such as labor market flexibility.

Poloz (1990) compares the real exchange rate flexibility of the Canadian provinces with those between France, Germany, Italy and the UK. His analysis finds greater variability of real exchange rates between Canadian provinces than the four EU countries. This result suggests that the real exchange rate operates as more of an adjustment mechanism within the currency union of Canadian provinces than between the EU regions. The lower variability of real exchange rates between the four EU countries may indicate the relatively larger role played by other adjustment mechanisms. This result suggests that the EU countries may satisfy OCA theory if factor mobility plays a relatively larger role in adjustment than real exchange rate changes.

Another study, Eichengreen (1990), compares the variability of real exchange rates in ten EC countries with those in four regions of the USA (the Northeast; North-central, South and West). Eichengreen finds that the real exchange rates of the EC countries are three to four times more variable than the real exchange rates between the four US regions. Comparing this general result with Poloz's result appears suggestive of contradiction. However, this apparent contradiction may lie in the differences between Canada and the USA as currency unions. For example, labor mobility may be greater in the USA than in Canada. Therefore, the latter makes greater use of the real exchange rate.

De Grauwe and Vanhaverbeke (1991, 114–18) undertake two comparisons of real exchange rate variability and labor mobility for the period 1977–85. The first comparison examines the variability of real exchange rates within and between five EU countries (France, Germany, the Netherlands, Spain and the UK) for the period 1977–85. This comparison yields the following results. First, real exchange rates are approximately two times more variable between countries than between regions of countries. This result suggests that flexibility in labor markets plays a relatively greater role than real exchange rate movements within countries than between countries. The second test compares real exchange rate variability between a number of countries participating in the EMS (Belgium, Denmark, France, Italy, the Netherlands, Spain, West Germany and the UK) and four countries belonging to the OECD which were not participating in the EMS (Greece, Japan, Portugal and the United States). Their comparison revealed that real exchange rates are less variable between the EMS countries than between the four chosen OECD countries. This result suggests that labor is relatively more mobile between EMS participants than non-EMS participants.

A third study, again by Eichengreen (1990), examined the relationship between real exchange rates by utilizing data on real share prices. Eichengreen compared the covariance of real share prices in Toronto and Montreal with the covariance of real share prices in Paris and Düsseldorf. The results of Eichengreen's study revealed that the ratio of share prices were five times more variable in Europe than in Canada. However, the data did indicate a convergence of share prices between Paris and Düsseldorf over time. This result indicates the presence of asymmetric shocks differentially affecting French and German companies as demonstrated by variances in real share prices.

5.3.2.2 Fiscal policy

The second adjustment mechanism suggested by OCA theory is fiscal policy. A variety of tools may be available to the fiscal authority to respond to exogenous shocks. These tools include transfer programs, insurance schemes, expenditures policies and the tax code. Such tools seek to alleviate the costs brought on by the shock and facilitate adjustment. These tools may be either automatic or discretionary.

Several studies have considered the role of fiscal policy in adjusting to economic shocks. These studies examine the use of the fiscal responses to shocks in existing currency unions, such as the USA and Canada. These fiscal policy responses consist of two components: an increase or decrease in tax liabilities and an increase or decrease in income transfers. These studies attempt to suggest whether a similar policy mechanism already exists or would be feasible within the EU to assist in the operation of the EMU.

Sala-i-Martin and Sachs (1991) use regression analysis to estimate the fiscal policy response of the federal government to negative shocks to the nine regions of the USA (as defined by the US Census Bureau). Their analysis reveals that a one-dollar decrease in regional per capita income leads to a 34-cent decrease in tax liability and a 6-cent inflow of transfers. This response reflects the redistribution of income from relatively well-off regions to relatively adversely affected regions. Sala-i-Martin and Sachs suggest that the same one-dollar decline in per capita regional income would only lead to a reduction in EC tax liability of 0.5 cents. This response stems in large part from the limited extent of EU tax policy. Further analysis needs to examine national fiscal provisions in response to adverse shocks in order to estimate the combined effects of taxes and transfers at both the national and EU levels.

Von Hagen (1993b) disputes Sala-i-Martin and Sachs' findings. He suggests that federal taxes and transfer play a much smaller role in the process of domestic adjustment. Rather than providing a 30–35 percent offset to income reductions fiscal policy at the federal level offsets 10 percent of the decline in per capita regional income.

Bayoumi and Masson (1991) conducted a study similar to Sala-i-Martin and Sachs (1991) for the case of Canada. Their findings report that the Canadian tax and transfer system offsets 35 percent of a one-dollar reduction in income. Again this finding suggests a larger role of the central Canadian authority in alleviating the financial burden of shocks than the central EU authority. Under such circumstances individual countries of the EU may bear a higher proportion of adjustment costs than Canadian provinces. The ability of these countries to provide such expenditures will depend on the effects of the shock on their domestic tax base, their ability to borrow on financial markets and their ability to obtain transfers from other countries within the currency union.

5.3.2.3 Factor and output market flexibility

The third adjustment mechanism suggested by OCA theory consists of flexibility in factor and output markets. Flexibility in these markets denotes the possibility of price changes and the mobility of factors and outputs in response to exogenous shocks. Factor markets concern labor and capital markets. In addition to price flexibility and factor mobility, flexibility in factor markets includes flexibility in participation rates. Output markets concern the markets for goods at various stages of production.

A number of studies examine the flexibility in factor and output markets in the EU. Some studies use the USA as a benchmark from which to make comparisons. Other studies focus exclusively on countries within the EU. These studies report consistent findings.

The first general result concerns the relative mobility of labor in the USA versus the EU. The European Commission (1990) reports that the average annual rate of net migration within the USA (50 countries and Washington, DC) is 0.7 percent of the population; the corresponding rate in the EC (64 regions) is 0.2 percent.

Eichengreen and Frieden (1993) find that migration between US regions exceeds migration between countries of Europe. However, they note that this finding ignores the existence of the secondary labor market of (primarily unskilled) guest workers from outside of Western Europe. Eichengreen (1992a) finds that internal labor movements within US countries exceed movements within French départements and German Länder by a factor of two or three.

The second general result concerns the speed with which employment rates respond to shocks in the USA versus the EU. Employment rates respond much more quickly to shocks in the USA than in the EC. Eichengreen (1990, 79) reports that US regional unemployment rates react to each other 20 percent faster than EC national unemployment rates. Most migration results from permanent shocks to the regional economies (Eichengreen 1997c, 79). Statutory barriers and cultural differences may in part explain the slower response of labor within the EU (Eichengreen 1997b, 46).

Decressin and Fatas (1995, 1649) also find that European labor responds more slowly than American labor in the face of shocks. Labor in Europe responds first to shifts in demand through changes in participation rates rather than migration. The migration response only increases enough to outweigh the participation response three years after the arrival of a demand shift.[4]

The third general result concerns the relative speeds at which national labor markets within the EU respond to shocks. Eichengreen (1997b, 45) finds that the speed of adjustment varies across countries. He notes that France, the Netherlands and the UK make the fastest adjustments while Ireland, Italy and Belgium make the slowest. Statutory barriers and cultural differences may in part be responsible for these differential response speeds.

The fourth general result concerns the movement of labor between countries in the EU versus within countries. Decressin and Fatas (1995, 1649) find that employment shocks represent a large amount of the regional shocks that occur in Europe. However, regional migration rates are not significant given the occurrence of asymmetric regional shocks. Rather shifts in labor demand are met by changes in labor force participation rates. De Grauwe and Vanhaverbeke (1991, 124) report that inter-regional labor mobility in Europe does however exceed inter-country mobility within Europe. Krugman (1993, 254) also notes the limited role of migration as an adjustment mechanism in Europe. He suggests that real wages play a greater role in the adjustment process. He cites empirical evidence for the Netherlands and Belgium to demonstrate that real wage adjustments of a sufficiently large magnitude are viable responses to adverse economic circumstances. Relative unit labor costs fell by more than 20 percent in the Netherlands in the first half of the 1980s in response to recession. Relative unit labor costs fell by approximately 25 percent in Belgium later in the decade in response to similar circumstances.

Molle and Van Mourik (1988) provide a comprehensive analysis of migratory behavior within Western Europe for the period from 1958. Their analysis accords with the findings of the above-mentioned studies of limited intra-European migration. In spite of reduced barriers to internal immigration, Molle and Van Mourik report that migration between EC countries has declined since 1958.[5] Molle and Van Mourik note the role of culture and distance as factors preventing intra-European migration on a larger scale. They also point out that output movements may serve as substitutes for migration.

Capital market flexibility has received much less attention than labor market flexibility. In part, this state of affairs is due to the difficulty in tracking and attributing factor causation to capital movements. Similarly, international financial markets enable the rapid flow of funds across borders. Following EU legislation initiating the integration of internal capital markets (SEA, Single European Act of 1986), the task of monitoring internal capital movements became increasingly difficult.[6]

Flexibility in output markets has increased since the creation of the European Communities. The initial customs union agreement provided for the gradual reduction of barriers to trade. Subsequent agreements and member accessions increased the size and diversity of the internal market. The Single European Act (1986) provided for the complete integration of markets in labor, capital, factor inputs and output.

5.3.2.4 Openness

The fourth adjustment mechanism suggested by OCA theory concerns the degree of openness. This mechanism refers to the extent to which participating countries' economies engage in trade with other countries within the currency union. Openness affects the vulnerability of regional economies to shocks from outside.

The proportion of GDP derived from exchange with other countries can serve as a measure of openness. More specific relationships between a country and other members in a currency union may provide a more useful measure of the degree of openness of the country's economy to influences common to the currency area.

Table 5.1 Exports and imports as a percentage of nominal GDP

Year/ Country	1980 Imports	1980 Exports	1992 Imports	1992 Exports
Belgium and Luxembourg	61.6	73.2	71.2	74.8
Denmark	50.3	51.6	55.4	54.5
France	52.0	55.4	65.7	63.1
Germany	49.4	51.1	54.7	54.1
Greece	40.9	48.2	62.8	64.2
Ireland	75.3	76.0	71.9	74.2
Italy	46.2	51.6	58.8	57.7
Netherlands	54.7	73.5	58.8	75.4
Portugal	45.3	58.6	73.6	74.8
Spain	31.3	52.2	60.3	66.3
UK	40.9	45.0	50.7	55.5

Source: Adapted from Table 1: Country Trade with the EU Countries as a Percentage of Imports and Exports, respectively (Hoeller and Louppe (1994) from Eurostat).

Table 5.1 reflects increases in imports and exports between the countries participating in the European Communities from 1980 to 1992. These increases reflect the larger amount of exchange EC countries undertake with each other since their accession to the arrangement.

Fatas (1997) demonstrates the growing correlation between national business cycles of EU member countries and the aggregate EU business cycle. In part this growing correlation stems from increased trading relationships between EU member countries, as well as the reduced importance of national borders as barriers to exchange and as factors increasing domestic isolation from external economic influences. Fatas offers two possible reasons for the growing correlation between national business cycles. First, regional specialization is overtaking national specialization in production thereby reducing country-specific effects. Second, economic policy is becoming increasingly coordinated among EU countries. Fatas suggests that if this trend of economic integration and business cycle correlation continues, a single currency would represent a superior monetary arrangement to the current system of individual sovereign currencies.

5.3.2.5 Industrial and portfolio diversification

The fifth adjustment mechanism suggested by OCA theory consists of industrial and portfolio diversification. Industrial diversification refers to the range of industrial undertakings across productive sectors. The more industrially diversified a country or region, the less vulnerable it is to industry-specific adverse shocks. Portfolio diversification refers to the range of wealth holdings across industries and investment instruments of different risk. The more diversified a country or region's portfolio, the less vulnerable it is to shocks affecting a single type of wealth holding.

Atkeson and Bayoumi (1991, 198) examined how capital income recipients undertake portfolio diversification in comparison with labor income recipients. Their study reveals that capital income recipients avail themselves of portfolio diversification opportunities to a greater extent than labor income recipients. In fact, they find that labor income recipients undertake very little portfolio diversification. This finding may in part be explained by the relative difficulty of diversifying wealth that is tied up primarily in the form of human capital

Rouwenhorst (1999) examines country effects in equity returns in Western European countries from January 1978 through August 1998. This period covers the period of operation of the EMS and the period since 1992 when would-be euro-zone participants harmonized their monetary and fiscal policies in anticipation of joining the zone. This study finds evidence that country effects in equity returns have persisted in spite of the increased monetary and fiscal coordination that occurred during this period. That is, the bias of investors to hold domestic equities continues. The results of this study suggest that economic integration may not lead EU investors to avail themselves of the single currency union to undertake greater international portfolio diversification. Portfolio diversification within the EMU may therefore represent a limited means of adjustment to asymmetric shocks.

5.4 MOTIVATIONS FOR THE CREATION OF THE EMU

The motivations behind the development of the EMU fall into two categories. The first and larger category consists of domestic motivations. These motivations include all of the internal reasons EU countries advocate the creation of the currency union. These reasons are myriad but may be divided into two categories: macroeconomic and microeconomic. In addition to these economic motivations, various political concerns also drove EU decision-makers to promote EMU.

The foremost goal of EMU, price stability, captures one of the leading motivations behind EMU. Advocates of currency union tout price stability as a major potential benefit. Price stability may be conducive to economic and financial stability, as well as long-term growth. It is therefore important for a number of reasons. First, price stability increases the information content of prices. When less uncertainty surrounds prices investment increases as the task of long-term planning is facilitated. Second, price stability determined by a central monetary authority may reduce national political business cycles and thereby reduce short-term discretionary policies (Martino 1990, 529).

In addition, a number of additional macroeconomic reasons may drive the case for EMU. First, the existence of a single European currency within a number of countries eliminates exchange rate uncertainty between the currencies of these countries. The European Commission estimates the savings from the elimination of exchange risk to be approximately two percent of EU GDP (Currie 1992a, 252). Second, a common currency eliminates the possibility of competitive depreciations between participating countries. Third, the elimination of national exchange rates, which capture expectations of domestic economic policies, may reduce the direct costs to countries of domestic deficits (Bovenberg et al. 1991, 387). Fourth, participation in a currency union may act as an effective means of delivering monetary discipline (Frankel 1996,153; Giavazzi and Pagano 1988, 1055). Inflation-prone countries may benefit from the existence of a credible monetary policy. (However, these gains depend upon the decisions and behavior of the new monetary authority.) Fifth, inflation-prone countries may seek to loosen monetary policy beyond the preferences of the Bundesbank. Similarly all countries except Germany and the Netherlands may expect to enjoy lower interest rates under the new regime, if it achieves higher anti-inflation commitment and policy credibility than their own respective monetary institutions. Sixth, countries may expect to gain from the option of holding reserves in the common currency, expected to be third largest in the world behind the dollar and the yen (Martino 1990, 520–21). Finally, if the euro becomes widely used in international currency markets, EMU advocates note that the euro could become the third most circulated currency in the world. EMU members may enjoy the ability of the European Central Bank (ECB) to affect world interest rates (Catenaro 1997, 5).

Various microeconomic motivations behind EMU also exist. Perhaps the most widely cited benefit is the reduction in transactions costs associated with the elimination of multiple currencies. Two possible benefits arise from the replacement of national currencies with a single currency. First, resources devoted to currency conversion are freed up for alternative productive activities. Second, resources devoted to hedging against currency fluctuations between the affected currencies are also freed up for alternative uses. The European Commission's report on EMU, *One Market One Money* (1992, 21), suggests that these transactions costs amount to approximately 0. 5 percent of EU GDP. The report notes that these costs are greatest for the small, open economies of the EU, as well as the weakest economies (ibid., 28). The Commission also predicts savings from the reduction in administrative costs associated with multiple currencies.

EMU may also promote the realization of the Single Market Program. Goodhart (1996, 1087) suggests EMU may bolster the single market '[by eliminating] the calculation of regional balance of payments statistics ... [so that] the focus of attention will shift to the larger whole grouping [instead of particular regions or countries] ...' The single currency and single monetary policy may also facilitate internal EU transactions and exchange.

Several political concerns may also have motivated domestic decision-makers to support EMU. First, EMU would provide participants with access to larger credit markets in a single currency. National debt obligations issued in the common currency would compete with each other for a wider pool of funds. Larger credit markets might reduce the cost of credit, national risk factors notwithstanding. Second, participation in the currency union might represent an opportunity for domestic politicians to reduce inflation and to increase monetary policy credibility at lower political cost than otherwise. Third, some countries might have been attracted by the possibility of funding awards from the EU government. Such funds could be used to finance domestic expenditure policies. In the case of Ireland, the EU contributed funds to reduce the Irish deficit to assist it in meeting the convergence criteria for admission to EMU.

The second and smaller category consists of international motivations. Seeing the EU moving forward to currency union, various countries opted for participation in order to be able to contribute to decision-making processes on important political and economic issues. Similarly, countries might have feared economic discrimination by members of the future euro-club. Bolton and Roland (1997, 1060) make this point succinctly:

> An unpleasant implication of our analysis is that barriers to trade and factor movements between the European Union and neighboring non-Union countries play a role in cementing the Union. In the absence of such barriers, a country would be less willing to join the Union if it can obtain most of the economic benefits of the Union by staying out and not paying the political costs in terms of loss of sovereignty.

To the extent that the common currency signifies a barrier to trade, this same logic applies to EU countries' motivation for participation in EMU.

In addition, security concerns may have motivated countries to extend the political reach of the European Communities to monetary affairs. German reunification raised concerns among neighboring countries of the need to constrain Germany within a European framework. A common currency and monetary policy would serve to further fuse the economies of Western Europe.

5.5 COSTS OF PARTICIPATION IN EMU

EMU participants face two types of cost associated with the new currency arrangement. The first costs relate to domestic economic policy. These costs include the loss of domestic monetary and exchange rate policy. The second costs relate to microeconomic costs associated with the transition from the existing currency arrangement to the currency union. These costs include possible increases in currency market volatility and the redenomination of domestic information and pricing infrastructures.

5.5.1 Policy Costs

EMU participants face a number of policy costs. Several of these costs relate to changes in policy instruments available to participating countries and the effects on domestic economies while others relate to uncertainty surrounding the operation of the new institutional framework in which monetary policy is undertaken. The following paragraphs raise these issues in turn.

Participants in the EMU face three costs in terms of domestic economic policy instruments. These costs arise from the constraints participation in the currency union places on domestic monetary, exchange rate and fiscal policy. These constraints preclude participating countries from undertaking those policy measures which they might otherwise have chosen prior to membership in the currency union. By precluding countries from indulging their preferences, these constraints impose an implicit cost on countries.

Participation in the ERM has limited the monetary and exchange rate sovereignty of prospective EMU participants since each country's accession to the arrangement.[7] In order to maintain the value of their currencies within the ERM, countries have had to maintain fixed rates of exchange. To meet this objective, countries had to undertake monetary and exchange rate policies which would sustain these exchange rates. Viñals (1996, 1104) notes that 'Before mid-1992, most Member Countries seemed to have voluntarily relinquished making use of the nominal exchange rate as a tool for adjusting their economies, as exemplified by the extensive period – from January 1987 to August 1992 – without realignments in the ERM.' For this reason, the policy costs associated with the transition to full currency union are less than what they would otherwise have been in the case of a transition from sovereign currency arrangements.

In addition, participation in the ERM became easier after the speculative attacks on various EU currencies during 1992–93. Following these attacks, ERM participants agreed to expand the fluctuation margins of currencies within the system to ±15 percent. The EU currencies have not met with any speculative attacks since the widening of the margins that leave a large amount of room for changes in relative valuations.

Similarly the predominant desire of national governments to adhere to macroeconomic policies that would qualify them for admission to EMU has shifted the preferences of national decision-makers in the areas of monetary and exchange rate policy. In particular national decision-makers have chosen policies that increased the probability of their fulfillment of the admission criteria. For this reason countries have endeavored to satisfy the convergence criteria (discussed in the following section) as closely as possible. These efforts have, however, resulted in the creation of various alternative outlets to accommodate government spending. The discussion below highlights some of these efforts to reduce the size of official budget deficits.

5.5.1.1 Monetary policy

With the complete surrender of sovereign currencies countries face potential costs in three areas related to monetary policy. The first area concerns monetary policy as a means to affect the domestic economy. Countries no longer possess monetary policy as an instrument to boost or reign-in domestic economic activity. For example, national central banks can no longer adjust interest rates in order to affect domestic consumption and investment. The ECB will assume control over interest rates. Similarly, national central banks cannot independently set reserve requirements and engage in open market operations to affect the domestic money supply. In addition, countries can neither choose their own inflation targets nor fix the value of their exchange rate *vis-à-vis* outside currencies. Their exchange rate depends on the policies of the EU monetary authority.

The second and third areas concern government revenues from the money supply and wealth redistribution based on changes therein. First, national governments will no longer be able to collect seigniorage on the issuance of national currency. Rather, EMU participants will be left to divide the seigniorage that arises from the euro.

Second, the EMU-wide inflation rate may affect the distribution of wealth around the union. Low-inflation countries such as Germany and the Netherlands may experience a decline in real wealth if the inflation rate of the EMU exceeds their current national inflation rates.[8] Vaubel (1994c, 44) developed a model to test the inflation rates that Germany and the Netherlands would have experienced if the EMU had operated from 1975–92. His tests revealed that their respective inflation rates would indeed have been higher than they were. Losses due to an increased inflation rate might only be avoided if agents fully anticipate the new inflation rate and fully index the value of all wealth holdings. High-inflation countries will face costs associated with disinflation if the EMU-wide inflation rate is below their current inflation rates (Eichengreen 1997b, 40). For this reason, they will likely resist a very low inflation rate because such would increase the real cost of the repayment of the national debt.

5.5.1.2 Exchange rate policy

The loss of the exchange rate policy instrument constitutes an additional cost for EMU participants. Although ERM members exercised limited exchange rate independence, the instrument remained available to them albeit with the risk of violation of the ERM parity grid. In the face of asymmetric shocks countries could make use of exchange rate changes, or request a realignment of the central parity grid *vis-à-vis* the other currencies of the ERM. However, under EMU no such realignments can take place between countries. Participating countries possess a single currency and no possibility exists for a shift in the nominal valuation of exchange rates between countries by policy-makers. Rather real exchange rates may only vary as a result of changes in real factor and output prices.

The inability of policy-makers to intervene in exchange rates may be especially problematic in the face of asymmetric shocks, which may lead constituents to pressure their political representatives and leaders for assistance. De Grauwe (in Torres and Giavazzi 1993, 267) highlights this problem: 'Asymmetric shocks tend to have permanent effects on growth rates of regions and countries. The implications for EMU are that the macroeconomic adjustment problem in a future monetary union will be intense, because countries will no longer be able to use the exchange rate as a policy instrument ...' Whether the loss of exchange rate policy constitutes a large problem depends upon the ability of policy-makers to utilize alternative measures to assist in the adjustment processes facing their affected constituencies.

5.5.1.3 Fiscal policy

Fiscal policy constitutes another policy area in which EMU participants face constraints. The Treaty on European Union (TEU) (1991) set forth four convergence criteria that countries had to satisfy in order to qualify for admission to the currency union. Two of these criteria related to fiscal policy variables. The first criteria concerned domestic debt and the second domestic deficits. The convergence criteria defined permitted relative debt and deficit levels as a fraction of GDP. A number of countries failed to satisfy these criteria so EU decision-makers relaxed them to accommodate debt and deficit reduction trends as sufficient for admission.

In an effort to meet these criteria, countries have resorted to distortionary and myopic techniques. Countries have sought new sources of one-time revenues in order to reduce their national deficits. For example, in 1997 Italy imposed a euro-tax. This tax operated by providing accounting revenues in the current period although the revenues would not actually be collected until 1999. The French government sold several state enterprises in order to generate additional income. The German government considered, but decided against, revaluing the Bundesbank's holdings of gold reserves. It did, however, sell portions of its holdings in Deutsche Telekom. Ireland accepted contributions from the EU to assist with its government's expenditures.

Countries have engaged in these practices to satisfy the letter of the convergence criteria. However, countries' desires to qualify for entry to EMU may have led them to undertake less efficient spending, financing and organizational practices than they otherwise would have. These practices may have satisfied short-term political concerns but may prove costly over the long term.

Following the institution of the EMU, the Growth and Stability Pact (1996) obliges participating countries to maintain debts and deficits below certain GNP. Countries that are unable to rectify excessive deficits as defined by the Growth and Stability Pact face possible penalties. These penalties include deposits with the EU for up to two years and the conversion of these deposits into fines in the event that the excessive deficit is not corrected. If countries resort to less efficient spending, financing and organizational practices in order to satisfy debt and deficit restrictions than they otherwise would have, countries may incur additional costs associated with EMU participation. However, if EMU participation manages to increase fiscal efficiency and reduce wasteful expenditures, these fiscal limits may lead to net domestic savings over the alternative scenario in the absence of EMU.[9]

The combined effect of losses in policy autonomy in monetary, exchange rate and fiscal affairs may introduce differential costs to individual countries because of their different preferences regarding national policy instrument usage. For example, southern countries that tend to have higher inflation rates may be relatively worse off in the short run than they otherwise would have been. Italy, for example, uses inflation as a tax on its underground economy. Portugal and Spain, for example, use money creation as a means to gain seigniorage. Attempting to satisfy the convergence criteria required these countries to reduce domestic spending or reduce the growth of domestic money supplies. Similarly these countries may need to reduce domestic spending. This shift in policy from national preferences, in the absence of the proposed EMU, may lead to a reduction in gains from inflation. Countries accept these costs because of expected benefits from admission to the EMU. However, this admission does not come without a price.

Alesina and Grilli (1992) point out that policy shifts associated with EMU may be particularly costly for the periphery countries of the EU. They write that: 'In a situation in which the EEC is not completely unified economically and politically, different member countries may have substantially different preferences over the conduct of monetary policy. For example ... periphery countries ... may have to pay the highest costs of giving up their monetary independence.' Their suggestion assumes that monetary and exchange rate policy are relatively more important instruments of policy in these countries than in other EU countries. To the extent that these countries depend more on these instruments to affect the economy and to collect revenues, these costs may indeed be greater for peripheral countries. If EMU monetary policy is less inflationary than these countries prefer these countries may face yet another cost.

5.5.1.4 New institutional framework

Countries within the EMU and beyond also face costs because of the new institutional framework of the currency union. The first cost concerns the efficacy of the new central monetary authority and its relationship with national central banks, as well as with EU and national political institutions. Private and public sector actors face uncertainty regarding the decision-making practices and policy strategies of the new monetary authority. Similarly agents face uncertainty regarding the vulnerability of the monetary authority to political influence, that is, how independent the institution will in reality be.

If the appointment of the first European Central Bank (ECB) president is any indicator, the ECB is already subject to political pressures. On March 1, 1998 France and Germany reached a deal to appoint Dutchman Wim Duisenberg as first president of the ECB. Duisenberg accepted an eight-year term of office. However, he agreed to step down after four years in order to allow a French ECB president to replace him. France agreed to withdraw their nominee, Jean-Claude Trichet, in exchange for: (1) this gentleman's agreement from Duisenberg to step down; (2) the appointment of a French ECB vice president (Christian Noyer); and (3) the appointment of a French chairman of the European Bank for Reconstruction and Development (Philippe Lafayette).

The second cost, which closely related to the first, concerns the credibility of the new monetary authority. Economic actors face uncertainty regarding its commitment to its goals and announced policies until enough time has passed for the new institution to develop a reputation. Currie (1992a, 252) writes that: 'For analysing the transition, what is at stake is the means of determining the common monetary policy within Europe, and the possible implications for fiscal policy ... the primary issues concern the credibility of monetary and fiscal policy, and the institutional structures that best underpin that credibility ...' Only time will reveal the ECB's credibility to its commitments.

5.5.2 Additional Costs of Transition

Additional costs may arise during the transition from the existing currency arrangement and the early years of the EMU arrangement. These costs result from speculation arising from uncertainty, currency substitution and redenomination of information infrastructures and prices. These costs will depend upon the speed, timing and credibility of the transition process, as well as subsequent EMU monetary policies (Barrell 1992, 244).

Speculation may arise due to uncertainty faced by investors in financial markets. Such uncertainty may stem from the possibility of a final realignment of exchange rates between EMU participants' currencies, doubt concerning the institution of the euro and the lack of reputation of the new EU monetary authority.[10] Speculation may arise either prior to the transition to currency union or during the operation of the currency union for several reasons. First, if markets perceive the ECB's commitment to its strategy as less than complete, speculators may anticipate the ECB's actions given the incentives it faces as an institution. For example, speculators may expect time-inconsistent policies by the ECB. Second, if markets anticipate a revaluation of the euro *vis-à-vis* other currencies such as the dollar, speculators may shift their relative holdings of the concerned currencies. Third, if markets expect the withdrawal of any participant in the arrangement speculators may shift the relative composition of their holdings.

Portes (1996, 141–2) identifies three potentially costly problems, which may arise between the time when the euro is introduced and the time when national currencies are withdrawn from circulation. These problems derive from uncertainty surrounding the replacement of national currencies and payments systems and the timing of these events. The first problem Portes identifies concerns when the new EU payments system will take over payments transaction between EMU countries. The longer this transition, the more financial markets may fear a delay in the introduction of the common currency. The second problem concerns delays by EMU participants in converting national expenditures and debt to the euro. This potential problem poses similar risks for speculation. The third problem concerns the simultaneous operation of national currencies and the euro. During the period of simultaneous circulation of currencies individuals may continue to use more familiar national currencies, at least when not traveling to other EMU countries. If the euro does not obtain popular support, markets may perceive this as a negative signal and substitute away from euro holdings.

The new common currency arrangement will also require changes throughout the EU to information infrastructures and price listings. Information structures include accounting systems and banking software. In addition, new coins and currency need to be minted. In 2002, existing national currency and coinage will be removed from circulation. Price listings include menus, catalogs and tags on commodities at retail facilities. Prices need to be recalculated into euros and labels replaced accordingly. In places such as France, some merchants have already begun listing prices in euros as well as in francs. Nominal contracts also need to be redenominated in either the euro or another currency, such as the dollar or yen, which will exist after the transition. All of these changes will impose costs on EMU participants.

The elimination of 12 national currencies in exchange for the euro will also impose costs on participants in foreign exchange markets. First, such participants will face a reduced selection of currencies into which to diversify their holdings *ceteris paribus*. For example, Salin (1984, 175) writes that: 'Some of those who trade on the foreign exchange markets benefit from the possibility of choosing among different currencies. Thus when all currencies are depreciating, but at different rates, it is important for non-Germans, for instance, to be able to hold D-marks.' This cost will affect those investors who substituted any of the 12 currencies for holdings of their own or a different currency. Second, foreign exchange traders will lose revenues generated by currency conversion and trading.[11] Third, speculators in the 12 currencies will no longer be able to undertake speculation in these currencies against each other or other non-EU currencies.

5.6 TRANSITION TO EMU

The transition to EMU required the setting of participating countries' currencies' exchange rates with respect to each other and the replacement of these currencies with the euro. Three stages marked the transition to EMU: Stage I (July 1, 1990 to December 31, 1993); Stage II (January 1, 1994 to June 30, 1998); and Stage III (July 1, 1998 to the present).[12] Several considerations arose in the context of this transitional period. These considerations include the convergence of participating economies, the speed of the transition and possible sources of instability during this period.

5.6.1 Economic Convergence

OCA theory emphasizes the similar responses of regions to shocks as important in the determination of an optimum currency area. Such similarity ensures the ability of common policies to facilitate economic adjustment processes. Likewise, OCA theory emphasizes the role of flexibility in markets for factors of production and output, industrial and investment portfolios, and policy responses to adverse shocks. However, OCA theory does not make any suggestions regarding levels of debt, deficits, interest rates, inflation and unemployment.

In spite of the reduction of barriers to exchange within the EU, the consensus of economic observers is that the EU does not qualify as an optimum currency area. Empirical studies of European labor markets in particular find the adjustment mechanisms within the EU insufficient. Labor has not exhibited sufficient levels of mobility despite the elimination of many statutory barriers to movement. Where governments possess limited policy tools, the adjustment mechanisms posited by OCA theory assume a particularly important role. When these mechanisms fail to operate, asymmetric shocks may lead to strong domestic pressures for institutional change.

In contrast to this consensus, the following empirical studies indicate some convergence in interest rates and inflation rates. Dornbusch (1991, 306) notes that the inflation rates of EMS participants fell significantly since 1978. In addition, the differences between participants' inflation rates has narrowed. Dornbusch identifies three groups of countries with similar inflation rates. The first group consists of Germany, the Netherlands, Austria and Switzerland (not a participant in the EMS); the second group consists of Belgium, Ireland, Italy and the UK; and the third group consists of the southern countries, Greece, Portugal and Spain. Nölling (1993, 52) finds some convergence of interest rates between EMS participants. However, national debts and deficits persist. Frankel, Phillips and Chin (1993, 294) find that the gap between European interest rates narrowed between 1987 and 1991. They attribute these differentials in part to exchange rate realignment expectations.

Participation in the ERM has affected the responses of ERM members to shocks. Bayoumi (1992, 353) finds that it has led to prolonged time responses and greater conformity of responses. The loss of full monetary independence likely lies behind these responses.

5.6.1.1 Maastricht convergence criteria

EU leaders promoted economic convergence as a precondition for EMU. The TEU (1991) and the ESCB Statute contain a number of criteria for admission to the currency union. The criteria include limits on domestic debt and deficit levels, as well as limits on domestic inflation and interest rates. These criteria are as follows:

1. *National debt/deficit levels*: The level of a state's national debt at the time of examination does not exceed 60 percent of the country's GDP (at market prices). The level of a country's national deficit at the time of examination does not exceed 3 percent of the country's GDP (at market prices). (ESCB Statute, Section 6, Article 2; TEU, Article 109j (1) and Article 104c (6).)

2. *Domestic inflation rates (price stability)*: 'A Member Country has a price performance that is sustainable and an average rate of inflation, observed over a period of one year before the examination, that does not exceed by more than 1½ percentage points that of, at most, the three best performing Member Countries in terms of price stability. Inflation shall be measured by means of the consumer price index on a comparable basis taking into account differences in national definitions' (ESCB Statute, Section 6, Article 1).
3. *Domestic interest rates*: 'Observed over a period of one year before the examination, a Member Country has had an average nominal long-term interest rate that does not exceed by more than 2 percentage points that of, at most, the three best performing Member Countries in terms of price stability. Interest rates shall be measured on the basis of long-term government bonds or comparable securities, taking into account differences in national definitions' (ESCB Statute, Section 6, Article 4).

The economic motivation behind these criteria was to ensure that EMU participants would not impose the burdens of their debt on other participants and that participants' economies could adapt with relative ease to a common monetary policy.

In addition, the TEU and ESCB Statute set forth three additional criteria. First, countries had to belong to the ERM for at least two years prior to consideration for admission to the EU. During this period, members' currencies could not have experienced any realignments outside of the ±15 percent fluctuation margins (ESCB Statute, Section 6, Article 3). Second, national central banks had to be independent from domestic political institutions (TEU, Article 107). Third, national central bank regulations had to accord with the TEU and the ESCB Statute (TEU, Article 108).

Economic observers have raised a number of criticisms of the Maastricht convergence criteria. These criticisms fall into three categories. The first category questions the economic logic behind the selection of these criteria. OCA theory does not include these criteria as essential for the operation of a currency union. Satisfaction of these criteria does not ensure that countries will respond similarly to shocks and that countries possess sufficient adjustment mechanisms to respond to asymmetric shocks. Countries may satisfy the convergence criteria but possess very different domestic economic structures (De Grauwe 1996, 1093). For this reason, adjustment to disturbances may be very difficult.

Observers may question the absence of unemployment rates among the convergence criteria. Unemployment constitutes a matter of strong political contention within the EU. It seems as valuable a criterion as any of those chosen and possibly more so given its direct impact on individuals. The relative clarity with which large numbers of EU constituents could observe this variable likely discouraged politicians from choosing it as a criterion given their inability to rectify this problem and the difficulty with which unemployment figures could be manipulated in comparison with national accounting conventions.

The second category of criticisms emphasizes the heterogeneity of EU economies. This heterogeneity of GDP and domestic growth rates may justify different values of national debt, deficits, inflation and interest rates. Catenaro (1997, 15–16) finds that the public debt levels of 11 European countries are positively correlated with measures of political instability. This finding appears supportive of the argument set forth by Rogoff (1990) that incumbent governments utilize debt levels as a constraint on future governments. As public debt levels increase, domestic interest rates may also lead to changes in at least two of the variables included in the convergence criteria, as a result of perhaps a single political motivation.

Corsetti and Roubini (1993, 75–6) present five criticisms that reflect the questionable value of uniform criteria for heterogeneous economies. First, they note that the real burden of domestic debt repayment varies by country according to their respective domestic inflation rate. Second, they point out that the real burden of debt repayment varies according to the relative amount of national debts. Third, the convergence criteria ignore the burden of the debt and/or deficit for countries with different growth rates. Fourth, the criteria do not allow for cyclical and automatic stabilization expenditures. Fifth, the debt and deficit criteria combine national capital and current accounts. Buiter et al. (1993, 87) comment that no foundation exists for the determination of appropriate fiscal limits and no sound logic exists for the imposition of homogeneous criteria across heterogeneous countries. This criticism is particularly relevant to the case of asymmetric disturbances.

The third category of criticisms concerns the time inconsistency of incentives created by the criteria. De Grauwe (1996, 1095) cautions that countries may behave opportunistically to fulfill the criteria in order to gain admission to the EMU. Following admission countries will eventually have to deal with their domestic fiscal situations. In the context of the currency union national fiscal problems may turn into supranational problems at the level of the EU where the monetary interests of participating countries are integrated. De Grauwe (1996, 1095) also warns that the commitment of current politicians to fiscal and monetary restrictions in no way constrains their successors.

5.6.1.2 European Commission's application of the convergence criteria

The application of the convergence criteria is subject to critical evaluation, as well. The determination of countries' fulfillment of the convergence criteria ended up a political rather than an economic matter. The European Commission presented its decision on first-round EMU participants in March 1998. This decision represented the Commission's application of the criteria to the candidate countries. The Commission determined that 11 countries could participate in the single currency starting in 1999.

This decision relied on perverse interpretations of at least three of the convergence criteria. First, the Commission had to repeal outstanding Decisions regarding the unsustainability of government deficits. All of the first-round candidates for EMU carried Decisions against their fiscal situations prior to the issuance of the Commission's decision on first-round entrants. Second, a number of countries, including France and Germany, do not meet the debt requirement. Debt levels in Belgium and Italy exceed the 60 percent limit by a factor of two. The TEU provides an escape clause from the debt requirement which states that countries with a declining deficit may be considered to have met this criterion.

However, even this criterion did not apply in all cases. (Table 5.2 contains OECD estimates of public debt as a percentage of nominal GDP for selected years from 1993. This table demonstrates the directions of change in national debt levels.) Third, two countries had not participated in the ERM for two years prior to the Commission's decision: Finland and Italy. Finland still will not have satisfied this criterion by January 1999, while Italy barely satisfies it having reentered the ERM most recently in November 1996.

Table 5.2 Public debt as a fraction of nominal GDP

Country	1993	1995	1997	1999 (Proj.)
Austria	62.7	69.2	64.3	63.9
Belgium	135.2	130.8	121.9	114.6
Denmark	78.0	69.0	60.8	52.2
Finland	58.0	58.1	55.4	50.4
France	45.2	52.5	57.8	59.7
Germany	48.0	58.3	61.5	60.2
Greece	111.6	110.1	109.5	106.8
Ireland	96.3	82.3	65.2	47.5
Italy	119.1	124.2	121.6	117.4
Luxembourg	6.1	5.9	6.7	–
Netherlands	80.8	78.6	70.9	65.8
Portugal	64.3	69.1	65.3	61.9
Spain	60.5	66.0	69.3	67.1
Sweden	76.0	78.0	76.9	70.6
United Kingdom	47.8	53.1	52.3	49.4

Source: Table 3: EU Member Country Debt Levels according to Maastricht criteria (*OECD Economic Outlook*, 64, December 1998, Annex Table 61, Annex-251).

The Commission's perverse interpretation of the convergence criteria sets a dubious example for EU and EMU countries. The interpretation serves as a demonstration of the proclivity of EU institutions to surrender decisions in the monetary and economic spheres to political motivations. Corsetti and Roubini (1993, 76) suggest that such behavior distorts the incentives for EU countries to control domestic spending. This decision also raises the question of how much latitude EU and EMU participants have in determining national economic policy in spite of the constraints outlined in the TEU and the ESCB statute.

5.6.1.3 The Growth and Stability Pact

EU leaders amended the TEU and the ESCB Statute with the provisions for the Excessive Deficit Procedure (EDP) in June 1997. The Growth and Stability Pact outlines fiscal criteria that EMU participants must satisfy and a procedure for penalizing violations of these limits. These criteria consist of the debt and deficit ceilings set out in the Maastricht convergence criteria. These criteria stipulate that for any year a state's debt must not exceed 60 percent of its GDP and its deficit must not exceed 3 percent of its GDP.

If a country exceeds either of these criteria, the EDP may begin. Under this procedure, the Commission prepares a report on the state's debt and/or deficit. The Monetary Committee arrives at a decision based on this report. The European Council then announces the existence of the excessive deficit and the procedure continues. Upon determination of an excessive deficit a country must prepare a plan to remedy the excess, unless an exception to this course of action is appropriate. Exceptions are permitted for countries suffering from a decline in GDP of 2 percent or greater. For GDP declines of 0.75 percent to 2 percent the Council of Ministers may grant an exception from the procedure. If the European Council decides that an excessive deficit exists, countries may be required to make deposits of 0.2 percent to 0.5 percent of GDP with the EU. If the excessive deficit is not rectified within two years, these deposits may turn into fines not to be returned to the offending state.

Economic observers have pointed out a number of problematic aspects of the Growth and Stability Pact. The criticisms of the Maastricht fiscal convergence criteria also apply. Von Hagen and Eichengreen (1996,134) note that the EDP will deter countries from undertaking tax-smoothing and stabilization efforts which they otherwise would have. Instead, countries will lobby for the EU to take care of these matters centrally. Such a transfer of responsibilities would lead to an increase in power at the center. They point out that the EU can obtain additional funding for fiscal assistance programs through loans from the European Investment Bank. Von Hagen and Eichengreen (1996, 137) caution that the EU may run up deficits in order to meet the demands of EU member countries that exceed the amounts that countries would have run up individually. Eichengreen and Wyplosz (1998, 68) conclude that countries will undertake fiscal policies until they reach the limits set out by the Growth and Stability Pact in order to avoid penalties. For assistance needs beyond these limits countries may press the EU for funds. If EU deficits ensue, the consequences may be similar to those experienced by the USA during the years of its persistent large national deficits. Higher interest rates may follow, accompanied by a reduction in internal consumption and investment.

5.6.2 Speed of Transition

The Delors Report (1989) originally envisioned a more rapid transition to monetary unification than has occurred. In part, the slower speed that has occurred is due to Germany's insistence on the imposition of the convergence criteria set out by the TEU. Germany demanded these criteria in order to incorporate some semblance of economic prudence into the plan for a European monetary union such that countries with excessive debt and inflation could not enter the union and press for a high inflation rate. Such an eventuality was anathema to the conservative, anti-inflationary German Bundesbank and German population, which still harbors memories of the German hyperinflation of the early 1920s.

The transition has largely been affected by the speed of decisions within the EU institutions. These decisions have hinged upon the economic and political events within the respective countries most concerned with the institution of the currency union. Notably political events within France and Germany have played a central role. Political decisions in these countries and others such as Italy have been colored by pressing domestic economic concerns, such as unemployment. Incumbent officials must address such concerns in order to retain the support of their domestic constituents given the electoral cycles in their countries.

5.6.3 Sources of Instability During the Transition

Several sources of potential instability exist during the transition to EMU. These sources stem from within the countries of the EU, as well as from abroad. For either case, the instability may result from either or both political and economic sources.

Political instability within the institutions of the EU and within the countries of the EU represents the first source of potential instability. Economic actors face uncertainty regarding the operation of the new EMU monetary authority, the ECB, and its interaction with EU and national government institutions. Similarly, actors face uncertainty regarding the possible behavior of the ECB *vis-à-vis* financial markets. Uncertainty also surrounds the extent to which political decision-makers will intervene in the transition.

Economic actors faced uncertainty *ex ante* regarding the extent that political actors would adopt discretion in the transition to EMU, such as regarding the fulfillment of the convergence criteria and excessive deficit procedures. The Commission's March 1998 report, which identified 11 of the first-round EMU participants, provided some indication of the propensity of the Commission if not other EU institutions as well to disregard empirical evidence. The political haggling involved in the appointment of the first ECB President, Wim Duisenberg, also demonstrates EU countries' willingness to politicize the operation of the monetary authority.

Economic instability within the EU and abroad represents the second source of potential instability. Economic instability may result from uncertainty in financial markets by wealth holders. Such instability may lead to speculative attacks or to currency substitution. Currency over- or undervaluations may also lead to speculative attacks or currency substitution. Investor expectations play a critical role in these events.

International economic and political instability may also lead to instability during the transition to EMU. For example, the current economic crisis in Eastern Europe and Asia affects the wealth holdings of EU citizens abroad, as well as the demand of EU and international investors for EU investment instruments. To the extent that the wealth of EU citizens falls because of such a crisis, a recession may set in. If this recession includes asymmetric, regional shocks, prospective EMU members may face domestic pressures for expansionary monetary policies or government transfers. If countries respond to these pressures through policies that affect their currency's relative valuation within the ERM, a realignment of EMU currencies may be necessary. After the transition, countries cannot pursue independent monetary policy. Domestic or EU-level transfers may be the only means of responding to regional shocks.

5.7 CONCLUSION

This chapter highlights the economic situation in the EU that serves as the background to EMU. The consensus among economists is that the EU as a whole does not satisfy the criteria for an optimum currency area. Economic disturbances affect regions differentially and inadequate adjustment mechanisms exist to respond to these disturbances. Furthermore, the convergence criteria outlined by the TEU are subject to serious criticisms. Perhaps the most important criticism is the blanket application of these criteria to heterogeneous national economies.

Certain groups of countries within the EU may form an optimum currency area. However, the Commission's decision regarding first-round participants considered the convergence criteria as the prerequisites to admission. These criteria differ from those of OCA theory and do not ensure the viability of a currency union among countries that satisfy them. In addition political discretion determined fulfillment of these criteria.

Two ingredients into EMU may be preparing a recipe for failure. First, the regions concerned do not possess the essential characteristics of a viable currency union. Second, the currency union, by its very nature, requires the surrender of national sovereignty in two policy areas – monetary and exchange rate policy – and the loss of additional sovereignty in fiscal policy. The resultant union may create a single currency area with regions possessing diverse policy needs. National politicians may refuse to relinquish these tools completely given their need to meet constituent demands for policy. In the face of major shocks, the result may be centrifugal internal forces which lead to the abandonment of the entire project.

NOTES

1. European Commission economists write that: 'The optimal currency theory was originally developed to define the optimal geographic jurisdiction of a given money; the Community more nearly faces the inverse task of defining the optimum economic and monetary competences of a given geographic jurisdiction' (1992, 28).
2. De Grauwe (1996, 1092) refers to a currency area comprised of all 15 members of the EU. He cites the following articles in support of this assertion: Eichengreen (1990), Bayoumi and Eichengreen (1992), Neumann and Von Hagen (1991) and De Grauwe and Vanhaverbeke (1991). In contrast, the following source espouses the contrary: Gros and Thygesen (1992).
3. De Grauwe (1996, 1092–3) continues: 'Whereas there is a strong consensus that the EU-15 should not form a monetary union, there is an equally strong conviction that there is a subset of European Union countries which form an optimum currency area ...' Decressin and Fatas (1995, 1628) suggest the 'possibility that certain regions within Europe of different countries may constitute OCA by virtue of their vulnerability to similar employment (for example) shocks ...'; Viñals (1996, 1106) also points out that: 'The general result (Bayoumi and Eichengreen, 1993) has been that while an EMU comprising all European countries would be rather costly given the predominance of asymmetric shocks, an EMU comprising a smaller and more homogenous group of countries – Germany, Belgium, Luxembourg, the Netherlands, Austria and possibly France – would be desirable.'
4. Participation rates adjust via changes in the number of part-time employees and changes in the criteria for retirement (Decressin and Fatas 1995, 1648–9).
5. However, they distinguish two periods of immigration from third countries. The first period from 1959–73 marks the emigration of Portuguese and Greeks to France, Germany and the United Kingdom. The second period from 1958–80s marks the arrival of immigrants from the former French colonies of North Africa in France and the arrival of Turkish Gastarbeiter in Germany.
6. Panic (1992, 150–1) reports that from the mid-1970s through the mid-1980s EC investment abroad consumed between 75 and 80 percent of EC investment capital. The single largest destination of these funds was the USA. The USA was also the single largest country invested in the EC.
7. Chapter 3 notes the dates of accession of the EU countries to the ERM.
8. Vaubel points out that: 'Alesina and Grilli (1992, 145) call this the problem of "how to keep Germany in". They argue that it probably cannot be solved unless European monetary policy is either geared to Germany's country-specific shocks (as in the pre-1993 ERM) or constrained to be even less inflationary than the policies of the Bundesbank.'

9. Roger Cohen (1997) Writes: 'Throughout Europe, the euro, like globalization, has proved unforgiving of the inefficiencies of what Germans call the Vaterstaat – the consoling father-state, always there when needed. It is forcing a radical reconsideration of the model of European society – one that is treacherous politically because it has been decreed by central bankers rather than demanded by voters.'
10. Eichengreen and Wyplosz (1993, 52) suggest that uncertainty regarding the process of monetary union contributed to the. speculative crises beginning in the fall of 1992: '... until the summer of 1992, anticipations of a smooth transition to monetary union had stabilized expectations and hence the operation of the EMS. At that point, the protracted process of negotiation and ratification allowed doubts to surface about whether the treaty would ever come into effect. This altered the costs and benefits of the policies of austerity required of countries seeking to qualify for European monetary union, leading the markets to anticipate that those policies would ultimately be abandoned.'
11. One estimate suggests that European banks will experience losses in profits from currency conversions and trading commissions of $5 billion.
12. Three important monetary events have taken place during these transitional stages. First, several countries joined the ERM. Second, a series of speculative crises in 1992–93 forced several currencies in the ERM to assume new values within the ERM parity grid. Third, as a result of these valuation changes, the fluctuation margins of the ERM expanded to ±15 percent for most countries. (Only Germany and the Netherlands retain narrow fluctuation margins of ±2.5 percent.)

6. Monetary and fiscal policy and institutions in the European Monetary Union

6.1 INTRODUCTION

The EMU introduced a number of changes into the operation of monetary and fiscal policy. EMU participants surrendered national monetary policy to the European Central Bank (ECB). Participants' fiscal policy faced limits on debt and financing arrangements as specified in the Treaty on European Union (TEU) (1991) and Growth and Stability Pact (GSP) (1996). This chapter looks at the implications of EMU for monetary and fiscal policy, and, the monetary and fiscal institutions of the new arrangement for EMU participants.

The chapter is organized as follows. The first half of the chapter looks at the implications of EMU for monetary and fiscal policy, respectively. The second half of the chapter looks at the organization and operation of the monetary and fiscal institutions, respectively. The final section concludes.

6.2 IMPLICATIONS OF EMU FOR MONETARY POLICY

The countries of the European Union (EU) have enjoyed monetary policy as an instrument of sovereign policy throughout the existence of the affiliation. However, sovereignty in monetary affairs has been reduced for some countries because of the successive attempts at the creation of a fixed exchange rate arrangement between EU currencies. Monetary policy in the EU has been limited by participation in the ERM since 1979.

Participation in the ERM and its predecessor, the snake, has prevented national governments from fully utilizing monetary and exchange rate policies directly to affect their domestic economies.[1] However, as the snake-in-the-tunnel clearly demonstrated, no fixed exchange rate system between countries is truly irrevocable, as proponents of the EMU plan advocate.[2] Fixed exchange rate arrangements do, however, increase the cost to countries of manipulating their nominal exchange rates for short-term gain and may introduce nominal stability into exchange markets.

Within the ERM, countries were prohibited from independently adjusting their exchange rates from those set forth within the official parity grid. The only exceptions to nominal exchange rate rigidity occurred during the official realignments. By committing to adhere to fixed parities, countries agree to limit their pursuit of monetary goals, which would lead to deviations of their currency's valuation from outside of the permitted fluctuation margins (since 1993, ±15 percent).

The proposed EMU will bring a change in the operation of monetary policy in the EU. EMU participants will experience the most change in the conduct of monetary policy as they surrender control over this aspect of their economies to the ESCB.[3] The experience of non-EMU participants will depend on the monetary targets and policies chosen by the ECB.

The euro will also represent a major new international currency. The ECB will bear the responsibility for undertaking the management of the euro *vis-à-vis* other world currencies. This responsibility includes attending to the relative valuation and movements of the euro on world currency markets. Similarly, it includes deciding on whether or not to permit currency flows to affect the internal money supply. The ECB may utilize sterilization operations to prevent currency movements from affecting the money supply within the EMU area.

6.2.1 Goals of EMU Monetary Policy

The TEU creates the European System of Central Banks (ESCB) as the monetary authority for the European Communities (EU). Article 105 (1) of the Treaty sets price stability as the primary goal of EU monetary policy. Furthermore, the ESCB must promote the overall economic objectives of the Community.[4] On October 13, 1998 the ECB specified the definition of price stability it would pursue. This strategy provides for an annual increase of the Harmonized Index of Consumer Prices (HICP) of less than two percent (ECB 1998).

The EMU replaces the system of sovereign monetary policy approaches within the EU with a single monetary policy approach. To the extent that the ECB's choice of instruments varies from that of national central banks, the new arrangement will constitute a change of approaches. This shift may differ from national preferences. However, many of the Member Countries have reshaped their monetary policies following the ratification of the TEU in 1992. The ensuing changes sought to model domestic monetary institutions and procedures after those of the proposed European monetary authority.

6.2.1.1 Role of monetary policy in adjusting to shocks

Monetary policy takes on a different role in the context of the EMU. No longer do countries possess the option of resorting to monetary and/or exchange rate policies that could, at the risk of penalty for violation of ERM parities, alleviate difficulties that arise from shocks. The loss of national monetary (and exchange rate) policy means that countries can no longer fashion policy to meet the demands of their domestic constituents.

Similarly the ECB cannot expand or tighten monetary policy within as limited a jurisdiction as a national central bank. For this reason, the ECB will not be able to offer monetary policy as a remedy for asymmetric shocks within regions or countries of the EU. Expansionary monetary policy by the ECB might only be justified in the face of depressed economic circumstances throughout the single currency area. Contractionary monetary policy by the ECB might only be justified in the face of inflationary pressures throughout the single currency area. In the event that economic conditions affect the EU less than universally, the governing EU institutions and the ECB must decide what (if any) shifts in monetary policy to implement. This decision will incorporate the differential effects of monetary policy throughout the union. This decision will depend upon the relative strength of different interests within the ECB and likely the EU's primary governing institutions.

The loss of national monetary policies may become especially contentious in the face of asymmetric shocks. Where these shocks affect sovereign countries differentially, these countries may request some form of assistance from the ESCB. The ESCB's responses are limited to monetary policy actions. The EU, however, might be able to arrange for fiscal transfers.

Article 103 of the TEU outlines the procedures for financial assistance from the EU to member countries. In the face of economic shocks, the provisions of this article might play a central role. Article 104 (TEU) prohibits the ECB from financing domestic deficits by any means. The ability of EMU monetary policy to assist in adjustments to regional disturbances is therefore very limited.

6.2.2 Tools of EMU Monetary Policy

In order to achieve its long-run monetary goals the ECB will make use of intermediate and operating targets. The ECB will then use those instruments available to it in order to meet these targets. The following paragraphs consider the choice of targets facing the ECB, as well as the choice of policy instruments with which to pursue these targets.

The ECB decided on its intermediate targeting strategy on October 13, 1998. This strategy consists of a monetary target accompanied by an inflation target. The monetary target assumes first position of the two targets. The ECB targets M3.[5]

The European monetary authorities possess several policy tools at their disposal. These tools include open market operations, standing facilities (discount rates) and minimum reserve requirements. Articles 18 and 19

(ESCB/ECB Statute) provide for the use of open market and credit operations, and reserve requirements, respectively. The ESCB can use these instruments to affect the supply of money and credit within the EMU.

Open market operations by the ESCB consist of the sale and purchase of five different kinds of instruments. These instruments include bond issuances, fixed-term deposits, foreign exchange swaps, outright transactions and reverse transactions. These instruments differ in frequency of issuance and maturity. Open market operations affect interest rates, as well as liquidity in financial markets.

Standing facilities of the ESCB consist of short-term lending and depository facilities from or with national central banks. The cost of overnight lending or the payment for overnight deposit is tantamount to the discount rate. The standing facilities serve to affect overnight liquidity.

Minimum reserve requirements consist of the minimal deposits banking institutions must hold in deposit with the ESCB. Reserve requirements affect market liquidity and interest rates. The ESCB has not yet decided whether to make use of minimum reserve requirements.

The targets and instruments available to the ESCB closely resemble those presently in use by EU central banks. Many of these central banks have officially adopted price stability as their primary goal and employ short-term interest rate targets to maintain their position within the ERM. Table 6.1 provides an overview of the objectives and instruments of the EU central banks.

This table provides a cursory but telling look at the monetary policies of nine of the EU member countries. Six of the nine countries have explicitly taken price stability to be their long-term objective. Two of the other countries advocate preservation of the value of the currency, in other words, price stability. The ninth country, Denmark, focuses on retaining a stable relationship between its currency, the krona and the currencies participating in the ERM/EMU.

Table 6.2 from Kenen (1995) provides more specific evidence of the monetary policy instruments used by 11 EU countries. This table reveals the predominance of open market operations as the instrument of choice.

The final tool available to policy-makers is the exchange rate. The ECB will bear the responsibility of maintaining the euro's value on international currency markets. The euro's exchange rate will affect the cost of imports relative to exports. Unsterilized intervention in currency markets may allow increases in the internal money supply and lead to inflation. In order to prevent such consequences the ECB may undertake sterilized intervention.

6.2.3 Political Economy of Monetary Policy

Monetary policy within a currency union is subject to similar pressures as domestic monetary policy due to the goals and desires of the political authorities. These pressures relate to cyclical policy effects, seigniorage issues, deficit

Table 6.1 Objectives and instruments of national central banks within the EU

Central bank policy/country	Long-term objective	Intermediate objective (s)	Operational targets /instruments	1st round EMU participant?
Austria	N/A	N/A	N/A	Yes
Belgium	N/A	N/A	N/A	Yes
Denmark	To maintain the value of the krona against the core European currencies		Short-term interest rates (repo & discount rates)	No
Finland	Stable money value		Open market operations with selected credit institutions + reserve requirement of 2% on demand deposits, 1.5% other deposits, 1% on all other liabilities	Yes
France	Price stability	Exchange rate and growth of a monetary aggregate (M3)		Yes
Germany	Safeguarding the currency	(Annual) monetary targets (M3)	Discount rates (overnight credit, Lombard policy, minimum reserve policy); securities repos (OMO); minimum reserve requirements of 1.5% on savings deposits and 2% on sight and time deposits)	Yes
Greece	N/A	N/A	N/A	No
Ireland	N/A	N/A	N/A	Yes
Italy	N/A	N/A	N/A	Yes
Luxembourg	N/A	N/A	N/A	Yes
Netherlands	Price stability	Exchange rate stability between NLG and DM	Overnight credit and open market operations; minimum (monthly) reserve requirements	Yes
Portugal	Price stability	Exchange rate	Overnight credit and open market operations; minimum reserve requirements	Yes
Spain	Price stability		Reserve requirement for credit institutions of 2%; daily and 10-day repos; overnight discount rate	Yes
Sweden	Price stability		Short-term interest rates (repo rate)	No
UK	Price stability	Inflation target	Interest rates	No

Source: This data was collected from the homepages of the respective central banks on September 15, 1998. N/A denotes that the information was unavailable on the Internet.

Table 6.2 Monetary policy instruments of 11 EU countries

Instrument	B	DK	G	H	ES	F	El	IT	NL	PO	UK
Reserve requirements for monetary policy purpose											
Used	No	No	Yes	Yes	Yes	Yes	Yes	Yes	No	Yes	No
Remunerated	–	–	No	Partly	No	No	Partly[a]	Partly	–	Partly	–
Standing facilities[b]											
Below market rate	Low	None	Med.	None	None	None	None	Med.	High	None	None,
Deposit facility	Low	Low	None	None	None	None	Med.	None	None	None	None
Penalty rate	Low	None	Low	Med.	Low	Low	Med.	Med.	Low	Low	Med.
Open market operations											
Outright	Low	High	Low	Med.	None	Med.	None	Med.	Low	High	High
Repurchase	High	High	High	Low	High	High	Med.	High	High	Med.	Med.
Forex swaps	Med.	Low	Low	Low	Low	None	High	Med.	Low	Low	None
Frequency[c]	High	Med.	Low	Med.	Med.	Med.	High	Med.	Low	Med.	High
Type of tender[d]	Both	Vol.	Both	Rate	Both	Rate	Rate	Rate	Vol.	Both	Rate

Notes:
[a] Below market rate.
[b] Ranked by importance in affecting supply of liquidity to the market.
[c] Low meaning about once a week; medium meaning several times a week; high meaning more than once each day.
[d] Volume of interest rate tender.

Source: Kenen (1995, Table 3-1, 62).

finance and inflation policy. In addition participants in a currency union face the option of withdrawal from the arrangement. Political pressures may have real effects on monetary policy, the statutory independence of the monetary authority notwithstanding.

A major difference between the political economy of monetary policy at the national versus EU levels stems from the different relationship between the executive and legislative bodies of the EU and the ESCB versus these bodies and the national monetary authorities. At the national level executive and legislative officials obtain power directly through national electoral procedures. These officials may then exert pressure on the national monetary authority whose jurisdiction coincides precisely with their political jurisdiction.

This link between electoral jurisdiction and the coincidence of political and monetary jurisdiction is broken at the EU level. In short the executive branch consists of the nationally elected or appointed leaders and ministers who comprise the Councils of Ministers and the appointees of the European Commission. National representatives within the Council do not face an electorate of the entire jurisdiction of the ESCB. Rather their constituents rest within the limited scope of their respective national boundaries. For this reason their interests will focus on national concerns. The extent to which these concerns coincide with EU monetary concerns will depend upon the relationship between the national economies and the monetary policy of the EU.

Furthermore, the appointees of the European Commission do not account to any electorate and therefore may be subject to an entirely different set of concerns than those of their respective countries of origin. Only European Parliament members obtain office through direct election. However, the European Parliament is the weakest body within the government of the EU and is the least able to affect the ESCB.

The vulnerability of EU monetary policy to cyclical variables then differs from that of national monetary policy. The absence of a single electoral cycle of key decision-makers at the EU level implies the absence of cyclical tendencies in monetary policy that coincide therewith. The dispersion of national electoral cycles will similarly prevent the appearance of cyclical tendencies in monetary policy. To the extent that an electoral cycle exists the break between it and monetary policy may lead to a reduction in the inflationary bias associated with elections (Williamson 1975 and Fratianni and Von Hagen 1993 cited in Vaubel in Cobham 1994, 48). Similarly, if no political party predominates at the EU level, incumbent and party usage of monetary policy may occur to a lesser degree than at the national level.

The generation and distribution of revenues from money creation represents a second area by which the political authorities may endeavor to affect monetary policy. The monetary authority may provide the government with revenues from at least two sources. The first of these sources is from the creation of money. Seigniorage accrues as the difference between the cost of printing money and its real purchasing power. Two forms of seigniorage exist for participants in the currency union: internal and external seigniorage. Internal seigniorage stems from the demand for and usage of the euro within the currency area. External seigniorage stems from the demand for and usage of the euro outside of the currency area.

The extent to which political actors seek to obtain revenues from seigniorage depends upon the amount of seigniorage available. Buiter et. al. (1993), for example, assert that: 'For individual member countries the distribution of the internal and external seigniorage of the ECB is also important.' If the euro grows to occupy a major role on global financial markets, seigniorage may emerge to be quite significant. However, empirical estimates of seigniorage revenue indicates its limited role to individual countries at present, as well as its limited potential in the context of a single EU currency. Buiter and Kletzer (1991) note that seigniorage does not constitute an important source of revenue for most EU countries. Italy prior to 1986 and the Southern European countries of Portugal, Spain and Greece are the only contradictions to this observation. Table 6.3 lists seigniorage amounts for 11 EU members from 1984–88.

Table 6.3 Seigniorage for 11 EU countries (1984–88)

Year/country	1984	1985	1986	1987	1988
Germany	0.3	0.3	0.6	0.8	1.0
France	0.8	0.1	–0.2	0.3	0.8
Italy	1.9	2.4	1.1	1.2	1.3
United Kingdom	–0.5	0.2	0.3	0.1	0.2
Belgium	0.1	–0.1	0.4	0.2	0.1
Netherlands	0.4	0.3	0.3	0.7	0.9
Denmark	0.3	4.6	–2.4	–1.1	0.8
Ireland	0.7	0.7	0.3	1.0	0.3
Greece	5.0	1.1	2.9	3.8	NA
Spain	0.9	0.8	1.5	5.0	1.4
Portugal	0.6	1.1	1.6	2.8	2.2

Source: Adapted from Giovannini and Mayer (1991, 231) and uses data from the IMF, International Financial Statistics.

Alogoskoufis and Portes (1991, 241) provide an estimate of potential seigniorage, which they admit is optimistic of 0.05 percent of EU GNP.[6] Estimates of euro seigniorage also depend upon the extent to which this currency ascends to a position of dominance within international currency markets. Alogoskoufis and Portes (ibid., 241) estimate that between 1982 and 1989 European currencies grew to occupy 17.5 percent of world currencies in use from 15.1 percent.

The second source of revenues from money creation comes from inflation. Inflation consists of increases in the price level and serves to reduce the nominal value of outstanding debt. For a government with significant nominal debt inflation may be attractive as one means of reducing the burden of repayment. De Grauwe (1996, 1096) points out that: 'As long as [any] country has a higher debt to GDP ratio, the incentive to create surprise inflation will be present.' In the context of a currency union it is unclear, however, which inflation rate might be targeted in order to reduce the level of a country's national debt. After all, as beneficial as inflation may be to one country it may be equally detrimental to another, depending on the composition of its national balance sheet.

Inflation may also serve as a means of taxing those sectors of the economy which would otherwise avoid explicit payment of taxes. Those economies that depend upon inflation as an instrument of tax policy may constitute an optimal currency area (Canzoneri and Rogers 1990, 420). Similarly, countries with different demands for the inflation tax may belong to different optimal currency areas.

Deficit finance constitutes another area where political actors seek to affect the monetary authority. The TEU as well as the Statute of the ESCB seek to prevent the occurrence of monetary financing of national debts. Article 104 (TEU) and Article 21 (ESCB/ECB Statute) explicitly prohibit the ESCB from extending credit at preferential rates or purchasing national debt instruments. So long as this provision holds, countries are left to depend directly on financial markets as sources of debt financing or public credit institutions as sources of loans. The ESCB is similarly prohibited from assisting in deficit finance at the EU level.

A currency union faces the additional risk of national withdrawals from participation. Unlike sovereign countries in which the monetary authority and arrangement constitutes a subordinate element of the government, monetary policy within a currency union of politically independent countries may be cause for withdrawal from the arrangement. Members of a currency union accept the common monetary policy as a part of the package of participation. If one or more countries deem its benefits from withdrawal in excess of its benefits from remaining, they may withdraw in favor of the nationally preferable arrangement of monetary sovereignty or participation in a more optimal currency arrangement. Or, if the adjustment mechanisms of the currency union fail to satisfy domestic constituents in the face of disturbances, pressure may arise for withdrawal from the common monetary arrangement. In this case, the currency union will decrease in membership. Such occurrences are not without precedent. Panic (1992,156–7) highlights the case of Slovenia:

> Slovenia, the wealthiest republic in Yugoslavia, which has just declared its independence, provides a timely reminder of this possibility ... A similar response [withdrawal from monetary union] can be expected also from the strongest members of such a union if they are required to make what they regard as an unreasonably large contribution towards sustaining it ... [continuing from above] the long-standing resentment of the Slovenes that, as they see it, their own economic welfare has suffered irreparably because of the contribution which they have had to make towards helping much poorer southern republics of Yugoslavia. Unable to persuade other members of the federation to agree to a major reduction in their fiscal contribution, they have exploited the earliest opportunity presented by dramatic changes in Eastern Europe to leave, with EC approval, the Yugoslav economic, monetary and political union.

Similarly, if the policies of the currency union lead to costly violations of national preferences regarding monetary and economic policy, withdrawals may result.[7] The dissolution of a number of earlier attempted currency unions demonstrates precisely this point.[8]

If a country key to the operation of the currency union considers withdrawal, this country may succeed in garnering a change in EU monetary policy. For example, if Germany considered withdrawal other currency union participants might be willing to negotiate measures to remedy the cause of Germany's concerns or to offer other conciliatory concessions. Fears over loss of monetary credibility might drive such efforts for the case of Germany.

6.3 IMPLICATIONS OF EMU FOR FISCAL POLICY

The countries of the EU retain nearly the same amount of sovereignty over fiscal policy under the EMU as they have enjoyed since the ratification of the TEU. Countries retain the right to most taxation, expenditure and debt issuance policies. The GSP (1997), however, introduced more explicit limits, along with procedures and penalties for dealing with national deficits. The policies introduced by the GSP attempt to prevent national fiscal imbalances from destabilizing the common currency regime.

Fiscal policy may assume a more important role after the transition to EMU because of the disappearance of sovereignty over national monetary and exchange rate policies. Although these policies had effectively been abandoned following the expansion of the fluctuation margins of the ERM in 1993, the possibility of resorting to them still existed. However, with the disappearance of national currencies and coinage, national accounting systems, and sovereign monetary policies, fiscal policy remains as the major macroeconomic instrument of adjustment for national governments.

6.3.1 Goals of EMU Fiscal Policy

National fiscal policy within the EU may continue to have the same general goals as prior to the EMU. Governments retain national fiscal authority. However, this authority faces statutory limits in order to retain the credibility of the ESCB and the stability of the common currency. These limits concern the accumulation of excessive deficits. An additional limitation already in existence following the Single European Act (SEA) involves taxation rates. The Single Market Program enabled factors full mobility within the EU and therefore offered the exit option to the tax base on a much wider scale than previously existed.

6.3.1.1 Role of EMU fiscal policy in adjusting to shocks

Fiscal policy faces several limits as an adjustment mechanism within the EU. First, Article 95 (TEU) prohibits discriminatory taxation on commodities imported from EU countries. This article precludes attempts at transferring fiscal burdens to producers outside of a single country. Second, factor mobility implies the mobility of the tax base (Bayoumi and Eichengreen 1993). Governments may therefore be unable to levy taxes not directly tied to services (Bovenberg et al. 1991, 378).[9] Bovenberg et al. (ibid., 379) note the problem caused by tax base mobility for domestic debt accumulation: 'servicing public debt by running a primary surplus will become increasingly difficult, because the taxes levied to create this surplus would cause tax bases to leave the country.' Eichengreen (1997c, 73–4) further points out that regional fiscal authorities will also be constrained by the level of tax rates in neighboring fiscal jurisdictions. Factor mobility enables movements to those regions offering that bundle of public goods that most suits factors' heterogeneous preferences for a given tax price. Possible solutions to this situation include insurance funds and transfers from the central budget of the currency union.

Limits on deficit finance constitute a third constraint on fiscal policy. Articles 103 and 104 (TEU) address the issue of excessive deficits, deficit finance and multilateral economic surveillance. Article 104 (TEU) and Article 21 (ESCB/ECB Statute) bar the ESCB from extending credit or accepting debt instruments of governments at any level within the EU. The Growth and Stability Pact (1997) further delineates the criteria for excessive national debt levels and procedures for handling such possibilities within the EU's institutional framework. Eichengreen (1997b, 46–7) also points out that: 'EC members with high debt-to-GNP ratios and low levels of reserves will have particularly little fiscal autonomy. Moreover, since EC members, like US countries, will retain sufficient autonomy to at least contemplate the option of default on their debts, they will face an increasing borrowing cost of external finance, which will further limit the length of time for which fiscal independence and monetary union are compatible.'

According to the GSP, a country's deficit is considered excessive if it meets the following criteria: (1) it exceeds 3 percent of annual GDP when annual GDP has not fallen by 2 percent or more; and (2) it is neither temporary nor declining. The Council of Ministers may also decide that deficits in excess of 3 percent are not considered excessive when GDP has fallen between 0.75 percent and 2 percent. This latter case becomes a matter of discretion. For excessive deficits which persist beyond two years the Commission may extract a punitive amount between 0.2 percent and 0.5 percent of GDP depending on the size of the excessive deficit. This amount will be due for each year the deficit remains. After two years of continuous deficit, the amount is forfeited and becomes effectively a fine.

The EU may provide fiscal regional assistance given its own budget constraints. The EU may undertake redistributive policies from relatively prosperous regions within the EU to relatively less prosperous regions *à la* Sala-i-Martin and Sachs (1991). Such transfers may be particularly relevant in the case of asymmetric shocks. However, such transfers depend upon the ability of the EU to collect sufficient revenues from the member countries.

6.3.2 Tools of EMU Fiscal Policy

Fiscal policy tools within the EMU are the same as those available to fiscal authorities under autonomous monetary arrangements. National governments retain taxation, expenditure and debt issuance policy instruments. However, these instruments may face additional market and/or constitutional limitations because of the single currency area.

The EU itself may be able to utilize fiscal policy instruments in a manner similar to national governments. However, the ability of the EU to so do depends upon the provision for such policies by the EU institutions in accordance with the TEU. The EU has undertaken a minimal amount of fiscal tasks. Della Posta (1993, 144) notes that 'the European Community budget isn't large enough to be used countercyclically.' The limited fiscal potential of the EU suggests the need for coordination of national fiscal policies among EMU participants. Such coordination would affect national debt levels, as well as automatic and discretionary responses to economic disturbances.

The EU's ability to generate revenue is very limited. It depends directly on its members for the collection of all of these revenues. In particular, it depends on these countries to turn over: (1) a portion of domestic VAT revenues; and (2) national contributions. Together these two sources comprise over three-quarters of the EU's annual revenues.

The expenditures of the EU budget demonstrate the areas in which the EU plays a fiscal role. Slightly over half of its revenues support the EU's Common Agricultural Policy. Approximately an additional 30 percent of the budget goes to support the Regional Development Fund, the Social Fund, the Cohesion Fund and other structural funds. The remainder of its revenues goes to support research, education, internal administration and aid to developing countries in East and Central Europe, Latin America and the Mediterranean.

The EU budget is relatively very small. The EU budget consists of approximately 1.0 percent of annual EU GNP. The EU budget pales in comparison to the annual budget of the US government, which is approximately 25 percent of US GNP. The EU's budget may increase following the completion of the Single Market Program. Goldstein and Woglom (1992) estimate the EU budget may rise to 3 percent of annual EC GNP.

The small size of the EU budget limits its potential to undertake fiscal adjustment policy in response to asymmetric shocks. Previously, the Very Short-term Financing (VSTF) facility and the Medium-term Financing (MTF) Facility were available to countries facing difficulties maintaining their currencies within the fluctuation margins of the ERM. With the disappearance of national currencies, these adjustment mechanisms will similarly disappear.

Article 199 (TEU) prohibits the EU from incurring debt. The annual budget is supposed to balance. However, EU expenditures in reality have exceeded revenues and deficits have occurred. To finance such deficits the EU depends upon loans from the European Investment Bank. Article 104 (2) (TEU) states that publicly owned credit institutions, unlike the ECB and its national representatives, may extend overdraft and credit facilities to EU public entities.

The EU budget does not have any reserve allocated for unexpected expenditures. In the event of adverse shocks, EU-level institutions possess limited response mechanisms. The ESCB might utilize monetary policy to respond to a global shock that affected the countries of the EU relatively symmetrically.

The EU might also consider the creation of an insurance fund to provide assistance in the face of unexpected disturbances. Such a fund might be especially valuable if rigidities prevent the operation of the various adjustment mechanisms suggested by OCA theory (Della Posta 1993, 143). The need for an EU-level insurance/stabilization fund may be greater under the following circumstances: (1) the EU budget is balanced or in debt and no extra funds are available to respond to shocks; (2) member countries are running debts, as well; and (3) member countries possess insufficient national insurance/stabilization funds.

An area-wide insurance fund might benefit adversely affected regions in the face of asymmetric shocks. Bayoumi and Masson (1998, 1027 [footnote 5]) point out that such a fund would be viable, 'unless the shocks they [the countries] respond to are perfectly correlated and the regional cycles perfectly synchronised, which is unlikely ...' In this improbable case a shock would have identical effects across the single currency area.

6.3.3 Political Economy of EMU Fiscal Policy

National fiscal policy assumes increased importance in the context of a currency union of sovereign countries. Fiscal policy remains one major area in which countries retain nearly autonomous control. For this reason, it remains an area of interest for domestic political actors. This interest arises in spite of the fact that economic and monetary integration imposes new constraints on national fiscal policies.

Political budget cycles may exist at two levels within a currency union. Existing political budget cycles at the national level may persist. Deficit spending, however, faces restrictions by centrally established deficit limits. In addition a political budget cycle at the EU level may develop. However, the latter is unlikely to arise for several reasons. First, the leadership of the EU does not obtain office on the basis of an electoral cycle. The Councils of Ministers are composed of representatives who are either elected or appointed from individual member countries. These countries maintain their own electoral schedules. A political budget cycle might not even evolve to accompany the cycle of the Presidency of the Council of Ministers. Countries alternate according to a predetermined ordering to this position for six-month terms of office. Second, members of the European Commission are political appointees and are not accountable to any electoral body. The only EU-level institution with regular elections is the European Parliament. However, this body retains limited fiscal powers of its own.

Deficit finance remains an important concern for political decision-makers particularly at the national level. Deficits constitute national expenditures in excess of revenues. Many countries depend upon the issuance of debt instruments or credit in order to finance their expenditures. The limits imposed by the TEU and the GSP restrict this possibility for obtaining purchasing power. Eichengreen and Bayoumi (1994, 791) make the important point that the combined effect of the limited fiscal role of the EU and the deficit limits on countries may be destructive to the EMU:

> Given their openness and the consequent small size of their fiscal multipliers, EC member countries should no more assume principal responsibility for fiscal stabilization in Europe than do country governments in the United States. But advocates of Maastricht cannot have it both ways: while there is no question that fiscal stabilization is more appropriately undertaken at the EC level, the treaty makes no provision for expanding the Community's fiscal role. Given that in post-EMU Europe the EC budget will in all likelihood remain small by US standards, providing little scope for automatic stabilization at the Community level, vigorously applying the

excessive deficits procedures of the treaty to the national budgets of member countries would leave post-Maastricht Europe with significantly less automatic stabilization than the US economic and monetary union.

These limits may be particularly devastating in the face of adverse shocks.[10] De Grauwe (1996, 1093–4) notes that fiscal limits may lead to national pressures on the ECB to assist in countries' adjustment to asymmetric shocks. If the ECB responds to such pressures, its independence and credibility might be put into question.

An additional concern arises in the context of persistent, excessive deficits. This concern relates to the effect of borrowing on interest rates. Two opposing factors may exert effects upon interest rates faced by national governments (Bovenberg et al. 1991, 377). On the one hand, the increased size of the market for euro-denominated issues might not lead to similar increases in interest rates. On the other hand, bond buyers might demand larger returns to hold participating countries' debt instruments due to the elimination of exchange risk as a consideration and the enlargement of the market for government debt issues. This enlarged market leads to more competition in the internal market for debt instruments.

Persistent budget deficits may also incline the executive bodies of the EU, the Council of Ministers and the Commission, to press the ECB to pursue more inflationary policies than it would otherwise choose on its own. Such pressures would test the independence of the ECB. Were the ECB to succumb to such pressures, EU exchange rate policy would come under the direction of the executive bodies as well (Bovenberg et al. 1991, 380).

The efforts of countries to satisfy the deficit aspect of the convergence criteria for admission to EMU may affect post-transition fiscal policies. Some countries accumulated debt in order to satisfy the inflation criteria (without resorting to inflationary finance) and to maintain their position within the ERM parity grid, such as Italy (Dornbusch in Giovannini and Mayer 1991, 314–6). Other countries, such as Germany, resorted to off-budget expenditures in order to satisfy the debt criterion. These actions imply that countries will need future revenues to repay these debts. Such needs will place upward pressure on EU interest rates and drive mobile factors to relatively lower cost locations (to avoid tax increases) within or even outside of the EU.

A currency union faces the additional risk of national withdrawals from participation. Limits on fiscal policy, notably deficits and tax policy, may place strains on domestic governments to satisfy domestic demands for the provision of public goods. If these demands cannot be met within the auspices of the currency union, the domestic electorate may favor withdrawal. Such could be the case where one or more countries are dissatisfied with EU redistribution policies and these countries do not receive satisfactory resolution from EU institutions. Bolton and Roland (1997, 1084) suggest that fiscal policy may become an area of major contention.

Revenue generation and collection at the EU level has long been a matter of contention, regarding the balance between national contributions and the EU's source of revenues. Two factors may motivate this. First, EU and individual countries compete with each other for revenues. Second, EU member countries compete with each other in terms of net contributions. No country wants its net contributions to exceed its net benefits.

6.4 MONETARY AUTHORITY OF THE EMU

The TEU identifies the European System of Central Banks (ESCB) as the monetary authority of the EMU. This institution consists of the European Central Bank and the central banks of the EU members. The ESCB possesses statutory independence from all governments, national and EU, and bears sole responsibility for determining EU monetary policy.[11]

6.4.1 Responsibilities of the ECB and the ESCB

Article 105.2 (TEU) and Article 3.1 (ESCB/ECB Statute) identify four tasks to be carried out by the ESCB in its capacity as monetary authority. First, the ESCB, is responsible for determining EU monetary policy and conducting operations with the purpose of meeting EU monetary objectives. Price stability is the primary goal of the ECB. Second to this goal is the task of promoting overall EU economic policy in accord with Article 2 (TEU). Second, the ESCB is responsible for handling foreign exchange transactions in accordance with Article 109 (TEU). Third, the ESCB is responsible for maintaining EU participants' official foreign exchange reserve holdings. Fourth, the ESCB is responsible for facilitating the internal payments system (TARGET) between member countries. Article 105.5 (TEU) and Article 3.3 (ESCB/ECB Statute) provide for another responsibility. The ECB is responsible for the supervision of the financial system and credit institutions. In addition Articles 4 and 5 (ESCB/ECB Statute) provide the ECB with the duty of advising EU and national institutions on matters relating to monetary policy, and the collection of statistical data related to the operation of the financial markets and monetary policy.

6.4.2 Organization and Distribution of Power of the ESCB

The monetary institutions of the EMU are the ECB and the national central banks of the respective EU members. These institutions together form the

ESCB. Articles 9 and 14 (ESCB/ECB Statute) provide for the operation of the ECB, and the national central banks within the ESCB. The ECB assumes responsibility for determining and directing EU monetary policy upon the beginning of Stage III of EMU when it replaces the European Monetary Institute (EMI). The national central banks continue to operate, however, no longer independently of each other within the EMS. Rather they operate as national agents of the ESCB. These banks carry the responsibility of executing EMU monetary policy within their national jurisdictions, overseeing the operation of the domestic financial systems, and collecting statistical data from their national economies and financial systems.

Article 106.3 (TEU) provides the ECB with two top-level institutions. These bodies are the Governing Council and the Executive Board. The Statute of the ECB and ESCB and Articles 109a and 109b (TEU) contain the provisions governing these bodies. The former contains more extensive provisions than the latter. Article 10 (ESCB/ECB Statute) provides for the Governing Council, Article 11 (ESCB/ECB Statute) for the Executive Board and Articles 45–47 (ESCB/ECB Statute) for the General Council. The latter is a temporary body charged with representing the interests of EU countries exercising their right to derogation from EMU.

The Executive Board consists of a President, Vice President and four additional members. The members of the Executive Board attain office through appointment by the Heads of Country or Government of the member countries. These appointments result from a recommendation by the Council of Ministers following consultation with the European Parliament and the Governing Council. Members enjoy an eight-year, non-renewable term of office. Only citizens of the EU may receive appointments.

The Executive Board assists the Governing Council in determining and preparing EMU monetary policy in several ways (Article 12 ESCB/ECB Statute). First, the Executive Board undertakes research and planning for upcoming Council sessions. Second, the Executive Board implements monetary policy based on General Council decisions. Third, the Executive Board informs national central banks of their respective responsibilities in EMU monetary policy. Finally, the Executive Board assists the Governing Council with overall ECB operating policy. These tasks include the capital of the ECB, the key for capital subscription, the transfer of foreign reserve assets to the ECB, the allocation of monetary income of national central banks, the allocation of the net profits and losses of the ECB, and derogation from the initial allocation of monetary income of national central banks.

The Governing Council determines ECB policy. Article 12 (ESCB/ECB Statute) outlines the duties of the Governing Council. The duties include the determination of the operating goals of the ESCB, the choice of monetary policy instruments and the Rules of Procedure of the institutions of the ECB. In addition to determining EMU monetary policy and ECB operating policy, members of the Governing Council, meaning national central bank governors, along with members appointed by the Council of Ministers, handle Executive Board members' terms and conditions of employment (Article 11.3 ESCB/ECB Statute).

The Governing Council consists of the Executive Board and the governors of the central banks of the participants in EMU. Two voting procedures operate within the Governing Council depending on the issue at hand (Articles 10.2 and 10.3 ESCB/ECB Statute). Under the first voting procedure, each member of the Governing Council possesses one vote. Simple majority rule determines vote outcomes. Under the second voting procedure, a system of weights determines each member's vote. Each central bank governor receives a vote in proportion to its central bank's contribution to the subscribed capital of the ECB. Executive Board members receive zero weights. In addition the President of the Council of Ministers and a delegate of the European Commission may attend meetings but not vote.

Each voting procedure applies to different issues. The first procedure (Article 10.2 ESCB/ECB Statute) applies to votes concerning the employment terms and benefits packages of the Executive Board (Articles 10.3 and 11.3 ESCB/ECB Statute). The second procedure applies to Articles 28, 29, 30, 32, 33 and 51 of the ESCB/ECB Statute. These articles concern the following matters, respectively:

- Article 28: ECB capital fund
- Article 29: Key for capital subscription
- Article 30: Transfer of foreign reserve assets
- Article 32: Allocation of monetary income of national central banks
- Article 33: Allocation of net profits and losses of ECB
- Article 5 1: Derogation from Article 32.

The respective articles of the statute provide extensive discussions of the matters.

The General Council operates within the ECB to accommodate EU members that are exercising their right to derogation. This body consists of the President and Vice President of the ECB and the governors of all of the central banks of the EU. The four other members of the Executive Board may participate in sessions of the General Council, but are prohibited from voting.

The national central banks of EMU participants operate under the auspices of the ESCB. These banks effectively serve as national representatives of the ESCB. It is the duty of these banks to carry out the policy of the ECB. National provisions determine the organization of each national central bank.

The TEU and ESCB/ECB Statute make only three requirements on national central banks. First, national central banks within the ESCB must be statutorily independent from governmental institutions at all levels, meaning EU, national, regional and local levels (Article 107 TEU and Article 7 ESCB/ECB Statute). National central banks must satisfy the criterion of independence by the end of Stage II when the ESCB forms. Second, Article 14.2 (ESCB/ECB Statute) mandates that national central bank governors serve a term of office of at least five years. A national government may only terminate a central bank governor's term if the governor 'no longer fulfills the conditions required for the performance of his duties or if he has been guilty of serious misconduct' (Article 14.2 ESCB/ECB Statute). Third, national central banks may perform tasks beyond those outlined in the ESCB/ECB statute unless a two-thirds majority of the Governing Council decides that these tasks violate ESCB policy.

6.4.3 Political Economy of EMU Monetary Policy-making

The relationship between the monetary authority, the ESCB and the political institutions of the EU determines the political economy of EMU monetary policy-making. The ESCB consists not only of the governing bodies of the ECB, but also the national central banks. The political institutions of the EU include the EU-level institutions, as well as the governments of each national, regional and local jurisdiction.

The independence of the ESCB concerns its ability to make decisions free from political pressures by EU and national governments. Political pressures may enter into ESCB decision-making and actions through a number of channels. First, appointees to the Executive Board are all political appointees. These appointees may endeavor to fulfill the wishes of their supporters within the Council of Ministers especially and the Parliament and Governing Council. The ESCB is directly accountable to the Council of Ministers, European Parliament and European Council. According to Article 109a (3) the President of the ECB must submit an annual report to these bodies. The Parliament may then debate the report. The Parliament may also call the President or other ECB members to speak before the relevant committees.

Second, the governors of the national central banks obtain their positions in accordance with national procedures that may be subject to political discretion in spite of statutory independence. These governors may espouse policies that satisfy the wishes of the incumbent political leadership or of the party that appointed them. As long as individual countries retain the power to dictate the terms and conditions of employment of central bank officials, the risk of political subversion of national central banks remains high.

In addition, the coincidence of political boundaries with monetary jurisdictions may place national central bank governors under more political pressure to respond to domestic concerns. Von Hagen and Süppel (1994, 781) highlight this possibility:

> In a federal monetary union, leaving the decision over monetary stabilization policies to the representatives of the individual countries always leads to inefficient monetary stabilization. The two reasons for this are that these representatives will want to use the common monetary policy to stabilize regional shocks, and that they face a greater degree of policy uncertainty making their response to aggregate shocks inappropriately small.

The case of the German currency union following German reunification is illustrative. Buiter and Kletzer (1991) point out that Chancellor Kohl subjugated the Bundesbank with his insistence on the instantaneous setting of the exchange rate of East German marks for West German marks at par. To avoid this coincidence of jurisdictions the ESCB might adopt an arrangement similar to the US Federal Reserve System. The Federal Reserve consists of 12 districts, none of which coincides with a single political jurisdiction.

Under the current arrangement, the governors of the central banks of the 11 first round candidates to EMU, along with the appointed officials of the ECB, will be responsible for monetary policy-making. Their interests will dictate the direction EMU monetary policy takes. Vaubel (1994c), among others,[12] suggests that the position of the median voter of the Governing Council will determine the outcomes of EMU policy decision processes.

The TEU and ESCB/ECB Statute contain a number of articles that provide for the independence of the ESCB. Giovannini (1995, 335–7) points out the following articles: Article 104 (TEU), Article 105 (TEU), Article 106 (TEU), and Article 107 (TEU). Article 104 prohibits the ESCB from providing overdraft or credit facilities to any governmental institutions within the EU. Article 105 identifies the foremost goal of the ESCB as price stability. By identifying such a goal, the TEU provides a statutory safeguard against political subversion of monetary policy-making. Article 106 bestows the ECB with 'legal personality'. Article 107 explicitly instructs the ESCB to refrain from soliciting or accepting advice from any governmental body within the EU. Article 107 also appears as Article 7 of the ESCB/ECB Statute.[13]

Several motives may drive political actors to exert pressure upon national and EU monetary authorities. First, countries with national debts may desire inflation or increases in the EMU inflation rate in order to reduce their national debt obligations. Second, countries may desire inflation in order to obtain revenues from seigniorage. Third, countries may desire to attempt to increase domestic output through an inflation surprise. Fourth, countries may desire assistance in response to regional shocks. The domestic electoral cycle may heighten these motivations.

In order to withstand political pressures and preserve the credibility of the ESCB, EMU monetary authorities may desire the adoption of policy rules. Policy rules for the ESCB, combined with the limits on national debt contained within the GSP, may strengthen the credibility of EMU monetary policy. Such rules may reduce the influence of political pressures upon monetary policy-making. Giovannini (1995, 341) suggests that the current objective of price stability serves as a constraint on the behavior of the ESCB. Yet this objective leaves considerable latitude in the choice of policy measures and short-term goals of the ECB.

Bovenberg et al. (1991, 381) warn that a rule may be undesirable in the face of economic disturbances, particularly asymmetric ones. A rule may inhibit the appropriate monetary response to adverse circumstances. Two alternatives to address this criticism include the adoption of a country-contingent rule and the appointment of a conservative central bank governor (Rogoff 1985).

EMU monetary policy-making may be subject to fewer pressures associated with electoral cycles. The limited ability of national representatives to affect ECB decisions may preclude the continuation of national electoral cycles. However, if the ECB desires to affect domestic electoral outcomes, it may seek to utilize short-term policy measures in order to favor its preferred candidate. Such measures may lead to an EMU political business cycle correlated with national elections. Vaubel (1994c) suggests that an EMU political business cycle will favor those countries that meet the following criteria: (1) their weight in Governing Council votes is large; (2) their electoral cycle coincides with that of EU-level elections; and (3) they can call early domestic elections relatively easily.

EMU monetary policy-making may also undergo pressures associated with the EU electoral cycle. However, given the limited powers of the EU's only directly elected institution, the European Parliament, no significant electoral cycle may develop. Unless the European Parliament obtains significantly greater power, the possibility of an EMU political business cycle driven by EU elections seems small.

6.5 FISCAL AUTHORITY OF THE EMU

The TEU makes no provision for a central EU fiscal authority within the EMU. Rather the three primary governmental institutions of the EU determine the limited EU fiscal policy. Existing national fiscal institutions retain their roles within their respective jurisdictions. However, national fiscal policies face deficit limits as outlined in the TEU (1991) and later specified in the GSP (1997).

6.5.1 Responsibilities of the EMU Fiscal Authority

The responsibility for fiscal policy decisions falls upon the three primary governmental institutions of the EU: the European Commission, the European Parliament and the Council of Ministers. Each institution plays a role in the decision process regarding the EU's annual budget.

The budgetary process of the EU takes place on an annual basis. Article 203 (TEU) outlines the process. The first step occurs within the respective institutions of the EU included but not limited to the three primary governmental institutions. Each institution prepares its own budget estimates for the coming calendar year. The Commission then collects these estimates and forms a complete draft of these individual budgets. The Commission presents this complete budget to the Council of Ministers for preliminary approval. The Council may suggest changes. Following the approval of at least a qualified majority within the Council, the budget draft moves to the European Parliament. A majority of the Parliament may undertake amendments to the budget draft. If the Parliament makes any amendments, the budget returns to the Council for review and approval. In this case, the budget returns to the Parliament for final approval following the Council's review. If the Parliament does not make any amendments, the budget stands.

6.5.2 Organization and Distribution of Power of Fiscal Authorities in the EMU

Fiscal policy rests primarily with the member countries of the EU. The EU possesses a very general framework for fiscal policy, limited as this policy is. No single, central institution is charged with responsibility in this area. The members of the EU opted for a continuation of the existing fiscal arrangements in spite of debates over possible fiscal reorganizations.

The absence of a central institution responsible for overseeing fiscal policy may weaken the proposed monetary union. Such an institution might operate within a variety of alternative fiscal arrangements. These arrangements include a fiscal federation and a fiscal union.

A central fiscal authority might benefit a monetary union by providing redistributive transfers across regions. Sala-i-Martin and Sachs (1991) warn: 'Without simultaneously creating a fiscal union responsible for the insurance function, a viable monetary union in Europe may not be possible.' The need for a system of centralized fiscal transfers will depend on the exact nature of economic disturbances (for example region-specific), the operation of alternative adjustment mechanisms (such as capital flows[14]) and the costs associated with the creation and operation of such a system.

6.5.3 Political Economy of EMU Fiscal Authority(ies)

The relationship between national fiscal authorities and national governments, as well as between the primary governing institutions, determines the political economy of fiscal policy-making within the EMU. National governments may endeavor to utilize fiscal policy to satisfy their constituents' interests. Similarly, actors within the primary governing institutions of the EU may endeavor to utilize the budget of the EU to satisfy their constituents' interests.

At the level of the individual country, fiscal policy may be subject to a number of political pressures. These pressures stem from the relationship between political officials and their respective constituencies. Taxation and expenditure policies may favor particular segments of the population or sectors of the economy. Expenditure policies may be automatic or discretionary, and may or may not respond to economic disturbances.

At the level of the EU, fiscal policy may also be subject to a number of pressures. These pressures stem from relationships similar to those between national politicians and their constituencies. The limited size of the EU budget precludes the amount of bargaining at the EU level as at the level of individual member countries. Politicians within each of the involved institutions will compete to put forward the interests of their respective constituents. Such advocacy will take place within each of the institutions involved in the budgeting process. Advocacy may fall along national or sectoral lines and may be successful in accordance with national budgetary contributions or relative national strength within the EU's primary institutions.

Von Hagen (1994) mentions two important aspects of the budgeting process. Both aspects apply to the individual country's fiscal process, as well as to the EU's fiscal process. First, citing Wildavsky (1975, 4), he notes that the budgeting process represents a venue for political bargaining and exchange. Through this process political actors endeavor to fulfill the demands of their supporters. Second, he reports that institutional representatives promote the growth of the budget of their respective institutions.

Von Hagen's points apply to the taxing, spending and revenue generation tasks of national and EU authorities in addition to the budgeting proceedings. National concerns regarding annual EU contributions are one example of competitive jurisdictional advocacy. Institutional budgetary requests at the EU level also follow the behavioral patterns of institutions at the national level. These institutions desire budgetary increases and institutional expansion.

Like national fiscal policies, the EU fiscal policies may be vulnerable to short-run political concerns. The EU budget is prepared on an annual basis. It may therefore be subject to myopic political pressures. The budget may to some extent satisfy these pressures. However, such practices may impede the EU from adopting policies conducive to longer-term growth and prosperity.

6.6 CONCLUSION

The EMU will introduce a number of changes in monetary and fiscal policy-making, and monetary and fiscal institutions. Most notably sovereign countries will surrender monetary policy to the ECB. This transfer of monetary authority will leave countries with one less major instrument of economic adjustment. Countries retain authority over national fiscal policy and retain national fiscal institutions. However, the GSP limits the discretion national governments possess in the area of budget deficits. For this reason, sovereignty over fiscal policy is less than complete.

The reduction in policy tools available to national governments in the monetary and fiscal spheres may lead to pressures for monetary and fiscal accommodation and assistance from EU-level institutions. However, national calls for assistance will face competition from the calls of other member governments. The ability of the EU to respond to national calls for assistance will determine its long-run success of the single European currency arrangement.

NOTES

1. For example Dornbusch (1991, 317) writes that: 'There is no longer significant monetary policy in Europe.' He continues by noting that two adjustment mechanisms have taken over where nominal exchange rates no longer can: 'Whether or not exchange rates are fixed is ... a question of wage behavior and fiscal policy ...'.
2. Barrell (1992, 249, Note 1) makes this point: 'There can be no such thing as an irrevocable union of currencies between independent countries, or even between regions of the country. The British–Irish monetary union of 1826–1979 is an obvious counterexample.' Frankel (1996, 157) also makes the same point: 'In practice there is, no such thing as "irrevocably fixed."'
3. Dornbusch (1991, 317) notes, however, that the surrender of sovereign monetary authority is not as significant a loss for individual countries as it may at first glance appear. Participation in the EMS has required countries to maintain their exchange rates within a limited range of fluctuation *vis-à-vis* other participating currencies thereby ruling out the possibility of monetary policy conducted without consideration for its impact on the relative valuation of domestic currencies within the EU.
4. Article 2 of the TEU sets forth the economic objectives of the EC: 'The Community shall have as its task, by establishing a common market and an economic and monetary union and by implementing the common policies or activities referred to in Articles 3 and 3a, to promote throughout the Community a harmonious and balanced development of economic activities, sustainable and non-inflationary growth respecting the environment, a high degree of convergence of economic performance, a high level of employment and of social protection, the raising of the standard of living and quality of life, and economic and social cohesion and solidarity among Member countries.'
5. The European Monetary Institute (EMI) examined five possible targets before reaching a decision. These targets included exchange rate pegging, interest rate pegging, nominal income targeting, monetary targeting and direct inflation targeting. Operating targets include interest rates. Money supply targeting consists of selecting one measure of the money supply and attempting to maintain the supply of money at a chosen level through the use of those monetary instruments available to the monetary authority. The monetary authority may choose from

several measures of the money supply ranging from the more narrow M1 to the more inclusive M3. The EMI advocated an intermediate money target à la Bundesbank for the ECB. According to its plan non-EMU participants would then target their exchange rates to the euro.

Inflation targeting consists of selecting the rate of growth of the price level and attempting to meet this growth rate using those monetary tools available to the monetary authority. The monetary authority may choose a zero inflation rate or a positive inflation rate, for example. Persson and Tabellini (1996) advocate inflation targets for the EU instead of monetary targets. They argue that an exchange rate target would not allow non-EMU participants sufficient latitude to accommodate economic disturbances. An inflation target in contrast, would facilitate adjustment to shocks to velocity. In addition, an inflation target would make any competitive devaluations and inflationary (above the target) policies more apparent. By making such actions more easily observable, an inflation target may prevent them.

6. They also point out that: 'Cohen (1971) estimated that the seigniorage extracted from the fact that pound sterling was still a major regional currency in the 1950s and 1960s was almost zero.' Although they estimate US seigniorage to be approximately 0.2 percent of 1988 US GNP, they caution that this amount far exceeds the likely amount the euro would earn.
7. Panic (1992, 156) reports that '... Politicians had no difficulties in throwing off the straight-jacket of the gold standard [in the early 1990s] when it stood in the way of financing large budget deficits' (Fratianni and Spinelli 1984, 417).
8. For examples of earlier efforts at European currency unions and their respective demises see Chapter 2.
9. Consider the following simple example. Country A consists of two regions, North and South. South suffers from a negative shock. Country A's government decides to tax North and redistribute the revenues from this tax to South. Economic agents in relatively prosperous North may move to South in order to avoid the tax burden and receive the government revenues. Or, agents in North may move to Country B, C or D. In the event that many agents leave North, country A will face difficulties in collecting funds internally with which to assist South.
10. Interestingly, however, empirical tests by Corsetti and Roubini (1992 in Della Posta 1993, 153) find that political determinants are responsible for national debts and deficits rather than fiscal adjustment policies in response to economic disturbances.
11. Article 109f (TEU) and the EMI Statute provide for a transitional institution, the European Monetary Institute (EMI), to direct preparations for the establishment of the ECB during Stage II of the transition to EMU. The ECB replaces the EMI at the end of Stage II and the EMI ceases to exist.
12. Michele Fratianni and Jürgen von Hagen (1992), *The European Monetary System and European Monetary Union*, Boulder: Westview Press; Alberto Alesina and Vittorio Grilli (1993), 'On the feasibility of a one-speed or multi-speed European monetary union', *Economic and Politics*, **5**, 145–65; Geoffrey Garrett (1993), 'The politics of Maastricht', *Economics and Politics*, **5**, 105–23; Paul de Grauwe (1993), 'The Political Economy of Monetary Union in Europe', CEPR Discussion Paper No. 842.
13. These articles state the following: 'When exercising the powers and carrying out the tasks and duties conferred upon them by this Treaty and the Statute of the ESCB, neither the ECB, nor a national central bank, nor any member of their decision-making bodies shall seek or take instructions from Community institutions or bodies, from any government of a Member Country or from any other body. The Community institutions and bodies and the governments of the Member countries undertake to respect this principle and not to seek to influence the members of the decision-making bodies of the ECB or of the national central banks in the performance of their tasks.'
14. However Eichengreen (1997b, 23) notes that: 'Some observers argue that the case for fiscal federalism will be rendered redundant by the elimination of capital controls. Europeans will be able to protect themselves against the impact on their incomes of region-specific shocks by holding diversified portfolios of financial claims on firms in other regions. However, US experience suggests that freedom to invest in other regions weakens at most slightly the rationale for fiscal federalism.'

7. A rational choice approach to the political marketplace of the European Union

7.1 INTRODUCTION

The Rational Choice approach to political-economic analysis sets forth two basic axioms as determinants of individual behavior. These axioms provide a general framework for analyzing the behavior of individuals within the context of the political marketplace, which consists of individuals in the roles of policy brokers, demanders and suppliers. This chapter reviews models of policy broker, demander and supplier behavior, and considers how demanders and suppliers drive brokers to respond to their preferences. This chapter highlights the case of the EU throughout.

This chapter employs the following organization. Section 2 briefly reviews the Rational Choice approach to political-economic analysis. Section 3 explains the concept of the political marketplace as an analogy to the commercial marketplace. The section extends this concept to the case of the European Union (EU). Section 4 examines the brokers of policy. The second half of this section considers the policy brokers of the EU, namely the Council of Ministers, the European Commission and the European Parliament. Section 5 examines the demanders and suppliers of policy. The second half of this section considers the policy demanders and suppliers of the EU, namely voters, interest groups and EU-level agencies. The latter agencies include the European Commission and the European Central Bank. Section 6 provides a brief description of the political marketplace for monetary policy in the EU. The final section concludes.

7.2 THE RATIONAL CHOICE APPROACH

The Rational Choice approach represents a set of assumptions available to social scientists for studying the behavior of individuals, groups and institutions. The primary assumption is that individuals act purposively in order to obtain identifiable goals. This approach has, however, recently undergone a number of formal attacks by its opponents.

7.2.1 Assumptions of the Rational Choice Approach

The Rational Choice approach to individual behavior asserts that individual actors strive to maximize their respective individual utilities. Actors undertake means which they expect to lead to the attainment of their preferred goals. The approach consists of two fundamental axioms that pertain to individuals' preferences and preference orderings.

The first axiom, completeness, states that individuals are able to rank order all of their preferences. Individuals are able to identify the relative desirability of possible alternatives and place these alternatives into an ordinal listing. The second axiom, transitivity, states that individual's preferences are fully transitive or consistent. Transitivity implies that if an individual prefers A to B and B to C, he must also prefer A to C.

7.2.2 Criticisms of the Rational Choice Approach

The Rational Choice approach faces a number of criticisms. These criticisms fall into two categories. The first category of criticisms concerns the assumptions of the approach. The second category concerns the practice of the Rational Choice approach by social scientists. Two types of criticism comprise this category: methodological and substantive.

The first criticism represents a limitation of the notion of rationality. At some times or under some circumstances actors may behave in a manner that would not result in the achievement of their most preferred outcome(s). For example, Hindess (1989, 6) notes that: 'In times of crisis, decisions may not appear rational to outside observers, as decision-makers make brisk decisions based upon faulty or partial analysis.' Under certain circumstances, search costs may lead individuals to adopt limited or bounded rationality. However, such limited rationality may not result in irrational behavior.

A second criticism concerns the assumption of preference consistency. Preferences may appear or in fact be inconsistent for at least two different reasons. First, actors' preferences may change over time. Second, preferences may be a function of perceived feasible alternatives. If the set of feasible alternatives varies, intransitivities between choices may arise.

Hindess (1989) offers a convincing response to the above general criticisms of the Rational Choice approach. He writes that: 'Rational Choice analysis does not maintain of course that action is always rational. Its claim rather is that the assumption of rationality is a powerful heuristic device. It is a useful simplification and it provides us with means of identifying the role of non-rational elements in human behavior' (167). The Rational Choice approach stands as an instrumental means of examining and endeavoring to better understand human behavior.

Defense of the assumptions of the Rational Choice approach may also be found in the methodological position taken by Milton Friedman in his 1953 article 'The Methodology of Positive Economics'. Essentially Friedman states that the value of a theory lies in its predictive abilities, not in the realism of its assumptions. Hindess (1989, 181) notes that Downs (1957) and Becker (1976) both take recourse to Friedman's stance in defense of the Rational Choice approach.

Green and Shapiro's *Pathologies of Rational Choice Theory* (1994) represents the most comprehensive presentation of the second category of criticisms regarding the practice of the Rational Choice approach. This section briefly identifies the methodological criticisms. It also notes the substantive criticisms. The latter will receive further attention within a subsequent section of the chapter.

Green and Shapiro (1996) identify five major methodological criticisms of the Rational Choice approach (Friedman 1996a, 5–6). These criticisms derive from what Green and Shapiro refer to as Rational Choice theorists' attempts to formulate a universal theory. The first major criticism alleges that Rational Choice theorists' hypotheses are unclear and lend themselves poorly to empirical evaluation. By the same token Green and Shapiro allege that Rational Choice theorists fail to reformulate those hypotheses that depend upon specific initial conditions in order to attain equilibrium. Furthermore they assert that Rational Choice theorists eschew reformulation of these hypotheses in spite of questionable explanatory power on account of the uncertainty accorded to initial conditions and the conditions necessary for equilibrium.

The second major criticism involves *post hoc* theory development. The authors complain that Rational Choice theorists reformulate their theories in response to unfavorable empirical results. The third major criticism is that Rational Choice theorists engage in arbitrary domain restriction. The authors object that Rational Choice theorists limit the range of explanation of their theories in order to eschew reformulating or abandoning theories in the face of contradictory evidence. The fourth criticism is that Rational Choice models are incapable of accounting for the size of predicted effects. Finally, Green and Shapiro accuse Rational Choice theorists of concentrating their research on finding evidence favorable to their hypotheses. When these efforts fail, Green and Shapiro assert that Rational Choice theorists reformulate their assessment of the data to accord with their models.

In response to Green and Shapiro's (1994) methodological attacks on the Rational Choice approach, Friedman (1996b) edited a volume of articles that attempts to address Green and Shapiro's criticisms. These articles illuminate limitations of Green and Shapiro's criticisms. In particular, they caution that: 'The problematic aspects of the pathologies pointed out by Green and Shapiro are not peculiar to rational choice, and rather apply to scientific enterprises in general' (Kelley 1996, 102–104). However, the authors do admit the existence of individual works which may indeed suffer from one or more of the pathologies.[1] However, these works do not lessen the value of the approach itself or the contributions of unaffected studies. Furthermore, they attempt to demonstrate the instrumental value of Rational Choice models in gaining a greater understanding of social processes.

The first major criticism raised by Green and Shapiro targets unclear hypotheses that are difficult to test. In particular Green and Shapiro criticize the use of unobservable variables. These unobservables make empirical testing difficult, if not impossible. Such unobservables might include beliefs and preferences (Diermeier 1996, 64). The fact that these variables do not lend themselves to quantification, however, does not justify their exclusion from scientific models. Fiorina (1996, 91) argues that: 'An empirical contribution can be many things, only one of which is state-of-the-art statistical analysis.' As long as they play an important role and have real effects, unobservable variables represent valid elements of any potential model.

Green and Shapiro also take issue with Rational Choice theorists' use of such concepts as equilibrium, instability and stability. They deem such terms vague and unclear. They warn that such concepts gravitate to the fore of modeling only in the absence of significant amounts of empirical data (Green and Shapiro 1996, 195; Murphy 1996, 167). Murphy (1996) concedes this criticism and accepts the need for caution in the use of such concepts.

Lohmann (1996) notes that these criticisms regarding Rational Choice hypotheses do not deliver fatal blows to the approach. In defense of the Rational Choice approach, she writes:

> [R]ational choice theorizing has the potential to identify and correct logical inconsistencies and slippages. It is thus valuable even if the resulting theories are not tested empirically ... The implications of rational choice theory often replace firmly held, yet logically self-contradictory, intuitions ... many theoretical implications of rational choice scholarship were strikingly powerful and counterintuitive when first expressed, including Arrow's (1951) paradox and Olson's (1965) free-rider problem (127, 130).

This exposition highlights the inherent value of the deployment of the Rational Choice approach.

Green and Shapiro's second criticism concerns *post hoc* theory development. They criticize Rational Choice theorists for formulating theories in the face of empirical observations. Subsequently, they assert that Rational Choice theorists reformulate theories if disconfirming evidence appears. Defenders of the Rational Choice approach note that *post hoc* theory development represents in actuality the refinement of theories in light of empirical facts. For example, Chong (1996, 45) defends such refinements: 'Modifications of Rational Choice theory are derided by Green and Shapiro for being *post hoc* explanations, yet such modifications are meant to improve the theory in the light of disconfirming evidence.' Diermeier (1996, 61) notes that: 'What Green and Shapiro call "*post hoc* theory development" Thomas Kuhn would call "puzzle-solving."'

The third criticism raised by Green and Shapiro concerns arbitrary domain restriction. Green and Shapiro's criticism refers to instances where they observe Rational Choice theorists willing to deploy their models 'wherever the theory seems to work' (Green and Shapiro 1996, 45). This criticism relates to the use of the *ceteris paribus* assumption to limit the range of circumstances under which a model to operates. However, this assumption is necessary given: (1) theorists' limited knowledge over relevant operative factors; (2) the impossibility of providing for all possible situations; and (3) the difficulty of managing a complex, multivariate model. In the absence of omniscience, the scientific task of simplifying, hypothesizing, testing and discovering remains. Fiorina (1996, 88) emphasizes this point.

Green and Shapiro's fourth criticism alleges that Rational Choice theories are unable to predict the size of expected effects. In particular, they challenge the inability of Rational Choice models to account for free-rider effects within interest groups and other collective organizations. Voter turnout also represents a puzzle for Rational Choice. However, the limited ability of Rational Choice to provide full explanations for social phenomena does not devalue its ability to increase our understanding of such occurrences (Chong 1996, 49).

The fifth criticism Green and Shapiro advance is that Rational Choice theorists focus on evidence favorable to their hypotheses. Chong (1996, 44–5) discounts this criticism by pointing out Rational Choice theorists' continued attention to models of voter turnout and collective action. The task remains for Rational Choice theorists and others to understand these issues and others for which satisfactory models do not exist. Disconfirming evidence serves to fuel such undertakings, as in any valuable scientific undertaking.

Green and Shapiro (1996) lodge four major substantive criticisms against the Rational Choice approach. These criticisms concern Rational Choice explanations of voter turnout, collective action and spatial models of legislative behavior and party competition. The following paragraphs contain a brief presentation of these criticisms. A later section explains these models and reviews their shortcomings in more detail.

Rational Choice models face serious difficulties explaining voter turnout. Individual cost–benefit calculations regarding voting behavior yield negative or infinitesimally small expected net benefits to voting. Downs (1957) presents a model of voter's expected net return from voting. Only in the event that this return is positive will voters rationally go to the polls. This model (explained later) cannot justify present and historical turnout rates. To remedy this problem Riker and Ordeshook (1968) expand Downs' model to include a civic duty variable in order to explain the decision to vote. This model can only remedy the paradox of voter turnout for excessively high values of the civic duty variable. Green and Shapiro cite this paradox as an example of Rational Choice theorists reformulating their theory in the face of contradictory evidence. Similarly, they emphasize the irrationality apparent in the paradox of voter turnout. Expected returns to voting fall far below the costs associated with information acquisition and voting.

Rational Choice models also encounter some difficulty explaining the formation of interest groups. The challenge inherent in such models is to explain how multiple actors overcome the costs of organization and cover the costs of operation in the face of the free-rider problem. Green and Shapiro note the difficulty of overcoming the common pool problem. With large numbers of members any individual member of a group has an incentive to shirk and free-ride on the contributions of others.

Olson (1965) offers perhaps the best example of a Rational Choice explanation for the formation of interest groups. He suggests that small, homogeneous groups of individuals will organize in order to provide selective benefits to group members. Smaller group size reduces the costs of monitoring and increases the cost of shirking by the individual. For example, peer pressure to contribute may operate successfully within a small enough group. Selective benefits enable the group to exclude non-members from the products of the group. Lobbying activities by such groups represent a by-product of the group's existence.

Green and Shapiro praise Olson's model and his work. Olson not only formulated the theory but also tested it empirically. His example stands out against others who Green and Shapiro fault for failing to undertake experiments that would test the ability of their models to formulate predictions. Green and Shapiro criticize many studies for relying upon historical evidence alone.

Rational Choice models of legislative behavior also face criticism. Rational Choice models predict instability due to continual cycles in majoritarian regimes. However, this instability is not observed empirically. Tullock attributes the observed stability of majoritarian regimes to the existence of such institutional features as logrolling and coalitions. Shepsle and Weingast (1987) note that rules of procedure may also serve to eliminate cycles within a legislature. Green and Shapiro suggest that these examples demonstrate the tendency of Rational Choice theories to seek support from unclear definitions, for example of stability and equilibrium (Friedman 1996a, 7).

Spatial models of party competition receive additional attacks from Green and Shapiro. Rational Choice theory employs the median voter theorem to identify the spatial position upon which electoral candidates will converge. Testing of these models exemplifies three of Green and Shapiro's methodological criticisms. First, Rational Choice theorists do not test these models against alternative hypotheses regarding the determination of candidates' apparent policy positions. Second, Rational Choice theorists tend to employ these models in such a fashion that they are able to explain any course of events. Third, spatial models utilize variables that are difficult to quantify. Models containing such variables do not lend themselves to statistical testing, in which Green and Shapiro place credence.

7.2.3 An Evaluation of the Rational Choice Approach

The Rational Choice approach stands as an important analytical framework. It offers a systematic approach to studying individuals' behavior using given information to attain identifiable goals (Kelley 1996, 97). It represents an improvement over earlier approaches taken by political scientists, including structuralism, functionalism and reference-group theory (Chong 1996, 42–3). The Rational Choice approach offers a general, more comprehensive framework for individual behavior that seeks to understand the instrumentality of decisions and the root causes of individual actions.

This study employs the Rational Choice approach for several reasons. First, the assumptions of the approach represent an intuitively appealing foundation. Second, the approach employs logically consistent assumptions capable of yielding theoretically insightful models of actions within the political marketplace. Third, the approach has the potential to reveal valuable information about apparently irrational individual behavior.

7.3 PUBLIC CHOICE IN THE POLITICAL MARKETPLACE

The Rational Choice approach originated with the study of individual behavior in private markets but is now applied to the behavior of actors within the political marketplace.[2] The latter consists of politicians, voters, interest groups, bureaucrats, other government agents and corporate entities. In the political marketplace, analogous to the private marketplace, actors obtain information, formulate decisions and undertake actions in accordance with the basic assumptions of Rational Choice. The institutions of the political marketplace enter consideration as they affect the constraints that actors face, along with the decisions they make and the actions they choose.

7.3.1 Public Choice and Politics as Exchange

Public Choice endeavors to apply the basic framework of economics to the political arena. Actors within the political marketplace correspond to the policy brokers, demanders and suppliers of the commercial marketplace. However, the exchange of goods and services supplied publicly replaces the exchange of commodities provided by private producers. Such goods and services include legislation and regulation. Payments occur in such media as money, such as in the commercial marketplace, as well as votes, time, advertising, income-earning opportunities and other valuable resources. Politics constitutes a locus of exchange between a myriad of consumers, producers and brokers.

In the political marketplace, the actors may differ but the motivations are similarly dominated by self-interest. Gwartney and Wagner (1988, 8–9) compare the role of the politician to that of the broker in the commercial marketplace and the role of the voter to that of the consumer in the commercial marketplace. Special interest groups occupy a position similar to voters. The politician seeks to please his supporters with political goods and services in exchange for votes, campaign contributions and other material support. The politician's utility depends upon his ability to maintain power, most notably through election and re-election. Voters and other brokers of political resources, such as political action committees and special interest groups, offer their votes and support in exchange for commodities produced through the political process.

Politicians identify their relevant consumer supporters based on the latter's usefulness in advancing the former's utility. Political decision-makers' utility functions consist of such arguments as power, prestige and income (Frey and Gygi 1991, 66). Political decision-makers specialize in utilizing the political process to meet the demands of various constituencies. These constituencies consist of the politician's consumer supporters such as special interest groups and individual voters. Special interest groups offer politicians various kinds of support including publicity, endorsements, campaign contributions and votes. Individual voters offer politicians their support in the form of votes and campaign contributions.

Political decision-makers seek to satisfy their constituents in order to advance their own interests. Decision-makers' policy stances and voting behavior depend upon: (1) the relevant electoral cycle; (2) the strength and position of the relevant opposition challenger; and (3) the length of horizon facing the respective political decision-maker. The electoral process is competitive and therefore requires politicians to offer constituents satisfactory policies lest a challenger provide a more preferred alternative and defeat the incumbent in the next election (Holcombe 1993, 96).

Political actors face competition from several sources (Vaubel 1991, 33). First, incumbent politicians and existing institutions encounter competition from other incumbents and institutions. Second, incumbents face competition from challengers and would-be challengers in future elections. Institutions face competition from interests advocating the creation of alternative institutions. Such competition depends upon the contestability of the political market. Sunk costs may reduce the ability of challengers to unseat incumbents. High incumbency rates suggest the difficulty for challengers to defeat incumbents. Third, individuals and institutions face competition from their counterparts in other jurisdictions. This competition is particularly relevant where constituents possess low-cost exit opportunities. Jurisdictional and inter-governmental competition may occur at local, regional and national levels.

The existence of competitive relationships may imply a number of consequences. First, competing individuals or institutions may engage in wasteful use of productive resources in competition. Second, competitive relationships may motivate political actors to attend to changing constituent desires and strive to satisfy their preferences. Holcombe (1993, 94) makes this point for the case of inter-governmental competition: 'When individuals have a choice of governments, either because they can move or because they can select the government they prefer through election, then the competitive setting will push governments to act as their constituents desire.' Third, competition within the political process may reduce the monopoly power of any single individual or institution to impose its will on its constituents. Competitive relationships may also lead to attention to the interests of small, organized groups within society.

7.3.2 The EU: An International Political Marketplace

The European Union represents an unusual political marketplace. It possesses a number of characteristics that distinguish it from the domestic political marketplace of any sovereign country. First, the political marketplace of the EU is international. It consists of sovereign countries that possess their own independent governmental institutions. As such the political actors of the EU juggle a larger number and variety of national, regional and economic interests. Second, the governing institutions of the EU bear responsibility for a more limited number of policy areas than the governing institutions of the member countries. Third, the EU has limited enforcement mechanisms within its areas of political jurisdiction. Unlike the case of national governments, the EU government does not serve as a monopoly broker of violence (Moe 1990). Fourth, the EU legislature (the European Parliament) enjoys a weaker linkage with voters than national parliaments.

Fifth, the linkage between the political bodies of the EU and the agents of the EU is much closer than in sovereign countries. For example, the European Commission works very closely with the Council of Ministers in initiating and developing policy. Until the Parliament's censure of the Commission in early 1999 the Commission effectively possessed more power than the European Parliament. Its relative strength reflected the Commission's evolution in the decades prior to the European Parliament's development into a central governing institution. Since the censure and subsequent resignation of the Commission, the Parliament has reduced the difference in strengths of the two institutions. Henceforth the Parliament and Commission may work together more closely. This relationship may even develop into an alliance with which the Council must reckon. Analysis of the individual and institutional actors of the EU within the political marketplace must incorporate the differences between this marketplace and national political marketplaces.

7.4 POLICY BROKERS

The executive and legislative institutions of government represent the brokers of policy at the most basic level. Within these bodies officials consider policy proposals and determine whether or not these proposals will become accepted policy. Directly, these bodies act upon legislative proposals from individual constituents or representatives of constituents. Indirectly these bodies may exert oversight of regulatory bodies that operate within the central government.

Individuals comprise the executive and legislative bodies. These individuals possess individual utility functions, which reflect those goods or services that provide them with positive utility and those goods or services that provide them with negative utility. Public Choice assumes that these individuals are rational utility-maximizers.

The utility functions of individual politicians affect their behavior within the political marketplace, Downs (1957) asserts that elected politicians endeavor to maximize their individual utility. Politicians' utility functions consist of such elements as income, power and prestige from their official position. In order to advance these interests, politicians engage in behavior that will increase the likelihood of re-election or reappointment. Subsequently the elements of politicians' utility functions expanded to include post-political career remuneration opportunities (Rowley et al. 1995, 94).

The re-election or reappointment constraint drives politicians to endeavor to satisfy a sufficient amount of constituents that offer votes, money and other resources in order to secure their future occupational goals. Concerns about post-political career remuneration opportunities also affect the political goods and services politicians offer. Politicians offer political goods and services to such constituents in exchange for votes, money and other valuable resources. Political goods include votes on legislation, the introduction of new policy proposals and access to policy-makers.

The policy positions of individual politicians stem from the preferences of their constituents, as well as the position of the party to which they belong. The relative importance of these two factors depends upon politicians' need for continued constituent support and the ability of parties to benefit and punish politicians within institutional proceedings. The principal–agent relationship characterizes the relationship between politicians and their constituents. Politicians receive constituent support in order to advocate and oppose policies in accordance with constituent preferences. Politicians lobby the case of their constituents in legislative debate and render their votes on behalf of their constituents. Continued constituent patronage and support of any politician depends upon constituents' ability to monitor politician behavior and punish shirking. Over time politicians develop reputations about their behavior. These reputations may serve as a valuable asset for incumbent politicians.

The relationship between a politician and the party to which she/he belongs possesses similar characteristics to the relationship between politicians and constituents. Wittman (1995, 21) describes the political party as the political market analogue to the franchise of the economic sector. Politicians join political parties in order to gain access to organizational and financial resources, as well as to utilize the party's name recognition with respect to its preferred stances on issues. Politicians incur certain obligations in exchange for the benefits they realize from affiliation with the party. For example, parties may demand that politicians support legislative or regulatory initiatives through roll-call votes or public statements. Politicians may also bear responsibilities within the party such as supporting fellow party members in their campaign efforts. Parties may monitor member behavior and reward or punish them for carrying out or shirking their responsibilities.

Political candidates compete with each other and incumbent politicians for office. Competition centers on these actors' positions on issues of interest to the demanders and suppliers of policy. The median voter theorem (Downs 1957) attempts to describe the positions that politicians or parties take on issues during the run-up to an election. Competing politicians seek to receive more votes than their opponents do in order to garner enough votes to win the election. For this reason, the median voter theorem posits that politicians or parties adopt policy positions that converge on the position of the median voter. The politician who comes closest to this position receives the votes of the median voter and those voters for whom this position represents the alternative closest to their preferred position. The median voter position garners more votes than any other single position within the relevant issue space.

The assumptions of the median voter theorem are subject to a number of limiting criticisms. Rowley (1984) highlights eight criticisms of the model which demonstrate its limited applications. First, the model posits the existence of only two competing parties. Second, policy issues lie along a single dimensional political spectrum. In the real world, political platforms consist of a myriad of issues and are multidimensional. Third, voters understand political candidates' or parties' policy positions. In fact, voters may have only limited or biased information about candidates' policy positions. Distortionary advertising campaigns may render voters unable to discern fundamental differences between candidates. Fourth, voters' preferences are single-peaked. Voters' preferences may or may not be single-peaked depending upon: (1) the issue; (2) their frame of mind; and (3) their expected relative position in society. Fifth, voters participate in elections. Empirical turnout rates debunk this assumption. Sixth, candidates or parties understand voters' preferences. Seventh, candidates or parties are able to locate themselves in issue space in accordance with voter preferences. Candidates compete with each other to locate their position in the center of policy space as necessary in order to adopt the median voter's position. Finally, voters possess an *ex post* enforcement capability to penalize candidates or parties that, once elected, shirk from their campaign commitments. Voter myopia sheds doubt on this assumption.

These criticisms demonstrate the limitations inherent in Downs' median voter theorem. His assumptions are rarely if ever satisfied in reality. However, the theorem does offer an intuitively appealing hypothesis regarding the positions taken by would-be politicians with respect to voter preferences. It advances the notion that the candidate or party that occupies the central position in policy space will rule for single-peaked voter preferences. It also emphasizes the strategic behavior undertaken by political candidates and parties jockeying for power.

7.4.1 Policy Brokers in the EU

The individual members of the Council of Ministers, the European Commission and the European Parliament constitute the primary brokers of policy within the European Union. These institutions, respectively, represent the executive and legislative bodies of the EU. These bodies enable policy proposals to enter consideration at the level of the EU and to become accepted policy through the various political procedures necessary for policy proposals to enter operation. These political procedures require the participation of all three primary governing bodies.

The Council and the Parliament are the only institutions comprised of officials elected by the population of the EU. For this reason, the members of these institutions are the only actors concerned with the re-election constraint. Members of the Council obtain their positions in accordance with national electoral and appointment procedures. Since 1979, Members of the European Parliament (MEPs) have obtained their positions through popular election by the citizens of the EU member countries.[3] Until 1979, national parliaments designated national representatives to the European Parliament from among their membership in accordance with nationally determined procedures.

The Council of Ministers is the general term for the three forms of ministerial arrangements in which national representatives convene. These arrangements represent separate but related institutions. The first Council of Ministers is known simply as the Council of Ministers or as the General

Council. This Council consists of the Foreign Ministers of the member countries. These ministers obtain their positions in accordance with national procedures involving the Head of Government or State and the party or parties that won the national election.

The second Council of Ministers is known as the Technical or Specialized Councils. These Councils consist of the government ministers from the member countries in the respective policy areas, such as Agriculture, Economy and Finance, and Environment.[4] The Council of Economic and Finance Ministers, referred to as ECOFIN, handles monetary and financial affairs. Similar to the case of the General Council members of the Specialized Councils obtain their positions through national procedures involving the Head of Government or State and his/her party(ies).

The third Council of Ministers is the European Council. This Council consists of the Heads of State or Government of each of the members and the President of the European Commission. Heads of State or Government reach office in accordance with national electoral procedures. These procedures typically involve electoral and party support. The European Council appoints the President of the Commission subject to European Parliament approval. The European Council is effectively the highest institution within the EU's governance structure. The duties of the European Council are to promote the development of the EU, provide direction to the specialized Council meetings, and facilitate the resolution of matters of dispute.

Of the three Councils, the European Council is the only one accountable to the electorate. Heads of State or Government are the only Council members elected by the populations of the EU member countries. These actors are responsible to both their domestic constituents and their party of affiliation. Other Council members possess accountability to the Head of State or Government and their party. For this reason, voters will hold Heads of State or Government responsible for decisions by the Council(s) of Ministers. The re-election constraint will dominate these actors' decisions. Heads of State or Government will hold other ministers responsible for their respective actions. Unsatisfactory decisions will meet with resignation requests, isolation and loss of party support. Future career opportunities for ministers depend upon their *ex officio* performance.

The number of representatives each country has in the European Parliament varies. At present, the Parliament consists of 626 elected members. Beginning with the 2004 term, this number will decline to 535 (Treaty of Nice, Annex 1, Article 2). This decline is in preparation for the accession of new members to the EU which will increase the number of MEPs to a maximum of 732 (TEC, Article 189, second paragraph). Table 7.1 depicts the number of seats per country. Members serve renewable five-year terms of office.

Table 7.1 Number of European Parliament seats by country

Country	No. of seats (till 2004)	No. of seats (from 2004)	No. of seats (after expansion to 27 members)
Germany	99	99	99
France	87	72	72
Italy	87	72	72
United Kingdom	87	72	72
Spain	64	50	50
Netherlands	31	25	25
Belgium	25	22	22
Greece	25	22	22
Portugal	25	22	22
Sweden	22	18	18
Austria	21	17	17
Denmark	16	13	13
Finland	16	13	13
Ireland	15	12	12
Luxembourg	6	6	6
Poland	–	–	50
Romania	–	–	33
Czech Republic	–	–	20
Hungary	–	–	20
Bulgaria	–	–	17
Slovakia	–	–	13
Lithuania	–	–	12
Latvia	–	–	8
Slovenia	–	–	7
Estonia	–	–	6
Cyprus	–	-	6
Malta	–	–	5
Total	626	535	732

MEPs attain office in accordance with national electoral procedures. No uniform electoral system exists within the European Parliament. Electoral systems differ along two dimensions. First, systems possess constituencies of different sizes. These constituencies correspond to entire countries or multiple, smaller districts within a single country. Second, systems employ different decision rules such as first-past-the-post and proportional representation. Table

7.2 depicts the electoral systems prior to German reunification and the accession of Austria, Finland and Sweden.

Table 7.2 National European Parliament electoral systems

Country	No. of MEPs	Electoral system	No. of constituencies
Belgium	24	Party list PR + pref. vote	3
Denmark	16	Party list PR + pref. vote	1
Germany	81	Party list PR	10 + 1[a]
Greece	24	Party list PR	1
Spain	60	Party list PR	1
France	81	Party list PR	1
Ireland	15	STV*–PR	4
Italy	81	Party list PR + pref. vote	5
Luxembourg	6	Party list w/vote splitting	1
Netherlands	25	Party list PR + pref. vote	1
Portugal	24	Party list PR	1
United Kingdom†	81	Single member plurality	78 + 1[b]
Total	518		

Notes:

[a] One seat for Berlin. Following German reunification, the number of seats in Germany has increased.

[b] Northern Ireland consists of a single constituency with three seats elected by STV–PR.

* STV = single transferable vote.

† Beginning with the European Elections in June 1999, the UK will use a system of proportional representation to select MEPs.

Source: Adapted from Bowler and Farrell (1993, 49); originally created by Nugent (1991, 143).

Of those countries using party list proportional representation (PR), some use national lists (Denmark, France, Greece, Luxembourg, the Netherlands, Portugal and Spain) and some regional lists (Belgium, Germany and Italy). The following four countries allow preferential voting for individual candidates: Belgium, Denmark, Italy and the Netherlands (Bowler and Farrell 1993, 50). Countries such as France and Germany also impose minimum threshold requirements of 5 percent for parties to obtain or maintain seats within the Parliament. The UK and Ireland employ multiple electoral districts which differ from those districts used for national elections.

The different electoral systems for membership in the European Parliament have several implications for the relationship between political candidates, politicians and voters. In particular, electoral systems affect the ability of voter-principals to monitor politician–agents and the ability of voter–principals to punish politician–agents for shirking. For example, party lists sever the direct link between prospective candidates and their potential constituents. This gap reduces the accountability of politician–agents to their voter–principals, Under party-list systems, voters have a lower incentive to inform themselves about individual candidates. Rather, they inform themselves of different party platforms.

The gap between prospective candidates and constituents under party-list systems also discourages candidates from courting support from among the dispersed voters of the electorate and rather to direct their efforts at currying favor with officials within the party. Under party lists, candidates may also prefer to solicit support from organized interests rather than individual voters given the expected net benefits of such actions. Bowler and Farrell (1993, 62), however, do not find significant evidence of the latter for the case of the EU. Nevertheless, they do find that politicians in candidate-based systems, as opposed to party-list systems, attend more closely to the concerns of individual voters (ibid.).

Electoral district size also affects the principal–agent relationship between political actors and voters. The costs of monitoring politician behavior may rise with district size. Similarly, the accountability of politicians may decline in larger districts. For these reasons, politicians in relatively large districts may prefer to neglect the concerns of local and regional voters in favor of attending to the concerns of organized interests. Similarly, politicians from relatively small districts attend more closely to constituent concerns. Attention given to organized groups may generate larger expected net gains for politicians and political candidates where these groups offer necessary material resources and large blocs of votes (Taagepera and Shughart 1989, 56; cited in Bowler and Farrell 1993, 53). Bowler and Farrell (1993, 56–7) confirm the hypothesis that MEPs from district-based electoral systems pay more attention to local concerns. They also find that marginal list members and non-party candidates pay closer attention to the interests of individual voters (ibid., 59).

The European Parliament is organized into transnational political groups. Eight EU-level party groups comprise the national representatives who hail from approximately 100 different parties in their respective member countries. Members typically vote along political group lines. By this means, the supranational institution attempts to reduce the pull of national loyalties. Within political groups, however, MEPs often group with their fellow country representatives (Faina Medin and Puy Fraga 1988, 152). Their position involves balancing between three different constituencies: first, national or local constituents; second, national political parties; and third, EU political groups (ibid., 153). Closer links with and stronger monitoring and enforcement mechanisms by national constituents will affect representatives' relative loyalties.

Voters have four means of revealing their preferences to their MEPs. First, they have the power of the ballot. Second, they may petition the European

Parliament about matters of concern. Third, they may appeal to the European Parliament's ombudsman (Article 138e. 1–4 TEU). Fourth, they may express their preferences to national parliamentarians who can then convey them to MEPs during joint parliamentary meetings.

The European Parliament possesses several important powers in the legislative process. Two of these powers lie within two of the EU's legislative procedures. The cooperation procedure permits the Parliament to revise legislative drafts after the Commission's initial proposal and the Council of Ministers' initial review of this proposal. However, the Treaty of Amsterdam essentially eliminated this procedure. The codecision procedure grants the Parliament equal power with respect to the Council of Ministers. The Parliament and Council appoint an equal number of representatives to a conciliation committee charged with the task of devising a policy proposal. If the Parliament is unsatisfied with the final proposal, it may veto it and the proposal is effectively dead in the water. Parliamentary approval is also necessary for issues subject to the assent procedure. Such issues include provisions surrounding the European Central Bank.

The Parliament plays a key role in the EU's budgetary process. First, the President of the Parliament is responsible for signing the EU's annual budget into law. Second, the Parliament's Committee on Budgetary Control monitors the Commission's administration of the annual budget. The duties of this committee include oversight to deter fraud and investigation of alleged fraudulent activities.

The Parliament also plays a decisive role in the appointment of the Commission. Every five years the Council of Ministers appoints new Commissioners and a new President to serve in the European Commission. These appointments do not take effect until Parliament grants its approval of the appointments. In addition, the Parliament has the right to censure the Commission and consequently to dissolve the incumbent Commission (Article 144 TEU).

The European Parliament recently tested the censure motion in response to charges of fraud, waste and nepotism within the Commission. On Thursday January 14, 1999, the motion failed to receive the requisite majority to dissolve the sitting Commission. Subsequently, the Parliament appointed a panel of five lawyers and former public auditors from Belgium, France, the Netherlands, Spain and Sweden to conduct an investigation into allegations of fraud, mismanagement and nepotism within the Commission. The panel's report found the Commission collectively responsible for corrupt behavior within its administration. The report singled out three Commissioners: President Jacques Santer of Luxembourg, Vice-President Manual Marin of Spain and Edith Cresson of France. Following the release of the report on March 15, 1999, the entire Commission resigned before the Parliament could vote to disband the body.

The resignation of the Commission following the Parliament's investigation sets a new precedent. Previous threatened, rejected or withdrawn attempts at censure took place in 1972, 1976, 1977 and 1989–90 (Jacobs and Corbett 1990, 203). These attempts resulted from differences of opinion between the two institutions and the desire of relatively small political groups within the Parliament to gain attention (ibid.). However, none of these attempts resulted in the censure or resignation of the Commission.

The resignation of the Commission has several implications. First, it highlights the increase in oversight power of the Parliament over the Commission. This greater institutional accountability may deter commissioners from engaging in and tolerating similar mismanagement in the future. Second, it may strengthen popular perceptions of democratic accountability within the supranational bodies of the EU. Third, it may lead to greater cooperation and possibly collusion between the Parliament and Commission as they seek to preserve and promote their opportunity sets as supranational institutions.

The European Parliament also possesses the power to investigate any EU institution or body following a petition by at least 25 percent of its membership. Article 138c (TEU) sets out that the European Parliament may appoint a temporary Committee of Inquiry to ascertain whether or not the institution or body under investigation violated EU law. Only where the case is the subject of an ongoing investigation may the European Parliament not initiate such an inquiry.

The European Commission represents an anomalous institution in the EU by virtue of its dual roles as policy broker, demander and supplier. Its role in the four legislative procedures assures it a position within the legislative backbone of the EU despite the potential for conflicts of interest due to its role as bureaucratic demander and supplier.[5] The Commission serves as a *de facto* gatekeeper for much of EU policy. The four EU legislative procedures rely on the Commission to initiate and prepare policy proposals for consideration by the Council of Ministers and the Parliament.

The Commission consists of 20 members including a President. The members of the Commission are appointees from the member countries whose nominations are subject to approval by the European Parliament (Article 158.2 TEU). The members of the European Council appoint the President of the Commission, subject to the Parliament's approval (Article 158.2 TEU). This appointment procedure highlights the principal–agent relationship between Commissioners and the Council and Parliament. In this relationship, the Council and Parliament enjoy relatively low costs of monitoring the actions of their appointees in the Commission. The Parliament also possesses a potentially powerful device for punishing shirking by the Commission: censure. Renewable terms may also serve to drive Commissioners, at least in part, to attend to the concerns of their principals. The link between the Commission and the EU electorate is tenuous at best depending upon the extent to which the Council and the Parliament extend the demands of their constituents to the Commission.

The Council, Commission and Parliament represent the brokers of policy within the context of the EU and the EMU. The members of the institutions exchange policies for votes and other valuable resources that contribute to the maximization of individual politicians' utility functions. The policies supplied represent the policies demanded by different consumers within the political marketplace.

7.5 DEMANDERS AND SUPPLIERS OF POLICY

The demanders and suppliers of policy within the political marketplace include voters, interest groups and government agencies. These actors demand and supply policies that protect or promote their respective interests. In exchange for preferred policies, these actors offer political brokers votes, campaign contributions, post-political career remuneration opportunities, political expertise and other valuable resources.

The demanders and suppliers of policy serve as the driving forces behind policy. Individual citizen-actors participate in government directly by voting and indirectly through financial contributions to political causes and membership in interest groups. Individual citizen-actors also participate directly through employment with government agencies.

7.5.1 Voters

Individual voters represent sources of two valuable political resources: votes and money. Voters may use these resources to attract the attention of politicians in order to advance their interests through the political process. After all, politicians understand the need for constituent support in order to maximize their personal utility functions. Votes are necessary to secure victory in any electoral process and money is essential to finance campaign expenditures.

The motivation behind individual voting behavior represents a puzzle for students of political economy. Rational individuals determine whether to vote in elections based on their expected net benefits from registering their preferences at the polls. This decision involves some calculation of the expected net effects of alternative policies and/or candidates. These expectations depend upon information voters possess and how they make use of it to form expectations.

The rational ignorance hypothesis suggests that voters rationally remain uninformed regarding candidates' policy platforms. Voters do not inform themselves because they understand that the cost of information acquisition exceeds the expected benefit from voting. The probability that their individual vote will be decisive in any election is extremely small, so any direct benefit from their vote is negligible, if even positive. For the member countries of the EU, the probability of any individual's vote affecting the outcome of a national election is small. For elections of MEPs, the probability is equally small so long as they are elected on a countrywide basis. In this case, the benefit to information acquisition may be negative. Only where the expected net benefits to voting are positive does information acquisition and going to the polls appear rational. Furthermore, if voters anticipate net benefits from voting it is rational for them to inform themselves about the issues, candidates and parties.

Wittman (1995, 9–17) raises a case against the rational ignorance theorem. He suggests that individuals are not ignorant of election issues and candidates' positions. Rather, individuals are informed. Individuals utilize low-cost sources of information to learn about candidates. Party affiliation, analogous to a brand name, informs voters of a candidate's position on pivotal issues, such as defense, abortion and race policy. Voters also acquire information from broadcast, print and electronic media, as well as through everyday conversations.

Language differences within the EU may increase the costs of information search, acquisition and dissemination. Presently official documents are available in the following 11 languages: Danish, Dutch, English, Finnish, French, German, Greek, Italian, Portuguese, Spanish and Swedish. Speakers of such regional languages as Catalan, Flemish, Gaelic, Romansch and Welsh may find themselves at an informational disadvantage.

Wittman (1995, 12–15) argues that limited and sometimes biased information does not lead voters to make irrational selections in the polling booths. He (ibid., 107) points out that: 'Asymmetric information and inability to monitor opportunism does not imply that principals on average underestimate the opportunism by their agents or overestimate the quality of services provided.' If constituents possess rational expectations, they will include new information into their perceptions of politician behavior and they will not make systematic errors in their predictions of politician behavior.

Another criticism of the rational ignorance theorem targets the assumption that individuals only acquire information on candidates' policy positions in order to inform their voting decision. Individuals may in fact derive other valuable uses from such information. For example, information that bears on possible real economic consequences of alternative electoral outcomes my assist individuals in long-term planning decisions. Individuals may also derive satisfaction from acquiring information and engaging in informed conversations with others.

Individual voters may rationally gather information if the election outcome has the potential to significantly affect their individual utility. Such voters may focus their information-gathering efforts on understanding the positions of the candidates on one or more issues that affect them strongly. For the example of trade protection, Rowley et al. (1995, 151) argue that: 'Voters who stand to gain or to lose significantly from trade protection will be rationally well informed about such matters. They will be immune to persuasive advertising on such issues by interest groups or by politicians.' For example, an industrial tycoon may be especially concerned with potentially costly environmental legislation proposed by one candidate. Senior citizens may also carefully scrutinize the positions of political candidates on Social Security and Medicare policy given the importance of these issues to their individual utilities.

Several motivations may explain voters going to the polls despite the low probability of casting the decisive vote. These are expressive, retrospective, prospective, pocketbook, sociotropic and instrumental motivations. First, expressive motivations attribute the act of voting to individuals' desires to satisfy the socialistic tendencies within their consciences. Brennan and Buchanan (1983) offer the following example of expressive voting. Individuals vote for candidates who advocate redistribution policies to aid the poor. Second, retrospective and prospective motivations attribute the act of voting to voters' desires to register their preferences on past or expected future candidate performance. Voting may serve to express voters' approval or displeasure with certain policies or actors. For example, voters may reward or punish candidates because of past policy choices. Such voting behavior is known as retrospective voting. Similarly, voters may select candidates based on expected future political outcomes. Such voting behavior is known as prospective or strategic voting. Third, individual economic concerns may drive voters to the polls. Pocketbook voting is when individuals vote out of concern for the expected effects of particular policies on their individual wealth. Fourth, national economic concerns may also drive voters to the polls. Sociotropic voting occurs when individuals turn out to register their preferences regarding candidates whose policies may differentially affect national economic interests (Van Winden 1988, 13). Fifth, voters may go to the polls for reasons unrelated to the issues on the election platforms. Instrumental voting consists of voter turnout attributable to a cause separate from the selection of competing candidates. For example, individuals vote out of a feeling of civic responsibility.

The decision to vote may result from an individual's calculation of the expected net benefits from going to the polls. The individual's voting calculus consists of several elements. First, it consists of the costs an individual may incur as a result of informing him/herself, taking time off work and traveling to the polls. These costs may occur with certainty or with a lower probability depending upon a host of factors. For example, a schoolteacher may not have to report for work on election days, in which case she/he may not face the cost of lost wages or vacation time from going to the polls. However, the opportunity cost of going to the polls in terms of time, the cost of transportation and any other activity in which she/he could have engaged remains. If inclement weather threatens, the expected cost of voting may be higher than otherwise. These costs may, however, be significantly lower if the individual serves as a polling station volunteer and prefers this activity to any other at that time. However, the lower costs faced by volunteers affects a relatively small number of voters who turn out.

Only if the expected net benefits from the election of one candidate or party are significantly greater than those benefits under any other candidate will voters go to the polls and register their preferences (Borooah 1988, 63). Otherwise, individuals may succumb to the temptation to free-ride on others' efforts. In the case where electoral outcomes may have strong adverse effects for individuals or groups of voters, their turnout may be relatively high. Such effects may concern individual wealth and redistribution policies.[6]

The individual's voting calculus also includes the net benefits an individual expects from voting. Such benefits may depend upon the individual's vote being the decisive vote in the election. The individual may expect one candidate to advocate policies more closely in line with his/her preferences than any other candidate. The election of such a candidate would increase the individual's utility more than the election of any other candidate. The probability of any person's vote being the decisive vote in an election is, however, miniscule in large democracies. For this reason, expectations of being the decisive vote do not explain voter turnout. Satisfaction from participating in the electoral process may, however, offer an alternative explanation of voter turnout. This factor depends upon the weight that individuals place on participation relative to any other use of their time in their opportunity set.

Downs (1957) presents a formal model of the calculus involved in the individual's decision of whether or not to vote. The following equation depicts Downs' model:

$$R = PB - C.$$

Where R = net present value of voting; P = probability that the individual's vote is decisive; B = present value of the difference in the individual's utility between the two candidates; C present value of cost of voting. Individuals will only vote if the net present value of R is positive. Only for unrealistically high values of P and/or B can this equation be positive. The probability that any individual's vote will be decisive is approximately

$$\frac{1}{\text{number of registered voters in the population}}.$$

For modern countries with populations in the millions and hundreds of millions this probability is negligible. As the number of voters increases, P falls. The expected net benefit from voting becomes negative and the act of voting appears irrational. Downs' model is unable to explain actual voter turnout rates. The puzzle of explaining voter turnout constitutes the paradox of voting.

Recognizing the inability of Downs' model to account for voter turnout rates in the USA, Riker and Ordeshook (1968) extended Downs' model to include an additional variable representing the satisfaction an individual derives from complying with the ethic of voting. The following equation depicts Downs' revised model:

$$R = PB - C + D.$$

D represents the additional variable, also known as civic duty. This model might explain voter turnout for high values of D. However, this variable does not lend itself to empirical testing.

The paradox of voter turnout may in part be explained through recourse to the logic inherent in the model. If the expected net benefits from voting to any individual were not positive, no one would rationally go to the polls. However, if no one went to the polls, any single individual or a small number of individuals could increase their expected net benefits by in fact voting. Under such conditions, the probability of their vote being decisive would be much higher and consequently their expected net benefits from voting, as well. The above models assume that the probability of any individual's vote being decisive is exogenously tiny. However, this probability is a function of overall voter turnout, which is endogenous to the model (Lohmann 1996,143).

Green and Shapiro (1996) criticize the Rational Choice approach for its inability to account for the paradox of voting. Downs' model's prediction of zero turnout is refuted empirically. Furthermore, Green and Shapiro oppose attempts by Rational Choice theorists to downplay the costs of voting in attempts to salvage the Downsian model. They also denounce the addition of the civic duty variable because it renders the model untestable.

Ferejohn and Fiorina (1974) and Palfrey and Rosenthal (1985) attempt to remedy the paradox of voting. Ferejohn and Fiorina (1974) utilize a minimax model to examine the individual's voting decision. For a given election between two candidates, the individual may choose between one of three courses of behavior. First, he may vote for the first candidate whom he prefers to the second candidate. Second, he may vote for the second candidate. Finally, the voter may abstain. The individual voter selects that course of behavior that minimizes his maximum regret. This model overcomes the problem of voting only if one's vote is likely to be decisive.

Palfrey and Rosenthal (1985) utilize a game theoretic model in which voters decide whether to vote or to abstain. If voters are perfectly informed, they turn out in large numbers. Such turnout yields an outcome equivalent to that which would be reached by a random toss of a coin. All voters would be better off if everyone abstained from voting and allowed a coin toss to decide the election outcome. However, such abstention could not be enforced.

Palfrey and Rosenthal (ibid.) also consider their model under the assumption of imperfectly informed voters. Voters face three sources of uncertainty. First, they do not know the policies that candidates would actually pursue if elected. Second, they do not know whether other voters will vote or abstain. Third, they do not know the voting costs faced by other voters and the preferences of these other individuals. Voters determine their course of action for given expected actions by others representing a Nash equilibrium outcome. Voter turnout can only be explained by recourse to noninstrumental motivations (Lohmann 1996,146,148).

7.5.2 Interest Groups

Interest groups are organizations of individuals with similar concerns along one or more issue dimension. Interest groups may consist of individuals with similar occupations, hobbies, religious denominations, race, age or physical afflictions. These and other similarities serve as the basis for collective action on the part of members. Interest groups attempt to promote the unique concerns of their members.

Interest groups endeavor to advance the interests of members through various activities. Such activities include information-gathering and distribution projects, social activities, fund-raising for charitable causes or research and lobbying politicians on issues of concern. Groups typically serve a narrow subset of the population.

Interest groups offer politicians several valuable resources in exchange for political support. First, individual members may vote on behalf of sympathetic political candidates or incumbents. Second, individual members and interest groups may offer campaign contributions to help finance a politician's bid for election or re-election. Third, interest groups may provide low-cost advertising. Fourth, interest groups may provide policy expertise.

Interest groups are vulnerable to the potential problems of any collective activity. The single greatest challenge is overcoming the free-rider problem. This problem affects collective action at the stage of group formation, as well as during group operation over time. The free-rider problem occurs when one enjoys the benefits of the group's action without contributing to the costs. This problem is most likely to occur when the group includes a large number of members and when the products of group efforts exhibit the public good characteristic of non-exclusivity. For a large membership, the costs of monitoring contribution and punishing shirking may be very high. Under such circumstances, individuals may be able to enjoy the group's products without paying for them.[7] In order to overcome the free-rider problem, interest groups must be able to exclude non-contributors.[8] Where monitoring is less than perfect a strict and credible punishment threat may prevent individual shirking behavior. Similarly, repeated interactions may ensure individual cooperation (Chong 1996, 40).

If the group excludes non-contributors, the group must monitor member contributions and punish individuals who shirk. Monitoring ensures that the group can observe individual contributions. Non-contributors may be excluded from future access to the collective good or otherwise penalized.

To circumvent the free-rider problem small homogeneous groups that offer concentrated benefits may form. Small groups reduce the costs of monitoring individual behavior and enforcing cooperation. Small groups also raise the possibility of peer pressure as a means of enforcing individual contribution. Chong (1996,42) notes that: 'Monitoring is feasible in these smaller groups, and cooperation or defection can be rewarded or punished in the context of everyday interaction with friends and associates.' Concentrated benefits reduce the public good aspects of group products and may enable members to exclude benefits to non-contributors.

The existence of many interest groups demonstrates the ability of some organizations to overcome the free-rider problem. In spite of the risk of free-riders, imperfect information regarding individual contribution and limited enforcement mechanisms groups form and undertake the provision of various collective goods. The explanation for this occurrence lies in the positive expected net benefits to group organizers.

Olson (1965) presents a Rational Choice model of interest group formation. He suggests that viable interest groups consist of a relatively small membership possessed of similar interests. Olson overcomes the inherent irrationality of collective action by attributing group formation to individual cost–benefit analyses that yield members positive expected net benefits (Chong 1996, 40). Individuals enjoy selective benefits from belonging to the group. These benefits exhibit the basic characteristics of a public good: they are nonrival and nonexclusive. Olson suggests that small, homogeneous groups enjoying selective benefits enable groups to overcome the problems of collective action. In the absence of such benefits only coercion could prevent members from free-riding. Coercion may represent the only means to prevent shirking in relatively large groups. Political lobbying activity ensues as a by-product of the existing organizational framework.

Stigler (1974) criticizes Olson's model because if demand exists for the selective benefits, the private market might provide them at lower cost.

However, he attempts to reconcile this critique with Olson's model. First, he suggests that no free-rider problem exists. Rather, a cheap-rider problem might exist given that no good is available without cost. Second, individuals may form or join a collective entity in order to ensure that the body comes into existence in order to provide the desired goods or benefits. Otherwise, the risk exists that no such entity would develop and the individual's expected future gain is lower. Similarly, if an individual does not participate in the formation and operation of the collective group, it risks potentially higher opportunity costs in the event that the good(s) or benefit(s) is provided at an insufficiently small scale.

Interest group activities need not only include applying pressure to individuals within government to affect policy decisions. However, these organizations provide a relatively efficient means of so doing given the sunk costs already incurred as a result of the group's formation. Interest groups also possess an organizational network that may be utilized relatively easily to mobilize members on political issues. Political activity by interest groups includes information gathering on relevant issues, public promotion of preferred policies, lobbying sympathetic incumbents and political candidates, fundraising to contribute to sympathetic politicians and campaigning against antithetical politicians (Mitchell and Munger 1991, 425).

Narrow interest groups have one major advantage over large groups and unorganized individuals in the attainment of benefits through the political establishment. They are able to reap benefits disproportionate to the costs of provision of these benefits. Interest groups secure political concessions for which the cost is spread over a larger population. No single member of this population bears more than a small portion of the cost of these concessions and therefore does not undertake action against it. In many cases, the large population is rationally unaware of the price they pay for such concessions. The cost of information acquisition inhibits them from informing themselves. Similarly, the cost of undertaking action against such concessions is prohibitive for the individual. For these reasons, the small in number are able to exploit the great (the paradox of interest group power).

Interest groups may interact with political actors in order to undertake mutually beneficial exchanges. Interest groups offer politicians votes, money, advertising, post-political career remuneration opportunities and political expertise in exchange for access, votes and favorable policies. The latter might include the introduction of desired policy proposals, the protection of existing legislation that generates monopoly power, the protection of other policies favorable to the relevant interest groups, and the prevention of potentially harmful governmental investigations. Politicians respond to the offers of interest groups in order to maximize their individual utilities, which may include re-election constraints and other personal goals. Their responses depend upon their own internal calculations of their expected gains from advancing the interests of one interest group versus the cost of such behavior in terms of lost support from other interest groups and voting constituents.[9]

Interest groups attempt to extract economic profits from the government through rent-seeking activities. Rent-seeking occurs when individuals, singly or in groups, expend resources to obtain gains through the political process in excess of the opportunity cost of owning a resource. Lobbying of political decision-makers by interest groups to receive such returns constitutes rent-seeking (Tollison 1982). Groups undertake rent-seeking activities in order to obtain favorable policy outcomes through the political process. Rent appropriation exemplifies a successful bargain between one or a group of politicians and one or a group of private interests. In exchange for desired outcomes, interest groups offer politicians future votes, campaign contributions and access to other valuable resources. A political market effectively develops.[10] Rent-seeking theory suggests that actors may spend up to the full present discounted value of expected future benefits in pursuing such gains.[11]

Special interest groups engage in rent-seeking activities to gain benefits through the political process for which they do not bear the full cost (Gwartney and Wagner 1988, 22). Narrow interests invest in information acquisition on matters that affect them. They then utilize this knowledge to affect political outcomes by lobbying politicians in order to earn rents. Politicians attend to interest group lobbying in exchange for votes, campaign contributions and organizational support to aid in future electoral races (Holcombe 1993, 97).

Becker (1983) presents a model of interest group competition in which two groups of actors compete with each other for government transfers in a zero sum game. The first group pays taxes that finance the subsidy received by the second group. The subsidy received by the second group is smaller than the amount of taxes paid by the first group due to deadweight costs associated with the collection of taxes.

The first and second groups compete with each other for political influence. Both groups endeavor to minimize the deadweight costs associated with tax collection and subsidy provision. The group that produces political pressure relatively more efficiently increases its subsidy or decreases its tax. Group size affects group efficiency in two potentially offsetting ways. Smaller groups are better able to control free-riding. However, larger groups are more likely to enjoy the benefits of economies of scale in the provision of political pressure.

Becker suggests that his model is applicable to any situation characterized by competing interest groups. In addition to the tax and subsidy example, he suggests expenditures on defense and environmental policy as relevant applications. His analysis may also extend to issues of monetary policy. For example, net creditors may compete with net debtors to influence monetary policy. While the former prefer less inflationary policy in order to maintain the real value of their wealth, the latter prefer inflationary policies in order to increase the value of their wealth by reducing the real amount of their outstanding liabilities.

Becker's model is subject to several criticisms. First, the model depends upon a perfectly competitive market. Second, the model assumes taxpayers and subsidy recipients face zero information costs. Third, the model assumes zero transaction costs. Fourth, Becker's model ignores the role played by voters. He justifies this decision with his opinion that: 'Voter preferences are frequently not a crucial independent force in political behavior' (1983, 396). Finally, the model does not provide for any policy broker. Becker adopts the Chicago School approach that advances the notion that institutions do not matter.

Green and Shapiro raise several criticisms about Rational Choice theorists' attempts to formulate models of collective action. They note that these models lack the following lines of reasoning: (1) doing one's part; (2) every little bit counts; and (3) cheaters do not win. Any of these examples might assist attempts to explain observed collective action.

The effectiveness of interest groups in advancing their interests through the political process depends on the preferences and actions of their competitors. In addition to competition between interest groups, voters and government agencies compete with interest groups to influence political outcomes. All three types of actor possess resources of value to political decision-makers that they may use in order to advance their preferences through the political process.

Becker (1983, 396) discounts the notion of competition for policy between voters and interest groups. He suggests that interest groups affect voter preferences through various sources of information. By this means interest groups are able to sway voters in favor of their preferred policies. Interest groups take advantage of rational ignorance on the part of voters. Such preference manipulation may generate additional political power for successful interest groups.

Mitchell and Munger (1991) advance the opposite stance from Becker. They assert that voters exert greater influence over politicians under the following circumstances. First, relatively better informed voters wield more power in the political marketplace than less informed interest groups (ibid., 431).[12] Second, institutional conventions such as legislative committees provide a clear and direct link between elected committee members and voters. Politicians gravitate to those committees that address issues of particular concern to their constituents. Committee members attend to the concerns of voters from their constituencies before they attend to those of special interest groups. Clearly, however, this assertion depends upon the value of resources voters have to offer politicians relative to special interest groups and politicians' net expected benefits from alternative courses of action.

7.5.3 Bureaucracies and Agencies

Bureaucracies are governmental institutions that bear responsibility for regulation or policy in one or more issue areas. Executive or legislative institutions charge bureaucracies with the execution of legislation and implementation of regulations in various policy areas. Bureaucrats rely upon the executive and/or legislative institutions for all or most of their financial needs.

Criticisms of bureaucratic organizations focus on three potential problems inherent with a hierarchic agency dependent upon its principal for financial resources (Rowley et al. 1995, 133). First, bureaucrats will utilize the agency and its resources to advance their own interests. Such actions may include attempts to increase the size and responsibilities of the bureaucracy in order to increase bureaucratic power and attempts to increase the size of the discretionary budget of the bureau. Second, the hierarchic structure may encourage and reward unnecessarily wasteful behavior by individuals within the agency. The amount of waste and inefficiency inherent within the organization will depend upon the incentive structure that members face. Third, bureaucrats may hide or distort valuable information to suit their purposes and attempt to usurp control from their institutional overseers in order to gain a freer rein over their activities.

Bureaucrats, like individual actors, possess their own utility functions. The elements of their utility functions include monetary income, perquisites, patronage and power (Rowley et al. 1995, 152). These elements constitute economic goods for bureaucrats who utilize their official positions to promote their individual interests. A distinction arises between those bureaucrats most interested in financial security as an end and those most interested in power and extracurricular benefits (ibid., 136). The former bureaucrats clearly seek to maximize the funds they receive from their executive and/or legislative superiors. The latter bureaucrats may prefer to expand the size and scope of the agency in order to increase its relative power. Both kinds of actor endeavor to increase the discretionary budget at their disposal in order to direct expenditures to their preferred bundle of goods.

Government agencies serve two constituencies. First, they serve their executive and/or legislative overseers. Second, they serve individuals, firms and interest groups that participate in or are affected by the policies for which the agency is responsible.

A principal–agent relationship characterizes the association between bureaucracies and other agencies, and their executive or legislative superiors. The executive or legislative institutions occupy the position of principal and the bureaucracy the position of agent. Where the government consists of an executive and legislative branch, the bureaucracy possesses two principals. The existence of two principals with potentially different interests may facilitate strategic behavior by the bureaucratic agency. The more distinct the preferences of these bodies, the more latitude the bureaucracy may enjoy as it pits one principal against the other. The bureaucracy may also pit various coalitions within the legislature against each other in order to promote its interests (Wittman 1995, 112).[13]

The principal–agent relationship suffers from two potential problems. These problems are monitoring of the agent's behavior by the principal(s) and preventing agent shirking through a credible punishment or enforcement mechanism. If the principal and the agent do not share the same interests, shirking by the agent may become a serious problem. The agent may pursue his/her interests instead of those of the principal. The former problem results from the principal's inability to fully observe the agent's behavior. Furthermore, the agent may have superior information about his area of expertise and costs of production than the principal. Thus, a problem of asymmetric information arises. Even were the principal able to fully monitor the agent, this would represent a costly undertaking that might eliminate any net gains expected to spring from the relationship.

Niskanen (1971) presents two models of strategic bureaucratic behavior. Both models rely upon the possession of superior information by members of the bureaus regarding their costs of production. The first model posits a demand-constrained bureau. Under this constraint, the bureau provides the requisite level of output. Total output exceeds the optimal quantity that could be produced under efficient conditions and results in wasteful expenditures. The second model presents a model of a budget-constrained bureau. Under this constraint the bureau seeks to minimize the costs of production in order to retain the balance for purchases it desires. Not surprisingly bureaus prefer to face demand constraints rather than budget constraints. The former provides them with greater budgetary discretion.

Niskanen's models face several criticisms. First, Wittman (1995, 106) points out that budget maximizing is unlikely to be of the magnitude suggested by critics of bureaus except at the level of top-ranking officials. Second, to the extent that bureaus' balance sheets are subject to principal scrutiny, wasteful expenditures may lead to tighter budgets over time. For example, public outcry against US federal government expenditures on thousand-dollar toilet seats led to various programs aimed to curtail such wasteful spending. Third, the behavior of any bureaucracy depends upon the specific reward-cost structure it faces. This structure may change over time. Thus, Niskanen's models may apply to different bureaucracies more than others at any given time. Finally, bureaucrats may prefer to maximize their discretionary budget rather than their total budget.

Banks (1989) and Banks and Weingast (1992) formulate a model that addresses the final criticism. They offer a model of bureaucratic behavior in which the bureau attempts to maximize the difference between revenues and expenditures. In this way, the bureau endeavors to maximize its discretionary income or its rents. By maximizing discretionary income, members of the bureaucracy are able to allocate additional revenues in accordance with their own preferences. Executive and legislative branch members understand the tendency for bureaucracies to inflate their budgetary needs. For this reason, they often, although not always, allot a budget below the amount requested by the agency. However, legislative oversight committees may consist of members from constituencies with relatively high demand for the output of bureaus (Niskanen 1971). In such cases, oversight committees might push for larger budgets than bureaucracies themselves in order to benefit their constituents.

In order to prevent agency shirking, principals depend upon one or more credible enforcement mechanism(s). The executive and/or legislative branch(es) may implement monitoring arrangements and mechanisms by which they can directly penalize shirking behavior by the bureaucracy. Monitoring arrangements may include oversight committees and external auditors. Enforcement mechanisms depend upon the ability of these institutions to affect those elements valued by members of the bureaucracy. Control over budgetary appropriations, salaries, hiring and appointment procedures and other benefits represent potential means of penalizing bureaucratic shirking. In addition the executive and/or legislative branch(es) may wield the threat of dissolution of the agency perhaps in favor of a private alternative, the threat of a reduction in agency jurisdiction, merger with another agency, or reduction of policy discretion enjoyed by the agency. Interest groups may also monitor bureaucratic behavior. They may threaten to inform the relevant executive or legislative authority of inappropriate bureau activities.

Two alternative approaches describe the relative power of bureaus versus the legislature and vice versa. The first approach consists of the theory of bureau dominance (Niskanen 1971). This theory asserts that legislative overseers' concern with re-election distracts them from effectively monitoring governmental bureaus. Legislators perceive a weak link between their efforts at monitoring and constituent support. Bureau monitoring becomes a public good to legislators and they are unwilling to expend valuable resources for that purpose. Limited oversight enables bureaus to pursue their goals on a looser rein than otherwise. However, in the event that bureau shirking attracts the attention of a legislator's constituents, she/he will pay much more close attention to the actions of the bureau.

The second approach consists of the theory of congressional (legislative) dominance (Weingast and Moran 1983). This theory asserts that the legislature possesses several means of controlling bureaucratic behavior. These means reduce the need for close oversight. First, each bureau competes with others for budgetary allocations. Second, the executive and/or legislature may control high-level appointments within the bureaus. Finally, the executive and/or legislature may reduce the size of or eliminate perceived inefficient and/or unnecessary bureaus. Both theories relate to the US example in particular, but may be extended to other cases for alternative institutional circumstances.

A legislative committee system represents one example of institutional oversight mechanism. Within a committee system, legislators serve on one or more policy committees. Each committee possesses sole responsibility for one or more policy areas. Members self-select to those committees that offer them the greatest expected net returns (Shepsle 1975). Committee assignments often reflect the interests of legislators' constituents. Legislators utilize committee responsibilities to protect and promote constituent interests in order to maintain and increase support. Where constituent interests involve bureaucratic policies, bureaus may find themselves subject to relatively close committee monitoring.

Committees represent important power brokers within the US Congress. These bodies possess near monopoly power over their respective policy jurisdictions. For this reason, they serve as repositories of policy expertise and gatekeepers of legislative proposals in their policy areas. The committee system endures in part because of deference between members of different committees.

Government bureaus may also collude with legislators and special interest groups to promote policies in order to generate mutual benefits. Such relationships are known as iron triangles. These relationships are likely to spring up where special interests have captured committees within the legislature and voters do not observe the actions of such affiliations adversely affecting their interests. If voters understand the contribution of elected representatives to iron triangles, they may turn their resources against incumbent politicians.

The executive branch may also possess some means of monitoring and controlling bureaus. First, the executive may possess power of appointment. In this case, political appointees may act in the interests of their executive benefactor(s) out of loyalty or out of concern with increasing the likelihood of subsequent appointments. Second, the executive may be able to unsettle the operations of iron triangles. Weingast (1981) suggests that a strong executive representing public sentiment may be able to exert powerful pressures on the players in the triangle in order to end publicly unfavorable policies or activities.

7.5.4 Policy Demanders and Suppliers in the EU

The individual voters, interest groups, bureaucracies and corporate entities of the EU constitute the primary demanders and suppliers of policy within the EU. Voters include individuals from each of the respective 15 EU member countries. Interest groups include organizations from the member countries, respectively, as well as transnational organizations that comprise members from across the Union. The European Commission represents the largest administrative bureaucracy within the EU. The European Central Bank represents the EU's bureaucracy responsible for monetary policy.

Vaubel (1994b) offers the following insights into voter behavior in the EU. These insights bear on the case of a principal–agent relationship between voters and elected EU officials. First, he notes that voters are typically less aware of EU policy than national policies (228). He offers the following striking example: 'Only 24 percent know that, ultimately, the Council of Ministers decides about EC legislation (Eurobarometer 37, 1992 I).' The relatively higher cost of information acquisition may explain voters' apparent rational ignorance. Voters incur costs to learn about domestic political events that affect them more directly and quickly than EU policy proceedings. To further obtain information on EU policy would place additional demands on their time and possibly require resorting to additional sources of information that follow EU events. Perhaps it is not surprising that voters in higher-income member countries are better informed than their counterparts in lower-income member countries (Vaubel 1994b, 228). Policy information is also of a higher quality in member countries with: (1) higher income; (2) geographic proximity to Brussels; and (3) national referenda (ibid.).

Voters face different decision calculations in the context of the EU. The calculus of voting depends upon the country in which the voter goes to the polls. The election of Heads of State or Government determines the calculus concerning the Council of Ministers. The election of representatives to the European Parliament depends upon the respective country. This calculus differs from the calculus voters face in national elections. For example, in countries that employ national electoral districts, the probability of affecting a vote depends upon voter turnout, as well as the electoral system, such as first-past-the-post, single transferable vote or proportional representation, as well as any minimum thresholds for election. These factors complicate the decision calculus that voters face and thereby obfuscate the probability of any individual's vote being decisive. Furthermore, policy and politician monitoring becomes more expensive at the supranational level than at the national level.

Voter turnout rates in the EU have declined across all but three of the first 12 member countries since the introduction of direct elections to the European Parliament in 1979. Table 7.3 presents voter turnout rates for the 1979, 1984 and 1989 Parliamentary elections.

These results demonstrate the decline in overall voter turnout in European Parliament elections. They also demonstrate the variability in turnout rates across the EU. The high turnout rates in Belgium and Luxembourg stem at least in part from compulsory voting laws.

Low turnout rates may stem from the low probability of any vote in European Parliamentary elections determining policy. Each individual votes for either one party or one candidate to represent him/her in the European Parliament that consists of over 600 members. No single Parliament member has much power over policy because of the body's large membership and its limited but growing

Table 7.3 European Parliament voter turnout

Country	Year	Voter turnout (%)
Belgium	1989	90.7
	1984	92.2
	1979	91.4
Denmark	1989	46.2
	1984	52.4
	1979	47.8
France	1989	48.7
	1984	56.7
	1979	60.7
Germany	1989	62.3
	1984	56.8
	1979	65.7
Greece	1989	79.9
	1984	77.2
	1981	78.6
Ireland	1989	68.3
	1984	47.6
	1979	63.6
Italy	1989	81.0
	1984	83.4
	1979	84.9
Luxembourg	1989	87.4
	1984	88.8
	1979	88.9
Netherlands	1989	47.2
	1984	50.6
	1979	58.1
Portugal	1989	51.2
	1987	72.4
Spain	1989	54.6
	1987	68.9
United Kingdom	1989	36.2
	1984	32.6
	1979	32.3
Total	1989	57.2
	1984	59.0
	1979	62.5

Source: Adapted from Table 2 in Jacobs and Corbett (1990, 24) from European Parliament Summary of Results.

role in EU policy-making. Party-list systems and national districts prevent an individual's vote from potentially playing a determining role in the election of a candidate.

Low turnout rates may also stem from the second-order nature of party elections at the European level (Westlake 1994, 98). European Parliament elections do not involve contests between candidates for individual positions of leadership such as Heads of State or Government. European elections also do not revolve around issues with the same potential impact as those involved in local, regional and national elections. Rather than exert their energies in European Parliament elections, constituents may prefer to turn out for elections of politicians that affect them more directly and who they can more easily observe and reward/punish.

The re-election constraint may be of limited relevance to members of European Parliament given their relatively high rate of turnover. Jacobs and Corbett (1990, 43) estimate the average stay in office for MEPs at three and a half years. This calculation takes into account the accession of Greece, Spain and Portugal during ongoing five-year terms. They also report that in 1989 nearly one-half of new members elected were not incumbents. However, MEPs from the UK and Germany serve relatively longer terms than those MEPs from other countries. In part, these turnover rates result from the electoral systems employed. They may also be evidence of MEPs utilizing their positions as stepping-stones to other official positions, particularly within national legislatures (Westlake 1994, 105).

In selecting Heads of State or Government, EU voters consider candidates' positions on many policy issues. EU policy may constitute a secondary concern to domestic issues such as healthcare, unemployment and industrial policy. The latter issues affect voters more directly than many areas of EU policy such as agriculture. Where EU policy affects voters equally directly, information may be less clear and easily understood as political brokers attempt to obfuscate transfers from large groups of uninformed actors to narrow groups to maximize their expected net political gains.

Incumbent politicians understand voters' rational ignorance and are aware of low turnout rates. For these reasons, the re-election constraint will not likely serve to prevent shirking by politicians. They may be relatively free to pursue personal or party goals, as well as attend to the desires of concentrated interest groups that offer specific rewards. Similarly, if elected politicians can identify and target the interests of the small number of voters that actually do go to the polls, they can effectively protect their positions.

Interest groups represent the second major category of policy demanders and suppliers. These groups exist at the national and transnational levels within the EU. The former consists of various organizations devoted to local, regional, national, industrial, occupational and social issues within national boundaries. The latter include members with similar interests from around the EU. Transnational groups may benefit from reduced transaction costs by lobbying for EU dominion over issues in order to lower the cost of lobbying multiple national governments (Vaubel 1994b, 238). Andersen and Eliassen (1991) note that since 1987 transnational groups have increasingly carried out lobbying at the EU level.

The EU represents a fertile playing field for special interest groups. Vaubel (1994b, 238) reports that: 'At least 72 percent of the EC budget (Vaubel 1994a) and at least 78 percent of EC legislation (Peirce 1991a, Table 3) are devoted to interest groups.' Furthermore, groups can tap into a wealth of resources from existing national networks to affect future EU policy and regulations. They benefit from the sunk costs incurred in the past by interest group founders.

Interest groups primarily target the European Commission with their lobbying efforts. The Commission attracts special interest attention because of its central role in policy initiation. The Commission is responsible for providing proposals for all new policies to the Council of Ministers. Such proposals may result from Council requests or from Commission initiatives alone. The European Commission is particularly prone to interest group lobbying for policy proposals in order to increase EU regulation in order to justify expansion in its size and budget. Interest groups can collude with the Commission to promote their respective interests at the expense of the unorganized masses of EU voters. Interest groups may target Commissioners directly or more likely members of their cabinet staffs (Andersen and Eliassen 1991, 180).

The Council of Ministers represents the second target of interest group lobbying efforts. Interest groups lobby national leaders at home, as well as through their permanent representatives at the EU, the Council of Permanent Representatives (COREPER) of the Council of Ministers. Heads of State or Government may request policy proposals from the Commission in response to interest group pressures and reach favorable decisions on such matters. Heads of State or Government may be more likely to promote special interest legislation at the EU level than at national levels given the expected lower costs of such acts due to higher levels of voter ignorance about EU policy proceedings. At the level of the EU, Heads of State or Government may more easily publicly downplay the role of legislation that takes from the many to give to the few.

Interest groups have long paid the least attention to the European Parliament. Until 1979, it consisted of members of national parliaments. National interest groups could lobby MEPs more easily through national avenues. Since 1979, however, members attain office through direct election and therefore receive attention separately from members of national parliaments. However, interest groups may find their net rewards greater from focusing on Heads of State or Government in the Council of Ministers who play a greater role in EU policy than individual MEPs (Andersen and Eliassen 1991, 175). The attention received by members of the European Parliament has, however, increased with the growth of its role in policy determination since 1987. Relative ignorance by the electorate also favors special interest lobbying of the EU legislature.

The European Commission constitutes the largest bureaucratic agency in the EU with over 15,000 employees. The European Commission currently consists of 20 Commissioners appointed from among the EU member countries for renewable five-year terms of office (Art. 158.1 TEU).[14] Commissioners are typically former high-ranking national officials. Commissioners have included former members of national parliaments, former MEPs and former national ministers. Each country has at least one representative in the Commission (Article 157.1 TEU). The following countries have two representatives: France, Germany, Italy, Spain and the UK. Article 157.1 (TEU) states that Commissioners must act independently of national and other political institutions. Similarly, it instructs member countries to refrain from efforts to influence Commissioners. Adherence to this article may depend upon expected individual and national net benefits, given the difficulty of observing and proving partial behavior. Each Commissioner heads up one or more of the 26 policy jurisdictions of the Commission, known as Directorates-General.

The Commission's behavior accords with the general predictions of the theory of bureaus. The bureau has undertaken expansion along several dimensions. First, Vaubel (1994a, Table 3 in Vaubel 1994b, 235) notes that it has increased the size of its staff by nearly ten times since 1960. Second, the bureau offers highly attractive compensation packages to those fortunate enough to obtain one of the coveted positions with the institution. Vaubel (1994b, 235) again states that: 'The clearest sign of a control problem is the fact that net salaries in the CEC are so much higher than in the national administrations (Section 2.2) and that job applications with the European Commission exceed vacancies by a factor of 47' (Staufenbiehl 1992, 384). Third, the bureau has expanded the scope of its regulatory jurisdiction to new and additional policy areas.

Additional regulation benefits the Commission in at least two ways. First, it offers justification for increases in the size of its budget and its staff. Second, it creates an additional source of special interest patronage. Special interest groups will spend up to the expected net present value of regulation to gain favorable policies. Commissioners gravitate to those policy areas that are especially relevant to their countries of origin (Kuhn 1993 in Vaubel 1994b, 236). By this means, they can endeavor to promote the interests of domestic groups. Such behavior may stem from Commissioners' desires to gain the support of domestic constituencies for future political campaigns or to expand their post-Commission career remuneration opportunity set.

The Commission has also been supportive of policies to expand the scale and scope of EU policies. Such expansion serves the interests of the Commission by ensuring the continued existence of the EU and increasing the demand for their services as an administrative agent. Faina Medin and Puy Fraga (1988, 151) point out that: 'The CEC and its bureaucrats, European Commissioners or lower level civil servants, have a very strong direct interest in the success of the whole integration process.' For example, as Commission President Jacques Delors spearheaded the committee responsible for initiating the transition to EMU. The EMU represents a long-term project that even if unsuccessful will ensure the continued existence of the Commission for the medium term.

The European Commission is ultimately responsible for its actions to the European Parliament. The latter has three means of controlling the Commission's behavior. First, it must approve the candidates to the positions of Commission President and the Commissioners. Second, the Budgetary Control Committee of the European Parliament monitors the budgetary expenditures of the Commission, which acts as agent responsible for expenditures of the EU government. Third, the European Parliament possesses the right of censure of the Commission. Following a two-thirds majority in favor of a censure motion, the entire Commission must resign. The European Parliament recently passed a censure motion of the European Commission.

The Commission is also accountable to the Council of Ministers. The latter wields the power of the purse over the officials and staff of the Commission. Each year the Commission must submit a proposal for the salaries of its employees to the Council of Ministers. The Commission computes these salaries by a complex formula known as *la méthode* (Cini 1996,122).

The European Central Bank (ECB) acts as the monetary agent of the EU. The ECB is the monetary authority for the European Monetary Union (EMU). As such, the ECB is responsible for deciding upon monetary policy within the EMU.

The Governing Council directs the ECB. The Governing Council consists of the members of the Executive Board of the ECB and the governors of the central banks of the EMU participant countries. As discussed in Chapter 5, the Council of Members nominates candidates for the Executive Board; subsequently, the European Parliament and the Governing Council must approve these nominations.

Executive Board members act primarily as agents of the Heads of State or Government of EMU participant countries. National central bank governors are agents of their respective national governments. For this reason, the actions of the Governing Council and ultimately EMU monetary policy may reflect the preferences of the Heads of Government or State of EMU participants. If the re-election constraint is binding, these individuals will advocate monetary policies favored by their voting and supporting constituencies.

The vulnerability of the Governing Council to political pressure flies in the face of provisions for independence of the European System of Central Banks.

Any of a number of economic circumstances might drive Heads of State or Government to pressure Governing Council members to expand monetary policy. Such circumstances include pressure from voters or interest groups due to adverse economic circumstances. Much less likely is the occurrence of pressures for monetary tightening. In fact, the TEU provides the EU governing institutions with the task of determining the direction of economic policy within the EU. This task could be driven by the desires of political actors to promote their own interests in response to various sources of pressure.

Future efforts at political manipulation of the ECB, in spite of various provisions for monetary authority independence, should come as no surprise to observers of the progress towards EMU. The following examples from Chapter 4 demonstrate the propensity of EU politicians to treat monetary policy and appointments within the ECB as issues up for negotiation and interference. First, the European Commission loosely interpreted the Maastricht convergence criteria in selecting countries to participate in the first round of EMU. Second, participants in the ERM decided to widen the permitted fluctuation bands in order to accommodate currency movements driven by market pressures. Third, the appointment of the first ECB president represented a compromise between France and Germany. This compromise included an agreement for the first president, Wim Duisenberg, to step down halfway into his eight-year term in order to allow a Frenchman to replace him.

7.6 THE POLITICAL MARKETPLACE FOR MONETARY POLICY IN EMU

Monetary policy represents an important policy tool, as well as an important political commodity. Governments may attempt to influence the monetary authority in order to advance the interests of one or more important constituencies. Monetary policy plays a critical role in the wealth, positive or negative, held by individuals, firms and governments. Monetary policy affects interest rates, inflation rates and exchange rates. These variables affect domestic borrowing and lending, as well as net wealth holdings by creditors and debtors. Under the assumption that more wealth is preferred to less, monetary policy clearly represents an important if not controversial matter of policy.

The marketplace for monetary policy involves several actors. First, the Council of Ministers, predominantly, and the European Parliament, negligibly, serve as the brokers of policy. As such, they attempt to secure agents that will respond to their demands as they seek to gain and retain support from their various constituencies. Second, voters, interest groups and corporate entities serve as the demanders and suppliers of policy. Net creditors and net debtors respectively prefer tighter or looser monetary policies. Voters' monetary policy preferences also depend upon the budgetary situation of their governments and the impact of this situation or any change from it on their individual expected net wealth. The EU's primary bureaucratic agent, the Commission, promotes policy that it perceives beneficial to its expected long-term growth and viability. Finally, the ECB serves as the agent of the policy brokers, notably the Council of Ministers. The Heads of State or Government decide among themselves the agenda and structure of the ECB in order to serve their often myopic interests.

7.7 CONCLUSION

The Rational Choice approach offers a powerful set of assumptions regarding individual behavior. These assumptions and the behavioral predictions that ensue from them provide a useful framework for explaining and anticipating individual behavior under a variety of circumstances. Opponents of the approach have levied a number of criticisms against it. However, the approach remains a valuable explanatory and suggestive framework for understanding individual behavior.

The approach may be combined with the notion of politics-as-exchange. The latter suggests that rational actors interact in the political marketplace analogously to individual interaction in the commercial marketplace. In the former context brokers, demanders and suppliers meet to exchange resources of value to each other. Policy brokers include members of the executive and legislative branches of government. In the case of the EU these bodies are the Council of Ministers, the European Parliament and the European Commission. Individuals within these institutions are effectively agents of policy demanders and suppliers. For this reason, they are subject to the pressures placed upon them by these individuals and groups. Policy demanders include voters, interest groups, government agencies and corporate entities. The European Commission constitutes the largest government agency within the EU. It occupies a unique role as policy broker, demander and supplier. In these roles, respectively, it plays an active part in initiating policy and expanding the scale and scope of EU powers. The ECB represents the monetary agent of the government of the EU. Policy demanders, suppliers and brokers exchange political support for policies.

NOTES

1. Fiorina (1996, 85) for example writes: 'Many of the critical observations they make about specific studies are on the mark. Nevertheless, I completely disagree with their bottom line.' Kelley (1996, 103) also acknowledges the validity of Green and Shapiro's criticisms in some cases and recommends that Rational Choice theorists learn from observations. Furthermore,

Lohmann (1996, 130) adds that: 'Some early Rational Choice theorists indulged in a cultist universalism that denies the legitimacy of alternative modes of inquiry, and some still do so today. But the field has matured ... Today many Rational Choice theorists believe that Rational Choice can explain part, but not all, of what goes on in any given political domain ... ' Kelley (1996, 103).

2. Schofield (1996, 190), however, notes that Condorcet applied the elements of Rational Choice theory to the formation of government institutions at the end of the 1700s.
3. Council Decision and Act of September 20, 1976 on Direct Elections first provided for the direct election of members of the European Parliament.
4. Other Technical Councils exist in the following areas: internal market, research, industry, development, labor, social affairs, fisheries, education, telecommunications, consumer affairs, health, culture and justice and home affairs.
5. The four legislative procedures are: the consultation, cooperation, codecision and assent procedures.
6. Frey (1971), for example, examines the relatively higher turnout in elections of individuals with relatively higher income.
7. Stigler (1974), however, argues that there is no such thing as a free-rider. Rather he asserts that cheap-riders enjoy relatively lower cost than other contributors to collective goods. The existence of cheap-riders reflects the fact that any action incurs costs.
8. Where the cost of exclusion exceeds the benefits, groups may rationally undertake no action to exclude non-contributors.
9. The politician's calculation of expected net benefits from promoting the interests of one group over another is analogous to the calculation performed by Peltzman's (1976) regulator. In the Peltzman model the regulator responds to votes and money from groups on both sides of the regulated issue in forming his decision of the optimal amount of regulation.
10. It is important to note, however, that political outcomes, which represent successful pursuit of self-interest by politicians and/or private groups or individuals, may simultaneously serve the public interest. Economists have traditionally considered the public interest to be that outcome reached through a constrained optimization problem in which economic efficiency is maximized (Dillon et al. 1991).
11. McChesney (1997) suggests that political actors do not sit idly by awaiting offers from rent-seekers. Rather, they actively solicit private resources in exchange for political outcomes. He terms the resources expended by private actors in this sense political market rents.
12. Denzau and Munger (1986) found this result.
13. Wittman (1995, 112) presents the following examples of models of strategic behavior by bureaucratic agents in the face of preference divides between the legislature and the executive, or between members of the legislature: Hill (1985); Hammond, Hill and Miller (1986); and McCubbins, Noll and Weingast (1990). He further notes one potential remedy for avoiding the problem suggested by McCubbins, Noll and Weingast (1989). They recommend the legislature and executive jointly agree to the individual appointed to lead the bureaucratic agency.
14. Vaubel (1994b, 232) observes that more and more Commissioners have prior experience as national ministers and Council of Ministers members. For this reason, as Council members they may have promoted legislation to increase the size and scope of the Commission and its duties. Such growth accorded with their long-term interests.

8. Institutions and monetary policy

8.1 INTRODUCTION

The Council of Ministers, European Commission and European Parliament comprise the executive and legislative framework of the EU. The Council of Ministers and the European Parliament comprise the policy brokers within the political marketplace of the EU. The Commission acts as policy broker, demander and supplier. Voters and interest groups comprise the rest of the demand and supply sides of the EU political marketplace. The Treaty on European Union (TEU) endows the brokers with certain powers in the field of monetary affairs. Brokers employ these powers to advance their own interests. This chapter demonstrates how these institutions can utilize their powers to affect monetary policy in response to voter and interest group demands.

The chapter employs the following organization. Section 2 reviews two types of institutional determinants of political outcomes: agenda control and decision rules. Sections 3, 4 and 5 consider the organizational structure, decision rules and role in the monetary policy process of the Council of Ministers, European Commission and European Parliament, respectively. Section 6 briefly identifies the channels for institutional impact upon monetary policy. The final section concludes.

8.2 INSTITUTIONAL DETERMINANTS OF POLITICAL OUTCOMES

The outcomes of decision processes depend on at least two institutional features. These features are agenda rules and decision rules. The former concerns who decides which issues decision-makers debate and vote on. The latter concerns the relevant level of approval necessary for a proposal to gain acceptance. These features may affect the equilibria of political markets.

8.2.1 Agenda Rules

Agenda rules relate to the order in which issues come up for a vote, the individual or collective nature of issue votes, the existence of veto rights and the presence of an agenda setter. An agenda setter controls the order in which proposals come up for consideration and may thereby determine the final decision outcome.

An agenda setter has the potential to determine policy outcomes by at least two different means. This potential stems from the gatekeeping authority the agenda setter possesses and the agenda setter's ability to admit or restrict proposals subsequent to his own. Gatekeeping authority refers to the power to admit or reject any or all proposals to compete against the *status quo*. The ability to admit or reject proposals subsequent to his preferred alternative depends upon whether the agenda setter is subject to an open or a closed rule. Under the former, the agenda setter may consider other proposals subsequent to his own. Under the latter, the agenda setter will not consider proposals subsequent to his own.

In institutions prone to vote cycling, the agenda setter possesses the ability to determine the outcome of the decision process. The agenda setter may prepare the voting sequence in such a manner to secure victory for his most preferred alternative. (Voting sequence is simply the order in which decision-makers vote on issues.) The agenda setter may also decide which issues come up for discussion by decision-makers. By preventing certain issues from reaching the agenda, the agenda setter effectively reduces the set of possible political outcomes.

Veto rights denote the power of an individual decision-maker, an agenda setter or an institution to reject a proposal. Veto rights may apply to the introduction of a proposal to the decision process, the *ex ante* veto, as in the gatekeeping power of an agenda setter or following the outcome of a pair-wise competition, the *ex post* veto. The *ex post* veto is more valuable than the *ex ante* veto because it serves as a final control over the outcome of the decision process. Other veto rights may exist at any stage during the legislative process.

8.2.2 Decision Rules

Decision rules identify the relevant number of votes necessary for a proposal to pass. Several general types of decision rules exist. First, unanimity rules require that all voters favor a proposal in order for it to pass. Second, simple majority rules require that at least (N+1)/2 voters favor a proposal in order for it to pass. Finally, supra-majority rules require that some number of voters greater than (N+1)/2 favor a proposal in order for it to pass. Examples of supra-majority rules include two-thirds, three-quarters and four-fifths majority rules.

In their 1962 classic, *The Calculus of Consent*, Buchanan and Tullock identify the two basic costs of collective decision-making. They term the first costs decision costs. These costs arise from bargaining between participants in the election in order to gather sufficient votes to pass the proposal. As the number of votes required for passage of a proposal rises, decision costs increase. For example, a unanimity rule requires full consent. If all but one or a few voters favor a proposal, this voter acquires the power to engage in a strategic holdout. By this means, the last voter(s) may attempt to extract additional benefits from the consenting majority. The second costs are external costs. These costs represent the costs faced by individuals who oppose the passing proposal. As the number of votes required for passage of a proposal rises, external costs decrease. Using these two cost concepts, Buchanan and Brennan suggest the optimal collective decision rule as the number or proportion of votes that minimizes the sum of the two costs.

Different voting rules imply different costs for advocates and opponents of particular legislation. Opponents of legislation that passes under a less than unanimity rule face the costs of adjusting to the policy environment resulting from the new legislation. Policy opponents expect the legislation to impose net costs on their constituents. The latter may protest against a government that passes legislation against its interests. Transfers from net gainers to net losers may assuage the latter from protesting such policies. Where policy brokers disperse the costs of concentrated benefits across a relatively large number of individuals, the latter may raise no protest against these costs. Two reasons may explain this phenomenon. First, the latter may be unaware of these costs. Second, they may acknowledge these costs but refrain from protesting against them due to the cost of the requisite organization and action.

Unanimous decision rules prevent the passage of legislation with such external costs, *ceteris paribus*. However, unanimous rules introduce the potentially costly possibility of strategic holdout. In the absence of consensus, unanimous rules may also result in situations of gridlock where full approval is not forthcoming. Such gridlocks may delay or prevent the passage of legislation thereby imposing additional costs upon proponents of the bill(s) and their constituents.

8.3 COUNCIL OF MINISTERS

The Council of Ministers consists of three distinct but closely related affiliations of ministerial-level national representatives. These bodies determine the direction of EU policy. The members of the General and Specialized Councils focus on those issues within their respective policy domains. The European Council focuses on matters of overall direction, matters of conflict and matters with far-reaching consequences.

The European Council constitutes the highest level of these representatives, Heads of State or Government. This institution has the ability to single-handedly drive EU policy because of its near independence from and control of the other two EU-level government institutions, the Commission and the Parliament.

European Council members are also more senior within their national governments and within their parties than the members of the other Councils. European Council members are accountable to their voter constituents, their supporting interest groups, corporations and their party of membership. The Council's historical record of making or breaking Community initiatives subject to the discretion and preferences of Heads of Government or State attests to the power of this body.

8.3.1 Organizational Structure of Council

The Council of Ministers consists of the three types of Councils and possesses its own internal hierarchy and bureaucracy. The three types of Councils are the General Council of Foreign Ministers, the specialized Technical Councils and the European Council. The President of the Council tops the internal hierarchy. The internal bureaucracy consists of the Committee of Permanent Representatives and the General Secretariat.

A President leads the Councils of Ministers, respectively. The President is the representative from the member country that currently holds the Council Presidency rotation. For example, if the UK holds the Council Presidency, the UK Agriculture Minister presides over the Council of Agricultural Ministers. Similarly, the British Prime Minister presides over the European Council and the British Foreign Chancellor leads the Council of Foreign Ministers. The Council Presidency rotates among member countries on a predetermined basis.

Each Council Presidency determines the policy agenda during his/her term of office. Each Presidency term lasts six months. The European Council summit during the final month of this term represents the last chance of a given Council President to advance his policy preferences during that term.

The three Councils of Ministers enjoy a relatively extensive administrative support structure. This structure consists of the General Secretariat, the Council of Permanent Representatives (COREPER) I and II, and various ambassadors, deputies, committees and working groups. These bodies comprise national delegates, as well as EU-level bureaucrats.

The General Secretariat supports the Secretary-General of the Council of Ministers (CM RoP Article 21). The General Affairs Council (of Foreign Ministers) unanimously selects a Secretary-General (Article 151.1–2 TEU and CM RoP Article 17.1). Where the Council cannot unanimously decide, the European Council may intervene. The position of Secretary-General possesses no predetermined fixed-term length. No Secretary-General has served less than seven years total. The longest serving Secretary-General, Christian Calmes, served from 1952–73.

The Secretariat serves as a liaison between the Council Presidency and the Councils, as well as between the Council and the Commission and individual member countries (Hayes-Renshaw and Wallace 1995, 571). The General Secretariat includes ten Directorates-General (A through J). Directorate-General G is responsible for economic and monetary affairs.

The Committee of Permanent Representatives is a standing group of senior diplomats from member countries whose primary duty is to prepare issues for presentation and debate in Council meetings (CM RoP Article 16).[1] COREPER consists of two separate and distinct bodies: COREPER I and II. Both bodies comprise permanent representatives from all EU member countries. The latter consists of ambassadors' deputies. The Deputy Permanent Representative from the country currently holding the Council Presidency leads COREPER II. COREPER I consists of ambassadors. The Permanent Representative from the country currently holding the Council Presidency leads COREPER I. Representatives from the Council Secretariat and the Secretariat General of the Commission, along with representatives from the relevant Directorate(s)-General of the Commission attend COREPER meetings.

Over time, COREPER has accumulated significant power within the Council. Members of COREPER may stand in for national representatives in Council meetings and thereby express their positions (Bieber and Palmer 1975, 311). For this reason, interest groups may attempt to influence the members of COREPER. Members have also acquired increasing power over the Commission because of their proximity to individual Council members. Given the lack of accountability to voters, their governments and other EU institutions, members of COREPER are left to attempt to advance their interests within the Council bureaucracy relatively unencumbered.

COREPER groups meet at least once a week to discuss issues of policy. The General Secretary prepares the agenda of COREPER with the Council Presidency. COREPER II handles four policy areas: General Affairs, Development, Economics and Finance, and Budget-related issues. COREPER I handles all other issues.

Working groups assist COREPER in researching various policies. In 1995, over 150 working groups existed (Hayes-Renshaw and Wallace 1995, 561–2). COREPER representatives present working group reports and offer recommendations to the Council.

The Antici Group consists of representatives from the permanent representations of each member country. These representatives gather weekly to schedule meetings, draft minutes of and organize the agenda for meetings of COREPER II. Representatives of the Council and Commission Secretariats also attend meetings of the Antici Group. Another group of representatives, known as the Deputies' Deputies, similarly assists COREPER I.

The Economic and Financial Committee also exists to inform the Council and the Commission of monetary affairs within the EU (Article 109c TEU). The Committee consists of two appointees from each of the member countries, the Commission and the European Central Bank (ECB). The duties of the Economic and Financial Committee specifically include delivering opinions regarding monetary issues in response to Council, Commission or its own initiatives, reporting on the economic and financial conditions of member countries and the EU as a whole, and reviewing the movement of capital and payments within the EU (Article 109.2 TEU).

8.3.2 Institutional Procedures

The Councils of Ministers meet on a regular basis to debate and decide on policy issues facing the EU. The General Council and the Technical Councils meet at least twice a month in Brussels.[2] The European Council meets at least twice a year in the country that holds the Council Presidency.

Each Council Presidency is responsible for preparing the agenda for meetings during its term (CM RoP Article 2). The respective ministers from the country holding the Presidency develop the agenda in their policy domain with assistance from the General Secretary of the Council and his cabinet. In addition, individual Council members and the Commission may submit items for inclusion.

The Council of Ministers employs three different decision rules depending on the issue at hand. These rules are unanimity, qualified majority and simple majority. For votes to take place, a quorum of eight members is necessary. Members may decide to abstain in lieu of participating in votes.

Majority decisions in the Councils follow a system of weighted votes. The number of votes a country possesses depends upon the size of its population. Each country casts its votes as a block. Table 8.1 lists the member countries and their respective voting weights since the creation of the European Communities. The table reflects the periodic enlargements of the Communities. These weights currently range from 29 votes for the largest countries to four votes for the smallest country.

The Treaty of Nice (2000) anticipated the need for the reweighting of votes in the Council given expected future enlargements (Annex II, 2). This reweighting will increase the total votes to 345. The votes of the existing 15 members will remain unchanged. Table 8.2 lists the number of weighted votes the future members will possess.

As a result of these new votes, the qualified majority becomes 258 plus either a majority of members or two-thirds of the membership, as given in Table 8.2. In addition, a qualified majority must represent a minimum of 62 percent of the EU's population.

The Council employs qualified majority voting (QMV) in several areas related to monetary affairs (Boudreaux and Lipford 1998, 146). First, the Council decides on the overall economic policy of the EU by QMV (Article 103.2 TEU). Second, the Council employs QMV to adopt changes to the central

Table 8.1 Voting weights in the Council of Ministers

Country/Year	1958 (EC6)	1973 (EC9)	1981 (ECI0)	1986 (EC12)	1995 (EC15)	2005 (EC15)
France	4	10	10	10	10	29
Germany	4	10	10	10	10	29
Italy	4	10	10	10	10	29
Belgium	2	5	5	5	5	12
Netherlands	2	5	5	5	5	13
Luxembourg	1	2	2	2	2	4
Denmark	X	3	3	3	3	7
Ireland	X	3	3	3	3	7
United Kingdom	X	10	10	10	10	29
Greece	X	X	5	5	5	12
Portugal	X	X	X	5	5	12
Spain	X	X	X	8	8	27
Austria	X	X	X	X	4	10
Finland	X	X	X	X	3	7
Sweden	X	X	X	X	4	10
Total	17	58	63	76	87	237
Qualified majority	12	41	45	54	62	169*
% of Total	70.59	70.69	71.43	71.05	71.26	71.31

Note: A qualified majority of 169 plus a majority of members is necessary for proposals originating in the Commission. A qualified majority of 169 plus a two-thirds majority is necessary for all other proposals.

Source: Adapted from the following tables: (1) Annex II: Qualified Majority System in Fiona Hayes-Renshaw 1996, 163; (2) Table 10.2: Composition of the EU Council Votes in Lane, Maeland, and Berg 1996,168; and (3) Treaty of Nice, Annex I, Article 3.1.

parity grid of the ERM (Article 109.1 TEU). Third, the Council decides by QMV what, if any, assistance to provide to an EU country experiencing balance-of-payment problems (Article 109h.2 TEU).

However, Council members usually strive to attain consensus in decision-making. Such efforts are especially apparent at the level of the European Council. It prefers unanimous consent to majority decisions because of the perceived benefits of full support for a legislative decision. The Vienna Convention on International Agreements demands each sovereign country approve the provisions of any international arrangement in which it participates. Failing such approval, the arrangement fails to bind in the relevant country. This protection preserves the hegemony of domestic governments within national political jurisdictions. Furthermore, countries may refuse to

Table 8.2 Voting weights of future EU members

Country	Voting weights
Poland	27
Romania	14
Czech Republic	12
Hungary	12
Bulgaria	10
Slovakia	7
Lithuania	7
Latvia	4
Slovenia	4
Estonia	4
Cyprus	4
Malta	3
Total	108

cooperate in future legislative negotiations and thereby threaten the long-term survival of the EU as a political arrangement. In situations lacking consensus, the Council may postpone its decision until later (Bieber and Palmer 1975, 311).

8.3.3 Role in Monetary Policy-making

The Council of Ministers participates in the process of EU monetary policy-making in several ways. First, the Council of Economics and Finance Ministers (ECOFIN) is responsible for adopting legislation related to monetary policy, including various policy guidelines. Such legislation includes changes to the Statute of the ECB/ESCB (Article 106.5 TEU), changes in the ESCB's supervisory responsibilities of credit and financial institutions (Article 105.6 TEU), and changes in the relationship of the euro with third-country currencies (Article 109.1 TEU). ECOFIN is also responsible for ensuring macroeconomic policy coordination among EU countries. The Economic and Financial Committee serves to inform the Council on these and related issues. Second, the European Council nominates candidates to serve on the Executive Board of the ECB. Third, the Council of Ministers is also responsible for setting the overall direction of economic policy within the EU as outlined in the TEU.

The European Council has repeatedly played an important role in the transition to EMU. First, it appointed the Werner Commission in 1970 to prepare a plan for economic and monetary union. Second, it undertook the decision to proceed with the EMS (Tsoukalis 1989, 66). Finally, German Chancellor Kohl placed the matter on the agenda for the European Council summit during his Council Presidency in 1988 (Sandholtz 1993, 126). This summit appointed the Delors Committee that later developed the original plan for the three-stage transition to EMU adopted in Maastricht in December 1991.

8.4 EUROPEAN COMMISSION

The European Commission plays a central role in the legislative process of the EU. It is responsible for initiating policies before the Council of Ministers and preparing policy proposals in response to Council requests. The Commission consists of a large bureaucratic structure with a vast appetite for expanding its jurisdiction. Interest groups favor the Commission as a target for their attentions because of its role in preparing EU policy proposals.

The accountability of the Commission to the Council of Ministers and the European Parliament limits its ability to serve as gatekeeper to EU policy in a number of ways. First, Commissioners are Council appointees and only attain office with parliamentary approval. Second, the Council must approve the Commission's salaries each year. Third, the Commission submits monthly and annual reports to the Parliament. Fourth, the Parliament also has the power to pass a resolution of censure of the Commission and may demand the resignation of all Commissioners. The Parliament's oversight of the Commission constitutes the EU electorate's only means of checking the activities of the Commission. All of these features restrict the Commission's autonomy.

8.4.1 Organizational Structure

The members of the Commission are responsible for formally initiating EU policy proposals. The European Commission is organized into 26 Directorates-General. The latter correspond to various policy jurisdictions. Each Commissioner is responsible for at least one Directorate-General. A Director leads each Directorate-General. The Directorates-General relevant to monetary affairs include Directorate-General II (Economic and Financial Affairs), Directorate-General XV (Internal Market and Financial Services) and Directorate-General XXI (Taxation and Customs Union).

The number of Commissioners is currently 20. The following member states have two Commissioners: France, Germany, Italy, Spain and the UK. The remaining states have one. From January 1, 2005, each member state will have one Commissioner. The Council of Ministers may change this number following a unanimous vote (Treaty of Nice, Annex I, Article 4.1). This number will change once 27 countries belong to the EU. From that time, the number of Commissioners will be less than the number of EU member countries. The

Council will decide on this new number. Countries will hold Commission memberships according to a rotation system yet to be developed by the Council (Treaty of Nice, Annex I, Article 4.2).

A President tops the internal hierarchy of the Commission (Article 158 TEU). The Council appoints the President subject to Parliament's approval. The President serves a renewable five-year term. The Commission may also appoint one or two Vice-Presidents (Article 161 TEU). The Amsterdam Treaty (1997) allows the Commission President to reject national nominees to the Commission. It also permits him to select policy responsibilities for individual Commissioners. The President is responsible for providing policy direction to the Commission, overseeing the Secretariat-General of the Commission and representing the Commission before other EU and international institutions.

Each Commissioner possesses his own cabinet of seven officials. The members of these cabinets serve to inform the Commissioners of research conducted by their relevant Directorate-General(s) and notify them of proposals of interest from Directorates-General other than those for which they are responsible. A chef-de-cabinet heads each cabinet and acts as chief liaison between the Commissioner and the rest of the cabinet.

The close communication between Commissioner and cabinet renders the latter an important target of interest group attentions (Andersen and Eliassen 1991). Interest groups employ two strategies for targeting Commissioners. First, they target Commissioners responsible for Directorates-General of the relevant policy jurisdiction. Second, they target Commissioners based on common national interests. Interest groups can affect policy proposals by lobbying the Commission while it prepares new proposals. Gorges (1993, 76, 78) notes that:

> ... the Commission tends to consult interest groups with the aim of collecting technical information to use in developing legislation ... The Commission ... does grant them [EC-level organizational representatives of interest groups] something of a representational monopoly by seeking to consult with them first, by including them in the elaboration of policy, by furnishing them with the earliest possible info, and by providing them with the resources necessary to participate in EC policymaking (technical support such as interpreters, meeting rooms, per diem expenses, etc).

The lack of accountability to voters and the inability of voters to supply those commodities demanded by the bureaucratic Commission enable interest groups to take the front seat in policy development with the Commission.

The Secretariat-General supports the General Secretary of the Commission. The Secretariat-General prepares documents for and plans meetings of the College of Commissioners. The body also organizes meetings of the Commission with other EU and international institutions. The Secretariat-General is accountable to the President of the Commission. The position of

General Secretary possesses no predetermined fixed term length. The longest serving General Secretary, Emile Noel, held office from 1958–87.

8.4.2 Institutional Procedures

The European Commission meets on at least a weekly basis. The President of the Commission heads these meetings (Article 3 CEC RoP). The entire Commission debates and votes on policy proposals developed from Directorate-General reports. Each Commissioner presents the case for proposals within his policy jurisdiction.

The President of the Commission prepares the agenda of each session with the assistance of the General Secretariat (Article 15 CEC RoP). Weekly agenda include matters that belong to the Commission's annual program, as well as its quarterly rolling program (Article 4 CEC RoP). The weekly agenda provides an outline of issues for debate. Individual Commissioners may submit items for addition to the agenda or request the withdrawal of items from the agenda. Majority votes within the full Commission determine the inclusion or exclusion of individual requests.

Legislative proposals originate within the relevant Directorate-General. One official within the Directorate-General, the rapporteur, bears responsibility for drafting the proposal. Following completion of an initial draft the rapporteur submits the proposal draft to the cabinet of the Commissioner responsible for the relevant Directorate-General. The proposal must attain the approval of the cabinet before it progresses further. Subsequently the relevant cabinet presents the proposal to other cabinets for consideration. Upon the approval of all cabinets, the proposal advances to the agenda of the College of Commissioners for debate and a vote.

Steunenberg (1994) presents a model of the Commission's decision whether or not to initiate a proposal that it prefers to the *status quo* for a given level of consensus within the Council. He assumes that actors possess perfect information and are therefore able to foresee the consequences of their actions. Representatives of the Commission regularly attend meetings of the Council of Ministers and contribute to COREPER meetings (Tsoukalis 1989, 66). Three possible situations exist:

1. A qualified majority within the Council exists which prefers a change from the *status quo*.
2. A qualified majority within the Council does not exist which prefers a change from the status quo.
3. A consensus within the Council exists which prefers a change from the *status quo*.

In the first case, the Commission will initiate the proposal. A qualified majority in the Council may not amend this proposal because it lacks the requisite consensus to make such changes. In the second case, the Commission does not initiate the proposal. In the third case, the Commission will initiate its proposal as long as it expects any amendments introduced by the Council to be Pareto improvements.

The European Commission employs an absolute majority rule for decision-making (Article 163 TEU; CEC RoP Article 6). The Commission's Rules of Procedure specify that the requisite quorum equals a simple majority of the number of Commissioners provided for by the TEU (CEC RoP Article 5). These rules imply that six Commissioners out of 20 can decide on a proposal in the presence of the minimum quorum of 11. In addition to voting on a proposal the Commission can also refer it back to the Directorate-General for revision or postpone a vote until a later date.

Well-developed proposals that possess the support of significant interests seem likely to typically garner the support of at least an absolute majority for several reasons. First, Commissioners stem from diverse national backgrounds and given each country's low representation (one or two members out of 20) seem unable to advance one country's interests without significant vote trading. Second, Commissioners each represent one or more different policy areas. Each Commissioner has his own interest in advancing policy within his Directorate(s)-General. Supporting the policy of another Commissioner need not infringe upon his jurisdiction. Commissioners seem more likely to support each others' demands for widened jurisdictions and increased budgets in order to expand the Commission as an institution. Thus, Commissioners may adopt the interests of the institution above all other interests, depending upon their long-term individual objectives. Commission approval will likely, however, not be forthcoming for ill-prepared proposals, excessively frivolous proposals and proposals that do not receive the support of one or more large interests. The advancement of such proposals to the Council would likely place the Commission in disfavor with Council members who are already busy with their own agenda.

8.4.3 Role in Monetary Policy-making

The Commission partakes indirectly in monetary policy-making within the EMU in several ways. First, the Commission serves as official EU observer of member countries' economic policies. Second, the Commission supplies recommendations regarding member country deficits under the Excessive Deficit Procedure. Finally, the Commission sends a delegation to G8 meetings to represent the EU.

The Commission possesses the power to directly affect monetary affairs through its role as policy initiator. The Commission submits policy proposals to the Council of Ministers for consideration and possible eventual adoption. Such proposals originate within the relevant Directorate-General. Directorate-General II focuses on EU economic and monetary affairs. In addition, Directorate-General XXI attends to matters of tax policy and Directorate-General XV focuses on financial services.

Article 106.5 (TEU) highlights the Commission's role in making changes to the Statutes of the ESCB. The Commission may either present such a proposal for amendments to the Council or the Council must consult the Commission in case of Council-initiated proposals. The Commission plays a similar role in the extension of supervisory duties of credit and financial institutions of the ECB (Article 105.6 TEU) and the establishment of international exchange rate arrangements involving the euro (Article 109.1 TEU).

The Commission has long been a proponent of monetary integration. First, Sandholtz (1993, 126) notes that: 'The CEC had proposed monetary integration to complement the common market as early as 1961' Second, Commission Vice-President Raymond Barre chaired the committee that prepared the two Barre Reports on a European monetary system in 1969. Third, Commission President Roy Jenkins called for renewed efforts at European monetary integration following the demise of the snake in 1977. His calls led to the establishment of the European Monetary System (EMS). Fourth, Commission President Jacques Delors managed to gain Council appointment as head of the committee that prepared the original plans for the European Monetary Union (EMU) in 1989. Commission leadership has played an important role in advancing the cause of EMU. This record accords with the Commission's interests of expanding the scope and scale of EU jurisdiction and thereby ensuring its future raison d'être.

8.5 EUROPEAN PARLIAMENT

The European Parliament is the EU's largest elected representative body. Members meet in committees to prepare and debate policy proposals brought before them. Unlike other parliamentary bodies, the European Parliament does not have the power to initiate, draft and pass legislation. Rather it participates in this process along with the Council of Ministers and the European Commission.

8.5.1 Organizational Structure

The European Parliament consists of an internal hierarchy, along with a system of Political Groups and a system of committees. The internal hierarchy provides general direction and administrative support to the Parliament. The Political Groups gather individual members into associations of similar political preferences. Committees bear responsibility for policy development in their respective area(s) of specialty.

The President and 14 Vice-Presidents head the internal hierarchy of the European Parliament. Together the President and Vice-Presidents comprise the Bureau of the Parliament. These individuals hold office for renewable two-and-a-half-year terms. Their terms of office begin in the month of July following full parliamentary elections in June every five years, and during the month of January halfway through each five-year term.

MEPs formally attain positions within the Bureau by election (Article 140 TEU). However, the leading parties in the Parliament typically decide among themselves the candidate for the Presidency. A formal election provides rubber-stamp approval to the chosen candidate. For the 1989 parliamentary term, the Socialists and the European People's Party decided *ex ante* to place individuals from their parties, respectively, in this position (Jacobs and Corbett 1990, 88). Officially, any group of 13 members may suggest nominations for the post. The election of Vice-Presidents follows a competitive electoral process. However, Political Groups usually provide candidates in proportion to their presence in the Parliament (ibid.).

The President of the Parliament possesses several important responsibilities (Westlake 1994, 195). First, he presides over the plenary sessions of the European Parliament. Second, he assembles the conciliation committee and co-signs final reports required by the codecision procedure. Third, the President renders his signature to grant final approval of the EU's annual budget. Fourth, the President presides over meetings of the Conference of Political Group Presidents. Finally, the President represents the Parliament in interactions with other EU and international institutions.

The European Parliament organizes members into committees to address particular policy issues. Committee composition generally reflects the relative composition of the Parliament in terms of Political Groups. However, Political Groups may engage in position trading whereby they exchange their claims to representation on different committees (Tsebelis 1995, 58). Political groups may also gain influence on committees by appointing representatives as substitute members. The latter may participate fully in committee meetings and may even vote in the place of one or more of their Political Group's full committee members (ibid.).

The Parliament currently possesses 20 committees. Two of these committees possess subcommittees. These committees include the Committee on Budgets (30 members), the Committee on Economic and Monetary Affairs, and Industrial Policy (49 members), the Committee on External Economic Relations and the Committee on Budgetary Control. Members serve as full members of one or more standing committees. Approximately two-thirds of MEPs serve on one committee. The remaining members serve on two committees (Tsebelis 1995, 57). In addition, they may serve as substitute members of additional committees. A number of temporary committees also operate at different times.

An elected chairman and one to three vice-chairmen lead each committee. These chairmen act together as the committee's bureau. Chairmen and vice-chairmen serve two-and-a-half-year terms of office that coincide with those of the President and Vice-Presidents of the Parliament. Political Groups distribute chairmanships in accordance with the d'Hondt system of proportional representation (Jacobs and Corbett 1990, 96). Political Groups receiving chairman and vice-chairman positions nominate candidates from their respective parties for the position. Group members then validate these nominations through a token election. A credible *ex post* punishment threat protects nominees from any challengers (Tsebelis 1995, 58).

Committee chairmen meet ensemble in the Conference of Committee Chairmen (Westlake 1994, 194). This body attempts to determine which policy issues belong on the agenda of the European Parliament. It presents its proposals before the Conference of Political Group Presidents.

Committee systems may endow committee members with an inordinate amount of power in their respective policy domains. Shepsle and Weingast (1987) highlight the strategic powers of committees within the US Congress. They report the following stylized facts (in Rowley et al. 1995, 116). First, committees acquire gatekeeping powers and agenda control over issues within their domain. Second, committees amass relevant policy expertise. Third, committees possess near monopoly power over legislative proposals in their policy domain. Committees respect and do not infringe upon the domains of each other.

The stylized facts concerning the committee system of the US Congress describe the committee system of the European Parliament to a much lesser extent. Members within the relevant committee may introduce issues for consideration. The appropriate committee then appoints a rapporteur who is responsible for preparing a report on the matter. In this way, the committee members affect the Parliament's agenda and accumulate policy knowledge. However, the Parliament must respond to proposals initiated by the Commission and Council through the relevant legislative procedure. For this reason, Parliament does not control its agenda, cannot serve as legislative gatekeeper and does not possess monopoly power over legislation.

Eight Political Groups comprise the European Parliament. These Groups correspond to associations of members of national political parties with similar ideologies. The Parliament currently consists of the following Political Groups: the Group of the Party of European Socialists, the Group of the European People's Party, the Group of the European Liberal, Democrat and Reform Party, the Group Union For Europe, the Confederal Group of the European United Left/Nordic Green Left, the Green Group in the European Parliament, the Group of the European Radical Alliance and the Group of Independents for a Europe of Nations.

Membership of a Political Group is not mandatory. However, membership may convey valuable privileges. These privileges are procedural and administrative in nature. The former privileges include several valuable powers (Westlake 1994, 189). First, Political Groups may raise questions before the Council or Commission. They may also respond to resolutions from the Commission, Council of Ministers or European Council. Second, they may request a parliamentary debate be held. Third, they may request an item be added to the Parliament's plenary agenda. Political Group Presidents may act as representatives of their Groups in such interactions. For example, they periodically meet with the President of the Parliament to discuss issues and submit suggestions for the agenda of future plenary sessions. They also assign speaking time in plenary sessions and grant rapporteurships (Jacobs and Corbett 1990, 46).

Political groups also enjoy four administrative privileges. First, they receive financial assistance to cover the costs of support staff, office space and office equipment. Such assistance corresponds approximately with Groups' relative presence within the Parliament. The Parliament devotes approximately 15 percent of its budget to administrative expenses. Second, Political Groups receive financial assistance from the European Information Campaign to inform voters about upcoming elections.

The Parliament also provides administrative and procedural privileges to MEPs unattached to a Political Group. These representatives receive administrative support in accordance with their presence in the Parliament. Two unattached members may also attend but not vote at meetings of the Enlarged Bureau, which consists of the Bureau and the Presidents of the Political Groups. The Enlarged Bureau assists in the preparation of the Parliament's agenda. One representative of the unattached members may also attend the meetings of the Conference of Political Group Presidents. The Conference settles the final agenda of the Parliament. Unattached members also appoint representatives to committees and receive their share of speaking time (Jacobs and Corbett 1990, 74).

Since 1979 the two dominant Political Groups have been the Socialist (the Group of the Party of European Socialists) and Christian Democrat Groups (the Group of the European People's Party) (Westlake 1994, 186). These Groups together command a majority of representatives within the European Parliament. To the extent that the members of these parties attain national electoral success, they may similarly dominate national elections and thereby hold positions as Heads of State or Government and occupy the Council of Ministers.

A General Secretariat supports the Secretary-General of the European Parliament. The Parliament's Bureau appoints the Secretary-General for a term of fixed length. The General Secretariat serves as the administrative support system for the Parliament. It includes seven Directorates-General that handle various aspects of the administration of the Parliament. These Directorates-General include: Directorate-General I (Sessional Services), Directorate-General II (Committees and Delegations), Directorate-General III (Information and Public Relations), Directorate-General IV (Research), Directorate-General V (Personnel, Budget and Finance), Directorate-General VI (Administration) and Directorate-General VII (Translation and General Services). These Directorates contrast with those of the Council Secretariat and the Commission that focus on various policy domains.

8.5.2 Institutional Procedures

The European Parliament meets in plenary session for one week every month in Strasbourg. During this time the Parliament debates and votes on matters before it. Interpretation occurs in all 11 official languages during plenary sessions. During the rest of the month MEPs spend approximately two weeks in committees in Brussels. They spend the remaining week meeting within Political Groups, with domestic party officials and with various policy demanders and suppliers.

The European Parliament differs from other parliamentary institutions in the brevity and staggering of its plenary sessions. These sessions last less than three months per year. This brevity, along with the staggered nature of sessions, implies that the Parliament operates more slowly than other parliamentary institutions. In addition, the body is not at the ready to respond to sudden Council, Commission or other political announcements or events (Westlake 1994, 203).

The European Parliament conducts its policy work through its system of committees. These bodies prepare policy proposals in response to Council, Commission or internal requests. Parliamentary committees do not observe strict rules for adding items to their agenda (Tsebelis 1995, 59).

The Parliament possesses 20 committees. The Parliament possesses only a few subcommittees, along with various working groups and temporary committees. The most relevant subcommittee for this study is the Subcommittee on Monetary Affairs. The latter belongs to the Committee on Economic and Monetary Policy and Industrial Affairs.

The European Parliament enters the legislative process once a legislative proposal appears before it. The source of such a proposal may be the Council or the Commission. The Parliament may also undertake policy reports calling for a proposal. Such proposals or calls for policy reports go immediately to the relevant committee. The Parliament submits the completed reports to the

Commission to request a formal policy proposal by the Commission. One or more other committees may also be requested to prepare an opinion on the issue.

Upon receipt of a legislative proposal, the committee charges one member to serve as rapporteur. Political Groups utilize a system of points based on their relative representation within the Parliament to bid for rapporteurships on specific issues. The highest bidding Political Group wins the rapporteurship in charge of the preferred legislative bill (Tsebelis 1995, 59). It is this person's responsibility to research and draft the proposal. Committees charged with rendering an opinion on an issue before another committee select one member to serve as draftsman. This person researches and drafts the committee's opinion.

The rapporteur presents the completed proposal draft to the committee. Following committee approval, the rapporteur brings the draft before the entire Parliament during a plenary session. One or more Commission representatives may attend at this session.

MEPs and Commission representatives may suggest amendments to the draft and the rapporteur must revise the draft accordingly. The committee again votes on whether to accept the amended draft. This draft then goes before the full Parliament as an A series document for a vote up or down.

The legislative process varies according to which legislative procedure applies. These procedures include the consultation, cooperation, codecision and assent procedures. The Parliament also allows committees to adopt alternative procedures such as the simplified procedure in order to accelerate the process.

The President of the Parliament and the Conference of Political Group Presidents prepare the agenda for plenary sessions. The agenda is subject to change for procedural reasons such as failure to meet the quorum, referral of a report back to committee or due to unexpected events such as the arrival of specific requests by the Council or Commission (Jacobs and Corbett 1990, 131). A quorum of at least one-third of MEPs must be present for any vote to be taken. One or more Commission and Council representatives may also attend plenary sessions. These representatives receive a time allotment to participate in parliamentary debates. However, they may not vote.

The European Parliament uses a variety of decision rules during plenary sessions. The Treaty on Establishing the European Communities and the Parliament's Rules of Procedures outline these decision rules. These rules include simple, absolute and one-third majority rules. In addition, a quorum rule may accompany these minimum thresholds. Table 8.3 highlights the decision rules employed by the Parliament for legislative matters excluding the budget.

Table 8.3 Legislative decision rules of the European Parliament

Subject	Majority requirement
Request for a legislative initiative	Absolute
Request for the Commission to withdraw a proposal	Parliament's President must automatically request withdrawal where a proposal fails to secure a simple majority of the votes cast
Amendment of the Council Common Position (cooperation or codecision procedure)	Absolute
Intention to reject the Council's Common Position (codecision)	Absolute
Confirmation of intention to reject the Council's Common Position (codecision procedure)	Absolute
Rejection of the Common Position (cooperation or codecision procedure)	Absolute
Request to Commission to withdraw its proposal (cooperation procedure)	Absolute
Approval of the conciliation committee's joint text (codecision procedure)	Simple
Rejection of the Council text (codecision third reading)	Absolute
Assent on accession	Absolute

Source: Adapted from Table 5 in Westlake (1994, 261–3).

Regarding most matters the Parliament employs an absolute majority rule (Article 141 TEU). Majority rule reduces the need for consensus building. However, the limited role of the Parliament within the EU's legislative process may render this apparent cost-saving measure needless. After all, the ultimate decision-maker, the Council, prefers to attain unanimous consent for its decisions.

One problematic aspect for decision-making within the Parliament is the relatively high rates of absenteeism (Westlake 1994, 102). Lack of sufficient attendance can and has prevented votes from taking place. However, high-profile decisions such as approval of the annual budget usually manage to attract the requisite quorum. Reasons for low attendance include the party-list systems employed by many states. Party-list systems make MEPs directly accountable to the parties rather than constituents. MEP neglect of Parliamentary attendance further weakens the role of the body within the EU government and discourages voter turnout.

8.5.3 Role in Monetary Policy-making

The European Parliament possesses very limited powers in the sphere of monetary policy-making. It is able to debate matters of economic and monetary policy, as well as to prepare own-initiative reports in these areas. The Sub-committee on Monetary Affairs bears responsibility for researching and presenting such studies. The Council of Ministers requires the assent of the European Parliament in order to grant the ECB additional supervisory responsibilities of credit and financial institutions (Article 105.6 TEU) and to amend the Statute of the ESCB (Article 106.5 TEU). The Council must also consult the Parliament in order to enter any international exchange rate agreements (Article 109.1 TEU).

8.6 CHANNELS FOR INSTITUTIONAL INFLUENCE UPON MONETARY POLICY

The executive and legislative institutions can affect monetary policy-making by several means. First, they can legislate changes to the Statutes of the ECB/ESCB. Such changes might include specific changes regarding the monetary targets of the ECB. Second, they can legislate changes in the TEU. Such changes might include the goals of EU economic and/or monetary policy (Article 2 TEU). Similarly, they can legislate on the role of the euro in international exchange rate arrangements.

The executive and legislative institutions can also utilize their powers over the monetary authority in order to influence its decisions. The Council of Ministers, particularly the European Council, can apply pressure to its appointees on the Executive Board and the members of the Governing Council of the ECB. The members of Executive Board, meaning its President, Vice-president and four additional members, attain office through appointment by the Heads of State or Government of the member countries. Subsequently these appointments must meet with approval from the European Parliament and the Governing Council. The Council might propose changes to the composition of the Executive Board if dissatisfied with its performance. Similarly, the Council might delay Executive Board appointments until the ECB adopts its policy preferences. The Council might also amend the term lengths of Executive Board members. The President of the Council, along with a representative from the Commission, may attend meetings of the Governing Council, although they may not vote. Their attendance may provide sufficient pressure to secure policies in line with Council preferences.

Furthermore, the ECB is directly accountable to the Council of Ministers, European Parliament and European Council. According to Article 109a (3) the President of the ECB must submit an annual report to these bodies. The Parliament may then debate the report. The Parliament may also call the President or other ECB members to speak before the relevant committees. Failure of Executive Board members to satisfy Council demands might meet with dissolution of the Board or other punitive responses. Given the accountability of its Executive Board to the Council, its statutory independence seems less than sufficient to insulate it from political pressure.

National central bank governors and Executive Board members may vote according to the preferences of their respective Head of State or Government. The former in particular may advance their country's leader's preferences given the need for national support and cooperation in maintaining their position and acting as monetary agent of their country. Executive Board members may be less loyal to national interests given their election by national and international representatives alike. However, their behavior will likely depend upon their preferred future career path and earning opportunities.

Studies of the Federal Reserve System of the USA reveal several sources of political influence on bank policies. Such influence stems from within the Fed's decision-making hierarchy, as well as from the executive and legislative branches. Alesina and Sachs (1988) find evidence relating monetary policy with the presidential electoral cycle. Their results note that liberal Presidents tend to advance more expansionary policies, while conservative Presidents tend to advance policies that are more contractionary. National central bank governors and Executive Board members may promote expansionary or contractionary policy in line with the preferences of their national leader. Grier

(1991, 1996) and Chopin et al. (1996a) find a positive correlation between the partisan ties of the leadership of Congressional Banking committees and the direction of money growth. In particular Grier (1996) finds that monetary base growth increases following changes in Senate and House Banking Committee leadership to greater liberality. He employs the Americans for Democratic Action (ADA) scores to measure leaders' liberality. These results are suggestive of the influence of Committee leaders over the decisions of the Federal Reserve. Conservative and liberal Congressmen alike depend on their constituents for electoral support and therefore advocate the latter's preferences in their various legislative roles in order to advance their personal goals. The behavior of US Congressmen may evidence the direction of policy biases in favor of electoral constituents by elected EU officials within the Council of Ministers and the European Parliament.

EU countries may further attempt to exert influence within the Governing Council in accordance with their respective contributions to the bank's capital assets. Article 28 of the ESCB/ECB Statute states that EMU participants will provide the ECB with ECU 5,000 million upon its inception. Countries will provide this amount in accordance with a system of weights, the formula for which Article 29.1 (ESCB/ECB Statute) outlines. This article states the following calculation for capital subscription weights:

- Fifty percent of the share of its respective Member State in the population of the Community in the penultimate year preceding the establishment of the ESCB.
- Fifty percent of the share of its respective Member State in the gross domestic product at market prices of the Community as recorded in the last five years preceding the penultimate year before the establishment of the ESCB.

Table 8.4 lists the respective contributions from each country.

The top five contributions provide nearly 80 percent of the ECB's capital. Germany alone provides nearly one-quarter of the bank's capital followed by France, Italy and England with contributions of 16.8703 percent, 14.9616 percent and 14.7109 percent respectively. These countries might attempt to wield influence in proportion to their contributions, as a sort of *quid pro quo*. Article 29.3 directs the countries to review these provisions for adjustment every five years.

Article 33 of the ESCB/ECB Statute provides for the allocation of net profits and losses within the ESCB. The Governing Council distributes any net profits between the ESCB's general reserve fund and the subscribers of the ECB (Article 33. 1 ESCB/ECB Statute). The general reserve fund receives up to 20 percent of any net profits up to 100 percent of its assets. The subscribers receive the remainder of the net profits based on the proportion of their contributions. The ECB covers net losses first with the general reserve fund, and second from the relative revenues received by subscribers up to their respective contributions (Article 33.2 ESCB/ECB Statute).

Table 8.4 Capital subscription rates to the ECB

Country	Shares in ECB's capital key (%)
Germany	24.4096
France	16.8703
Italy	14.9616
United Kingdom	14.7109
Spain	8.8300
Netherlands	4.2796
Belgium	2.8885
Sweden	2.6580
Austria	2.3663
Greece	2.0585
Portugal	1.9250
Denmark	1.6573
Finland	1.3991
Ireland	0.8384
Luxembourg	0.1469

Source: Adapted from European Monetary Institute/European Central Bank, www.ecb.int/about/abshare.htm, October 13, 1998.

8.7 CONCLUSION

The governing institutions of the EU possess a number of ways to affect internal monetary policy. These ways include directly legislating monetary policy objectives and indirectly eliciting preferred policies from the ECB. The accountability of ECB leaders to the governing institutions, particularly the European Council, may render the ECB vulnerable to political pressures from these sources. In response to constituent pressures, the governing institutions might resort to various means in their role of policy purveyors in order to remedy unpopular economic circumstances. The European Council in particular plays a decisive role in major policy matters. The link between Heads of State or Government and national electorates will drive European Council members to promote the interests of their domestic constituents. This chapter highlights both the legislative and extra-legislative means by which such goals might be achieved within the sphere of monetary policy.

Any attempts politically to influence monetary policy will be subject to high levels of approval within the EU. The European Council will serve as the primary field on which countries wage battles over monetary issues. Given the heterogeneity of economic situations around the union, demands for monetary policy changes will vary in timing, degree and duration. Unanimous consent within the Executive Board, Governing Council and European Council may be difficult, if not impossible, to secure for monetary policy under certain circumstances. Qualified majority support may also be difficult to secure. Monetary integration may serve as the catalyst to the disintegration of the growing European economic and political union.

NOTES

1. The Merger Treaty (1965) formally recognized the Committee of Permanent Representatives as the administrative support for policy development within the Council (Bieber and Palmer 1975, 312).
2. During the months of April, June and October, however, the Councils hold their meetings in Luxembourg.

9. Macroeconomic shocks to the European Monetary Union

9.1 INTRODUCTION

The viability of the European Monetary Union (EMU) depends upon its ability to accommodate pressures on the economies of its constituent countries. Shocks to aggregate supply and demand will test the ability of various mechanisms to stabilize European Union (EU) economies. Historical performances of EU economies may shed light on the ability of individual countries to respond to macroeconomic shocks. Differences in these abilities and the structure of domestic economies may give rise for calls for differential monetary policy responses that stretch the seams that bind the common currency arrangement.

This chapter employs the following organization. Section 2 provides a general discussion of shocks to aggregate demand and supply and their effects on the economy. Section 3 presents empirical findings on macroeconomic shocks to the economies of the EU over the past 30 years. Section 4 briefly examines the relationship between macroeconomic shocks and European labor markets. Section 5 considers different types of adjustment mechanisms. Section 6 identifies the gainers and losers from asymmetric shocks. The final section concludes.

9.2 SHOCKS TO AGGREGATE DEMAND AND SUPPLY

Economic shocks are changes in any of the underlying variables which affect aggregate demand and supply and lead to shifts in these curves. Such shocks affect important elements of the economy. Affected elements include prices, output and employment. Changes in these variables may affect different segments of the economy differentially. Such differences exist in timing, magnitude and location. Asymmetric shocks result in a wider variety of effects than symmetric shocks. Such asymmetry may result from heterogeneous economic structures, regulations and preferences. Shocks to aggregate demand and supply may lead to calls for adjustment assistance by adversely affected regions and sectors.

9.2.1 Aggregate Demand Shocks

Aggregate demand consists of the aggregate amount of goods and services that consumers desire for a given level of prices. The aggregate demand curve depicts the relationship between the quantity of products consumers want and different price levels. The curve slopes downward because of the negative relationship between output and the price level. Aggregate demand may shift in response to changes in one or more of its determinants. These determinants include money demand, government purchases and consumer preferences.

Changes in the money supply shift the curve outward or inward. Expansionary monetary policy that leads to increases of the money supply causes the aggregate demand curve to shift outward. Expansionary monetary policy leads to lower interest rates and costs of credit. Outward movements of the demand curve denote consumers' willingness to spend more money for a given quantity of purchases. Reduced money demand can also shift the aggregate demand curve outward as consumers prefer to use their money for purchases rather than to acquire and hold money balances. Reduced money demand leads to a rise in consumption.

Contractionary monetary policy that results in decreases of the money supply causes the aggregate demand curve to shift inward. Contractionary monetary policy leads to higher interest rates and costs of credit. Inward movements of the demand curve denote consumers' willingness to spend less money for a given quantity of purchases. Increased money demand can also shift the aggregate demand curve inward as consumers prefer to hold money rather than to make purchases. Increased money demand leads to a decline in consumption.

Government fiscal policy and consumer demand may also cause the aggregate demand curve to move. Expansionary fiscal policy in such forms as government purchases or tax reductions may shift the demand curve outward. Contractionary fiscal policy in such forms as reductions in government purchases or tax increases may shift the demand curve inward. Increases in consumer demand for consumption and/or investment may shift the demand curve outward. Decreases in consumer demand for consumption and/or investment may shift the demand curve inward.

The following simple examples depict the general implications of positive and negative shocks to aggregate demand for output, prices (the price level) and employment. Consider first the effects of a positive shock to aggregate demand. The aggregate demand curve shifts outward to reflect the increased aggregate demand. For a horizontal short-run aggregate supply curve or an upward-sloping aggregate supply curve, output increases above the level of full employment. Increased input and capacity utilization enables this output increase. Unemployment falls. Over time, the economy cannot sustain production above the level of full employment. Wages and prices increase until output returns to its original level in the long run.

Next, consider the effects of a negative shock to aggregate demand. The aggregate demand curve shifts inward to reflect the reduced aggregate demand. In the short run, demand falls at the existing price level. Decreased input and capacity utilization follows. Unemployment rises. Over time, wages and prices fall until output returns to its full employment level.

Governments may employ various stabilization policies to facilitate the adjustment of the economy to shifts in aggregate demand. Adversely affected regions and sectors may demand such accommodation from elected representatives. Stabilization tools include monetary and fiscal policy as well as regulatory policy. In the case of a negative demand shock, the monetary authority may reduce the cost of credit and lower the return on money holdings in order to stimulate investment and consumption. The fiscal authority may also consider expansionary fiscal policies to return economic activity to its full employment level.

These tools, however, face limitations. In the context of a single currency area, domestic monetary policy no longer ranks among the stabilization tools available. Only exchange rate manipulations of the common currency *vis-à-vis* the currencies of the rest of the world remain a possibility. The desirability of such actions depends upon, among other factors, the degree of economic homogeneity of the relevant monetary domain. Fiscal policy may remain as a national stabilization tool subject to statutory debt limits and the market's willingness to purchase additional credit instruments. However, it cannot serve as a straightforward substitute for monetary policy.

9.2.2 Aggregate Supply Shocks

Aggregate supply consists of the amount of goods and services available in the economy for a given level of prices. The aggregate supply curve depicts the relationship between the quantity of commodities available and different price levels. The slope of the aggregate supply curve depends upon the responsiveness of output production to changes in aggregate demand.

The slope of the aggregate supply curve has been a matter of theoretical and empirical debate. According to the Keynesian approach, the short-run aggregate supply curve slopes upward. This upward-sloping curve reflects market frictions and rigidities, as well as informational imperfections that prevent instantaneous responses to price and wage shocks. The Classical approach in contrast espouses a vertical aggregate supply curve characteristic of the perfect information, market-clearing model.

The consensus in the literature now holds that the short-run aggregate supply curve slopes upward. The long-run curve, however, is vertical at the level of output that corresponds to the full employment of available factor inputs and technology. Over the long run the position of the curve reflects the operation of real, not nominal, determinants. The question of what timeframe constitutes the long run remains.

The neo-Keynesian and neo-Classical frameworks comprise the two opposing approaches to the slope of the aggregate supply curve and prolonged adjustment periods. Both frameworks reflect theoretical advances over their predecessors: the Keynesian and Classical approaches. Neo-Keynesian explanations of the short-run aggregate supply curve employ models of sticky wages and prices. Sticky wage models include staggered contract models (Taylor 1980), indexed wage models (Fischer 1977), efficiency wage models (Yellen 1984; Shapiro and Stiglitz 1984) and union bargaining models (Blanchard and Fischer 1989; Manning 1993; Phipps 1992). These models rely on one or more rigidity for the less than instantaneous response of wages to price shocks. Sticky price models include the menu costs model (Mankiw 1985), near rational behavior models (Akerlof and Yellen 1985) and staggered price models (Taylor 1979; Blanchard 1983; Ball and Cecchetti 1988). These models also attempt to explain less than instantaneous price responses to price shocks.

Neo-Classical explanations of the short-run aggregate supply curve rely upon agents with imperfect information. The worker misperception model asserts that workers confuse an unanticipated price-level increase with an increase in the real wage (Friedman 1998). Employment rises in the short run due to the decline in real wages. Over the long run, however, workers realize that real wages have fallen and demand higher wages. Labor supply falls. The producer misinformation model asserts that individual producers confuse nominal and real prices (Lucas 1973). Producers misperceive a positive demand shock that leads to an increase in the aggregate price level with an increase in demand for their product. They respond to a positive shock by increasing output and factor inputs, notably labor, in the short run because they mistakenly believe that the real cost of labor has fallen. Producers later reduce their labor demand correspondingly.

An empirical study of the aggregate supply curve for OECD countries using data from the 1960s through 1990s finds that neo-Keynesian explanations of wage and price stickiness account for an upward-sloping short-run aggregate supply curve (Madsen 1998). Price and wage sluggishness leads to slow adjustment to demand shocks and therefore real effects on the economy. Tests of neo-Classical theories of aggregate supply demonstrate that both unexpected and expected shocks had real effects on wage and price adjustment. However, the evidence indicates that adjustment occurs more slowly than the worker and producer misperception models imply. Madsen's findings for the neo-Keynesian ridigity and neo-Classical imperfect information theories of aggregate supply evidence the real effects of demand shocks for durations of greater than one year.

The aggregate supply curve may shift in response to a number of real factors. These factors may lead to outward or inward shifts of the aggregate supply curve. Outward shifts correspond to positive shocks to aggregate supply. Positive shocks include any change in the underlying determinants of aggregate supply that reduce the cost of producing a unit of the good or service. Examples of positive shocks include technological improvements that increase productivity and reduce the cost of production, the elimination of costly regulations and the availability of new or additional factor inputs. Inward shifts of the aggregate supply curve correspond to negative shocks to aggregate supply. Negative shocks include any change in the underlying determinants of aggregate supply that increase the cost of producing a unit of the good or service. Examples of negative shocks include natural disasters and physical conflicts that destroy factor inputs, production facilities or infrastructure, the introduction of costly regulations and the introduction of artificial barriers to competition, such as the creation of monopolies or cartels.

The following simple examples depict the general implications of positive and negative shocks to aggregate supply for output, prices (the price level) and employment. Consider first the effects of a positive shock to aggregate supply. The positive shock causes the short-run aggregate supply curve to shift down (if horizontal) or right (if upward-sloping). Productivity and output rise. The original quantity of output is available at lower prices. Consumers therefore increase aggregate consumption and output rises. Unemployment falls. Permanent positive shocks to aggregate supply such as resource discoveries and technological improvements shift the long-run aggregate supply curve right to a higher level of full employment output.

Next, consider the effects of a negative shock to aggregate supply. For a fixed level of aggregate demand, a negative shock to aggregate supply causes a horizontal short-run aggregate supply curve to shift up or an upward-sloping short-run aggregate supply curve to shift left. As the aggregate supply curve shifts along the aggregate demand curve, the price level rises and output declines. The fall in output results in a level of production below the level possible at full employment and an increase in unemployment. Over the long run, the price level eventually may fall to its earlier level corresponding to full employment.

Government policy may assist in the adjustment process of the economy to negative supply shocks. Adversely affected sectors and regions may lobby the government for assistance. The two primary adjustment tools of the government are monetary and fiscal policy. In response to a negative shock, the monetary authority may endeavor to provide a boost to aggregate demand in order to jump-start the economy. The monetary authority may stimulate aggregate demand through expansionary policy that reduces the cost of credit to borrowers and reduces money demand to encourage investment and consumption. The government may also attempt to stimulate the economy through tax cuts and/or government purchases. Over the long run, governments may also adopt regulatory changes to assist the adjustment process.

9.2.3 Asymmetric Shocks

Macroeconomic shocks to aggregate demand and supply may have wide-ranging effects. These effects depend upon the shock's source, duration, timing, location, magnitude, the structure of the economy affected by the shock and the operation of one or more adjustment mechanisms. Differential effects may occur both within and across national boundaries.

The EU is vulnerable to asymmetric shocks, which affect countries and regions differentially because of the heterogeneity of its constituent economies. Asymmetric shocks may be country- or industry-specific. In the former case, shocks affect one or more countries differentially because of characteristics peculiar to that country. Examples of sources of country-specific shocks include labor market regulations, tax structures, individual preferences and regulatory policy.

A common monetary policy could also affect countries differentially due to national preferences regarding saving and spending. Currie (1997), for example, notes that British households have a higher interest elasticity of demand than German households. For this reason, the British economy may respond more strongly to changes in interest rates.

Industry-specific shocks affect industries differentially because of characteristics peculiar to that industry. Sources of industry-specific shocks include factor market regulations, technological developments, tax and regulatory policy and changes in the relative prices of factor inputs. One example of a shock due to regulatory policy change is the closure of British coalmines during the 1980s.

Vulnerability to country- and industry-specific shocks depends upon differences in the sources of these shocks across countries and industries and the mechanisms available for adjustment. Real and nominal rigidities in particular may serve to propagate the effects of shocks over time. However, some national differences particularly concerning regulatory policy have declined following the implementation of the Single Market Program and successive efforts to adopt common regulations across the EU. Nevertheless significant differences remain.

9.3 EMPIRICAL STUDIES OF ECONOMIC SHOCKS TO THE EMU

A number of studies attempt to examine the occurrence and effects of different economic shocks to the EMU. These models seek to identify the types and frequency of shocks, as well as the adjustment processes of the relevant countries and regions. These models consider the behavior of such variables as real exchange rates, annual GDP (nominal and real), consumer price indices, output and monetary aggregates. The evidence found using these models bears directly on the viability of the EMU as a single currency area.

9.3.1 Aggregate Demand and Supply Shocks

The economies of the member countries of the EU have experienced a number of shocks to aggregate demand and supply over the past 30 years. Such shocks include the oil price rises of the 1970s, the German reunification of 1990 and different periods of contractionary US Federal Reserve policy. These shocks affect domestic economic variables and may lead to hardships for European consumers and producers.

Optimum currency area theory suggests that regions facing similar economic shocks may represent a viable single currency area. A common monetary policy would be suitable to respond to economic disturbances affecting the region. In order to determine whether the countries of the EU comprise an optimum currency area, economists have undertaken a number of studies of the correlation of demand and supply shocks affecting the region.

Two empirical measures may be useful in determining whether or not two or more countries are subject to similar shocks. The first measure consists of the correlation of demand and supply shocks between these countries. The more correlated demand and supply shocks between countries are, the more likely that these countries could adhere to a common monetary policy. The less correlated demand and supply shocks between countries are, the less symmetric the relevant disturbances are and the less likely that these countries could adhere to a common monetary policy. Rather, countries subject to different shocks would retain independent monetary policy that they could employ to suit their respective circumstances. The second measure consists of the relative sizes of shocks affecting the countries. The more similar the size of the shocks, the more likely that a common policy response would suffice. The greater the difference in the size of shocks, the more likely that different policy responses would be necessary.

Bayoumi and Eichengreen (1993) attempt to capture the symmetry of shocks hitting 11 EU countries to assess the viability of a common currency among these countries. They estimate correlation coefficients for demand and supply shocks between Germany and ten EU member countries for the period 1963–88. The findings of their report are detailed in Table 9.1.

This table reveals relatively close correlations of supply shocks affecting France, Belgium, the Netherlands and Denmark with Germany. It also reveals the relatively close correlations of demand shocks affecting France, Belgium and Denmark with Germany. However, the correlations of demand shocks of these countries with Germany are less than the correlations of supply shocks.

Table 9.1 Correlation coefficients for demand and supply shocks between Germany and 10 EU countries (1963–88)

Country	Supply shocks	Demand shocks
Germany	1.00	1.00
France	0.54	0.35
Belgium	0.61	0.33
Netherlands	0.59	0.17
Denmark	0.59	0.39
United Kingdom	0.11	0.16
Italy	0.23	0.17
Spain	0.31	–0.07
Ireland	–0.06	–0.08
Portugal	0.21	0.21
Greece	0.14	0.19

Source: Adapted from Bayoumi and Eichengreen (1993), Table 7.4, p. 211: Correlation Coefficients between Germany and 10 EU Countries (1963–88).

Table 9.1 also reveals low correlations of supply and demand shocks for the remainder of the EU countries with Germany. The UK, Ireland, Portugal and Spain in particular return low correlation coefficients. These results suggest a division of EU countries with respect to the correlation of supply and demand shocks.

Bayoumi and Eichengreen (1993) also attempt to find the relative sizes of shocks affecting these 11 countries. Using the same data set they arrive at the results detailed in Table 9.2.

This table reveals that Germany, Denmark and the Netherlands experience supply shocks of the same magnitude. Belgium experiences supply shocks of a similar magnitude. The United Kingdom, Spain and Portugal face supply shocks of rather greater magnitude. The results for demand shocks show that Germany, France, Belgium and the Netherlands face similarly sized shocks as Spain, Greece and the UK. Ireland and Portugal face the greatest standard deviation of demand shocks followed by Italy and Denmark.

Funke (1997) undertakes a more inclusive analysis of the correlation of demand and supply shocks between European countries using annual data from 1970–93. His results indicate that the demand and supply shocks affecting EU countries over this period were relatively asymmetric. The highest demand shock correlations occurred between the following pairs of countries: France and Germany, the Netherlands and Luxembourg, Belgium and Austria, Luxembourg and Belgium, and Luxembourg and Germany. The highest supply shock correlations occurred between the following country pairs: Germany and Austria, the Netherlands and Germany, Germany and Austria, Italy and France, and Belgium and the Netherlands. The lowest demand and supply shock correlations involved countries at the periphery of Europe: Denmark, Finland, Greece, Italy and Poland.

Table 9.2 Relative size of supply and demand shocks affecting 11 EU countries

Country	Supply shocks	Demand shocks
Germany	0.017	0.014
France	0.012	0.012
Belgium	0.015	0.016
Netherlands	0.017	0.015
Denmark	0.017	0.021
United Kingdom	0.026	0.017
Italy	0.022	0.020
Spain	0.022	0.015
Ireland	0.021	0.034
Portugal	0.029	0.028
Greece	0.030	0.016

Source: Adapted from Bayoumi and Eichengreen (1993), Table 7.6, p. 215: Standard deviations of AS & AD shocks (sizes of shocks).

Funke's study also compares demand and supply shocks to West German Länder with demand and supply shocks affecting EU countries. He chooses the German Länder as a benchmark currency union with which to compare the countries of the EU. Funke finds the correlations of supply and demand shocks between German Länder to be much higher than in the case of EU countries.

Funke suggests that the lower demand and supply shock correlations between EU countries relative to the corresponding correlations between German Länder evidences the occurrence of asymmetric shocks affecting these countries. He attributes the varied incidence of these shocks to product, factor input and export market differences (ibid., 466). He anticipates that further differentiation will ensue from the Single Market Program. Subsequently, he expresses doubt that the 16 countries together comprise an area suited to a single currency and a common monetary policy.

Von Hagen and Neumann (1994) examine the behavior of real exchange rates to determine the symmetry of economic disturbances affecting European countries. They note that the real exchange rate between two countries can reveal the occurrence of asymmetric shocks due to its role as an adjustment mechanism. For example, a relatively stable real exchange rate is evidence of similar shocks affecting two countries. If the real exchange rate is unstable, its relationship suggests the occurrence of asymmetric shocks.

Von Hagen and Neumann (1994) examine the variance of the real exchange rates between six German Länder and eight European countries. They employ seasonally unadjusted price and exchange rate data for the Länder and countries shown in Table 9.3. The German Länder again serve as the benchmark monetary union.

Table 9.3 West German Länder and European countries studied by Von Hagen and Neumann (1994)

German Länder	European countries
Bavaria	Austria
Baden-Württemberg	Belgium
Berlin	Denmark
Hesse	France
Northrhine-Westphalia	Italy
Saarland	Luxembourg
–	Netherlands
–	UK

Von Hagen and Neumann (1994) utilize the standard deviations of real exchange rate shocks measured by price level changes to indicate the correlation of economic disturbances between Länder and between Länder and European countries. Table 9.4 reports the results of analyses to identify changes in the real exchange rates at both monthly and quarterly intervals for four sample periods.

The standard deviation of real exchange rate changes at both monthly and quarterly frequencies are relatively close between the German Länder for all periods. Through the early 1980s, the European countries exhibit greater standard deviations of real exchange rate changes *vis-à-vis* the German Länder. However, their relative standard deviations show declines. In part, the reduction in standard deviations may be due to membership in the European Monetary System (EMS) or adherence to a Deutschmark exchange rate peg, and the reduction of further trade barriers between EU countries. Von Hagen and Neumann (1994) conclude that Austria, Belgium, France, Germany,

Table 9.4 Monthly and quarterly exchange rate changes

	BA	BE	BW	HE	NW	SA	A	B	DK	F	I	L	NL	UK
Monthly real exchange rate changes														
1973–78	16	21	16	17	17	19	51	90	123	167	225	95	96	217
1979–82	11	17	12	13	12	13	36	91	86	101	98	96	44	204
1983–86	12	20	11	12	11	13	31	45	60	55	66	47	31	165
1987–89	7	10	8	10	7	7	21	21	43	28	59	21	24	126
Quarterly real change rate changes														
1973–78	26	34	24	31	27	27	100	182	187	379	492	163	142	414
1979–82	24	28	18	20	18	20	71	208	185	209	172	189	102	465
1983–86	15	28	14	15	15	18	53	71	96	109	119	84	45	379
1987–89	9	14	8	10	8	8	34	36	60	43	111	34	44	125

Source: From Von Hagen and Neumann (1994), Table 1, p. 238: Standard Deviations of Real Exchange Rate Shocks [average over six German Länder, 1/1000].

Luxembourg and the Netherlands represent members of a viable single currency area based on real exchange rate evidence.

Chamie et al. (1994) undertake several tests to estimate the impact of supply and demand shocks (both real and nominal) affecting the USA and 13 European countries. They also examine the speed of adjustment to shocks given existing nominal rigidities. Their study considers shocks to nine regions within the USA, as well as to the USA as a whole. They compare the US results with the results for the European countries. Their data consists of measures of the money supply (M1) and indices of industrial production and consumer prices from 1970:1–1994: 4.

Chamie et al. (1994) first attempt to estimate the amount of output variance attributable to supply and demand shocks. They estimate the contributions of the different shocks for multiple time horizons ranging from 1 quarter to 48 quarters. Their results indicate that supply shocks affect output in the short run to a greater extent in Europe than the USA. Supply shocks contribute half of the variance in output in the first quarter in the UK, Spain, the Netherlands, Sweden, Norway, Portugal and Greece. The inclusion of the UK, the Netherlands and Norway may stem from the relative importance of the oil and natural gas sectors to their economies. Supply shocks account for over 50 percent of output fluctuations in the remaining countries (Germany, France, Italy, Belgium, Switzerland and Austria) only after at least four quarters. Shocks to real demand have their greatest impact on the following countries within the first two quarters: Germany, France, Italy, Belgium and Switzerland. Nominal shocks play the greatest role in Belgium and Switzerland. However, their impact pales in comparison to the supply and real demand shocks.

Next, the authors estimate the symmetry of disturbances to supply and demand (see Table 9.5). They decompose the structural shocks to each region or country into common and specific stochastic components. They then measure and present the relative contribution of the common component to the region- or country-specific component. Countries that experience similar contributions of the common component face relatively symmetric shocks.

The common component of structural supply shocks contributes approximately the same amount to output variability in France, the Netherlands, Belgium and Austria. The common component explains a much larger amount of output variance for Germany and Switzerland. The common component of structural shocks to real demand contributes similarly to output variability in France, Belgium and the Netherlands. The common component again explains much more of Germany and Switzerland's output variance. Shocks to Germany may comprise the largest single element of the common component. These European countries, with the exceptions of Germany and Switzerland, face much more asymmetric shocks relative to the nine US regions.

Table 9.5 Symmetry of supply and demand shocks

Countries	Relative contribution of common component (%)	
	Supply shocks	Real demand shocks
Germany	51	51
France	12	22
United Kingdom	18	13
Italy	5*	5*
Spain	25	12
Netherlands	13	26
Belgium	14	20
Switzerland	44	37
Austria	12	11
Sweden	1*	4*
Norway	0*	0*
Portugal	5*	28
Greece	7*	0

Note: Shocks that are not statistically related to the common component at a 5% significance level.

Source: Adopted from Chamie et al. (1994), Table 4: Variance Decomposition of Structural Shocks – European Model with 13 Countries.

The authors then examine the speed of adjustment to shocks given the existence of nominal (price) rigidities. They estimate the slope of the short-run aggregate supply curve for 12 European countries and the entire USA. For higher levels of nominal rigidities, the supply curve is more vertical. Monetary policy can play a greater role in affecting output when the aggregate supply curve is vertical. Chamie et al. (1994) report the supply curve slopes in Table 9.6.

Average quarterly inflation exhibits a positive relationship with the slope of supply curves reflecting relative nominal flexibility in countries with relatively high inflation. The following European countries have the flattest supply curves: France, Austria, Switzerland, Germany and Belgium. The last three of these countries have greater nominal rigidities than the USA as evidenced by the slopes of their supply curves. The more flexible countries correspond to those of the European periphery. In these regions, prices may respond more quickly to economic disturbances.

Chamie et al. (1994) also examine the role of shocks in the long run where the aggregate supply curve is vertical. For supply, real demand and nominal shocks to output the USA responds more slowly than the European countries. For the case of shocks to prices, the USA responds only slightly more quickly than Germany, Switzerland, Austria and Belgium. Prices in Italy and Spain

Table 9.6 Supply curve slopes and average quarterly inflation

Country	Slope of supply curve	Average quarterly inflation
Portugal	5.84437	0.04301
United Kingdom	2.22443	0.02337
Spain	1.68577	0.02918
Greece	0.73819	0.04230
Sweden	0.45550	0.02049
Italy	0.30609	0.02876
Netherlands	0.28639	0.01070
France	0.22837	0.01881
Austria	0.14008	0.01129
United States	0.13255	0.01543
Switzerland	0.07594	0.00956
Germany	0.06436	0.00876
Belgium	0.06306	0.01396

Source: Adapted from Chamie et al. (1994), Table 6, p. 21: Slope of Short-term Supply Curve.

take even longer to adjust to shocks. The authors attribute the difference in adjustment time between European countries and the USA to the nominal exchange rate as a means of adjustment in the former.

9.3.2 Shocks within the European Monetary System

The EMS has apparently led to convergence in the responses of participating countries to economic shocks. One reason for the similarity of responses stems from the exchange rate parity grid within the Exchange Rate Mechanism ERM. This grid limited countries' ability to manipulate their real exchange rate in response to shocks.

An examination of the adjustment processes of EMS members by Bayoumi and Taylor (1995) yields several results. First, participation in the ERM has not affected the kinds of shocks hitting the participating economies. Second, EMS membership has led to increased similarity of responses by participants. Third, price and output responses have slowed in countries participating in the arrangement. The authors attribute the slowdown in price and output responses to the limitations of participation in a fixed exchange rate system (1995, 326).

The EMS may have facilitated coordination of monetary policy actions between member countries for the given period. Ultimately, however, it was a fixed exchange rate arrangement in which countries retained sovereignty over monetary and fiscal policy as ultimate tools of adjustment. Governments could therefore undertake policies that led to revaluations of their currency *vis-à-vis* other currencies within the ERM grid in response to constituent pressures. In fact, revaluations took place on numerous occasions, as Table 9.7 demonstrates.

Table 9.7 Exchange rate adjustments during the EMS (1979–92)

Date	Currency	% Realignment
3/13/79	EMS began	
9/24/79	DEM	+2
	DKK	–2.9
12/3/79	DKK	–4.76
3/23/81	ITL	–6
10/5/81	DEM, NLG	+5.5
	FRF, ITL	–3
2/22/82	BEF	–8.50%
	DKK	–3
6/14/82	DEM, NLG	+4.25
	ITL	–2.75
	FRF	–5.75
3/22/83	DEM	+5.5
	NLG	+3.5
	DKK	+2.5
	BEF	+1.5
	FRF, ITL	–2.5
	IEP	–3.5
7/22/85	BEF, DKK, DEM, FRF,	+2
	IEP, NLG ITL	–6
4/7/86	DEK NLG	+3
	BEF, DKK	+1
	FRF	–3
8/4/86	IEP	–8
1/12/87	DEM, NLG	+3
	BEF	+2
1/19/89	Entry of ESP	
1/8/90	ITL (narrow band)	–3.7
10/8/90	Entry of GBP	
4/6/92	Entry of PTE	
9/14/92	ITL	–7.0
9/16/92	ITL & GBP withdraw	
	ESP	–5.0
11/22/92	PTE, ESP	–6.0

Source: Adapted from Gretschmann et al. in Gretschmann, ed. (1993), Table 1, p. 36: Chronology of the EMS. [Original Source: Bank of England 1992.]

Only three of the countries participating in the EMU revalued on more occasions than they devalued. In contrast, three countries devalued on more occasions than they revalued, one country (Italy) devalued seven times before withdrawing, one country entered late and withdrew in less than four years following two devaluations, and one country (the UK) withdrew within less than two years of joining. Monetary policy as a sovereign policy tool appears to have played an important role. Without the ability to adjust domestic monetary conditions the system may not have functioned as long as it did.

9.4 MACROECONOMIC SHOCKS AND THE EUROPEAN LABOR MARKETS

European labor markets may be particularly vulnerable to the effects of adverse shocks. Since the 1970s, European unemployment has exhibited an upward trend. A number of factors contribute to labor market rigidities and therefore the limitations of labor market flexibility as a mechanism of adjustment to economic disturbances. For this reason, the effects of economic shocks on labor markets represent an issue of concern in the context of the EMU.

9.4.1 Unemployment: a Western European Problem

Unemployment has been a growing problem for the economies of Western Europe since the 1970s. The rise of this problem follows the expansion of governmental regulations of European labor markets (Siebert 1997, 50). Not only have the overall numbers of unemployed been on the rise, but these numbers have also been increasingly persistent. As these trends persist, the potential destabilizing effects of adverse shocks become increasingly of concern. Table 9.8 presents the number of laborers, employed and unemployed, for the years 1981 through 2000 (projected) for the EU.

This table reflects the increase in the EU labor force from the accession of new countries to the EU. It also reflects changes in the unemployment rate. The overall trend in EU unemployment is upward.

The relatively high rates of European unemployment may be the result of various institutional characteristics of European labor markets. These institutions include collective bargaining, unemployment benefits and other forms of labor market legislation. The latter include job security legislation, employment-related taxes, mandatory benefits provisions and minimum wage legislation. These institutions affect labor demand, supply and the wage-setting process (Siebert 1997, 43).

Table 9.8 European Union employment statistics (1982–2000) (in millions)

Year	Labour force	Employment	Unemployment	Unempl./Labour (%)
1982	146.7	134.2	12.5	9.31
1983	147.7	133.6	14.1	10.55
1984	149.0	133.9	15.1	11.28
1985	150.0	134.5	15.5	11.52
1986	151.4	135.6	15.7	11.58
1987	152.4	137.1	15.3	11.16
1988	153.8	139.4	14.4	10.33
1989	154.8	141.7	13.1	9.24
1990	156.2	144.0	12.3	8.54
1991	165.3	151.4	13.9	9.18
1992	164.9	149.1	15.8	10.60
1993	164.8	146.6	18.2	12.41
1994	165.2	146.2	19.0	13.00
1995	165.5	147.0	18.5	12.59
1996	166.2	147.4	18.8	12.75
1997	166.9	148.2	18.7	12.62
1998 (proj.)	167.4	149.7	17.7	11.82
1999 (proj.)	168.2	150.8	17.4	11.54
2000 (proj.)	169.0	151.9	17.0	11.19

Source: Adapted from *OECD Economic Outlook*, 64, December 1998. Annex Table 23, Labour Force, Employment and Unemployment, p. A-247.

Collective bargaining consists of union negotiations regarding various aspects of the employee–employer relationship. Most notably, collective bargaining concerns the determination of wages, non-wage benefits, termination conditions and post-employment compensation. These factors affect the wage and non-wage costs of labor faced by employers. As these costs rise, employers hire fewer employees and unemployment rises.

Collective bargaining plays an important role in the EU. Only two Western European countries do not possess strong trade unions: the United Kingdom and Switzerland (not currently an EU member) (Nickell 1997, 62). Union influence depends not only upon union presence in a country but also on its power to affect wages beyond its unionized membership. The union coverage ratio represents the amount of the labor force over which union agreements extend. Table 9.9 presents measures of union density and coverage within a number of OECD countries.

Table 9.9 Union density and coverage

Country	Union density (%)	Union coverage index*
Austria	46.2	3
Belgium	51.2	3
Denmark	71.4	3
Finland	72.0	3
France	9.8	3
Germany (W)	32.9	3
Ireland	49.7	3
Italy	38.8	3
Netherlands	25.5	3
Norway	56.0	3
Portugal	31.8	3
Spain	11.0	3
Sweden	82.5	3
Switzerland	26.6	2
United Kingdom	39.1	2
Canada	35.8	2
United States	15.6	1
Japan	25.4	2
Australia	40.4	3
New Zealand	44.8	2

*Note:** Numbers in the Union Coverage Index column correspond to the following percentages of the labor force covered by collective bargaining by unions: 3 = greater than 70% of workers; 2 = between 25 and 70% of workers; 1 = less than 25% of workers.

Source: Adapted from Nickell (1997), Table 4, p. 61: Features of OECD Labor Markets 1, 1989–94, Union Density adapted from Table 5, p. 63: Features of OECD Labor Markets A 1989–94 (source: see bottoms of tables).

This table reflects the wide extent of union coverage within the EU. None of the listed EU countries have a lower union coverage ratio than the USA. Nickell (1997, 47) and Layard et al. (1991) find a positive relationship between unemployment rates and measures of union coverage. However, Nickell (1997, 68) notes that higher levels of coordination in wage negotiations between unions and employers may prevent increases in the unemployment rate due to union pressure for increased compensation and employment protection.

The unemployment benefit systems of European countries affect the incentives that unemployed laborers face to return to active employment. Two aspects of unemployment benefits bear directly on the incentives to seek re-employment by displaced workers. The first aspect concerns the percentage of full-time wages that workers receive as compensation while unemployed: the benefit replacement rate. The greater this percentage is, the lower the incentive to return to gainful employment is.[1] The second aspect concerns the duration of unemployment compensation. The longer the availability of benefits, the lower is the return to remaining unemployed.[2] Table 9.10 presents the benefit replacement rates and benefit duration for selected OECD countries.

Table 9.10 Benefit replacement rates and duration

Country	Benefit replacement rate (%)	Benefit duration (years)
Austria	50	2
Belgium	60	4
Denmark	90	2.5
Finland	63	2
France	57	3
Germany (W)	63	4
Ireland	37	4
Italy	20	0.5
Netherlands	70	2
Norway	65	1.5
Portugal	65	0.8
Spain	70	3.5
Sweden	80	1.2
Switzerland	70	1
United Kingdom	38	4
Canada	59	1
United States	50	0.5
Japan	60	0.5
Australia	36	4
New Zealand	30	4

Source: Adapted from Nickell (1997), Table 4, p. 61: Features of OECD Labor Markets I, 1989–94; Union Density adapted from Table 5, p. 63: Features of OECD Labor Markets II, 1989–94.

Although three EU countries offer lower benefit replacement rates, all EU countries provide benefits for at least as long as the USA. Only Italy offers an apparently less comprehensive benefits plan than the USA.

Other forms of labor market legislation that affect unemployment are job security legislation, employment-related taxes, mandatory benefits provisions and minimum wage legislation. The more that such legislation increases the cost of labor, the greater the corresponding unemployment rate. Job security legislation consists of legislation that prescribes the hiring and firing procedures that employers must follow, as well as levels of compensation at severance. Employment-related taxes include payroll taxes. Mandatory benefits include healthcare and pension provisions. Minimum wage legislation dictates the lowest allowable wages employers may legally pay laborers.

Restrictive labor market legislation has a negative effect on overall employment. It serves to increase the effective cost of labor and subsequently reduce the demand for laborers. Citing a 1993 OECD study, Nickell (1997, 49) reports job security legislation to be a leading cause of European unemployment. Similarly, Jackman (1995, Table 7) finds a positive correlation between countrywide minimum wage coverage and high unemployment rates for the following EU countries: Belgium, France, Greece, Portugal and Spain (Nickell 1997, 51).

High unemployment rates represent only one side of the European unemployment problem. The other side of the problem consists of the growing persistence of unemployment in the EU. Table 9.11 lists long-term unemployment rates for European countries as a percentage of total unemployment in 1992.

Long-term unemployment comprises over a third of total unemployment in 9 out of 15 EU countries. Table 9.12 from Englander and Egebo (1993) highlights changes in the percentage of long-term unemployed for nine EU countries over time.

For all but three countries (Denmark, the Netherlands and the UK), long-term unemployment has risen between 1983 and 1990. Viñals and Jimeno (1998, 42) point out that long-term unemployment in the EU may increasingly consist of both structural and cyclical unemployment due to the lengthy duration of unemployed episodes.

The persistence of relatively high unemployment rates may stem from several features of the European labor markets. These features raise the cost to employers of utilizing labor as a factor input. The unemployment benefit system, along with collective bargaining practices and other labor market legislation, increase the cost of labor to producers. For this reason, they lead to reductions in the demand for labor. Obstfeld and Peri (1998, 230) write that the relatively high costs of labor ‘discourage job creation, increase “wait” unemployment and make underground activities more attractive.’ So long as employers cannot

Table 9.11 Long-term unemployment in the EU (1992)

Country	Long-term unemployment as a percentage of total unemployment in 1992
Europe	41.2
Belgium	59
Denmark	27
Germany	33.5
Greece	49.7
Spain	44
France	34.6
Ireland	58.9
Italy	58.2
Luxembourg	17.5
Netherlands	17
Austria	44
Portugal	31.1
Finland	8.2
Sweden	8.1
United Kingdom	35.4

Source: Adapted from Mehrez and Valla (1998), Figure 3. [Original source: Eurostat 1992.]

adjust labor costs and quantity quickly, especially in the downward direction following negative shocks, the demand for labor will be lower than would otherwise be the case. Differences in these mechanisms across countries may in part explain differences in the persistence of unemployment across regions.

In addition, Bean (1994, 532) identifies four persistence mechanisms in European labor markets. Two of these mechanisms affect the demand side of the market and two the supply side. He notes two constraints on shifts in the demand curve for labor. First, firms economize on their demand for labor because of the relatively high costs of hiring and firing employees. Second, firms utilize labor and capital in fixed proportions and are therefore slow to adjust to shocks affecting either factor. On the supply side, Bean places the blame on labor itself. The first mechanism he identifies rests on the insider–outsider theory of unemployment.[3] According to this theory, insiders set wages above the market-clearing level. Negative shocks displace incumbent insiders and reduce their numbers leading to greater current and future unemployment due to the difficulty of outsiders finding work. Second, he submits that

Table 9.12 Long-term unemployment measures for the years 1983 and 1990

Country/Year	Share of long-term unemployed in total unemployment (%)	Share of long-term unemployed in total unemployment (%)
	1983	1990
Germany	39.3	49.0[1]
France	42.2	43.9
Italy	57.7	70.4[1]
United Kingdom	47.0	40.8[1]
Spain	52.4	54.0
Netherlands	50.5	49.9[1]
Belgium	66.3	76.3[1]
Denmark	33.0	25.9[1]
Ireland	36.9	67.3[1]

Note: [1] Data for 1989.

Source: Adapted from Englander and Egebo (1993), Table 4 p. 20: Labour market rigidity in ERM countries.

unemployed workers become locked out of the labor market with the passage of time due to skill depreciation and reduced search efficacy.[4]

9.4.2 Labor Market Flexibility as a Macroeconomic Adjustment Mechanism

Optimum currency area theory notes the importance of labor market flexibility as one type of macroeconomic adjustment mechanism. Flexibility in labor markets provides for the requisite change in relative prices necessary for real exchange rates to change. Labor markets may adjust to shifts in labor demand through flexibility in wages, location and participation rates.

Flexibility in labor markets may allow producers to adjust wages and the number of laborers employed, and to more quickly and less expensively respond to economic shocks and return production to full employment levels. Without labor market flexibility, producers hire fewer employees to reduce expected labor-related costs. Subsequently unemployment reaches higher levels than it would in a more flexible labor market. Similarly, inflexible labor markets may lead to prolonged adjustments to economic disturbances and, ultimately, a slow return to equilibrium.

The first dimension along which labor markets may adjust to economic disturbances consists of the wage rate. Flexible wages enable employers to raise or lower the wage paid to workers without hindrance. In reality, however, wages tend to exhibit downward rigidity preventing employers from lowering wages in response to negative disturbances. Collective bargaining and various legislative provisions may bolster the downward rigidity of wages and other labor-related costs. Employers may respond to such limitations by hiring fewer workers and utilizing relatively more temporary employment contracts to lower their expected labor costs.

The second dimension along which labor markets may adjust consists of inter-regional migration. European migration rates, however, are relatively low both within and between countries, particularly in comparison with the USA. Low migration rates have persisted in spite of the reduction of barriers to movement between EU countries (Molle and Van Mourik 1988, 336). Possible causes of low migration include language and culture barriers, limited pension portability and uncertainty regarding skill recognition.

Gros (1998) suggests that thin housing markets may also play a role in explaining relatively low migration rates within Europe. He notes that: 'Housing and labor are the most regulated markets in most [EU] member states ...' (1998, 77). He observes a negative relationship between owner-occupied housing and inter-regional migration. Increased flexibility in European housing markets might facilitate migration within the EU in response to adverse shocks.

The third dimension along which labor markets may adjust consists of labor force participation rates. These rates vary across the EU: for example, participation rates hover around 50 percent for Ireland, Italy and Spain (*OECD Employment Outlook* 1996, 5). However, the Scandinavian countries and Portugal experience participation rates closer to 70 percent (ibid.).

Decressin and Fatas (1995) find that participation rates respond more quickly to shocks to labor demand than unemployment rates and migration. During the first three years following such a shock, changes in participation rates represent the principal adjustment mechanism within the labor market. The authors contrast this result with that of the USA where migration carries the greatest amount of the burden of adjustment in the short run.

9.4.3 Regional Labor Market Characteristics and Performance

Labor market characteristics and performance vary across the EU. Explanations for such variation lie in differences in regional regulations and preferences. These variations provide further evidence of the division of the EU into a core and periphery.

Unemployment rates vary across the EU. Table 9.13 presents aggregate unemployment rates for EU countries for selected years between 1985 and 1995, along with a projection for 1999.

Table 9.13 Unemployment rates for EU countries for selected years between 1985 and 1999

Country	1985	1990	1995	1999 proj.
Austria	4.2	4.7	5.9	6.0
Belgium	12.4	9.6	13.1	11.5
Denmark	9.0	9.6	10.3	6.0
Finland	5.0	3.5	17.2	9.7
France	10.2	8.9	11.5	11.2
Germany	8.0	6.2	9.4	10.8
Greece	7.8	7.0	10.0	9.8
Ireland	16.8	12.9	12.1	8.4
Italy	8.6	9.1	12.0	12.1
Luxembourg	1.7	1.3	3.0	3.2
Netherlands	9.2	6.0	7.0	4.2
Portugal	8.7	4.7	7.2	5.3
Spain	20.9	15.7	22.7	17.8
Sweden	2.8	1.6	7.7	6.3
United Kingdom	11.6	5.9	8.6	7.4

Source: Adapted from *OECD Economic Outlook*, 64, December 1998, Annex Table 21: Unemployment rates: commonly used definitions.

Five of the 12 countries entering the first round of EMU have unemployment levels in the double digits. In contrast, none of the three non-participants has unemployment in the double digits.

Siebert (1997, 41) suggests that the labor markets of EU countries fall into four categories based on performance. The first category consists of the Netherlands and the United Kingdom. Both countries have experienced declining unemployment since the middle of the 1980s. The second category consists of Germany, which is a unique position given the accession of the Eastern Länder in 1990. Compared to the first category, Germany has undertaken few institutional changes aimed at reducing unemployment.

The third and fourth categories contain the remainder of the EU countries. The third group includes France, Italy, Spain, Greece and Austria. These countries have done little to reform their labor markets. The fourth group consists of Sweden, Finland and Norway (not yet an EU member). These countries began reforms of their welfare systems in the 1990s. Denmark and Belgium fall between the French–German and French–Dutch categories, respectively.

Regional differences in unemployment result from differentiated economic structures, areas of production and legislation. Viñals and Jimeno (1998) estimate that region-specific factors account for approximately two-thirds of the conditional variance of regional unemployment rates in Europe for periods under five years (Obstfeld and Peri 1998, 224). This result does not distinguish between the incidence of asymmetric shocks across regions and the incidence of symmetric shocks yielding differential effects due to regional economic heterogeneities. To address this uncertainty they model the effects of a symmetric shock on different countries. Approximately three-quarters of EU unemployment results from country-specific shocks in this model. In contrast Eichengreen (1993, 145) finds that labor market disturbances are not significantly different across European countries. His finding suggests that differences in national labor markets account for regional differences in unemployment rates.

Variation in labor-related costs may in part explain differences in unemployment rates and persistence across the EU. Mehrez and Valla (1998, 7) point out differences in non-wage labor costs for several EU countries (see Table 9.14).

Table 9.14 Non-wage labor costs

Country	Non-wage labor costs as a percentage of total labor costs
Belgium	50.9
Denmark	16.9
Germany	44
Greece	39
Spain	44.7
France	48.6
Ireland	29.6
Italy	49.7
Luxembourg	32.3
Netherlands	45.4
Portugal	44
United Kingdom	27

Source: Adapted from Mehrez and Valla (1998), Figure 4. [Original Source: *European Economy*, 62, 1996.]

Non-wage labor costs represent the lowest percentage of total labor costs in Denmark and the United Kingdom. Non-wage labor costs correspond to the highest percentage of total labor costs in Belgium, Italy and France.

Migration rates differ between countries of northern and southern Europe. DeGrauwe and Vanhaverbeke (1991, 222), for example, find that labor is domestically less mobile in southern European countries. However, the higher rate of self-employment in southern countries may counterbalance lower labor mobility (Nickell 1997, 59). Low migration combined with high unemployment may increase the persistence of unemployment.

Differences in labor market performance within and across the countries of the EU may also result from variation in the composition of productive sectors across regions (Eichengreen 1993, 133). Regional labor market performance reflects the performance of the economic sectors in which it is employed. For example, negative shocks to the coal, oil and natural gas industries may adversely affect industries that depend on these resources as factor inputs. Subsequently production may fall in regions whose industries employ these resources and local unemployment may rise. Similarly, a fall in consumer demand for manufactured products may adversely affect regions that concentrate in the production of manufactured goods.

Eichengreen (1993) highlights the regional disparity in labor market performance for the United Kingdom and Italy. An approximate North–South division characterizes regional differences in labor market performance for both countries. In the UK, the North possesses a higher concentration of manufacturing and energy-sector-dependent firms. The South in contrast specializes in light manufacturing and services. The performance of the regional labor markets reflects the fortunes of their respective production sectors. The North fared much worse than the prosperous South during the 1980s.

Differences in labor market performance in Italy correspond to the fortunes of the industries of the North and South. However, in contrast to the UK the North of Italy has been relatively more prosperous than the South. The economy of northern Italy concentrates on the production of services and manufacturing. The economy of southern Italy concentrates on agriculture and heavy industry.

Labor markets may serve as a limited mechanism of adjustment to economic shocks within the EU. European labor markets are less flexible than their counterparts in the USA. This inflexibility stems from a combination of collective bargaining arrangements and national legislation affecting the terms of employment. Empirical evidence further suggests that laborers have a low propensity to migrate in response to adverse shocks. Furthermore, differences in industrial composition across regions and other barriers prevent rapid adjustment in labor markets. For this reason, the countries of the EMU may rely on other mechanisms of adjustment.

9.5 GAINERS AND LOSERS FROM ASYMMETRIC SHOCKS: SOURCES OF PRESSURES ON MONETARY POLICY

Asymmetric economic disturbances imply differential effects on different constituencies within the EU. For this reason, both gainers and losers may exist within EMU. Politicians will encounter pressures for policy responses to economic disturbances from those constituencies that are adversely affected. These pressures will vary positively with the extent to which the shocks adversely affect these constituents and inversely with the effect to which other adjustment mechanisms successfully operate. The effects of shocks and their distribution depend upon the economic activities across the EMU.

9.5.1 Economic Activities

The countries of the EMU engage in a variety of economic activities. Economic disturbances will likely affect the regions of EMU differentially because of this

Table 9.15 Primary, secondary and tertiary activities in the national economies of the EU

Country	% GNP from agriculture	% GNP from industry	% GNP from services
Austria (1996)	1.5	31.6	66.9
Belgium	2.0	28.0	70.0
Denmark (1994)	4.0	27.0	69.0
Finland (1995)	7.0	37.0	56.0
France (1994)	2.4	26.5	71.1
Germany (1995)	1.1	34.5	64.4
Greece (1994)	11.0	25.0	64.0
Ireland (1995)	8.5	38.3	53.2
Italy (1994)	3.3	33.0	63.7
Luxembourg (1995)	5.0	21.0	74.0
Netherlands (1996)	4.0	18.0	78.0
Portugal (1995 est.)	6.0	36.0	58.0
Spain (1995 est.)	3.6	33.6	62.8
Sweden (1993)	2.0	27.0	71.0
United Kingdom (1996 est.)	1.8	31.4	66.8

Source: Adapted from *The World Factbook 1998*. Central Intelligence Agency; http://www.odci.gov/cia/publications/factbook/index.html

Table 9.16 Areas of agricultural and industrial production in EU countries

Country	Areas of industrial production	Areas of agricultural production
Austria	Food products, iron, steel, machines, textiles, chemicals, electrical products, paper and pulp, tourism, mining, motor vehicles.	Grains, potatoes, sugar beets, wine, fruit, dairy products, livestock (cattle, pigs, poultry); sawn wood.
Belgium	Engineering and metal products, motor vehicle assembly, processed food and beverages, chemicals, basic metals, textiles, glass, petroleum, coal.	Sugar beets, fresh vegetables, fruits, grain, tobacco, beef, veal, pork, milk.
Denmark	Food processing, machinery and equipment, textiles and clothing, chemical products, electronics, construction, furniture, other wood products, shipbuilding.	Grain, potatoes, rape, sugar beets, meat, dairy products, fish.
Finland	Metal products, shipbuilding, pulp and paper, copper refining, foodstuffs, chemicals, textiles, clothing.	Cereals, sugar beets, potatoes, dairy cattle, fish.
France	Steel, machinery, chemicals, automobiles, metallurgy, aircraft, electronics, mining, textiles, food processing, tourism.	Wheat, cereals, sugar beets, potatoes, wine grapes, beef, dairy products, fish.
Germany	Western Germany: iron, steel, coal, cement, chemicals, machinery, vehicles, machine tools, electronics, food and beverages. Eastern Germany: metal fabrication, chemicals, brown coal, shipbuilding, machine building, food and beverages, textiles, petroleum refining.	Western Germany: potatoes, wheat, barley, sugar beets, fruit, cabbage, cattle, pigs, poultry. Eastern Germany: wheat, rye, barley, potatoes, sugar beets, fruit, pork, beef, chicken, milk, hides.
Greece	Tourism, food and tobacco processing, textiles, chemicals, metal products, mining, petroleum.	Wheat, corn, barley, sugar beets, olives, tomatoes, wine, tobacco, potatoes, meat, dairy products.

Ireland	Food products, brewing, textiles, clothing, chemicals, pharmaceuticals, machinery, transportation equipment, glass and crystal.	Turnips, barley, potatoes, sugar beets, wheat, meat, dairy products.
Italy	Tourism, machinery, iron, steel, chemicals, food processing, textiles, motor vehicles, clothing, footwear, ceramics.	Fruits, vegetables, grapes, potatoes, sugar beets, soybeans, grain, olives, meat, dairy products, fish.
Luxembourg	Banking, iron, steel, food processing, chemicals, metal products, engineering, tires, glass, aluminum.	Barley, oats, potatoes, wheat, fruits, wine grapes, livestock products.
Netherlands	Agroindustries, metal and engineering products, electrical machinery and equipment, chemicals, petroleum, fish, construction, microelectronics.	Grains, potatoes, sugar beets, fruits, vegetables, livestock.
Portugal	Textiles, footwear, wood pulp, paper, cork, metalworking, oil refining, chemicals, fish canning, wine, tourism.	Grain, potatoes, olives, grapes, sheep, cattle, goats, poultry, meat, dairy products.
Spain	Textiles and apparel (including footwear), food, beverages, metals, metal manufactures, chemicals, shipbuilding, automobiles, machine tools, tourism.	Grain, vegetables, olives, wine grapes, sugar beets, citrus fruits, beef, poultry, dairy products, fish.
Sweden	Iron, steel, precision equipment (bearings, radio and telephone parts, armaments), wood pulp, paper products, processed foods, motor vehicles.	Grains, sugar beets, potatoes, meat, milk.
United Kingdom	Production machinery including machine tools, electric power equipment, automation equipment, railroad equipment, shipbuilding, aircraft, motor vehicles and parts, electronics and communications equipment, metals, chemicals, coal, petroleum, paper and paper products, food processing, textiles, clothing, other consumer goods.	Cereal, oilseed, potatoes, vegetables, cattle, sheep, poultry, sheep.

Source: Adapted from *The World Factbook 1998*. Central Intelligence Agency; http:// www.odci.gov/cia/publications/factbook/index.html

diversity. These economic activities fall into three categories: agriculture, industry and services. Table 9.15 presents the percentages of national GNP from each of these categories of activity.

Services represent the leading category of economic activities across the EU. Industrial activities comprise the second largest component of GNP followed by agriculture. The latter only represents more than 5 percent of GNP in four countries: Finland, Greece, Ireland and Portugal.

Individual countries may be especially vulnerable to shocks to particular industries. Such vulnerability depends upon the industrial diversification of the country, as well as the relative income from different production sectors. Table 9.16 depicts the areas of industrial and agricultural production for the countries of the EU.

Diversity marks the economic activities of the EU as a whole. However, individual countries or groups of countries emphasize production of primary, secondary and tertiary commodities.

To the extent that countries' industrial structures render them subject to asymmetric industry-specific shocks, they may suffer disproportionately from the loss of monetary policy as an independent adjustment mechanism. Consider the example of the oil and natural gas-producing countries within the EU. These countries are the Netherlands and the UK. (Norway is also an oil and natural gas producer, although currently not a member of the EU.) An increase in world oil and natural gas prices would benefit these countries which are net exporters of these commodities but harm the rest of the countries that import these fuels. If the ECB responded to this supply shock with expansionary monetary policy, the net importers might benefit at the expense of the net exporters for whom revenues from these exports represent an important source of income and might fall if the (euro) exchange rate depreciates.[5]

The economies of the EU countries also vary according to the relative importance of capital and labor factor inputs. In addition, the labor they use varies in level of skill. Table 9.17 depicts the ratio of exports to imports for five categories of relative factor input utilization.

This table demonstrates the diversity of factor input utilization within the EU. The Mediterranean countries of Greece, Spain and Portugal display comparative advantages in labor-intensive production, along with Ireland. The rest of the EU possesses comparative advantages in either or both of capital and R&D-intensive industries.

In addition to the differences in relative factor input utilization, countries differ by relative export/import ratios. Table 9.18 highlights those industries for which exports exceed corresponding imports for EU countries. The identified countries may face particularly adverse consequences if these export industries experience negative shocks depending upon the proportion of national revenues from the affected industries.

Table 9.17 Factor intensity in national economies

Country-group	B+L	DK	D	GR	E	F	IRL	I	NL	P	UK
Capital and R&D intensive sectors	110	61	118	25	85	105	112	65	103	49	109
Capital-intensive sectors	147	216	83	83	118	105	143	120	310	41	85
Skilled labour-intensive sectors	83	101	197	27	68	152	41	120	88	31	130
Labour-intensive sectors	75	88	37	196	379	71	52	345	52	416	87
Less capital and labour-intensive	141	108	186	29	53	103	48	189	89	36	137
COMPARATIVE ADVANTAGES											
Capital intensity	X	X			X		X		X		
Labour intensity				X	X			X		X	
R & D intensity			X			X	X				X

Source: Adapted from Table 6.4: Comparative advantages of each Member State in the 40 sectors – Relative export/import ratio in the five groups, Social Europe, Special Edition, *European Economy* (1990, p. 51). Source: Commission Services.

Table 9.18 Sectoral production based on factor input usage

Capital- and R&D-intensive sectors	B+L	D	F	IRL	NL	UK	–
Capital-intensive sectors	B+L	DK	E	F	IRL	I	NL
Skilled labour-intensive sectors	DK	D	F	I	UK	–	–
Labour-intensive sectors	GR	E	I	P	–	–	–
Less capital and labour-intensive sectors	B+L	DK	D	F	I	UK	–

Source: Adapted from Table 6.4: Comparative advantages of each Member State in the 40 sectors – Relative export/import ratio in the five groups, Social Europe, Special Edition, *European Economy* (1990, p. 51). Source: Commission Services.

This table shows that exports exceed imports for the following countries in three or more of the above sectors: Belgium and Luxembourg, Denmark, Germany, France, Italy and the UK. These countries may harbor particular concern regarding EU exchange rate policy *vis-à-vis* the rest of the world, especially with important trading partners such as the USA. Such countries are particularly vulnerable to exchange rate risk.

The Single Market Program may compound the effects of industry-specific shocks if increasing specialization in production ensues at the national level (Englander and Egebo 1993, 12). Increased specialization would render countries more vulnerable to industry-specific shocks. Subsequently, a common monetary policy response to shocks would become increasingly unsuitable. In addition, the ECB must juggle the concerns of the various industries across the EU and may not be able to provide sufficient policy responses to all industries. However, if intra-industry specialization grows sufficiently, industry-specific shocks may affect wider jurisdictions resulting in less geographically concentrated effects and therefore similar pressure for monetary policy assistance from multiple countries (Obstfeld and Peri 1998, 143).

9.5.2 The Effects of Monetary Policy on Different Constituencies

Monetary policy represents one of the primary tools authorities possess for facilitating such adjustments. In spite of the ECB's statutory independence, institutional analysis and empirical observation reveal the potential vulnerability of this institution to manipulation to suit the demands of political expediency. Politicians within the EMU may attempt to use monetary policy as a means to respond to constituent pressures for assistance in preserving their holdings of wealth.

Monetary policy may impact EU constituencies differentially. Net creditors and net debtors harbor different preferences regarding monetary policy. Different preferences may reflect constituents' varying net wealth holdings, composition of wealth holdings, amount of leveraging and demand for foreign currency. For example, net creditors and net debtors harbor different preferences regarding monetary policy. Nowak (1993) distinguishes between three types of industry: interest rate sensitive industries, inflation sensitive industries and foreign exchange sensitive industries. Table 9.19 below provides examples of these industries.

Table 9.19 Monetary policy effects on different industries

Interest rate sensitive industries	Inflation sensitive industries	Foreign exchange sensitive industries
Government bond dealers and brokers	Net real asset holders	Export
Stock brokerage	Real estate	Import
Banking	Inventory accounting	
Real estate	Stock market	
Construction	Financially leverage firms and industries	
Automobile		
Financially leveraged firms and industries, e.g., agriculture and other cyclical industries		

Source: Adapted from Nowak (1993, 148–59).

Interest rates and inflation affect the cost of capital and the value of wealth holdings, respectively. High interest rates raise the cost of capital. Positive rates of inflation reduce the real value of wealth holdings. High inflation may be especially problematic for unindexed or incompletely indexed investments. Exchange rates affect individuals and firms that demand foreign currency. Domestic currency appreciation reduces the relative cost of foreign currency and vice versa.

Nowak (1993, 156–7) provides several examples of sectoral effects of changes in interest rates and inflation. Highly leveraged industries tend to be especially sensitive to changes in interest rates and inflation. Such industries include utilities, heavy industries (such as glass, oil, steel, aluminum), shopping malls and durable goods manufacturing industries (such as furniture, textiles, clothing). In addition, industries that rely upon long-term financing arrangements are more sensitive to inflation rates than industries that make greater use of short-term debt instruments. In contrast, less leveraged industries such as service-oriented businesses (for example, law and accounting firms, brokerage houses, restaurants) experience fewer benefits from changes in the price level.

9.5.3 Regional Divisions

Individual countries and regions of countries may experience an uneven distribution of shocks domestically because of regional differentiation in economic activity. Vandermotten (1997) divides Western Europe into 14 types of economic region. He uses an ascendant typological analysis to accommodate the proportion of different economic activities in GDP to distinguish between regions. These regions are: (1) central metropolitan; (2) secondary metropolitan; (3) heavy industrial region; (4) other central region; (5) peri-central Paris basin; (6) peri-central Germany; (7) peri-central third Italy (North and central Italy); (8) peri-central Scandinavia; (9) intermediate; (10) alpine; (11) peripheral metropolitan; (12) poor periphery; (13) Scandinavian periphery; and (14) East Germany. These classifications include separate regions of various countries with similar economic structures.

Central metropolitan regions represent those locations with the greatest per capita GNP. These regions include a number of large cities from around the EU. These cities are London, Paris, Amsterdam, Brussels, Stockholm, Rome, Madrid, Frankfurt, Munich, Hamburg and Milan. The economies of these cities consist predominantly of financial and other service industries. Secondary metropolitan areas are slightly less prosperous than central metropolitan regions. These regions include such cities as Bremen, Berlin, Gothenburg, Malmo, Copenhagen, Vienna, Genoa and Marseilles.

The heavy industrial and other central regions consist of those regions that engage in various manufacturing industries. These regions include the former centers of production of the Industrial Revolution. These regions include the so-called rust belt areas of northern England, South Wales, the Saar region, the Ruhr area, Nord-Pas-de-Calais and the Asturias, Cantabria and the Basque regions of Spain. Other regions within these categories such as Flanders, Alsace and Franconia engage in chemical and mechanical engineering and perform accordingly better than the industrial centers.

Lower per capita GDP and population distinguish the peri-central regions of the Paris basin, Germany, and North and central Italy from the metropolitan and industrial regions mentioned above. The regions of northeast Belgium and northern Spain also fall under this category. These regions concentrate in labor-intensive production. Relevant industries include agriculture and textile and chemical manufacture. The intermediate and alpine regions closely resemble the peri-central regions. However, the former possesses yet lower per capita GDP and populations.

The peripheral regions of Western Europe consist of those regions with the lowest per capita GDP. The economies of these regions include a relatively high percentage of primary activities. Productivity in these industries is low in comparison with similar industries in other regions. Manufacturing industries are few. The poorest peripheral regions include southern Italy (the Mezzogiorno), nearly all of Greece and Ireland and much of Portugal and Spain. Eastern Germany also belongs to the periphery but has marginally greater GNP than these regions. Northern Sweden and Finland possess somewhat greater per capita GNP than both Eastern Germany and the peripheral regions along the Mediterranean and Ireland.

GNP per capita varies widely between the countries of Western Europe. Table 9.20 presents these differences.

Table 9.20 Per capita national GDP

Country /Region	1990 Pop. (millions)	1960 GDP per capita	1966 GDP per capita	1973 GDP per capita	1982 GDP per capita	1987 GDP per capita	1990 GDP per capita
UK	57.3	121	110	103	96	102	99
NL	15.0	114	109	109	103	100	100
B	10.0	96	97	102	102	101	104
L	0.4	134	121	121	111	119	123
FRG	62.7	123	119	115	116	116	116
CH	6.8	175	165	155	138	136	134
OE	7.7	94	94	97	105	103	106
F	56.6	106	109	112	115	111	111
IT (North & Central)	37.8	102	104	106	116	117	119
El	3.5	56	54	55	62	61	68
P	9.8	38	42	54	53	51	55
SP	39.0	58	70	76	71	72	74
I (South)	19.9	53	60	63	70	70	66
H	10.2	34	41	50	51	48	46
DK	5.1	115	116	110	108	112	107
NO	4.2	90	89	84	100	110	101
SW	8.6	120	121	114	111	112	107
FI	5.0	86	87	94	100	103	104
GDR	16.0	–	–	–	–	–	6

Source: GDP per inhabitant, compared with the West European average. Adapted from Vandermotten in Blotevogel and Fielding (1997), Table 3.1, 52–3. [Original Sources: OECD, Eurostat, National Statistics.]

For 1990, a division exists between countries whose per capita GDP exceeds the West European average and countries whose per capita GDP falls below this level. The Southern European countries, along with Ireland, southern Italy and Eastern Germany, exhibit per capita GNP levels below the West European average. The remainder of the countries' and regions' per capita GDP exceeds this level. This division evidences the differences of relative economic strength between Western European countries and suggests the origins of differential pressures on monetary policy.

9.5.4 Core Periphery Division

These empirical findings highlight the similarities and differences of economic shocks in terms of size, correlation and persistence across the EU. Similarities between one or more countries particularly in terms of shock correlation suggest that these regions might be suitable participants in a currency union. A common monetary policy might facilitate adjustment to symmetric shocks. Countries that experience significantly different shocks, however, are better suited to maintaining individual monetary policy that considers their unique structures and vulnerabilities.

The studies presented earlier suggest a division of the countries of the EU into two groups. The first group consists of those countries whose shocks are relatively correlated. The second group consists of those countries whose shocks are relatively uncorrelated. The former group stands as the most viable subset of EU countries for participation in a currency union based on the theory of optimum currency areas.

The literature on EMU refers to the group of countries with relatively correlated shocks as the core.[6] This group centers on Germany and includes those countries whose currencies and economies are closely tied with the Deutschmark and the German economy. These countries include Belgium, Luxembourg, Austria and the Netherlands. These countries have had relatively close economic relations for many years. Belgium and Luxembourg forged a monetary union following the end of World War II and Austria unofficially began pegging its schilling to the Deutschmark in the 1970s. The Netherlands has maintained close trading ties with Belgium and Luxembourg since the post-World War II period and its currency has long shadowed the Deutschmark. The core also usually includes France, which is the second of the two large economies in the group.

The literature on EMU refers to those EU countries whose shocks are relatively uncorrelated with Germany and other members of the core as the peripheral countries. This group consists of the Southern countries of Greece, Italy, Portugal and Spain. Ireland, the UK and the Scandinavian countries of Finland and Sweden also fall outside the core on most criteria.

The following empirical studies report on the distinction between core and periphery. First, Bayoumi and Eichengreen (1993) find that the following countries experience supply and demand shocks that are relatively closely correlated with shocks affecting Germany: France, Belgium, the Netherlands and Denmark. Their results find that shocks to the UK, Italian, Spanish, Irish, Portuguese and Greek economies are much less correlated or negatively correlated with the Germany economy. They find that the economies of Germany, the Netherlands and Belgium also experience shocks of very similar sizes. The remaining countries experience larger supply shocks. The core countries experience demand shocks of similar sizes to the UK, Spain and Greece. The remaining countries face larger shocks to demand.

Funke (1997) finds a similar division of the effects of shocks between the core and periphery. The countries of the core experience relatively high correlations between supply and demand shocks. Similar shocks to the remaining countries are less high and less consistent across pairs of countries. Von Hagen and Neumann (1994) also find evidence of the core periphery distinction in the standard deviations of real exchange rates between eight European countries.

Chamie et al. (1994) uncover further differences in the timing of output variance subsequent to shocks between the core and periphery countries. Peripheral countries respond more quickly to supply shocks than core countries. In contrast, the latter experience the greatest variation of output due to real demand shocks sooner than the rest of EU countries. The authors also report that a common component explains variation in output more closely for the core countries, including France, the Netherlands, Belgium, Austria Germany and Switzerland.

Furthermore, Von Hagen and Hammond (1998) observe that the peripheral economies are less diversified than France and Germany and are therefore subject to more asymmetric shocks. They suggest that for this reason their economies might suffer under a common monetary policy with members of the core countries. The Benelux countries and Austria, however, are subject to sufficiently similar shocks that a common monetary policy with France and Germany serve their needs satisfactorily.

The aforementioned studies point to the potential difficulties of a currency union comprised of countries from the core and periphery. The foremost reason against such a monetary arrangement lies in the economies' vulnerability to asymmetric shocks and subsequent need for differential policy responses. The need for differential policy responses might only be alleviated by sufficiently flexible factor and output markets.

9.6 ADJUSTMENT MECHANISMS TO ECONOMIC SHOCKS

The literature on optimum currency areas suggests a number of possible adjustment mechanisms for regions within a single currency area. These mechanisms assist regional economies in responding to macroeconomic disturbances. Such mechanisms include changes in the real exchange rate, factor and output market flexibility, wage and price flexibility, and industrial and portfolio diversification. In addition, monetary and fiscal policy responses by the respective authorities may promote union-wide and regional adjustment to shocks. Some of these mechanisms operate automatically, while others operate at the discretion of government institutions.

Political institutions face the challenge of discussing, devising and implementing mechanisms to assist their constituents following economic disturbances. Pressures from voters and interest groups lead politicians to advance automatic stabilizers, as well as to undertake discretionary adjustment policies in the face of shocks. The latter may be particularly attractive to politicians' myopic electoral cycle concerns of gaining and retaining constituent favor.

9.6.1 Automatic Adjustment Mechanisms

Automatic adjustment mechanisms consist of those variables that move without political intervention in response to economic disturbances. These mechanisms include those specified by optimum currency area theory. Mechanisms identified by optimum currency area theory include real exchange rate flexibility, fiscal policy, factor and output flexibility, and industrial and portfolio diversification. A number of additional adjustment mechanisms may also operate. These mechanisms include indexed contracts such as indexed wage agreements, private and public capital market insurance funds, the tax code and social programs that provide payments that are negatively correlated with individual income such as unemployment insurance and welfare programs. Earlier discussions of adjustment mechanisms highlight the limitations of these means of adjustment within the EU. An important benefit of automatic adjustment mechanisms is that they take effect without a lag in contrast with discretionary policy.

9.6.2 Discretionary Adjustment Mechanisms

Discretionary adjustment mechanisms include those responses legislated on an *ad hoc* basis to respond to economic disturbances. Discretionary policy responses to economic shocks fall under the jurisdiction of regional, national and EU governmental institutions. At the EU level, the Council of Ministers (particularly the European Council), the European Parliament and the European Commission assume responsibility for such decision-making. Members of the European Council and the General Council may form the staunchest advocates of discretionary adjustment mechanisms given their electoral accountability as self-interested politicians and party representatives to their domestic constituents.

Governments possess a number of discretionary adjustment mechanisms at their disposal. These mechanisms include monetary policy, fiscal policy and regulatory policy. Governments may utilize these policy tools to stimulate or dampen supply and demand or to assist adversely affected regions or sectors.

Within the sphere of monetary policy, governments face three possible policy tools. These tools constitute the tools of the central banker. The ability of elected officials to commandeer these tools depends upon their ability to wield power over the relevant monetary authority. In the context of the EMU, however, monetary policy is only available to the government of the EU and the ECB. National governments can only advance their interests via their representatives in the European Council and in the Governing Council of the ESCB. The ECB possesses the same policy tools at its disposal as any sovereign monetary authority: the discount rate, reserve requirements and open market operations.

Pressures for monetary policy responses to shocks will call for one of two types of responses. The first type of response is expansionary policy. The purpose of expansionary policy is to reduce the cost of credit and the value of outstanding debt. The monetary authority may undertake expansionary policy by one of three means. First, the monetary authority may reduce the cost of borrowing funds from the discount window by lowering the interest rate charged on the loans it makes. Second, the monetary authority may make additional open market purchases to increase the money supply. Third, the monetary authority may lower reserve requirements in order to induce banks to lower vault holdings and increase the amount of money in circulation. Individuals and groups with negative net assets favor expansionary policy in order to reduce the cost of paying off outstanding debt.

The second type of monetary policy response is contractionary policy. The purpose of contractionary policy is to increase the cost of credit and the value of outstanding debt. The monetary authority may undertake contractionary policy by one of three means. First, the monetary authority may increase the cost of borrowing funds from the discount window by raising the interest rate charged on the loans it makes. Second, the monetary authority may make additional open market sales in order to reduce the money supply. Third, the monetary authority may raise reserve requirements in order to induce banks to increase vault holdings and reduce the amount of money in circulation. Individuals with positive net assets favor contractionary policy in order to maintain or raise the value of assets held and credits extended.

Discretionary adjustment mechanisms are subject to a number of limitations. One problem includes attaining sufficient support from political jurisdictions with competing interests. Net beneficiaries of policies will support them while net losers will oppose them. For the case of fiscal policy, constituencies that make net contributions to public coffers may resist increases in tax liabilities to support additional transfers to other constituencies. On the other hand, net recipients may lobby for the continuation of existing transfers and press for additional transfers in the face of new economic difficulties. The costs of such competition fall under the rubric of rent-seeking costs.

Another problem with discretionary policy is time lags. Hayes-Renshaw and Wallace (1995, 568) highlight the problem of time lags within the legislative process of the EU:

> Another gauge of productivity has to do with the time it takes for decisions to emerge; the time-lag between proposal and decision; and the response rate to events or new issues ... No study has been published covering more recent years, but an unofficial inside estimate recently indicated a time-lag between CEC proposal and final Council legislation of around a year and a half.

This indicates the additional time now demanded by the more complicated exchange of positions with the EP. These problems may be accentuated at the level of the EU.

Within the sphere of fiscal policy, governments have several policy tools at their disposal: taxation, expenditure and redistribution policy. Governments may undertake expansionary policy in order to stimulate the economy and contractionary policy to slow the economy. Expansionary measures may include reductions in tax rates and increases in government expenditures. Contractionary measures may include increases in tax rates and reductions in government purchases.[7] Redistributive measures may serve to increase the incomes of adversely affect constituencies with revenues from relatively prosperous constituencies.

The ability of the EU to undertake fiscal stabilization policy is, however, bound by two constraints. First, at the level of the EU, a relatively small budget exists with which to finance expenditures and undertake transfers. Second, at the level of individual countries, the debt limits provided by the Growth and Stability Pact (GSP) restrict the accumulation of debt.

An expanded centralized fiscal policy at the EU level may be necessary to undertake stabilization policy given the limited operation of automatic adjustment mechanisms. In order to remedy the limited budget, the EU government may request additional contributions from member countries. The MacDougal Report (1977) estimated that an EU budget of 5–7 percent of EU GNP would be necessary to support the fiscal needs of EU members (Obstfeld and Peri 1998, 237). However, any attempts to increase the relatively limited EU budget in order to accommodate fiscal pressures for assistance throughout the EU will likely meet with resistance at the national level. The deadlock among EU leaders at the summit of the European Council in December 1998 over proposed budgetary increases to finance EU expansion provides one example of such resistance.

Several possible outcomes exist to remedy the limits of EU fiscal policy to respond to shocks. First, the EU may dissolve the GSP to allow the persistence and growth of national debts. In this event, the ultimate constraint on national debt would come from financial markets. Second, the EU may retain the GSP but decide to interpret its restrictions loosely. Such action is not without precedent. The European Commission did not strictly apply the Maastricht debt criterion to EMU candidates.

Third, the GSP limits on national debt may lead to pressures for EU-level fiscal assistance (Obstfeld and Peri 1998, 222). For example, the Cohesion Fund and the growth of Structural Funds enabled the Maastricht Treaty on EMU to gain the requisite support (ibid., 244). However, the Treaty on European Union prohibits the EU from operating beyond its budget. But, EU annual budgetary expenditures have already exceeded revenues for more than one fiscal year. In addition, unlike many national constitutions the TEU also prohibits the ESCB from purchasing government debt. Once again financial markets will draw the line on the amount of government debt issues.

An additional case for a greater centralized EU fiscal role comes from the USA. Englander and Egebo (1993) note that federal fiscal transfers play a more important role in regional assistance than state transfers. In the absence of the functioning of these or other adjustment mechanisms, pressures for national constituencies may arise against continued participation in the EMU.

The countries of the EU face limited adjustment mechanisms with which to respond to economic shocks. These limits exist at the levels of both national and EU-level governments. The arrangements of the EMU impose limits beyond those facing sovereign countries. For this reason, citizens may place pressures upon nationally elected officials to withdraw from the arrangement if shocks affect wealth negatively. Such pressures appear particularly likely if national constituents perceive withdrawal and a return to sovereign economic policies as a remedy for economic woes.

9.7 CONCLUSION

Asymmetric shocks to the diverse economies of the EMU represent a threat to the development and future success of the single currency arrangement. Asymmetric shocks may adversely affect one or more industries or regions differently. Affected industries will rely upon various possible adjustment mechanisms to remedy the consequences of such disturbances. Accommodation depends upon market flexibility, economic diversification and policy intervention. Within the EU, these mechanisms offer limited adjustment possibilities. The abandonment of national currencies represents the loss of one key adjustment tool: monetary policy. Unsatisfactory adjustment to asymmetric shocks may drive constituents to pressure national politicians for a return to national policy measures up to and including a return to sovereign currencies. Such a return would also formally release national fiscal policy from the constraints of the EU's GSP.

NOTES

1. For example, see Layard et al. (1991); and, OECD (1996, Chapter 8).
2. For example, see Layard et al. (1991, Table 6, Row 3); and, OECD (1996, Chart 7.1B).
3. For more on the insider–outsider theory of unemployment see Lindbeck and Snower (1988) and Blanchard and Summers (1986).
4. For more on skill depreciation and reduced search efficacy models of prolonged unemployment see Blanchard and Diamond (1994) and Layard and Nickell (1987), respectively.
5. The effect of a fall in the euro exchange rate on revenues from oil and natural gas imports would depend upon the price elasticity of demand for these commodities by foreign consumers.
6. Forni and Reichlin (1997, 224–5) search for a common component in measures of the dispersion of output growth across the EU. They find that no group of EU countries satisfies the restriction that this common component explains 70 percent or more of the variation in output growth. To achieve this level of correlation, they must incorporate regions of various countries belonging to both the core and the periphery.
7. The expansionary or contractionary effects of tax and expenditure policy may depend on the existence of a crowding-out effect and the impact of such a policy on individual consumption and production incentives.

10. Political implications of macroeconomic shocks

10.1 INTRODUCTION

Macroeconomic shocks represent one destabilizing force that may affect the European single currency area. Given the area's economic heterogeneity, such disturbances may give rise to differential pressures for discretionary adjustment measures by affected constituencies. These pressures may lead to divergent policy preferences by national political decision-makers. Such divergences may irreparably fracture the fragile equilibrium among national leaders that has so far enabled the arrangement to continue forward.

This chapter employs the following organization. Section 2 considers the responses of affected constituencies to macroeconomic shocks and the pressures they subsequently place on national and EU institutions. Section 3 briefly introduces one spatial modeling technique: the win-set approach. Section 4 presents a win-set model of EU institutions and depicts possible internal dynamics in response to constituent pressures. Section 5 examines likely position shifts within the EU institutions following asymmetric shocks and the likely implications of these shocks for the European Monetary Union (EMU). Section 6 concludes.

10.2 CONSTITUENT RESPONSES TO MACROECONOMIC SHOCKS

Macroeconomic shocks generate effects for various economic variables that affect political constituents. These variables include such measures of economic performance as the inflation rate, the unemployment rate, per capita GDP, the exchange rate and the rate of growth of income. Changes in these variables introduce various implications for individual economic agents: in particular such changes imply improvements or reductions in individuals' wealth-earning and preservation opportunities. For this reason individual constituents respond to changes in these variables in order to maximize their expected utility.

Individuals and groups may pressure political decision-makers at both the national and EU levels for [monetary] policy responses to economic disturbances. Actors may register their preferences directly to elected officials through personal communication, votes, migration and campaign support. Subsequently elected officials may introduce, amend or protect policies in order to retain constituent support. Such efforts may include influencing the monetary authority to pursue a particular policy approach. In addition multinational corporations may apply pressure and offer support to EU and EMU participants' governments. Elected officials that do not satisfy the demands of voters, interest groups and multinational corporations risk defeat at subsequent elections.

10.2.1 Economic Performance and Government Support

Constituent support of incumbent government depends upon a number of factors. Foremost among these factors is economic performance. Various measures of economic performance reflect the environment in which individuals seek income-earning opportunities and endeavor to preserve and increase wealth. Individuals attribute responsibility for the strength or weakness of the domestic economy reflected by these indicators to decision-makers within the government. Consequently they reward or punish elected decision-makers at the ballot box.

Incumbent governments understand the role of economic performance in electoral success. They therefore attempt to undertake policies to improve these measures in the period before an election. They seek to increase the incumbent leader or party's chances of re-election. However, the effects of economic performance on government support vary across countries.

The literature on political business cycles examines the relationship between electoral cycles and policy measures. Political business cycle models hypothesize that politicians, notably the president and legislature, promote expansionary monetary and fiscal policies in the period approaching an election in order to give the appearance of their ability to create a strong economy and thereby garner necessary electoral support. Theoretical models are subject to the Lucas critique (Lucas 1976), as well as criticisms of the assumption of voter myopia. Empirical evidence in support of these models is mixed.

Individual voters' choice of candidate depends on several factors. These factors include the macroeconomic performance of the incumbent politician or party's platform, the platform of the opposition candidate or party and the individual's party affiliation. Constituents employ macroeconomic indicators to assess the incumbent politician or party's macroeconomic policy performance. Individual party affiliation may encapsulate multiple aspects of an individual's political preferences including religion, class, ideology, education, profession and net wealth. Party preferences may serve as low cost sources of information for voters in the face of rational ignorance.

Elected politicians must be clearly accountable for policy decisions in order for constituents to hold them responsible (Powell 1983, 108). Otherwise, constituents may not reward/punish them at the ballot box. Powell (ibid.) finds that the correlation between economic performance and government support is weaker in multiparty systems where it is more difficult for constituents to hold individual decision-makers or parties responsible.

Aggregate measures of economic performance conceal the distributional effects of macroeconomic policies and shocks. Such effects determine the political preferences of different constituencies. The relative size and strength of these constituencies affects their ability to affect political decision-makers and ultimately policy.

Consider the case of inflation. Inflation is a measure that leads to changes in the real value of wealth. The relative strength of creditors and debtors will affect the policies espoused by domestic leaders. The relative political strength of high-income versus low-income constituents will also affect national inflation, as well as unemployment preferences. Wealthier individuals tend to be relatively more averse to inflation than unemployment and the opposite for less wealthy constituents (Lewis-Beck 1988, 21).

10.2.2 Empirical Evidence of the Positive Correlation Between Economic Performance and Government Support within Western European Countries

Empirical evidence of the correlation between economic performance and government support as expressed by voters at the ballot box reveals a positive relationship. These studies employ such measures of economic performance as the inflation rate, the unemployment rate, the growth rate of real income, the burden of taxation, the exchange rate and GDP. The inflation rate, the unemployment rate and the burden of taxation exhibit negative relationships with government support. GDP and the growth rate of real income exhibit positive relationships with government support. The relationship between the exchange rate and government support depends upon the relative size of GDP comprised by exports and imports.

Government support decreases following a decline in economic performance. Lewis-Beck (1988, 104) finds that economic concerns affect individuals' voting choice most strongly in the following Western European countries (in descending order): the UK, Spain, Germany, France and Italy. For his purposes, economic concerns are both backward- and forward-looking. That is, voters anticipate candidates' and parties' future policies. Lewis-Beck (1988, 24) also identifies empirical studies of Australia, West Germany, the UK and the United States that find the governments of these countries employed expansionary policies prior to elections in which they acknowledged a real possibility of defeat.

Political economists have undertaken a number of country-specific studies of the relationship between measures of economic performance and government support within the EU. These studies confirm the hypothesis of a positive relationship between economic performance and government support. However, the performance measures that are most important in determining government support vary across countries.

Several studies examine the case of France. Among the performance indicators considered were the inflation rate, the unemployment rate, the growth rate of real income and the exchange rate. Lewis-Beck (1988) and Rosa (1980) report that of the inflation rate, the unemployment rate and the growth rate of real income, the inflation rate had the largest effect on presidential popularity. In contrast, Hibbs (1981) and Lafay (1984) report that the unemployment rate and the growth of real income have the strongest effects.

Lafay (1984) considers the 1981 French presidential election. He separates the effects of four measures of economic performance into short- and long-term impact. Inflation plays the greatest role over the long run whereas the unemployment rate and the exchange rate affect short-run policy assessments. The growth rate of real disposable income enjoys a long-term effect on voters' assessment of government performance as voters look back over time.

Economic performance has also affected German executive and legislative elections. Kirchgässner (1976 and 1977, 19–20) finds that the inflation, unemployment and growth of real income rates affect incumbent support. Of these factors, the unemployment rate has the single largest impact on government popularity.

Frey and Weck (1983, 18) study the impact of macroeconomic performance on the support received by opposing parties in the four German Reichstag elections for the period 1930–33. The unemployment rate in particular led to the rise in popularity of the National Socialist (Nazi) Party over this period. They estimate that the Nazi Party would have received only 24 percent of the votes in the March 1933 elections as opposed to 44 percent, had the unemployment rate not increased from 14 percent to 52 percent between July 1930 and January 1933.

Governments in the UK have also borne the burden of accountability for domestic economic performance. Pissarides (1980, 19–20) finds that the inflation rate, the unemployment rate, the growth rate of real income and the burden of taxation affect public support of the incumbent government. The unemployment rate has the single greatest impact on constituent support. Whiteley (1985, 75) reports that macroeconomic performance was an important determinant of the outcome of the 1983 general election.

Economic performance affected government support and subsequently electoral outcomes in Denmark and Sweden, as well.[1] The inflation, unemployment and growth of real income rates significantly affected constituent support of Danish (Paldam and Schneider 1980) and Swedish (Jonung and Wadensjoe 1979) governments. The burden of taxation also played a role in Denmark. The unemployment rate was the most important factor in both countries.

Unemployment has ranked as the leading economic concern of Spanish citizens in post-Franco Spain (Lancaster 1985, 118). Inflation ranks as their third concern after terrorism (ibid.). Dissatisfaction of the Spanish electorate with the incumbent government's economic policy among other issues resulted in the victory of the major opposition party in Spain's 1982 general election.

Economic performance has played a lesser role in Italian executive and legislative elections (Bellucci 1985, 107). Rather, party affiliation has played a stronger role. However, economic performance is playing an increasing role in Italian elections.

10.2.3 Economic Performance and National Support for the European Union

Domestic economic performance also bears on national support for the EU. Using survey data on national support for the EU, Eichenberg and Dalton (1993) report that economic performance plays a statistically significant role. These authors use the following domestic economic measures: inflation, unemployment, an index of GDP, intra-EU trade as a percentage of total trade and EU budget returns. Inflation affects national support for the EU most strongly: an increase in inflation of 1 percent reduces support for the EU by 2 percent. After inflation, intra-EU trade as a percentage of total trade plays the next strongest role. Higher trade with EU countries corresponds with greater support for the EU. This finding is unsurprising given the facilitation of intra-EU trade provided by the economic arrangement.

The correlations found by Eichenberg and Dalton (1993) imply that macroeconomic shocks may affect constituent support for national governments within the EU. First, negative shocks that differentially affect unemployment and GDP may reduce constituent support for the EU in individual countries that face increased unemployment and decreased GDP. Such support shifts may be particularly apparent in national elections. Second, expansionary monetary policy by the European Central Bank (ECB) may gain the support of highly indebted countries at the expense of less indebted or net creditor countries. Thus a tradeoff in support may ensue from any policy that affects national macroeconomic variables differentially. Third, any monetary policy decision may gain support of one country's constituents at the expense of another country's constituents. If such changes in support occur near national elections, national decision-makers may take policy stances away from the European Council and/or ECB's position out of necessity to preserve their chances of re-election.

10.2.4 Impact of Economic Heterogeneity in the EU

The effects of economic disturbances vary across countries, regions and industries because of the economic heterogeneity within the European currency union. Economic heterogeneity within the EMU implies that economic disturbances will give rise to differential pressures from adversely affected countries, regions and industries. Different constituencies may demand divergent policies from those advocated at the central EU level particularly in the monetary and fiscal policy spheres. For this reason, elected politicians may face a choice between policies constituents demand that counter the policies and goals of the EU and losing in elections to candidates and parties that promise to deliver policies that respond to constituents' self-interested policy demands.

A study by Eichengreen (1990) illustrates the differential effects of real exchange rate shifts on regional unemployment rates in Great Britain and Italy. Eichengreen regresses real exchange rate shocks on the unemployment rates for ten regions within Great Britain and nine regional groupings within Italy. Controlling for business cycles and differences in real energy prices, he finds that the coefficients on the unemployment rates of these regions are of different signs. Over half of these coefficients differ from zero at statistically significant levels.

Eichengreen's results are important for a number of reasons. First, countries participating in EMU may face more real exchange rate shocks in the absence of national currencies. Subsequently, these shocks may result in greater calls for individualized policy responses than would have been the case for each country individually when it possessed its own currency. Second, Eichengreen's study draws attention to the greater variation of regional pressures that the ECB and more importantly the European Council will have to respond to. This variation may result in conflicting policy demands.

10.2.5 Real and Expected Economic Adversity: A Force Behind Constituent Mobilization

Adverse economic circumstances or the threat thereof represents a major factor behind political mobilization by individual constituents. Subsequently, such circumstances or shocks are one source of government pressure by voters, interest groups and corporate entities. Examples of this phenomenon abound in the history of EU member countries.

One extreme example of economic adversity giving rise to political change is the economic crisis in Germany during the 1930s. As noted earlier, Frey and Weck (1983, 18) estimate that the threefold increase in the German unemployment rate in the first three years of the decade aided the National Socialist party in its bid for the government.

A more recent example of economic adversity giving rise to political change is the election of President François Mitterand in 1981. Mitterand marginally defeated incumbent Giscard d'Estaing by securing 2.6 percentage points more in this election than in the 1974 election against the incumbent President. Using data from the European Community Consumer Survey subjective index of national economic well-being, Lewis-Beck (1980, 86–7) finds that the shift in support for Mitterand arose from a growth in the number of economically disaffected voters.

European constituents also utilized the ballot box to oust governments advocating austere domestic policies to improve chances of admission to the EMU. In December 1995 strikers turned out in force in Paris to protest against social security reforms intended to reduce the budgetary burden on the government. French voters later again demonstrated their unwillingness to sacrifice social benefits to qualify for EMU by voting out the incumbent government in favor of the Socialist opposition in the spring of 1997. In October of the same year the loss of coalition support by Communist party members brought down the Italian government led by Prime Minister Romano Prodi. Members of the Communist and other parties in the Italian Parliament reflected constituent concerns over welfare policy reforms proposed to generate expenditure savings for the government.

Additional examples of recent mobilization against reforms related to economic integration include protests by farmers (February 22, 1999) and railway employees (November 23, 1998). In each of these cases, affected groups mobilized to express their opposition to proposed policies. Over 40 000 farmers belonging to the European Farmers' Union (COPA) descended upon Brussels from across the EU to protest against proposed agricultural policy reforms that would reduce government subsidies and possibly destroy the livelihoods of many small farmers. Railway employees in 12 EU countries went on strike to protest against proposed deregulation of freight transport to allow increased competition. The strike caused major disruption in three of the countries experiencing strikes: France, Belgium and Greece.

These examples demonstrate the types of circumstances that place pressures upon incumbent governments. Incumbents must respond to constituent pressures or face displacement by political opponents. The question remains how long EU governments will be able to juggle voters' and constituents' domestic concerns with the demands of economic integration into the EMU simultaneously. As national governments sacrifice more domestic policy instruments, the balance becomes increasingly precarious.

10.3 SPATIAL MODELING TECHNIQUES: THE WIN-SET MODEL

Spatial models provide an analytical framework for institutional decision processes using a simple majority rule (Krehbiel 1988). These models stem from the literature on positive political theory. Decision-makers vote on pairs of policies to reach a final decision. Three elements are essential to spatial models: (1) heterogeneous, but stable individual preferences; (2) multidimensional policy issues; and (3) the rules of procedure of the relevant decision-making institutions. Spatial models combine these elements to develop a multidimensional framework that captures the relevant decision process. Political economy scholars often limit the focus of these models to a representative sample of decision-makers in order to retain the tractability of the model. The results of such techniques serve as valuable explanatory tools. Spatial models may be useful in analyzing inter-institutional decision processes as well as intra-institutional proceedings.[2]

Spatial models require knowledge about the nature of the representative decision-maker's utility function, policy preferences and relevant issue dimensions.[3] The issue dimensions at hand, as well as the policy options available, determine the choices decision-makers face. Political decision-makers must choose from a range of policy choices. These policies incorporate the preferences of constituents, special interest groups, corporate entities and politicians. Preferences affect the choices of decision-makers within their respective institutions.

10.3.1 The Win-set Model

The win-set framework models the decision process for multiple policy issue dimensions (Shepsle 1986a). The simplest and most graphically tractable model incorporates two issue dimensions. Points in this two-dimensional issue space represent possible combinations of policies x and y.

The win-set framework utilizes heterogeneous actor preferences to demonstrate voting coalitions capable of defeating the *status quo*. Each actor possesses a strictly quasi-concave utility function in the issue space. A single bliss point represents the actor's most preferred combination of policies x and y. A single point in the win-set diagram illustrates the *status quo* for the given policy areas. Concentric circles, depicting contours along the actor's utility function, emanate from each individual's bliss point denoting successively lower utility levels as the distance of the point corresponding to the *status quo* in two-dimensional issue space grows from the respective individual's bliss point.[4] Actors' relevant indifference curves intersect the *status quo*. Points closer to an actor's bliss point reflect greater individual utility. Actors' utility functions overlap to depict sets of policy combinations that one or more actors prefer to the *status quo*. These actors represent a coalition that favors one of these alternative combinations to the given policy combination. Institutional rules permitting, these actors may initiate a vote to bring about a policy change in their favor.

Figure 10. 1 demonstrates a win-set diagram for two policy issues, x and y, and for three actors, A, B and C. $x^{status\ quo}$ and $y^{status\ quo}$ denote the existing levels of policy X and Y, respectively. Q denotes the current policy combination. Points A, B and C represent the bliss point of each of the actors. Overlapping regions depict policy combinations that a majority of actors prefer to the *status quo*. These regions are called win-sets.

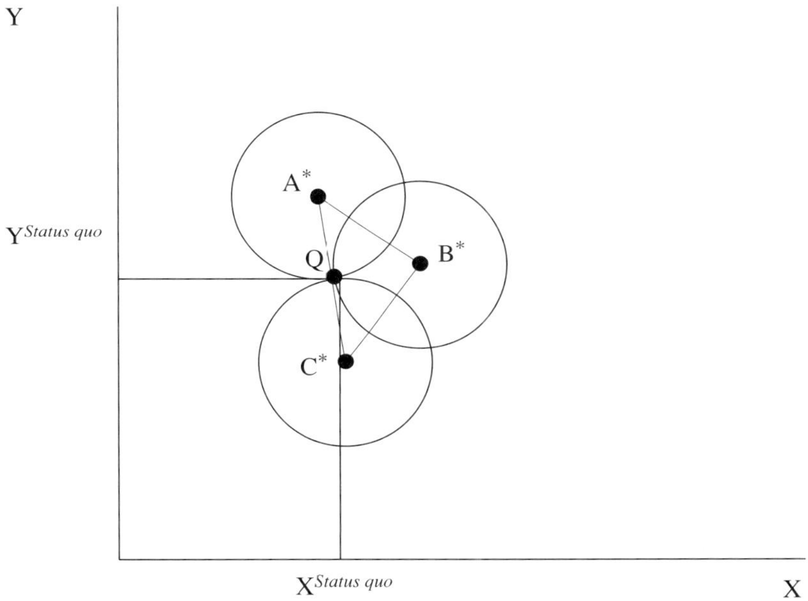

Key: * optimum or bliss point.

Figure 10. 1 Basic win-set diagram

Lines connecting two actors' bliss points represent the locus of tangent points of the actors' indifference curves. Along these lines, one actor can increase his utility only at the expense of another actor's utility. These points are Pareto optimal.

The win-set model is useful for identifying coalitions of actors who could garner the relevant vote majority to introduce and support an alternate policy combination in a vote between the actors. The number of votes required to change from the *status quo* depends on the operative decision rule. Rules include unanimity, simple majority, qualified majority and supra-majority.

Two conditions must be met for a coalition to achieve a change from the *status quo*. First, one or more of the actors interested in the change must be able to place his proposal on the agenda. Second, one or more win-sets must exist.

Consider the following example with three actors and a simple (2/3) majority decision rule. Figure 10.2 illustrates this example. Those areas where the indifference curves of two actors overlap represent regions containing policy points that a majority (2/3) of the actors prefer to the *status quo*. By supporting such a proposal, these actors could improve their utility.

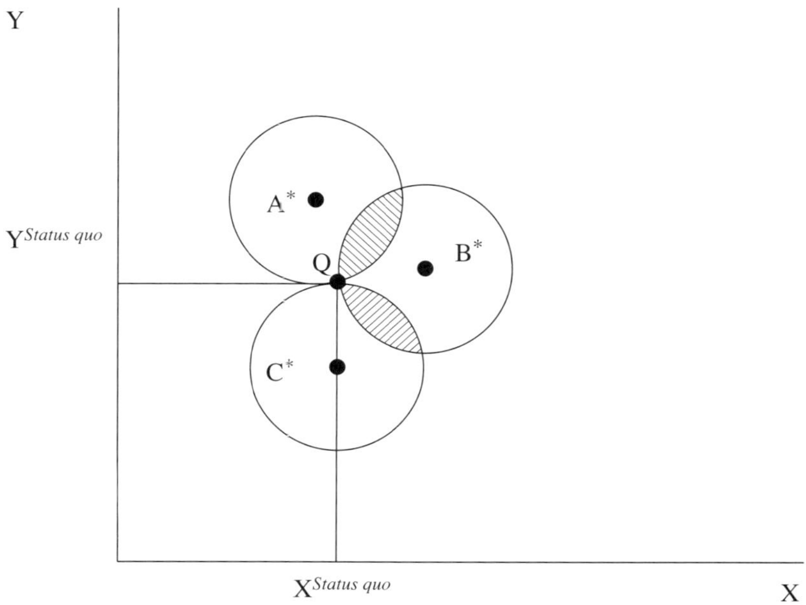

Key: * optimum or bliss point.

Figure 10.2 Possible coalitions within the win-set diagram

Figure 10.2 demonstrates two possible coalitions that satisfy the majority rule requirement. The overlapping region between A and B's indifference curves and the overlapping region between B and C's indifference curves represent possible win-sets.

Any outcome may be unstable because either member of the winning coalition might enter a new coalition with the third individual to defeat the policy chosen by the first coalition. In the absence of any institutions to prevent later votes and subsequent vote trading, vote cycling may result. As the number of individual participants increases, the number of possible coalitions rises (Mueller 1989; Ordeshook 1986).

The win-set diagram depicts the *status quo* and the actors' preferences at a single point in time. Over time, however, the actors' preferences may change.

A movement of the bliss point ensues from such preference changes. This new bliss point represents the peak of the actor's utility function. The indifference curve belonging to the relevant actor continues to go through the *status quo*. However, the relevant indifference curve may be further or nearer to the individual's most preferred point. This type of change may lead to a change in the win-sets. In this case, old coalitions may fall apart and new coalitions arise. The changes in coalition members may lead to policy changes unless blocked by institutional rules which may lead to a structure-induced equilibrium.

Figure 10.3 depicts a change in preferences by one actor. B's bliss point shifts from B^* to B^{**}. Correspondingly, a different indifference curve of B's goes through the *status quo*. As a result of B's change in preferences, the win-set consisting of A and B disappears. However, the win-set consisting of B and C enlarges.

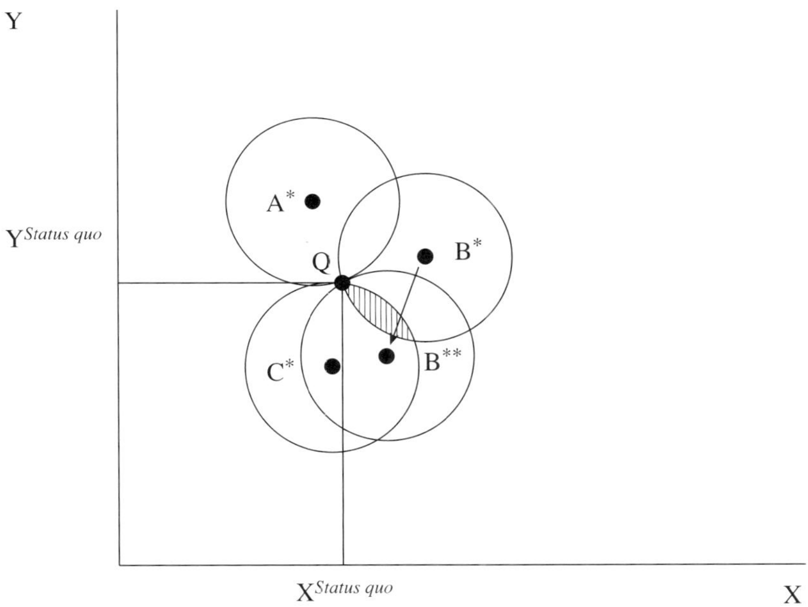

Key: * optimum or bliss point.
** optimum or bliss point after a change in preferences by one actor.

Figure 10.3 A preference change by one actor within a win-set diagram

For a sufficiently small preference change by B, some win-set between A and B may remain. This diagram shows the case of a larger preference change. It may also happen that more than one actor's preferences change resulting in a relocation of multiple bliss points and utility curves. This case again raises the possibility of the elimination of existing and creation of new win-sets.

10.4 EUROPEAN UNION INSTITUTIONS AND THE WIN-SET MODEL

The win-set framework may be useful in analyzing the behavior of actors within the EU. These actors harbor heterogeneous preferences and may behave strategically in order to achieve policy outcomes closer to their preferred combination. Over time, the preferences of these actors may change. Subsequently, they will pursue policies that reflect these changes.

10.4.1 The European Council in the Win-set Model

The European Council is the single most powerful institution at the level of EU decision-making. It consists of elected individuals from each member country. These individuals meet together at least twice annually. It is their responsibility to determine the direction of overall EU policy. This determination includes the definition of the economic goals of the EU. These goals are the objectives that, in theory at least, determine the monetary policy chosen by the ECB.

Electoral constraints will drive national leaders to choose economic goals that reflect the preferences of domestic constituents. With the introduction of the euro and the fixed rates of exchange between participating currencies, the economic goals of the EU are intimately tied to the economic fortunes of constituents across the single currency area. Monetary policy no longer exists as a sovereign tool of adjustment. Fiscal policy exists in a more limited form as a sovereign tool because of the constraints on deficits imposed by the Growth and Stability Pact (GSP). For these reasons, national leaders must utilize the political marketplace of the EU to advance the economic demands of their constituents.

National leaders have two ways to respond to aggregate demands for particular monetary policies. First, they can affect the economic goals of the EU defined in the Treaty on European Union (TEU). They alone can make the necessary amendments to this treaty to revise these goals. Second, they can pressure members of the Governing Council of the ECB. Each country's interests may enjoy representation (and advocacy) within the Governing Council in at least two ways. The first way consists of the head of the country's central bank who sits on the Council. The second way consists of the possibility of one of the six appointees to the Executive Board, a part of the Governing Council, originating from within its country. In either of these cases, the self-interest of these national representatives may motivate them to respond to pressures from their respective Head of State or Government.

The ECB may perceive political pressures for monetary responses in at least two ways.[5] First, individual actors within EU's governing institutions may directly contact members of the Governing Council and the Executive Board in order to express their policy wishes. Leading political decision-makers may signal their preferences to the ECB. Some of these preferences may be accompanied by veiled or overt threats.[6] Second, the ECB may perceive the wishes of leading political decision-makers given the preferences of their constituents and may of its own accord initiate policies in line with these wishes. In this case, the ECB directly responds to strong constituencies within the EMU, pre-empting direct institutional pressures. As far as decision rules on monetary policy decisions, the Governing Council operates within a black box similar to decision-making at the Federal Reserve Board.

Qualified majority voting within the European Council is the applicable decision rule for economic and monetary policy. It serves as the operative rule for decisions on the economic goals of the EU and for changes to the Statutes of the ECB/ESCB. Although the Council of Economics and Finance Ministers (ECOFIN) consists of national finance and economics ministers, overall economic policy determination remains within the jurisdiction of the European Council. Both the European Parliament and the Commission play a limited role in the passage of proposed changes to the Statutes of the ECB/ESCB. The European Parliament must grant its assent (Art. 106.5 TEU). The Council must also consult the Commission (Art. 106.5 TEU). The European Council, however, exercises nearly complete control over policy determination for reasons discussed in earlier chapters.

Agenda control within the European Council rests with the Council Presidency. As noted earlier, this office rotates between member countries every six months according to a pre-determined order.[7] The Council President may decide which issues to permit to reach the agenda of the Council. This power endows the Council President with gatekeeping power.

However, this power is not absolute for several reasons. First, the Council President holds this position for a limited period and may need to maintain cordial relations with other leaders in order for his preferred policies to make it to the agenda in future periods. Second, the Council President may only determine issues and policies that reach the agenda prior to Council meetings. During these meetings, members may raise issues and policies.

Consider the European Council within the win-set framework.[8] First, let us utilize three actors instead of the 15 that in reality comprise the Council. This simplification is necessary in order to maintain tractability. Second, let the relevant decision rule be two-thirds as an approximation of qualified majority. A qualified majority is necessary for the Council to change the overall economic policy of the EU (Article 103.2 TEU). Historically, the qualified majority rule within the European Council has required 71 percent of the cast votes in favor (see Table 8.1, p. 195). Two-thirds is a very close approximation. Third, let the relevant policy issues be the amount of domestic debt and short-term interest rates determined by the ECB. The latter serves as an approximation of the tightness of EU monetary policy. The former serves as an approximation of the tightness of EMU fiscal policy.

Note that levels of domestic debt face two explicit constraints. First, the GSP places limits on the amount of debt any country can accumulate and sustain. Deficits in excess of these limits may result in financial penalties. Second, financial markets place limits on government debt issue by their willingness to buy at a given price. Beyond a certain price, they may no longer be willing to purchase debt as a form of credit rationing.

Figure 10.4 depicts the positions of three members of the European Council. Q denotes the *status quo* of EU short-term interest rates and the total of domestic debt permitted by the GSP for a given year's GNP figures. Note that each country prefers higher or lower interest rate and debt levels. These differences

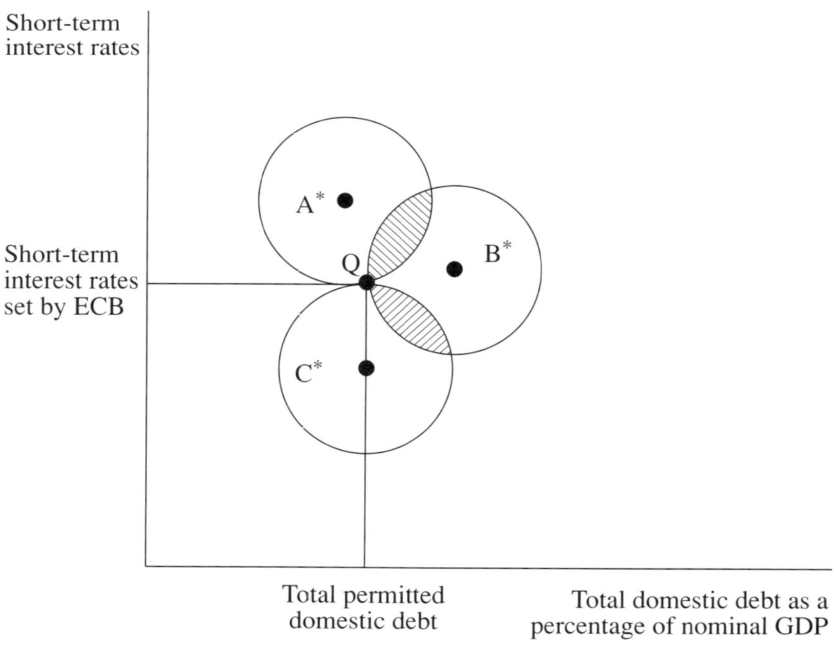

Key: * optimum or bliss point.

Figure 10.4 Monetary and fiscal policy within a win-set diagram

reflect the economic heterogeneity of their respective economies. In fact, if it were possible to condense the preference functions of all 15 members into three categories, this representation would more closely resemble reality and therefore be even more useful.

The win-sets in Figure 10.4 demonstrate that coalitions of A and B and B and C might be able to propose alternative policies that could defeat the *status quo* and make both of the parties in the winning coalition better off.

Consider the following hypothetical countries as the actors involved. Country A could be Germany with its historical preferences for relatively tighter monetary policy represented by higher short-term interests rates and relatively lower national debt. Country B could be France with its preferences for looser monetary policy and higher domestic debt levels. Country C could be Portugal with its preferences for lower interest rates and lower domestic debt than France. These examples are illustrative of the relationships between different countries within the EU. Another illustration could involve two core countries and one periphery country corresponding roughly to the proportion of countries in the respective groups.

10.4.2 From Constituent Pressure to Policy Change

Section 10.2 illustrates two links relevant to this analysis. First, it highlights the positive relationship between national economic performance and constituent support for elected decision-makers. Second, it highlights the positive relationship between domestic economic performance and support for the EU. These relationships imply that a reduction in national economic performance will lead to a decline in support for the incumbent national leadership, as well as support for participation in the EMU.

Heads of Government or State may hasten to respond to reductions in national economic performance for a number of reasons. First, expected gains from electoral participation following a negative shock may increase voter turnout. Increased expected voter turnout may increase the expected cost to politicians of not responding to constituent pressures for economic policy change. Second, politicians may fear that negative shocks give the appearance that they are not very successful at running the domestic economy and are therefore likely to receive less support in future elections. Whether or not individual leaders respond to constituent demands following adverse shocks will depend on whether individual and/or national economic concerns dominate other issues at the relevant election.

Interest groups within the EU are particularly expressive of their demands when faced with the threat of impending economic adversity. The possibility of such adversity might motivate them to demand adjustment or assistance policies to remedy their situations following economic shocks. Farmers' unions and trades' unions represent powerful interests that might bring pressure to bear on Heads of State or Government and ruling parties.

Pressures for stabilization and expansionary policy would emanate from the constituencies most strongly affected. Constituents might target national and European parliamentarians, as well as ruling government parties. Because national governments cannot adjust the direction of macroeconomic policy, such proposals must appear at the EU level. Heads of State and Government, members of the European Parliament and Commissioners can bring forward such proposals.

Heads of State or Government probably have the largest individual interest in responding to constituent demands given their position at the pinnacle of national politics. European Parliamentarians may also have interest in responding to such demands. However, MEPs represent large constituencies, in some cases equal to the size of their entire country, and are not likely to play a pivotal role individually. Nor are they likely to be the primary targets of constituent attention and ire.

Commissioners probably have the least interest in catering to constituent demands in the area of economic policy. First, the electorate plays no direct role in their appointment. Second, its role in economic policy is relatively limited, its central role in the development of the EMU since the Delors Report notwithstanding. However, the Commission maintains an interest in the survival and growth of the EU as a political entity. Herein lies its motivation in promoting policies that satisfy national policy demands in an area over which the EU exerts nearly sole authority.

10.5 POSITION SHIFTS FOLLOWING ASYMMETRIC SHOCKS AND THEIR IMPLICATIONS FOR EMU

Economic shocks to aggregate demand and supply may have asymmetric effects within the countries participating in the EMU. The economic heterogeneity as well as the limited adjustment mechanisms of these countries suggest that such differential effects are likely. Regional differences in economic activities, particularly industrial production, may promote such differences. Rigidities in the labor market represent one source of inflexibility to accommodate economic shocks

Asymmetric shocks that adversely affect national economic performance may lead to shifts in the economic and monetary policy preferences of affected EU constituents. Negative shocks may result in a shift of preferences to more expansionary monetary policy and a willingness to accumulate larger debt at least temporarily. In the two-dimensional win-set model described in the previous section, a movement of individual bliss points would reflect these preference changes. Policy brokers at the national and EU levels will likely respond to these shifts and the associated pressures if the former's interests are at stake. New coalitions may arise among countries with overlapping preferences.

10.5.1 The European Council within the Win-set Framework in the Face of Asymmetric Shocks

Asymmetric shocks to one or more national economies in the EMU may cause Heads of State or Government within the European Council to adopt new monetary and fiscal policy preferences. An exogenous shift in monetary and fiscal policy preferences within one or more countries may also give rise to calls for new policy proposals. These new preferences may give rise to calls for changes to the overall economic goals of the EU and/or the monetary policy pursued by the ECB. A win-set diagram can illustrate the initial policy combination within the EMU and the subsequent preferred policy positions of a representative sample in two-dimensional issue space. These dimensions are the amount of permitted domestic debt and the tightness of ECB monetary policy proxied by short-term interest rates.

Figure 10.5 shows the win-set diagram for three actors representing Heads of State or Government in two-dimensional issue space. Q denotes the *status quo*. A negative shock occurs. Actor B's bliss point shifts in response to the shock. The indifference curves through the initial *status quo* of actors A and B no longer overlap following the shock. This win-set disappears. However, the indifference curves of actors B and C overlap to create a new win-set after B's bliss point shifts. B and C would both prefer, or at least not object to, a policy proposal in the win-set created by their utility functions.

The new win-set offers a more expansionary policy combination than the original *status quo*. Such a policy may facilitate adjustment to the adversely affected constituencies within B's and C's countries. In particular, the loosening of the permitted debt ceiling would enable individual countries to expand domestic transfers. Such transfers may preempt labor migration which, as Obstfeld and Peri (1998, 243–5) note, may be unpopular in regions and/or countries that are net recipients of migrants.

In the event that B and C can introduce a proposal for some policy combination within the win-set, the *status quo* may change. Such a change could enable B and C to attain indifference curves closer to their individual bliss points. However, such a change would place A on a lower indifference curve and therefore reduce its country's utility. A's constituents would experience the kinds of external costs associated with decision-making identified by Buchanan and Tullock (1962). They may pressure their Head of State or Government for a return to the original policy combination. Lower interest rates

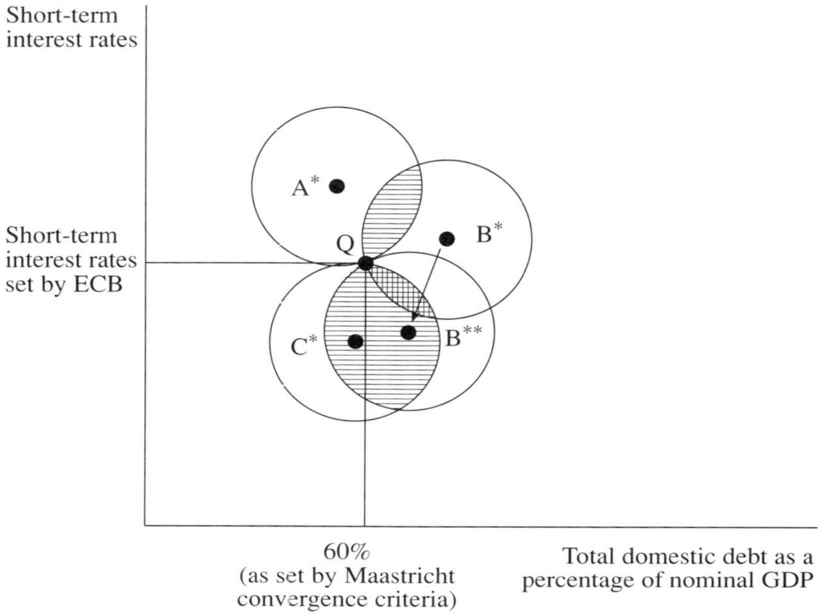

Key: * original optimum or bliss point.
** optimum or bliss point after a change in preferences by one actor.

Figure 10.5 Monetary and fiscal policy preference shifts by one actor within a win-set diagram

and larger debt in other EMU countries may reduce the wealth of net creditors in A and raise the risk of higher future inflation. Country A's constituents may experience frustration with the inability to fulfill their economic policy demands within the framework of the EU. Taken to the extreme such conditions may give rise to national demands for withdrawal from the arrangement and a return to a sovereign national currency.[9]

Movements of one or more actors in monetary and fiscal policy space may result in the formation of coalitions in favor of policy change. The direction of movement of these actors' bliss points demonstrates the new preferred policy combinations. Figure 10.6 illustrates the changes in monetary and fiscal policy preferences, respectively, that movements in different directions indicate.

Movements in northern and western directions reflect preference shifts toward relatively tighter monetary and fiscal policies. Movements in southern and eastern directions reflect preference shifts toward looser monetary and fiscal policies. Northeasterly movements reflect preference shifts toward tighter monetary and looser fiscal policy. Southwesterly movements reflect preference shifts toward looser monetary and tighter fiscal policy.

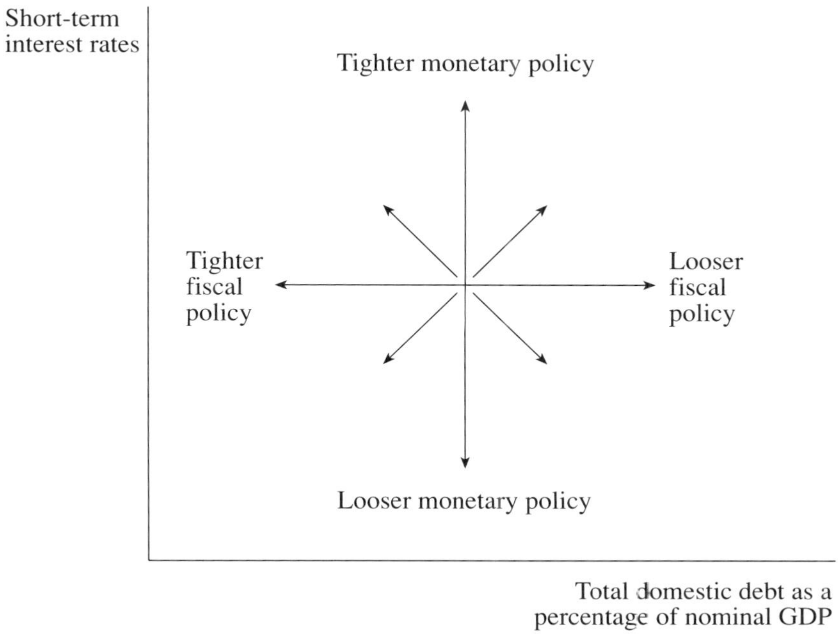

Figure 10.6 Monetary and fiscal policy directional shifts

EMU participants must secure changes in monetary policy by the ECB in order to achieve a change in short-term interest rates, whether higher or lower. EMU participants only need to press for an increase in permitted debt levels for fiscal policy preference shifts in excess of the given debt limit. Any preference shifts toward tighter fiscal policy remain at the discretion of the national government without the oversight of EMU authorities.

10.5.2 Possible Country Groupings within Monetary and Fiscal Policy Issue Space

Various groupings of EU countries may exist within monetary and fiscal policy issue space. These groupings may reflect similarities along the following dimensions: economic activities, labor market institutions and responses to economic shocks. Chapter 5, Sections 5.3 and 5.6 and Chapter 9 review the empirical evidence on these dimensions.

This evidence suggests three categories. These categories differ on the basis of vulnerability to similar supply and demand shocks, real exchange rate variability between the relevant currencies, speed of adjustment of prices following shocks, similarities of economic activities, relative labor intensity in production and similarity of GDP per capita. The empirical findings presented in Chapter 9, Sections 9.3, 9.4 and 9.6 generally support these categories. The first category, Group 1, consists of Germany, France, Belgium, Luxembourg, the Netherlands and Austria. The economies of these countries are relatively service-oriented and undergo similar responses to supply and demand shocks. The second category, Group 2, includes the southern peripheral countries: Greece, Ireland, Italy, Portugal and Spain. The third category, Group 3, consists of the lone Scandinavian country participating in EMU: Finland. (Norway and Sweden would also belong to this category based on the above criteria if they were participants in EMU.) The economies of the countries of the second and third categories are relatively more agriculture- and manufacturing-oriented. (The UK might well represent a fourth category of its own.)

The win-set diagram for these groupings may appear as in Figure 10.7.

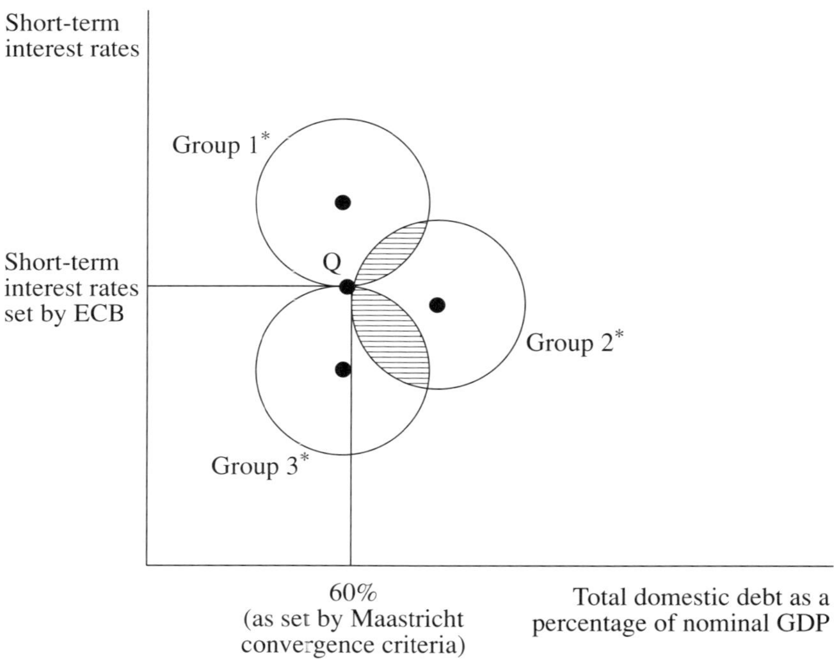

Key: * original optimum or bliss point.

Figure 10.7 Monetary and fiscal policy preferences for groups of countries based on historical data

This figure reflects the preferences of Germany's group for monetary and fiscal conservatism. The peripheral countries prefer relatively looser monetary and fiscal policy. Finland prefers looser monetary policy and desires a debt level below the maximum permitted by the GSP.

Consider the current example of the divergent performance of France and Germany. French GDP growth is currently just over 2 percent, in contrast with German GDP growth of a mere 0.4 percent. This divergence may give rise to deviations in monetary policy preferences, in particular. France may desire to maintain current monetary policy while Germany prefers a slight expansion of monetary policy to stimulate its economy. Consequently, the bliss points for the utility functions of each country will shift in opposite directions on monetary policy. Figure 10.8 depicts the current economic situation within the EMU.

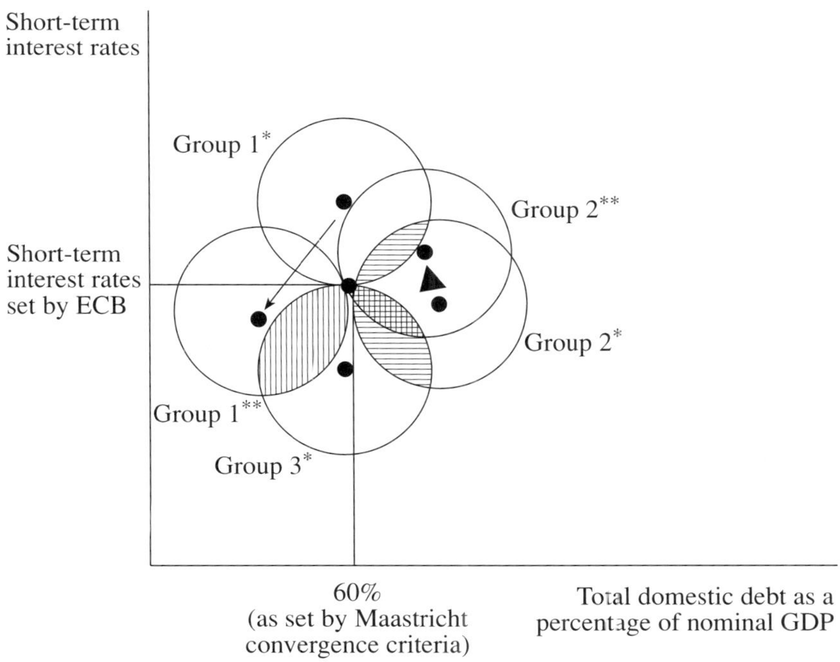

Figure 10.8 Monetary and fiscal policy preferences for groups of countries based on recent evidence

Figure 10.8 employs the following country groupings based on similarity of current economic performance: Germany, Italy, Belgium and Austria (Group 1); France, Spain and Ireland (Group 2); and Portugal, Finland, Luxembourg and the Netherlands (Group 3). The first group's preferences have changed towards looser monetary policy. Germany in part desires this change because of its weak economy at present. The second group's preferences have shifted toward slightly tighter monetary policy than they previously preferred. The third group's preferences remain completely unchanged. It prefers looser monetary and fiscal policy than the *status quo*. This stance leaves it a potential coalition partner with the first group. Figure 10.8 shows a wide area of possible policy combinations that Groups 1 and 3 might support together.

This example demonstrates the limitations of this framework because of the difficulty of categorizing countries on an *ex ante* basis because of economic differences across national economies and uncertainty regarding future economic developments within the EMU countries and beyond. The data employed by the studies examined in Chapters 5 and 9 are historical. Factors may weigh differentially in the performance of national economies at different times. In addition, economic divergences may evolve in the future from changes in current policy, regulations, economic structure, tastes, trading relations, technology and unanticipated shocks. Shocks may affect national economies differentially due to factors unique to each country. If the economic and monetary union leads to greater regional diversification, the effects of shocks may be all the more asymmetric. These differences may give rise to pressures for divergent monetary and fiscal policy combinations. For this reason, this framework remains useful for illustration purposes. It highlights the fact that economic heterogeneity raises serious doubt about the viability of a single currency among these countries.

For example, certain countries engage in relatively more international trade than other countries within the EMU. These countries will face differential consequences from expansions or contractions within their trading partners. Consider the current example of Germany. Its economy is nearly in recession partly because of the financial and economic crises in Asia and Russia.

Similarly, countries will face differential consequences from changes in the exchange rate between the euro and the national currencies of their trading partners. A tightening of monetary policy within the EMU will lead to an appreciation of the euro. Subsequently, exports from EMU countries become relatively more expensive. Foreign imports become cheaper. A loosening of monetary policy within the EMU will lead to a depreciation of the euro. EMU exports become cheaper and imports more expensive.

10.5.3 The Euro: A Currency without a Central Government

The discussion of the previous section points toward one unique and potentially problematic aspect of the EMU. The euro is a currency without a single central government. The supranational institutions of the EU are effectively agents of national governments. As such, these institutions may face divergent policy pressures from sovereign national governments. The success of the supranational institutions depends upon the adherence of national actors to the EU's institutional framework. Without the support of national governments, the EU institutions have little or no recourse to enforce policy upon them. Unlike sovereign governments, they do not have recourse to violence. However, after the replacement of national currencies with the euro they do control the currency in use at the national level.

The task of determining EMU monetary policy rests with the ECB. The independence of the ECB from political pressures from the European Council, most notably, and the Commission and Parliament will determine the amount of internal political uncertainty and divergent preferences that affects monetary policy in euro-land. National policy preferences may, however, enter policymaking within the ECB through the positions taken by national central bank heads and appointees in the Executive Board. In the absence of a stable policy direction, the euro may be more susceptible to fluctuations in its valuation to the detriment of its participants. Responses to shocks may be all the more complicated within the EMU due to greater internal economic heterogeneity.

Fiscal redistribution represents another major challenge within the EMU. Schneider and Wagner (1999, 5) note that without constitutional provisions for regional redistribution conflicts between EMU participants will likely follow adverse shocks. They (ibid.) caution that such conflict taken to the extreme may lead to withdrawal by one or more countries from the EMU.

10.5.4 The Withdrawal Option

The TEU contains no provisions for the withdrawal of any country from participation in the EMU. However, withdrawal stands as the natural alternative for countries that are unable to acquire monetary and fiscal policies that meet the demands of their constituents. For this reason, the option and related considerations deserve attention.

Bolton and Roland (1997) examine the role of fiscal policy and efficiency in the breakup and unification of countries. They use a majority rule for decisions and set the equilibrium tax rate according to the preferences of the voter with the median income. They determine that national pressures for breakup or unification depend upon the efficiency gains from unification versus the amount of income distribution across regions with heterogeneous income levels. If the government distributes income differentially across regions and the gains in efficiency from political union are small, a majority favors a breakup. These results imply that if wealth differences across EMU countries lead to fiscal (and monetary) policies that are on net more costly than the efficiency gains the arrangement creates, individual countries may opt for withdrawal from the arrangement. The loss of policy autonomy without offsetting efficiency gains drives countries to withdraw from political associations.

Intuition suggests that withdrawal from the EMU would be least costly while national currencies remain in circulation. From July 2002, the national currencies of participating countries cease to circulate. After that time, any withdrawal would require a country to introduce a new currency and encounter all of the associated start-up costs.

Withdrawal from the EMU by one or more participants would introduce a myriad of serious issues. First, withdrawal raises the issue of the refund of the capital subscription, the settlement of net capital profits and losses within the ESCB, and the transfer of property and other valuable resources between the ECB and the withdrawing country(ies). EU institutions would likely play a central role in the settlement of these issues. Second, countries that remain in the EMU may face financial penalties in the form of an interest rate premium on the euro by cautious financial markets. Third, any country that introduces a new sovereign currency faces the costs of designing, printing and distributing the new currency. In addition, accounting practices must be converted and financial measures in software, hardware and other equipment redenominated. The largest cost a country with a new currency may experience relates to establishing the credibility of the currency in world financial markets.

Important political questions also arise in case of a country's withdrawal from the EMU. Will the country continue to participate in the EU? Will Commissioners from the country retain their appointments within the Commission? Will MEPs retain their positions within the Parliament and their respective parties? Will the country continue to receive money from the EU's Structural Fund? Will the country continue to contribute to the EU's annual budget? These questions represent major issues that countries will face if any country withdraws from EMU.

10.6 CONCLUSION

The EMU consists of 12 countries with heterogeneous economies. These heterogeneities mean that the economies together experience a wider range of economic policy demands than any single country alone. Economic adversity may give rise to pressures for differential policy responses across the single currency area. Constituents of countries that do not perceive the central monetary policy response as satisfactory may pressure their leaders to withdraw from the arrangement in order to gain additional flexibility in macroeconomic adjustment policy.

NOTES

1. Miller and Listhaug (1985, 140) find evidence of the positive relationship between economic performance indicators and electoral outcomes in Norway (not yet an EU member).
2. Moser 1997 applies the spatial modeling technique to the legislative process of the EU. He offers a model of the role of the European Parliament in legislative proceedings using the cooperation procedure that involves the European Council and the European Commission. Subsequently Moser applies this model to legislation of a particular policy issue: car emission standards within the EU. He employs the concept of Nash equilibrium from game theory to accommodate the strategic behavior of the three EU institutions.
3. Krehbiel (1988, 261).
4. Circular indifference curves correspond to Euclidean preferences. Krehbiel (1988) discusses this and two other types of utility functions available to spatial models.
5. Frey and Schneider (1981) show that the German Bundesbank has yielded to political pressure in order to preserve its 'independence'.
6. Jones (1991a, 115) highlights such tendencies within the USA: 'A seemingly endless bombardment of Treasury attempts to influence Fed policy decision – with the Treasury's unsolicited advice nearly always tilted in the direction of easier money and lower Treasury borrowing costs – have been aimed at the Fed almost from its very beginning in 1913.' Havrilesky (1995a, 17, 19, 20) also notes political pressure upon the US Federal Reserve. Furthermore he finds that political principals in the Senate possess influence over Fed appointees, whereas House representatives enjoy no such influence: 'The confluence of economic and political disturbances in the early 1970s, in the early 1980s and in the 1993–94 brought about increases in legislative attacks on Federal Reserve prerogatives ... Thus, the state of the economy explains the joint proclivity of the executive branch to signal and the legislative branch to threaten the monetary authority ... These findings suggest that Fed officials do not respond to House members' concerns, but are sensitive to Senators' concerns regarding certain measures of the state of the economy. The apparent reason for this behavior is that Senators must confirm all Board appointments, while House members have no such power ...'
7. For the coming years the order is: Jun.–Dec. 2000 – France; Jan.–Jun. 2001 – Sweden; Jun.–Dec. 2001 – Belgium; Jan.–Jun. 2002 – Spain; Jun.–Dec. 2002 – Denmark; and Jan.–Jun. 2003 – Greece.
8. The following analysis is also capable of accommodating the Commission and Parliament. However, given the Commission's position as agent of the Council and the Parliament's limited role such an analysis becomes redundant. The bliss point and indifference curves of either or both of these institutions could be included. Their role in the decision process would be of no or only secondary value if included. The Council might only take their preferences into account in passing because the Council may choose to address the issue of economic policy goals or monetary policy in a manner that does not involve the interaction with either of these institutions. For an example of a win-set model of the EU's legislative decision processes, see Moser (1997).
9. George Soros writes that: 'In all likelihood the Euro will be introduced in 1999 as specified in the timetable ... People will direct all their anger and resentment over unemployment at the single currency. There may well be a political revolt – particularly in France, notorious for such rebellions – and it would likely take a nationalistic anti-European direction ... mounting popular discontent would likely sweep away present policies, including the single currency' (quoted in Eltis 1997).

11. Conclusion

11.1 REVIEW AND SUMMARY

This book is a comprehensive examination of the historical, economic and institutional foundations of the European Monetary Union. The EMU represents the latest attempt at monetary integration between the countries of Western Europe. It accompanies the Single Market Program and efforts at European political union. These economic and political attempts at integration find their roots in Western European desires to reduce the likelihood of conflict among Western European countries and aspirations to strengthen the economies of the region. These desires and aspirations date back to the last century and before.

Chapters 2 and 3 provide a survey of the history of Western European integration from the nineteenth century. A recurring pattern of attempts at economic integration followed by disintegration driven by strong domestic interests exists within Western Europe. In times of economic crisis, national interests have repeatedly supplanted supranational economic and monetary arrangements.

The introduction of a single currency and a common monetary policy follows legislative and regulatory changes aimed at the reduction and elimination of internal barriers to exchange. Advocates of currency unification argue that this additional step will further bolster the economies of the region. In addition, some proponents of economic and monetary unification anticipate that advances along these dimensions will promote political union and reduce the possibility of major conflicts between countries.

Critical to the viability of the EMU is the suitability of a common monetary policy for the economies of the participating countries. Optimum currency area theory suggests a number of criteria for the operation of a viable currency union. These criteria reflect similarities between participating economies, particularly in the presence of adverse shocks. Chapters 5 and 9 highlight the empirical similarities and dissimilarities of the economies of EU participants. The empirical evidence indicates that the EU as a whole does not meet these criteria. However, subsets of countries within the EU may indeed be candidates for membership in a more limited currency union based on historical evidence. These subsets may only be suitable if past economic and political circumstances remain unchanged. Future events may render these subsets unsuitable as well.

To the likely peril of the EMU, EU decision-makers ignored the empirical evidence in choosing participants for the first round of EMU in favor of political expediency. The European Commission employed discretion in determining the admission of participants based on candidates' fulfillment of the Maastricht Convergence Criteria.

The institutional framework plays a central role in the determination and operation of monetary policy within the EMU. Chapters 6, 7 and 8 examine the organization and operation of the relevant institutions: the Council of Ministers, the European Commission, the European Parliament and the European Central Bank. The dominance of the European Council stands out in this analysis.

Chapter 7 introduces the Rational Choice approach to the analysis of individual actors. This approach assumes that individuals are able to consistently rank order their preferences. A major benefit of this approach is that the implications for the behavior of individuals derived from one set of constraints may be applied to other actors faced with similar constraints.

This book analyzes the incentives facing political actors and their subsequent decisions analogous to the incentives and decisions facing actors within the commercial marketplace. Official decision-makers assume the role of policy brokers, while voters, interest groups and corporate entities assume the role of policy demanders and suppliers. Money, votes, advertising and post-political career remuneration opportunities constitute the media of exchange. Within this framework, the Council of Ministers, the European Commission and the European Parliament serve as the policy brokers. The European Commission may also take on the role of policy demander and supplier. The exchanges between these actors determine the policy decisions taken by national representatives within the EU institutions and by appointees within the Commission.

Finally, Chapter 10 employs the win-set framework to model the implications of heterogeneous national monetary and fiscal policy preferences within the EMU. This framework enables the identification of possible coalitions of actors supportive of changes in monetary and fiscal policy from the *status quo*. Of particular interest are the possible preference changes attributable to adverse economic shocks. Subject to institutional rules, changes in preferences by one or more actors may lead to a new vote on existing policy and subsequently to a change of policy. Given the electoral and financing link between national constituencies, interest groups and corporate entities and Heads of Government or State within the European Council, the framework used here suggests that a country disaffected by the decision of the requisite majority regarding monetary and fiscal policy may choose to withdraw from the EMU if its expected net benefits from returning to a sovereign currency are positive.

11.2 UNRESOLVED ISSUES

Western European governments have yet to undertake the needed fundamental reforms within European labor markets and tax structures. In the recent environment of economic growth in the USA and within the EU, countries have managed to see improvements in their fiscal situations. However, future threats of an economic slowdown stand as solemn reminders that the need for significant reform remains. As the economies of euro-zone countries become more closely bound within the single currency zone, the importance of these reforms cannot be understated.

Germany is taking steps in the right direction to loosen structural rigidities. In July 2000, its legislature passed a bill reducing the rate of tax on corporate profits from 40 percent to 25 percent. This act alone is expected to stimulate corporate growth and investment. In addition, German unemployment rates may decline as a result of production shifts from France to Germany following France's 1999 enactment of a 35-hour work week.

11.3 FUTURE RESEARCH DIRECTIONS

Political economists are pursuing research that explores the implications of the EMU as it evolves. One direction considers the implications of the EMU for international monetary institutions. Schneider and Wagner (1999), for example, explore the implications of the EMU and the recent economic crises in Asia for the International Monetary Fund. Another direction considers the implications of shocks to the EU for internal unemployment given existing labor market institutions. Blanchard (1999) and Blanchard and Wolfers (1999) suggest that the high and persistent unemployment characteristic of Western European labor markets will persist without changes in the relevant labor market institutions.

Another area of study concerns issues related to the operation of a currency without a central government. A natural question that follows on from the introduction of a supranational currency union such as the EMU is how durable it will be in the face of asymmetric shocks. If sovereign countries decide to withdraw from the arrangement, the EU has no means to prevent them. Unlike the national governments of its constituent members, the EU does not possess a monopoly over violence. It also has no police or military force at its direct disposal. National governments retain sovereignty in these areas.

Following the approach employed in this study, another extension concerns the implications of the expansion of EMU membership to current EU members, such as Denmark, Sweden, Greece and the UK. Their admission to the EMU may introduce new coalitions that reflect their respective preferences for monetary and fiscal policy. These coalitions may demand changes in these policies that run counter to one or more EMU participants. Some of these differences in preferences may be settled as a part of admission agreements between existing and prospective participants. Following admission, such policy changes may lead to the withdrawal of first round participants under extreme circumstances. Likewise, disaffected second round participants may subsequently opt to leave the union.

The proposed extension of EU membership to Eastern European countries suggests the opportunity for researching the suitability of these countries' economies for membership in the EMU. Such research might involve the re-estimation of models of responses to aggregate demand and supply shocks. In addition, the admission of these countries may have major implications for labor markets. The internal dynamics of the EMU in response to shocks may completely change following the opening of labor markets to the east.

The win-set framework in this book might provide two insights regarding the admission of Eastern European countries into the EMU. First, domestic debt levels and short-term interest rates for relevant countries may demonstrate whether they are suitable candidates for admission given the levels of these variables. Second, these variables may illustrate how the admission of Eastern European countries might affect the coalitions of countries already in the EMU.

11.4 OUTLOOK FOR THE FUTURE OF THE EURO

The euro's future looks certain to include challenges. Foremost among these challenges is the possibility of divergent growth between euro-zone member countries, most likely due to changes in the global economy. Of particular concern in the near term is the possibility of a global slowdown led by the US economy.

Second among the challenges facing the euro is the expansion of membership to would be EU members in Eastern Europe and along the Mediterranean. The addition of these countries would introduce further economic diversity within the region. Consequently, greater chances for asymmetric shocks and divergences in monetary policy preferences increase arise. The euro's future will indeed be a lively one.

References

Abelson, Robert P. (1996), 'The Secret Existence of Expressive Behavior', in Jeffrey Friedman (ed.), *The Rational Choice Controversy: Economic Models of Politics Reconsidered*, New Haven: Yale University Press, 25–36.

Akerlof, George A. and Janet Yellen (1985), 'A Near-rational Model of the Business Cycle, with Wage and Price Inertia', *Quarterly Journal of Economics*, **100** (Supplement), (5), 823–38.

Alesina, Alberto (1987), 'Macroeconomic Policy in a Two-party System as a Repeated Game', *Quarterly Journal of Economics*, **102** (3), 651–78.

Alesina, Alberto and Vittorio Grilli (1992), 'The European Central Bank: Reshaping Monetary Politics in Europe', in Matthew B. Canzoneri, Vittorio Grilli and Paul R. Masson (eds) (1992), *Establishing a Central Bank: Issues in Europe and Lessons from the US*, New York: Cambridge University Press.

Alesina, Alberto and Jeffrey Sachs (1988), 'Political Parties and the Business Cycle in the United States, 1948–1984', *Journal of Money, Credit and Banking*, **20** (1), 63–82.

Alesina, Alberto and Guido Tabellini (1993), 'Voting on the Budget Deficit', *Economics and Politics*, **5** (2), 145–65.

Alogoskoufis, George and Richard Portes (1991), 'International Costs and Benefits from EMU', in European Commission, *European Economy* (Special Edition), Brussels: Directorate-General for Economic and Financial Affairs.

Andersen, Svein S. and Kjell A. Eliassen (eds) (1996), *The European Union: How Democratic Is It?* London: Sage.

Andersen, Svein S. and Kjell A. Eliassen (1991), 'European Community Lobbying', *European Journal of Political Research*, **20** (2), 173–87.

Archer, Clive and Fiona Butler (1996), *The European Union: Structure and Process* (2nd edn), New York: St. Martin's Press.

Arrow, Kenneth (1951), *Social Choice and Individual Values*, New Haven: Yale University Press.

Atkeson, Andrew and Tamim Bayoumi (1991), 'Private Capital Markets and Adjustment in a Currency Union: Evidence from the United States', in Paul R. Masson and Mark P. Taylor (eds) (1993), *Policy Issues in the Operation of Currency Unions*, Cambridge: Cambridge University Press, 75–95.

Ball, Lawrence and Stephen G. Cecchetti (1988), 'Imperfect Information and Staggered Price-setting', *American Economic Review*, **78** (5), 999–1018.

Banks, Jeffrey S. (1989), 'Agency Budgets, Cost Information, and Auditing', *American Journal of Political Science*, **33** (3), 670–99.

Banks, Jeffrey S. and Barry R. Weingast (1992), 'The Political Control of Bureaucrats under Asymmetric Information', *American Journal of Political Science*, **36** (2), 509–24.

Barrell, Raymond (1992), 'The Prospects for Monetary Union in Europe', in Ray Barrell (ed.), *Economic Convergence and Monetary Union in Europe*, London: Sage Publications.

Barro, Robert J. (1990), *Macroeconomics* (3rd edn), New York: John Wiley & Sons, Inc.

Barsky, Robert B. and Jeffrey A. Miron (1989), 'The Seasonal Cycle and the Business Cycle', *Journal of Political Economy*, **97** (3), 503–534.

Bayoumi, Tamim (1992), 'The Effect of the ERM on Participating Economies', *International Monetary Fund Staff Papers*, **39** (2), 330–56.

Bayoumi, Tamim and Barry Eichengreen (1992), 'Shocking Aspects of European Monetary Integration', Discussion Paper No. 643, Centre for Economic Policy Research, London.

Bayoumi, Tamim and Barry Eichengreen (1993), 'Shocking Aspects of European Monetary Integration', in Francisco Torres and Francesco Giavazzi (eds) (1993), *Adjustment and Growth in the European Monetary Union*, Cambridge: Cambridge University Press, 193–229.

Bayoumi, Tamim and Paul Masson (1991), 'Fiscal Flows in the United States and Canada: Lessons for monetary union in Europe', Unpublished manuscript. International Monetary Fund.

Bayoumi, Tamim and Paul Masson (1998), 'Liability-creating versus Non-liability Creating Fiscal Stabilisation Policies: Ricardian Equivalence, Fiscal Stabilisation, and EU', *Economic Journal*, **108** (449), 1026–45.

Bayoumi, Tamim, Lucio Sarno and Mark P. Taylor (1999), 'European Capital Flows and Regional Risk', *The Manchester School*, **67** (1), 21–38.

Bayoumi, Tamim and Mark P. Taylor (1995), 'Macro-Economic Shocks, the ERM, and Tri-Polarity', *The Review of Economics and Statistics*, **77** (2), 321–31.

Bean, Charles R. (1994), 'European Unemployment: A Retrospective', *European Economic Review*, **38** (3–4), 523–34.

Bean, Charles, Richard Layard and Stephen Nickell (1987), *The Rise in Unemployment*, New York: Basil Blackwell.

Beck, Nathaniel (1994), 'An Institutional Analysis of the Proposed European Central Bank with Comparisons to the U.S. Federal Reserve System', in Pierre L. Syklos (ed.), *Varieties of Monetary Reforms: Lessons and Experiences on the Road to Monetary Union*, Boston: Kluwer Academic Publishers, 193–218.

Becker, Gary S. (1983), 'A Theory of Competition Among Pressure Groups for Political Influence', *Quarterly Journal of Economics*, **XCVIII** (3), 371–400. Reprinted in Charles K. Rowley (ed.) (1993), *Public Choice Theory Volume I: Homo Economicus in the Political Market Place*, Aldershot, UK and Brookfield, US: Edward Elgar Publishing, 375–404.

Becker, Gary S. (1976), 'Toward a More General Theory of Regulation: Comment', *Journal of Law and Economics*, **19** (2) 248–8.

Bellucci, Paolo (1985), 'Economic Concerns in Italian Electoral Behavior: Toward a Rational Electorate,' in Heinz Eulau and Michael S. Lewis-Beck (eds) (1985), *Economic Conditions and Electoral Outcomes: The United States and Western Europe*, New York: Agathon Press, 98–109.

Bergman, Michael, Stefan Gerlach and Lars Jonung (1993), 'The rise and fall of the Scandinavian Currency Union 1873–1920', *European Economic Review*, **37** (2–3), 507–517.

Bieber, Roland and Michael Palmer (1975), 'Power at the Top – the EC Council in Theory and Practice', *The World Today*, **31** (8), 310–318.

Blanchard, Olivier (1999), 'European Unemployment: The Role of Shocks and Institutions', Working Paper, http://web.mit.edu/blanchar/www/articles.html

Blanchard, Oliver J. (1983), 'Price Asynchronization and Price-level Inertia', in R. Dornbusch and M. Simonsen (eds), *Inflation, Debt, and Indexation*, Cambridge: MIT Press.

Blanchard, Olivier and Peter Diamond (1994), 'Ranking, Unemployment Duration and Wages', *Review of Economic Studies*, **61**, No. 3, 417–34.

Blanchard, Olivier and Stanley Fischer (1989), *Lectures on Macroeconomics*, Cambridge: MIT Press.

Blanchard, Olivier and Lawrence Katz (1992), 'Regional Evolutions', Brookings Papers on Economic Activity, **0** (1), 1–61.

Blanchard, Olivier and Lawrence H. Summers (1986), 'Hysteresis and the European Unemployment Problem', *NBER Macroeconomics Annual*, **1**, 15–78.

Blanchard, Olivier and Justin Wolfers (1999), 'The Role of Shocks and Institutions in the Rise of European Unemployment: The Aggregate Evidence', Working Paper, http://web.mit.edu/blanchar/www/articles.html

Blotevogel, Hans H. and Anthony J. Fielding (eds) (1997), *People, Jobs and Mobility in the New Europe*, Chichester: Wiley.

Board of Governors of the Federal Reserve System (1939), *The Federal Reserve System*, Washington, DC: National Capital Press.

Bolton, Patrick and Gerard Roland (1997), 'The Breakup of Nations: A Political Economy Analysis', *Quarterly Journal of Economics*, **112** (4), 1057–1086.

Bolton, Patrick and Gerard Roland (1996), 'Distributional Conflicts, Factor Mobility and Political Integration', *AEA Papers and Proceedings*, **86** (2), 99–116.

Borner, Silvio and Herbert Grubel (eds) (1992), *The European Community After 1992: Perspectives from the Outside*, Basingstoke: Macmillan.

Borooah, Vani K. (1988), 'Public Choice and Macroeconomic Policy', in Julien Van den Broeck (ed.), *Public Choice*, Dordrecht: Kluwer Academic Publishers, 61–90.

Boudreaux, Karol and Jody Lipford (1998), 'Group Size, Group Heterogeneity, and Voting Rules: An Application of the Buchanan–Tullock Model to the European Union', *European Journal of Law and Economics*, **5** (2), 133–52.

Bovenberg, A. Lans, Jeroen J.M. Kremers and Paul R. Masson (1991), 'Economic and Monetary Union in Europe and Constraints on National Budgetary Policies', *IMF Staff Papers*, **38** (2), 374–98.

Bowler, Shaun and David M. Farrell (1993), 'Legislator Shirking and Voter Monitoring: Impacts of European Parliament Electoral Systems upon Legislator–Voter Relationships', *Journal of Common Market Studies*, **31** (1), 45–69.

Brennan, Geoffrey and James M. Buchanan (1977), 'Towards a Tax Constitution for Leviathan', *Journal of Public Economics*, **8** (3), 255–73.

Brennan, Geoffrey and James M. Buchanan (1983), 'Predictive Power and the Choice Among Regimes', *Economic Journal*, **93** (369), 89–105.

Bresciani-Turroni, C. (1931), *The Economics of Inflation: A Study of Currency Depreciation in Post-war Germany, 1914–1923*, London: Allen & Unwin.

Broz, J. Lawrence (1997), *The International Origins of the Federal Reserve System*, Ithaca: Cornell University Press.

Buchanan, James M. and Gordon Tullock (1962), *The Calculus of Consent: Logical Foundations of Constitutional Democracy*, Ann Arbor: University of Michigan Press.

Buiter, Willem, Giancarlo Corsetti and Nouriel Roubini (1993), 'Excessive deficits: sense and nonsense in the Treaty of Maastricht', *Economic Policy*, **8** (16), 58–100.

Buiter, Willem and Kenneth M. Kletzer (1991) 'Reflections on the Fiscal Implications of a Common Currency', in Alberto Giovannini and Colin Mayer (eds) (1991), *Europe Financial Integration*, Cambridge: Cambridge University Press, 221–43.

Cafruny, Alan W. and Glenda G. Rosenthal (eds) (1993), *The State of the European Community: The Maastricht Debates and Beyond*, Boulder: Lynne Rienner Publishers, Inc.

Canzoneri, Matthew B., Vittorio Grilli and Paul R. Masson (1992), *Establishing a Central Bank: Issues in Europe and Lessons from the US*, New York: Cambridge University Press.

Canzoneri, Matthew B. and Carol Ann Rogers (1990), 'Is the European Community an Optimal Currency Area? Optimal Taxation Versus the Cost of Multiple Currencies', *American Economic Review*, **80** (3), 419–33.

Catenaro, Marco (1997), 'Fiscal Policy After Maastricht?' Working Paper, University of Sussex.

Central Intelligence Agency (1998), *The World Factbook 1998*, http://www.odci.gov/cia/publications/factbook/index.html

Chamie, Nick, Alain DeSerres and Rene Lalonde (1994), 'Optimum Currency Areas and Shock Asymmetry: A Comparison of Europe and the United States', Working Paper 94–1, Bank of Canada, Ottawa.

Chong, Dennis (1996), 'Rational Choice Theory's Mysterious Rivals', in Jeffrey Friedman (ed.), *The Rational Choice Controversy: Economic Models of Politics Reconsidered*, New Haven: Yale University Press, 37–57.

Chopin, Marc C., C. Steven Cole and Michael A. Ellis (1996a), 'Congressional Policy Preferences and the U.S. Monetary Policy', *Journal of Monetary Economics*, **38** (3), 581–5.

Chopin, Marc C., C. Steven Cole and Michael A. Ellis (1996b), 'Congressional Influence on U.S. Monetary Policy: A Reconsideration of the Evidence', *Journal of Monetary Economics*, **38** (3), 561–70.

Cini, Michelle (1996), *The European Commission: Leadership, Organisation and Culture in the EU Administration*, Manchester: Manchester University Press.

Cobbold, Lord (1994), 'A Rethink for the Ecu?' in Christopher Johnson and Stefan Collignon (eds), *The Monetary Economics of Europe: Causes of the EMS Crisis*, Rutherford: Fairleigh Dickinson University Press.

Cobham, David (ed.) (1994), *European Monetary Upheavals*, Manchester: Manchester University Press.

Cobham, David (1989), 'Strategies for Monetary Integration Revisited', *Journal of Common Market Studies*, **XXVII** (3), 203–218.

Cohen, Jon S. (1972), 'The 1927 Revaluation of the Lira: A Study in Political Economy', *Economic History Review*, **25** (4), 642–54.

Cohen, Roger (1997), 'Joining Euro Family, Every Member is Unhappy in His Own Way', *The New York Times*.

Colchester, Nicholas and David Buchan (1990), *Europower: The Essential Guide to Europe's Economic Transformation in 1992*, New York: Random House, Inc.

Congdon, Tim (1997), 'Why the Euro Will Fail', in Paul Temperton (ed.) (1997), *The Euro*, Chichester: John Wiley & Sons, 77–98.

Corsetti, Giancarlo and Nouriel Roubini (1993), 'The Design of Optimal Fiscal Rules for Europe after 1992', in Francisco Torres and Francesco Giavazzi (eds) (1993), *Adjustment and Growth in the European Monetary Union*, Cambridge: Cambridge University Press, 46–82.

Crawford, Malcolm. (1996), *One Money for Europe? The Economics and Politics of EMU*, New York: St. Martin's Press.

Currie, David (1997), *The Pros and Cons of EMU*, London: HM Treasury, www.euro-emu.co.uk/offdocs/prosandcons.html

Currie, David (1992a), 'European Monetary Union: Institutional Structure and Economic Performance', *The Economic Journal*, **102** (411), 248–64.

Currie, David (1992), 'Hard-ERM, Hard ECU and European Monetary Union,' in Matthew B. Canzoneri, Vittorio Grilli and Paul R. Masson (eds) (1992), *Establishing a Central Bank: Issues in Europe and Lessons from the US*, New York: Cambridge University Press, 127–47.

Currie, David and John Whitley (1994), 'What Route to European Monetary Integration?' in David Cobham (ed.), *European Monetary Upheavals*, Manchester: Manchester University Press, 167–87.

Curtis, Michael (1965), *Western European Integration*, New York: Harper and Row.

De Cecco, Marcello (1992), 'European Monetary and Financial Cooperation Before the First World War', *Rivista di Storia Economica*, **9** (1–2), 55–76.

De Cecco, Marcello (1989), 'The European Monetary System and National Interests', in Paolo Guerrieri and Pier Carlo Padoan (eds) (1989), *The Political Economy of European Integration: States, Markets and Institutions*, Savage: Barnes and Noble, 85–99.

De Cecco, Marcello (1987), 'The Gold Standard', in John Eatwell, Murray Milgate and Peter Newman (eds) (1987), *The New Palgrave: A Dictionary of Economics*, Vol. 2, London: Macmillan Press Ltd.

De Grauwe, Paul (1996), 'Monetary Union and Convergence Economics', *European Economic Review*, **40** (3–5), 1091–1101.

De Grauwe, Paul and Wim Vanhaverbeke (1991), 'Is Europe an Optimum Currency Area? Evidence from Regional Data', in Paul R. Masson and Mark P. Taylor (eds) (1993), *Policy Issues in the Operation of Currency Unions*, Cambridge: Cambridge University Press.

De Haan, Jakob and Jan-Egbert Sturm (1994), 'Political and Institutional Determinants of Fiscal Policy in the European Community', *Public Choice*, **80** (1–2), 157–72.

De Kock, M.H. (1974), 'Constitution and Administration of Central Banks, Including Ownership of Capital and Distribution of Profits', in M.H. De Kock, *Central Banking* (4th edn), New York: St. Martin's Press.

Decressin, Joerg and Antonio Fatas (1995), 'Regional Labor Market Dynamics in Europe', *European Economic Review*, **39**, 1627–55.

Dedman, Martin (1996), *The Origins and Development of the European Union: 1945–95: A History of European Integration*, New York: Routledge.

Del Mar, Alexander (1895), *History of Monetary Systems*, London: Effingham Wilson, Royal Exchange. Reprinted in 1969 by Augustus M. Kelley Publishers, New York.

Della Posta, Pompeo (1993), 'Fiscal Policy Implications of the European Union', in Wolfgang Gebauer (ed.), *Foundations of European Central Bank Policy*, Heidelberg: Physica-Verlag.

Denzau, Arthur and Michael Munger (1986), 'Legislators and interest groups: how unorganized interests get represented', *American Political Science Review*, 80, 89–106.

Destler, I.M. and C. Randall Henning (1989), *Dollar Politics: Exchange Rate Policymaking in the United States*, Washington, DC: Institute for International Economics.

Diermeier, Daniel (1996), 'Rational Choice and the Role of Theory in Political Science', in Jeffrey Friedman (ed.), *The Rational Choice Controversy: Economic Models of Politics Reconsidered*, New Haven: Yale University Press, 59–70.

Dillon, Patricia, Thomas L. Ilgen and Thomas D. Willett (1991), 'Approaches to the Study of International Organizations: Major Paradigms in Economics and Social Science', in Roland Vaubel and Thomas D. Willett (eds) (1991), *The Political Economy of International Organizations: A Public Choice Approach*, Boulder: Westview Press, 79–99.

Dornbusch, Rudiger (1988), 'Lessons from the German Inflation Experience of the 1920s', in Rudiger Dornbusch (ed.), *Exchange Rates and Inflation*, Cambridge: MIT Press.

Dornbusch, Rudiger (1991), 'Problems of Monetary Integration', in Alberto Giovaninni and Colin Mayer (eds), *European Financial Integration*, Cambridge: Cambridge University Press, 305–27.

Dowd, Kevin (1993), 'Does Europe Need a Federal Reserve System?', in Kevin Dowd, *Laissez-faire Banking*, London: Routledge, 265–80.

Dowding, Keith and Desmond King (1995), 'Introduction', in Keith Dowding and Desmond King (eds), *Preferences, Institutions and Rational Choice*, Oxford: Clarendon Press, 1–19.

Downs, Anthony (1957), *An Economic Theory of Democracy*, New York: Harper & Row.

Duisenberg, Willem F. (1999), 'The Eurosystem's Strategy for the euro', speech at a conference organized by *The Economist*, Rome (March 12), www.ecb.int/key/sp009312.htm

Eichenberg, Richard C. and Russell J. Dalton (1993), 'Europeans and the European Community: The Dynamics of Public Support for European Integration', *International Organization*, **47** (4), 507–34.

Eichengreen, Barry (1997a), *European Monetary Unification: Theory, Practice, and Analysis*, Cambridge: MIT Press.

Eichengreen, Barry (1997b), 'One Money for Europe? Lessons from the U.S. Currency Union', in Barry Eichengreen (ed.), *European Monetary Unification: Theory, Practice, and Analysis*, Cambridge: MIT Press.

Eichengreen, Barry (1997c), 'Shocking Aspects of European Monetary Unification', in Barry Eichengreen (ed.), *European Monetary Unification: Theory, Practice and Analysis*, Cambridge: MIT Press.

Eichengreen, Barry (1994a), 'Institutional Prerequisites for Economic Growth: Europe after World War II', *European Economic Review*, **38** (3–4), 883–90,

Eichengreen, Barry (1994b), 'Déjà vu All Over Again: Lessons from the Gold Standard for European Monetary Unification', Center for International and Development Economics Research, Working Paper No. C94–032, University of California, Berkeley.

Eichengreen, Barry (1993), 'European Monetary Unification and Regional Unemployment', in Lloyd Ulman, Barry Eichengreen and William T. Dickens (eds) (1993), *Labor and an Integrated Europe*, Washington, DC: Brookings Institution.

Eichengreen, Barry (1992a), 'Is Europe an Optimum Currency Area?', in Silvio Borner and Herbert Grubel (eds) (1992), *The European Community after 1992: Perspectives from the Outside*, Basingstoke: Macmillan, 138–61.

Eichengreen, Barry (1992b), *Golden Fetters: The Gold Standard and the Great Depression 1919–1939*, New York: Oxford University Press.

Eichengreen, Barry (1990), 'Is Europe an Optimum Currency Area? Evidence from Regional Data', Centre for Economic Policy Research Discussion Paper No. 478, in Herbert Grubel (ed.), *European Economic Integration: The View from the Outside*, London: MacMillan.

Eichengreen, Barry and Tamim A. Bayoumi (1994), 'The Political Economy of Fiscal Restrictions: Implications for Europe and the United States', *European Economic Review*, **38** (3–4), 783–91.

Eichengreen, Barry and Jeffrey Frieden (1993), 'The Political Economy of European Monetary Unification: An Analytical Introduction', *Economics and Politics*, **5** (2), 85–104.

Eichengreen, Barry, Jeffrey Frieden and Jürgen Von Hagen (1995), *Politics and Institutions in an Integrated Europe*, New York: Springer-Verlag.

Eichengreen, Barry and Charles Wyplosz (1998), 'The Growth and Stability Pact: More than a Minor Nuisance?' *Economic Policy*, **0** (26), 65–104.

Eichengreen, Barry and Charles Wyplosz (1994), 'How to Save the EMS', in Christopher Johnson and Stefan Collignon (eds) (1994), *The Monetary Economics of Europe: Causes of the EMS Crisis*, Rutherford: Fairleigh Dickinson University Press.

Eichengreen, Barry and Charles Wyplosz (1993), 'The Unstable EMS', *Brookings Papers on Economic Activity*, **1**, 51–139.

Eltis, Walter (1997), 'The Creation and Destruction of the Euro', Policy Study No. 155, London: Centre for Policy Studies.

Ellwood, D.W. (1991), 'The Marshall Plan and the Politics of Growth', in Peter M.R. Stirk and David Willis (eds) (1991), *Shaping Postwar Europe: European Unity and Disunity 1945–1957*, New York: St. Martin's Press.

Englander, Steven and Thomas Egebo (1993), 'Adjustment Under Fixed Exchange Rates: Application to the European Monetary Union', *OECD Economic Studies*, **20**, 7–40.

Eulau, Heinz and Michael S. Lewis-Beck (1985), *Economic Conditions and Electoral Outcomes: The United States and Western Europe*, New York: Agathon Press.

European Central Bank, Press Division (1998) *A Stability-oriented Monetary Policy Strategy for the ESCB*, http://www.ecb.int/press/pr981013_1.htm

European Commission (1992), *One Market, One Money*, Brussels.

European Commission (1990), 'Social Europe', *European Economy* (Special Edition), Brussels.

European Economy, (Special Edition, 1990), Commission of the European Communities, Luxembourg, Office for Official Publications of the European Communities, 1990–1992, No. 1.

Faina Medin, J. Andres and Pedro Puy Fraga (1988), 'A Framework for a Public Choice Analysis of the European Community', *Journal of Public Finance and Public Choice*, **6** (2), 141–58.

Fatas, Antonio (1997), 'EMU: Countries or Regions? Lessons from the EMS Experience', *European Economic Review*, **41** (3–5), 743–51.

Ferejohn, John and Morris P. Fiorina (1974), 'The Paradox of Not Voting: A Decision Theoretic Analysis', *American Political Science Review*, **68** (2), 525–36.

Ferejohn, John and Debra Satz (1996), 'Unification, Universalism, and Rational Choice Theory', in Jeffrey Friedman (ed.) (1996), *The Rational Choice Controversy: Economic Models of Politics Reconsidered*, New Haven: Yale University Press, 71–84.

Fiorina, Morris P. (1996), 'Rational Choice, Empirical Contributions, and the Scientific Enterprise', in Jeffrey Friedman (ed.) (1996), *The Rational Choice Controversy: Economic Models of Politics Reconsidered*, New Haven: Yale University Press, 85–94.

Fischer, Stanley (1977), 'Wage Indexation and Macroeconomic Stability', Carnegie-Rochester Conference Series on Public Policy, **5**, 107–47.

Flandreau, Marc (1996), 'The French Crime of 1873: An Essay on the Emergence of the International Gold Standard, 1870–1880', *Journal of Economic History*, **56** (4), 862–97.

Flandreau, Marc (1993), 'On the Inflationary Bias of Common Currencies: The Latin Union Puzzle', *European Economic Review*, **37** (2–3), 501–506.

Flandreau, Marc, Jacques Le Cacheux and Frederic Zumer (1998), 'Stability without a Pact? Lessons from the European Gold Standard, 1880–1914', *Economic Policy*, 26, 115–49.

Folkerts-Landau, David and Peter M. Garber (1992), 'The ECB: A Bank or a Monetary Rule', in Matthew B. Canzoneri, Vittorio Grilli and Paul R. Masson (eds) (1992), *Establishing a Central Bank: Issues in Europe and Lessons from the US*, New York: Cambridge University Press, 86–110.

Forni, M. and L. Reichlin (1997), 'National Forces and Local Economies: Europe and the United States', CEPR Discussion Paper No. 1632.

Forsyth, Douglas J., and Ton Notermans (eds) (1997), *Regime Changes: Macro-economic Policy and Financial Regulation in Europe from the 1920s to the 1990s*, Providence: Berghahn Books.

Frankel, Jeffrey (1996), 'Recent Exchange-rate Experience and Proposals for Reform', *AEA Papers and Proceedings*, **86** (2), 153–8.

Frankel, Jeffrey, Steven Phillips and Menzie Chin (1993), 'Financial and Currency Integration in the European Monetary System: The Statistical Record', in Francisco Torres and Francesco Giavazzi (eds) (1993), *Adjustment and Growth in the European Monetary Union*, Cambridge: Cambridge University Press, 270–306.

Fratianni, Michele (1988), 'The European Monetary System: How Well Has It Worked?' *Cato Journal*, **8** (2), 477–501.

Frey, Bruno S. (1971), 'Why Do High Income People Participate More in Politics?' *Public Choice*, **XI**, 101–105.

Frey, Bruno S. and Beat Gygi (1991), 'International Organizations from the Constitutional Point of View', in Roland Vaubel and Thomas D. Willett (eds) (1991), *The Political Economy of International Organizations: A Public Choice Approach*, Boulder: Westview Press, 58–78.

Frey, Bruno and Friedrich Schneider (1981), 'Central Bank Behavior: A Positive Empirical Analysis', *Journal of Monetary Economics*, **7** (3), 291–315.

Frey, Bruno and Hannelore Weck (1983), 'A Statistical Study of the Effect of the Great Depression on Elections: The Weimar Republic, 1930–33', *Political Behavior*, **5** (4), 403–20.

Frieden, Jeffrey, Daniel Gros and Erik Jones (1998), *The New Political Economy of EMU*, Lanham: Rowman and Littlefield.

Friedman, Jeffrey (1996a), 'Introduction Economic Approaches to Politics', in Jeffrey Friedman (ed.) (1996), *The Rational Choice Controversy: Economic Models of Politics Reconsidered*, New Haven: Yale University Press, 1–24.

Friedman, Jeffrey (ed.) (1996b), *The Rational Choice Controversy: Economic Models of Politics Reconsidered*, New Haven: Yale University Press.

Friedman, Milton (1998), 'The Role of Monetary Policy', [Collective Volume Article], *Economic Policy*, Vol. 1, Paul F. Whiteley (ed.), Elgar Reference Collection International Library of Comparative Public Policy, Vol. 6, Cheltenham, UK and Northampton, Mass: Elgar, 46–62.

Friedman, Milton (1984), 'Monetary Policy for the 1980s', in John H. Moore (ed.), *To Promote Prosperity: U.S. Domestic Policy in the mid-1980s*, Stanford, CA: Hoover Institution.

Friedman, Milton (1953), 'The Methodology of Positive Economics', in Daniel M., Hausman (ed.) (1984), *The Philosophy of Economics: An Anthology*, New York: Cambridge University Press, 210–44.

Funke, Michael (1997), 'The Nature of Shocks in Europe and Germany', *Economica*, **64** (255), 461–9.

Giavazzi, Francesco and Marco Pagano (1988), 'The Advantage of Tying One's Hands: EMS Discipline and Central Bank Credibility', *European Economic Review*, **32** (5), 1055–82.

Gildea, John A. (1990), 'Explaining FOMC Members' Votes', in Thomas Mayer (ed.) (1990), *The Political Economy of American Monetary Policy*, Cambridge: Cambridge University Press, 211–27.

Giovannini, Alberto (1995), *The Debate on Money in Europe*, Cambridge: MIT Press.

Giovannini, Alberto and Colin Mayer (eds) (1991), *European Financial Integration*, Cambridge: Cambridge University Press.

Goldstein, Morris and Geoffrey Woglom (1992), 'Market-based Fiscal Discipline in Monetary Unions: Evidence from the US Bond Market', in Matthew B. Canzoneri, Vittorio Grilli and Paul E. Masson (eds) (1992), *Establishing a Central Bank: Issues in Europe and Lessons from the US*, New York: Cambridge University Press.

Goodhart, Charles (1996), 'European Monetary Integration', *European Economic Review*, **40** (3–5), 1083–1090.

Goodhart, Charles (1993), 'The European System of Central Banks after Maastricht', in Paul R. Masson and Mark P. Taylor (eds) (19933), *Policy Issues in the Operation of Currency Unions*, Cambridge: Cambridge University Press.

Goodman, John B. (1992), *Monetary Sovereignty: The Politics of Central Banking in Western Europe*, Cornell: Cornell University Press.

Gorges, Michael J. (1993), 'Interest Intermediation in the EC After Maastricht', in Alan W. Cafruny and Glenda G. Rosenthal (eds) (1993), *The State of the European Community: The Maastricht Debates and Beyond*, Boulder: Lynne Rienner Publishers, Inc., 73, 78.

Gowa, Joanne (1983), *Closing the Gold Window: Domestic Politics and the End of Bretton Woods*, Ithaca: Cornell University Press.

Green, Donald P. and Ian Shapiro (1996), 'Pathologies Revisited: Reflections on Our Critics', in Jeffrey Friedman (ed.) (1996), *The Rational Choice Controversy: Economic Models of Politics Reconsidered*, New Haven: Yale University Press, 235–75.

Green, Donald P. and Ian Shapiro (1994), *Pathologies of Rational Choice Theory*, New Haven: Yale University Press.

Gretschmann, Klaus (ed.) (1993), *Economic and Monetary Union: Implications for National Policy-makers*, Norwell: Kluwer Academic Publishers.

Gretschmann, Klaus, Hans-Helmut Kotz and Olaf Sleijpen (1993), 'The European Monetary System: The Geography of Economics versus the Politics of Money', in Klaus Gretschmann (ed.) (1993), *Economic and Monetary Union: Implications for National Policy-makers*, Norwell: Kluwer Academic Publishers, 27–50.

Grier, Kevin B. (1996), 'Congressional Oversight Committee Influence on U.S. Monetary Policy Revised', *Journal of Monetary Economics*, **38** (3), 571–9.

Grier, Kevin B. (1991), 'Congressional Influence on U.S. Monetary Policy: An Empirical Test', *Journal of Monetary Economics*, **28** (2), 201–220.

Grier, Kevin B. (1986), 'Monetary Policy as Political Equilibrium', *Cato Journal*, **6** (2), 539–43.

Gros, Daniel (1998), 'External Shocks and Labour Mobility: How Important Are They for EMU?' in Jeffry Frieden, Daniel Gros and Erik Jones (eds) (1998), *The New Political Economy of EMU*, Lanham: Rowman and Littlefield Publishers, Inc., 53–82.

Gros, Daniel and Niels Thygesen (1992), *European Monetary Integration*, New York: St. Martin's Press.

Guerrieri, Paolo and Pier Carlo Padoan (1989), *The Political Economy of European Integration: States, Markets and Institutions*, Savage: Barnes and Noble.

Gwartney, James D. and Richard E. Wagner (eds) (1988), *Public Choice and Constitutional Economics*, Greenwich: JAI Press, Inc.

Hall, Robert E. (1978), 'Stochastic Implications of the Life Cycle-permanent Income Hypothesis: Theory and Evidence', *Journal of Political Economy*, **86** (6), 971–87.

Hammond, Thomas, Jeffrey Hill and Gary J. Miller (1986), 'Presidential Appointment of Bureau Chiefs and the "Congressional Control of Administration" Hypothesis', Paper presented at a meeting of the American Political Science Association, Washington, DC.

Havrilesky, Thomas (1995a), 'The Pressures on Monetary Policy: An Overview', in Thomas Havrilesky (ed.) (1995), *The Pressures on American Monetary Policy* (2nd edn), Boston: Kluwer Academic Publishers, 11–27.

Havrilesky, Thomas (1995b), 'Banking and Other Private Sector Influences on Monetary Policy', in Thomas Havrilesky (ed.) (1995), *The Pressures on American Monetary Policy* (2nd edn), Boston: Kluwer Academic Publishers, 255–87.

Hayes-Renshaw, Fiona (1996), *The Council of Ministers*, New York: St. Martin's Press.

Hayes-Renshaw, Fiona and Helen Wallace (1997), *The Council of Ministers*, New York: St. Martin's Press.

Hayes-Renshaw, Fiona and Helen Wallace (1995), 'Executive Power in the European Union: The Functions and Limits of the Council of Ministers', *Journal of European Public Policy*, **2** (4), 559–82.

Hibbs, Douglas A. (1981), 'Economics and Politics in France: Economic Performance and Mass Political Support for the Presidents Pompidou and Giscard d'Estaing', in Douglas A. Hibbs (1987), *The Political Economy of Industrial Economies*, Cambridge: Harvard University Press, 224–40.

Hill, Jeffrey (1985), 'Why So Much Stability? The Role of Agency-determined Stability', *Public Choice*, **46** (3), 275–87.

Hindess, Barry (1989), *Political Choice and Social Structure: An Analysis of Actors, Interests and Rationality*, Aldershot: Edward Elgar.

Hoeller, Peter and Marie-Odile Louppe (1994), 'The EC's Internal Market: Implementation and Economic Effects', *OECD Economic Studies*, **23** (4), 55–107.

Holcombe, Randall G. (1996), 'Vibert's Vision: Constitutional Theory in Search of a Constitution', *Constitutional Political Economy*, **7** (4), 281–91.

Holcombe, Randall G. (1993), *The Economic Foundations of Government*, New York: New York University Press,

Holtfrerich, Carl-Ludwig (1993), 'Did Monetary Unification Precede or Follow Political Unification of Germany in the 19th Century?' *European Economic Review*, **37** (2–3), 518–24.

Horstmann, Winfried and Friedrich Schneider (1994), 'Deficits, Bailout and Free Riders: Fiscal Elements of a European Constitution', *Kyklos*, **47** (3), 365–83.

Hubbard, R. Glenn (1995), *Money, the Financial System, and the Economy*, (2nd edn), Reading: Addison-Wesley Publishing Company, Inc.

Jackman, Richard (1995), 'Unemployment and Wage Inequalities in OECD Countries', Discussion Paper No. 235, Centre for Economic Performance.

Jacobs, Francis and Richard Corbett (1990), *The European Parliament*, Boulder: Westview Press.

Johnson, Christopher and Stefan Collignon (eds) (1994), *The Monetary Economics of Europe: Causes of the EMS Crisis*, Rutherford: Fairleigh Dickinson University Press.

Johnston, Mary Troy (1994), *The European Council: Gatekeeper of the European Community*, Boulder: Westview Press.

Jones, David M. (1991a), 'Unrelenting Political Pressures', in David M. Jones (1991), *The Politics of Money: The Fed Under Alan Greenspan*, New York: New York Institute of Finance, 111–20.

Jones, David M. (1991b), 'A New Central Bank for Europe', in David M. Jones (1991), *The Politics of Money: The Fed Under Alan Greenspan*, New York: New York Institute of Finance, 177–97.

Jonung, Lars and Eskil Wadensjoe (1979), 'The Effect of Unemployment, Inflation and Real Income Growth on Government Popularity in Sweden', *Scandinavian Journal of Economics*, **81** (2), 343–53.

Kane, Edward J. (1986), 'Politics and Fed Policymaking: The More Things Change the More They Remain the Same', in Eugenia Froedge Toma and Mark Toma (eds) (1986), *Central Bankers, Bureaucratic Incentives and Monetary Policy*, Dordrecht: Kluwer Academic Publishers, 185–98.

Keesing's Research Report (1975), *The European Communities: Establishment and Growth*, New York: Charles Scribner's Sons.

Kelley, Stanley, Jr. (1996), 'The Promise and Limitations of Rational Choice Theory', in Jeffrey Friedman (ed.), *The Rational Choice Controversy: Economic Models of Politics Reconsidered*, New Haven: Yale University Press, 95–106.

Kenen, Peter B. (1969), 'The Theory of Optimum Currency Areas: An Eclectic View', in R. Mundell and K. Swoboda, (eds), *Monetary Problems of the International Economy*, Chicago: University of Chicago Press.

Kenen, Peter B. (1995), *Economic and Monetary Union in Europe: Moving beyond Maastricht*, Cambridge: Cambridge University Press.

Kindleberger, Charles P. (1986), *The World in Depression 1929–1939*, Berkeley: University of California Press.

Kirchgässner, Gebhard (1977), 'Wirtschaftslage und Wählerverhalten', *Politische Vierteljahresschrift*, **18** (2–3), 510–36.

Kirchgässner, Gebhard (1976), *Rationales Wählerverhalten und Optimales Regierungsverhalten*, Ph.D. dissertation, University of Konstanz.

Kirschen, Etienne-Sadi with Henry Simon Block and William Bruce Bassett (1969), *Financial Integration in Western Europe*, New York: Columbia University Press.

Kitzinger, U.W. (1964), *The Politics and Economics of European Integration: Britain, Europe, and the United States*, New York: Frederick A. Praeger.

Krehbiel, Keith (1988), 'Spatial Models of Legislative Choice', *Legislative Studies Quarterly*, **13** (3), 259–319.

Krugman, Paul (1993), 'Lessons of Massachusetts for EMU', in Francisco Torres and Francesco Giavazzi (eds) (1993), *Adjustment and Growth in the European Monetary Union*, Cambridge: Cambridge University Press, 241–61.

Lafay, Jean-Dominique (1984), 'Political Change and Stability of the Popularity Function: The French General Election of 1981', in Heinz Eulau and Michael S. Lewis-Beck (eds) (1985), *Economic Conditions and Electoral Outcomes: The United States and Western Europe*, New York: Agathon Press, 78–97.

Lancaster, Thomas D. (1985), 'Economics, Democracy, and Spanish Elections', in Heinz Eulau and Michael S. Lewis-Beck (eds) (1985), *Economic Conditions and Electoral Outcomes: The United States and Western Europe*, New York: Agathon Press, 110–24.

Lane, Jan-Erik, Reinert Maeland and Sven Berg (1996), 'Voting Power Under the EU Constitution', in Svein S. Andersen and Kjell A. Eliassen (eds) (1996), *The European Union: How Democratic Is It*?, London: Sage.

Laursen, K. and J. Pedersen (1964), *The German Inflation, 1918–1923*, Amsterdam: North Holland.

Layard, Richard, Stephen Nickell and Richard Jackman (1991), *Unemployment Macroeconomic Performance and the Labor Market*, Oxford: Oxford University Press.

Layard R. and Nickell S. (1987), 'The Labour Market', in Rudiger Dornbusch and Stephen Nickell (eds), *The Performance of the British Economy*, Oxford, Clarendon Press.

Lewis-Beck, Michael S. (1988), *Economics and Elections: The Major Western Democracies*, Ann Arbor University of Michigan Press.

Lewis-Beck, Michael S. (1980), 'Economic Conditions and Executive Popularity: The French Experience', *American Journal of Political Science*, **24** (2), 306–23.

Lieberman, Sima (1992), *The Long Road to a European Monetary Union*, Lanham: University Press of America,

Lindbeck, Assar and Dennis J. Snower (1988), *The Insider-Outsider Theory of Employment and Unemployment*, Cambridge: MIT Press.

Lodge, Juliet (1984), 'The 1984 Euro-elections: A Damp Squib?' *The World Today*, **40** (8–9), 333–40.

Lohmann, Susanne (1996), 'The Poverty of Green and Shapiro', in Jeffrey Friedman (ed.) (1996), *The Rational Choice Controversy: Economic Models of Politics Reconsidered*, New Haven: Yale University Press, 127–54,

Lucas, Robert (1976), 'Econometric Policy Evaluation: A Critique', Carnegie-Rochester Conference Series on Public Policy, **1** (2), 19–46.

Lucas, Robert (1973), 'Some International Evidence on Output-Inflation Tradeoffs', *American Economic Review*, **63** (3), 326–34.

Madsen, Jakob B. (1998), 'New Keynesian versus New Classical Theories of Aggregate Supply: Evidence from the OECD Countries', *Scottish Journal of Political Economy*, **45** (33), 273–93.

Mally, Gerhard (1973), *The European Community in Perspective: The New Europe, the United States and the World*, Lexington: Lexington Books.

Mankiw, N. Gregory (1994), *Macroeconomics* (2nd edn), New York: Worth Publishers, Inc.

Mankiw, N. Gregory (1985), 'Small Menu Costs and Large Business Cycles: A Macroeconomic Model of Monopoly', *The Quarterly Journal of Economics*, **10** (2), 529–38.

Manning, Alan (1993), 'An Economic Analysis of the Effects of Pre-strike Behavior', in David Metcalf and Simon Milner (eds), *New Perspectives on Industrial Disputes*, New York: Routledge, 115–32.

Maor, Moshe (1995), 'Party Competition in Interlinked Political Markets: The European Union and its Member States', in Keith Dowding and Desmond King (eds) (1995), *Preferences, Institutions and Rational Choice*, Oxford: Clarendon Press, 114–33.

Martino, Antonio (1990), 'A Monetary Constitution for Europe?', *CATO Journal*, **10** (2), 519–23.

Masson, Paul R. and Mark P. Taylor (eds) (1993a), *Policy Issues in the Operation of Currency Unions*, Cambridge: Cambridge University Press.

Masson, Paul R. and Mark P. Taylor (1993b), 'Currency Unions: A Survey of the Issues', in Paul R. Masson and Mark P. Taylor (eds) (1993), *Policy Issues in the Operation of Currency Unions*, Cambridge: Cambridge University Press.

McChesney, Fred (1997), *Money for Nothing: Politicians, Rent Extraction, and Political Extortion*, Cambridge: Harvard University Press.

McCubbins, Mathew D., Roger G. Noll and Barry R. Weingast (1990), 'Slack, public interest and structure induced policy', *Journal of Law, Economics and Organization*, **6** (0), 203–212.

McCubbins, Matthew D., Roger G. Noll and Barry R. Weingast (1989), 'Structure and Process, Politics and Policy: Administrative Arrangements and the Political Control of Agencies', *Virginia Law Review*, **75**, 431–82.

McKinnon, R.I. (1963), 'Optimum Currency Areas', *American Economic Review*, **53**, (4), 717–25.

Mehnert-Meland, Ralph (1995), *Central Bank to the European Union: European Monetary Institute, European System of Central Banks, European Central Bank, Structures, Tasks and Functions*, London: Kluwer Law International.

Mehrez, Gil and Natacha Valla (1998), 'EMU: What if the Shocks are in the Labor Markets?' Working Paper, Working Paper Archive, Washington University at St. Louis, http://www.ssc.wisc.edu/econ/archive/wpa.html

Menkhoff Lukas (1997), *Monetary Policy Instruments for European Monetary Union*, Heidelberg: Springer-Verlag Berlin.

Miller, Arthur and Olga Listhaug (1985), 'Economic Effects on the Vote in Norway', in Heinz Eulau and Michael S. Lewis-Beck (eds) (1985), *Economic Conditions and Electoral Outcomes: The United States and Western Europe*, New York: Agathon Press, 125–43.

Mitchell, William C. and Michael C. Munger (1991), 'Economic Models of Interest Groups: An Introductory Survey', *American Journal of Political Science*, **35** (2), 512–46. Reprinted in Charles K. Rowley (ed.) (1993), *Public Choice Theory Volume I: Homo Economicus in the Political Market Place*, Brookfield: Edward Elgar Publishing, 405–40.

Moe, Terry M., (1990), 'Political Institutions: The Neglected Side of the Story', in Charles K. Rowley (ed.) (1993b), *Public Choice Theory Volume III: The Separation of Powers and Constitutional Political Economy*, Brookfield: Edward Elgar Publishing, 63–105.

Molle, Willem and Aad Van Mourik (1988), 'International Movements of Labour under Conditions of Economic Integration: The Case of Western Europe', *Journal of Common Market Studies*, **XXVI** (3), 317–42.

Moore, Carl H. (1990), *The Federal Reserve System: A History of the First 75 Years*, Jefferson: McFarland and Company, Inc., Publishers.

Moser, Peter (1997), *Checks and Balances in Democracies: Applications of the Positive Theory of Political Institutions to Decision-making in Switzerland, the European Union, and to Central Bank Independence*, 2nd revised manuscript, St. Gallen.

Moure, Kenneth (1996), 'Undervaluing the franc Poincaré', *Economic History Review*, **LIX** (1), 137–53.

Mueller, Dennis C. (1989), *Public Choice II: A Revised Edition of Public Choice*, Cambridge: Cambridge University Press.

Mundell, Robert (1961), 'A Theory of Optimum Currency Areas', *American Economic Review*, **51**, 657–65.

Munger, Michael C. and Brian E. Roberts (1990), 'The Federal Reserve and its Institutional Environment: A Review', in Thomas Mayer (ed.) (1990), *The Political Economy of American Monetary Policy*, Cambridge: Cambridge University Press, 83–98.

Murphy, James Bernard (1996), 'Rational Choice Theory as Social Physics', in Jeffrey Friedman (ed.) (1996), *The Rational Choice Controversy: Economic Models of Politics Reconsidered*, New Haven: Yale University Press, 155–74.

Murray, Philomena and Paul Rich (1996), *Visions of European Unity*, Boulder: Westview Press.

Neumann, M. and J. Von Hagen (1991), 'Real Exchange Rates Within and Between Currency Areas: How Far Away is EMU?', Discussion Paper, Indiana University, Bloomington, IN.

Nickell, Stephen (1997), 'Unemployment and Labor Market Rigidities: Europe versus North America', *Journal of Economic Perspectives*, **11** (3), 5–74.

Nicoll, William (1984), 'The Luxembourg Compromise', *Journal of Common Market Studies*, **23** (1), 35–43.

Nicoll, William and Trevor C. Salmon (1994), *Understanding the New European Community*, New York: Harvester Wheatsheaf.

Niskanen, W.A. (1975), 'Bureaucrats and Politicians', *Journal of Law and Economics*, **18** (3), 617–44. Reprinted in W.A. Niskanen (1994), *Bureaucracy and Public Economics*, Aldershot: Edward Elgar Publishing, 243–67.

Niskanen, W.A. (1971), *Bureaucracy and Representative Government*, Chicago: Aldine Press. Reprinted in W.A. Niskanen (1994), *Bureaucracy and Public Economics*, Aldershot: Edward Elgar Publishing

Nölling, Wilhelm (1993), *Monetary Policy in Europe after Maastricht*, transl. Brian Rasmussen with Allan Blunden, Alistair McCrae and Susan Powell, New York: St. Martin's Press.

Nordhaus, William (1975), 'The Political Business Cycle', *The Review of Economic Studies*, **42** (2), 169–90.

Nowak, Laura S. (1993), *Monetary Policy and Investment Opportunities*, Westport: Quorum Books.

Nugent, Neill (1991), *The Government and Politics of the European Community*, 2nd ed, Durham University Press.

Oatley, Thomas H. (1997), *Monetary Politics: Exchange Rate Cooperation in the European Union*, Ann Arbor: The University of Michigan Press.

Obstfeld, Maurice and Giovanni Peri (1998), 'Regional Non-adjustment and Fiscal Policy', *Economic Policy*, **0** (26), 205–47.

OECD (1996), *OECD Employment Outlook*, **59**, Organisation for Economic Co-operation and Development, Paris.

OECD (1998), *OECD Economic Outlook*, **64**, Organisation for Economic Co-operation and Development, Paris, A-211, A-213, A-251.

Olson, Mancur (1965), *The Logic of Collective Action*, Cambridge: Harvard University Press.

Ordeshook, Peter (1986), *Game Theory and Political Theory: An Introduction*, Cambridge: Cambridge University Press.

Overturf, Stephen Frank (1986), *The Economic Principles of European Integration*, New York: Praeger.

Padoa-Schioppa, Tommaso (1994), *The Road to Monetary Union in Europe: The Emperors, the Kings and the Genies*, Oxford: Clarendon Press.

Paldam, Martin and Friedrich Schneider (1980), 'The Macro-economic Aspects of Government and Opposition Popularity in Denmark, 1957–78', *National okonomisk Tiddskrift*, **118** (2), 149–70.

Palfrey, T.R. and H. Rosenthal (1985), 'Voter Participation and Strategic Uncertainty', *American Political Science Review*, **79**, 62–78.

Panic, M. (1992), *European Monetary Union: Lessons from the Classical Gold Standard*, New York: St. Martin's Press.

Pegg, C.H. (1962) 'Die Wachsende Bedeutung der europaeischen Einigungsbewegung in den Zwanzigen Jarhren', *Europe Archiv*, 24, 866.

Peirce, W.S. (1991), 'Unanimous Decisions in a Redistributive Context: The Council of Ministers of the European Communities', in R. Vaubel and T.D. Willett (eds), *The Political Economy of International Organization: A Public Choice Approach*, Boulder, CO: Westview, 267–85.

Peltzman, Sam (1976), 'Toward a more general theory of regulation', *Journal of Law and Economics*, **19** (2), 211–40.

Peretz, Paul (1983), 'Making Inflation Policy', in Paul Peretz (1983), *The Political Economy of Inflation in the United States*, Chicago: The University of Chicago Press.

Perlman, M. (1993), 'In Search of Monetary Union', *Journal of European Economic History*, **22** (2), 313–32.

Persson, Sven and Guido Tabellini (1996), 'Monetary Cohabitation in Europe', *AEA Papers and Proceedings*, **86** (2), 111–16.

Phipps, A.J. (1992), 'Trade Union Objectives, Strike Frequency and the Phillips Curve', *Australian Economic Papers*, **31** (58), 111–26.

Pierce, James L. (1990), 'The Federal Reserve as a Political Power', in Thomas Mayer (ed.) (1990), *The Political Economy of American Monetary Policy*, Cambridge: Cambridge University Press, 151–64.

Pissarides, Christopher A. (1980), 'British Government Popularity and Economic Performance', *Economic Journal*, **90** (3593), 569–81.

Pollard, Sidney (1981), *The Integration of the European Economy Since 1815*, University Association for Contemporary European Studies, London: George Allen and Unwin.

Poloz, Stephen S. (1990), 'Choosing an Exchange Rate Regime: The Challenge for Smaller Industrial Countries: Postscript: Exchange Rate Policy in Canada', collective volume article in *Choosing an Exchange Rate Regime: The Challenge for Smaller Industrial Countries*, Victor Argy and Paul De Grauwe (eds), International Monetary Fund, Washington, DC, pp. 374–77.

Portes, Richard (1996), 'Implementing EMU', *AEA Papers and Proceedings*, **86** (2), 139–42.

Powell, G. Bingham, Jr. (1983), 'The Science of Politics: Cleavages, Party Ideology and Accountability in Comparative Voting Behavior', Paper presented at the annual meeting of the American Political Science Association, Chicago.

Riker, William H. and Peter C. Ordeshook (1968), 'A Theory of the Calculus of Voting', *American Political Science Review*, **LXII** (1), 25–42. Reprinted in Charles K. Rowley (ed.) (1993), *Public Choice Theory Volume I: Homo Economicus in the Political Market Place*, Brookfield: Edward Elgar Publishing, 240–57.

Rogoff, Kenneth (1990), 'Equilibrium Political Budget Cycles', *American Economic Review*, **80** (1) 21–36.

Rogoff, Kenneth (1985), 'Can Exchange Rate Predictability Be achieved Without Monetary Convergence? Evidence from the EMS', *European Economic Review*, **28** (1–2), 93–115.

Romer, Christina D. (1986), 'Is the Stabilization of the Postwar Economy a Figment of the Data?', *American Economic Review*, **76** (3), 314–34.

Rosa, Jean-Jacques (1980), 'Economic Conditions and Elections in France', in Paul Whiteley (ed.), *Models of Political Economy*, London: Sage, 101–20.

Rosenthal, Glenda G. (1975), *The Men Behind the Decisions*, Lexington: Lexington Books.

Roubini, Nouriel and Jeffrey D. Sachs (1989), 'Political and Economic Determinants of Budget Deficits in the Industrial Democracies', *European Economic Review*, **33** (5), 903–38.

Rouwenhorst, K. Geert (1999), 'European Equity Markets and the EMU', *Financial Analysts' Journal*, **55** (3), 57–64.

Rowley, Charles K. (ed.) (1993a), *Public Choice Theory Volume I: Homo Economicus in the Political Market Place*, Brookfield: Edward Elgar Publishing.

Rowley, Charles K. (ed.) (1993b), *Public Choice Theory Volume III: The Separation of Powers and Constitutional Political Economy*, Brookfield: Edward Elgar Publishing.

Rowley, Charles K. (1984), 'The Relevance of the Median Voter Theorem', *Journal of Institutional and Theoretical Economics*, **140** (1), 104–26.

Rowley, Charles K., Willem Thorbecke and Richard E. Wagner (1995), *Trade Protection in the United States*, Brookfield, UT: Edward Elgar.

Sachs, Jeffrey D. and Xavier D. Sala-i-Martin (1989), 'Federal Fiscal Policy and Optimum Currency Areas', Paper presented at a conference on 'European Economic Integration: Towards 1992', Cambridge, MA: National Bureau of Economic Research.

Sala-i-Martin, Xavier and Jeffrey Sachs (1991), 'Fiscal Federalism and Optimum Currency Areas: Evidence for Europe from the United States', in Matthew B. Canzoneri, Vittorio Grilli and Paul R. Masson (1992), *Establishing a Central Bank: Issues in Europe and Lessons from the US*, New York: Cambridge University Press, 195–219.

Salin, Pascal (1984), *Currency Competition and Monetary Union*, Boston: Martinus Nijhoff Publishers.

Salmon, Trevor and William Nicoll (1997), *Building European Union: A Documentary History and Analysis*, New York: St. Martins Press.

Sandholtz, Wayne (1993), 'Monetary Bargains: The Treaty on EMU', in Alan W. Cafruny and Glenda G. Rosenthal (eds) (1993). *The State of the European Community: The Maastricht Debates and Beyond*, Boulder: Lynne Rienner Publishers, Inc., 125–42.

Schlaim, A. (1974), 'Prelude to Downfall: The British Offer of Union to France, June 1940', *Journal of Contemporary History*, **9** (3), 27–63.

Schmid, Gregory C. (1974), 'The Politics of Currency Stabilization: the French franc, 1926', *Journal of European Economic History*, **3** (2), 359–77.

Schneider, Friedrich (1996), 'The Design of a Minimal European Federal Union: Some Ideas Using the Public Choice Approach', in Jose Casas Pardo and Friedrich Schneider (eds) (1996), *Current Issues in Public Choice*, Cheltenham and Brookfield: Edward Elgar Publishing, 203–20.

Schneider, Friedrich (1985), 'Public Attitudes towards Economic Conditions and their Impact on Government Behavior', in Heinz Eulau and Michael S. Lewis-Beck (1985), *Economic Conditions and Electoral Outcomes: The United States and Western Europe*, New York: Agathon Press, 15–31.

Schneider, Friedrich and Alexander Wagner (1999), 'The Role of International Monetary Institutions after the EMU and after the Asian Crises: Some Preliminary Ideas Using Constitutional Economics', Universität Linz Working Paper 9903, Institut für Volkswirtschaftslehre.

Schneider, Ondrej (1999), 'Euro, Evropska Konvergence a Ceska Ekonomika', *Finance a Uver*, **49** (1). ('Euro, European Convergency and Czech Economy', with English summary.)

Schofield, Norman (1996), 'Rational Choice and Political Economy', in Jeffrey Friedman (ed.) (1996), *The Rational Choice Controversy: Economic Models of Politics Reconsidered*, New Haven: Yale University Press, 189–212.

Shapiro, Carl and Joseph E. Stiglitz (1984), 'Equilibrium Unemployment as a Worker Discipline Device', *American Economic Review*, **74** (3), 433–44.

Shepsle, Kenneth A. (1986a), 'The Positive Theory of Legislative Institutions: An Enrichment of Social Choice and Spatial Models', *Public Choice*, **50** (1–3), 135–78.

Shepsle, Kenneth A. (1986b), 'Institutional Equilibrium and Equilibrium Institutions', in Herbert F. Weisberg (ed.) (1986), *Political Science: The Science of Politics*, New York: Agathon Press

Shepsle, Kenneth A. (1975), 'Congressional Committee Assignments: An Optimization Model of Institutional Constraints', *Public Choice*, **22** (22), 55–78.

Shepsle, K.A. and Barry R. Weingast (1987), 'Why are Congressional Committees Powerful?' *American Political Science Review*, **81** (3), 929–45.

Siebert, Horst (1997), 'Labor Market Rigidities: At the Root of Unemployment in Europe', *Journal of Economic Perspectives*, **11** (3), 37–54.

Simmons, Beth A. (1994), *Who Adjusts? Domestic Sources of Foreign Economic Policy During the Interwar Years*, Princeton Studies in International History and Politics, Princeton: Princeton University Press.

Smith, Dale and Jürgen Wanke (1993), 'Completing the Single European Market: An Analysis of the Impact on the Member States', *American Journal of Political Science*, **37** (2), 529–54.

Smith, Rodney T. (1991), 'Canons of Public Choice Analysis of International Agreements', in Roland Vaubel and Thomas D. Willett (eds) (1991), *The Political Economy of International Organizations: A Public Choice Approach*, Boulder: Westview Press, 46–57.

Staufenbiehl, J.E. (1992), *Berufsplanung fuer den Management-Nachvuchs*, Staufenbiehl: Koeln.

Steunenberg, Bernard (1994), 'Decision Making under Different Institutional Arrangements: Legislation by the European Community', *Journal of Institutional and Theoretical Economics*, **150** (4), 642–69.

Stigler, George J. (1974), 'Free Riders and Collective Action: An Appendix to Theories of Economic Regulation', *Bell Journal of Economics and Management Science*, **5** (2), 359–65. Reprinted in Charles K. Rowley (ed.) (1993a), *Public Choice Theory Volume I: Homo Economicus in the Political Market Place*, Brookfield: Edward Elgar Publishing, 357–63.

Stirk, Peter M.R. (1996), *A History of European Integration since 1914*, London: Pinter.

Strakosch, Sir Henry (1937), 'The Money Tangle of the Postwar Period', in A.D. Gayer (ed.) (1937), *The Lessons of Monetary Experience: Essays in Honor of Irving Fisher*, London: George Allen and Unwin Ltd., 153–78.

Sugden, Robert (1981), 'The Tyranny of Majorities', *The Political Economy of Public Choice: An Introduction to Welfare Economics*, New York: Halstead Press, John Wiley & Sons, 176–203.

Taagepera, R. and M. Shughart (1989), *Seats and Votes: The Effects and Determinants of Electoral Systems*, New Haven: Yale University Press.

Taylor, John B. (1980), 'Aggregate Dynamics and Staggered Contracts', *Journal of Political Economy*, **88** (1), 1–23.

Taylor, John B. (1979), 'Staggered Wage Setting in a Macro Model', *American Economic Review*, **69** (2), 108–113.

Temperton, Paul (ed.) (1997), *The Euro*, Chichester: John Wiley & Sons.

Thygesen, Niels (1994), 'Towards Monetary Union in Europe – Reforms of the EMS in the Perspective of Monetary Union', in Christopher Johnson and Stefan Collignon (eds) (1994), *The Monetary Economics of Europe: Causes of the EMS Crisis*, Rutherford: Fairleigh Dickinson University Press.

Thygesen, Niels (1978), 'Inflation and Exchange Rates: Evidence and Policy Guidelines for the European Community', *Journal of International Economics*, **8** (2), 301–317.

Tollison, Robert D. (1982), 'Rent-seeking: A Survey', *Kyklos*, **35** (4), 575–602.

Toniolo, Gianni (1998), 'Europe's Golden Age, 1950–1973: Speculations from a Long-run Perspective', *Economic History Review*, **LI** (2), 252–67.

Torres, Francisco and Francesco Giavazzi (eds) (1993), *Adjustment and Growth in the European Monetary Union*, Cambridge: Cambridge University Press.

Tsebelils, George (1995), 'Decisionmaking Inside the European Parliament', in Barry Eichengreen, Jeffrey Frieden and Jürgen Von Hagen (eds) (1995), *Politics and Institutions in an Integrated Europe*, New York: Springer-Verlag, 42–64.

Tsoukalis, Loukas (1989), 'The Political Economy of the EMS', in Paolo Guerrieri and Pier Carlo Padoan (eds) (1989), *The Political Economy of European Integration: States, Markets and Institutions*, Savage: Barnes and Noble, 58–84.

Ulman, Lloyd, Barry Eichengreen and William T. Dickens (1993), *Labor and an Integrated Europe*, Washington: Brookings Institution.

Ungerer, Horst (1997), *A Concise History of European Monetary Integration: From EPU to EMU*, Westport: Quorum Books.

Van den Broeck, Julien (ed.) (1988), *Public Choice*, Dordrecht: Kluwer Academic Publishers.

Van Winden, Frans A.A.M. (1988), 'The Economic Theory of Political Decision Making: A Survey and Perspective', in Julien Van den Broeck (ed.) (1988), *Public Choice*, Dordrecht: Kluwer Academic Publishers, 9–42.

Vandermotten, Christian (1997), 'The Economic Framework of Migrations in Europe, 1960–90', in Hans H. Blotevogel and Anthony J. Fielding (eds) (1997), *People, Jobs and Mobility in the New Europe*, Chichester: Wiley, 51–68.

Vaubel, Roland (1994a), 'The Political Economy of Centralization and the European Community', *Public Choice*, **81** (1–2), 151–90.

Vaubel, Roland (1994b), 'The Public Choice Analysis of European Integration. A Survey', *European Journal of Political Economy*, **10** (1), 227–49.

Vaubel, Roland (1994c), 'The Breakdown of the ERM and the Future of EMU: Explanations, Predictions and Simulations from a Public Choice Perspective', in David Cobham (ed.) (1994), *European Monetary Upheavals*, Manchester: Manchester University Press, 32–60.

Vaubel, Roland (1991), 'A Public Choice View of International Organization', in Roland Vaubel and Thomas Willett (eds) (1991), *The Political Economy of International Organizations: A Public Choice Approach*, Boulder: Westview Press, 27–45.

Vaubel, Roland (1978), 'Real Exchange-rate Changes in the European Community: A New Approach to the Determination of Optimum Currency Areas', *Journal of International Economics*, **8** (2), 319–39.

Vaubel, Roland and Thomas D. Willett (eds) (1991), *The Political Economy of International Organizations: A Public Choice Approach*, Boulder: Westview Press.

Viñals, Jose (1996), 'European Monetary Integration: A Narrow or a Wide EMU?' *European Economic Review*, **40** (3–5), 1103–1109.

Viñals, Jose and Juan F. Jimeno (1998), 'Monetary Union and European Unemployment', in Jeffry Frieden, Daniel Gros and Erik Jones (eds) (1998), *The*

New Political Economy of EMU, Lanham: Rowman and Littlefield Publishers, Inc., 13–52.

Von Hagen, Jürgen (1994), 'Monetary Union and Monetary Policy: A Review of the German Monetary Union', in Pierre L. Siklos (ed.) (1994), *Varieties of Monetary Reforms: Lessons and Experiences on the Road to Monetary Union*, Boston: Kluwer Academic Publishers, 219–46.

Von Hagen, Jürgen (1993a), 'The Role of Budgeting Procedures for Improving the Fiscal Performance of the Member Countries of the EC', in Aaron Wildavsky and Eduardo Zapico-Goni (eds) (1993), *National Budgeting for Economic and Monetary Union*, Dordrecht: Martinus Nijhoff Publishers, 33–63.

Von Hagen, Jürgen (1993b), 'Monetary Union and Fiscal Union: A Perspective from Fiscal Federalism', in Paul R. Masson and Mark P. Taylor (eds) (1993a), *Policy Issues in the Operation of Currency Unions*, Cambridge: Cambridge University Press, 264–96.

Von Hagen, Jürgen and Barry Eichengreen (1996), 'Federalism, Fiscal Restraints, and European Monetary Union', *AEA Papers and Proceedings*, **86** (2), 134–46.

Von Hagen, Jürgen and Michele Fratianni (1992), *The European Monetary System and European Monetary Union*, Boulder: Westview Press.

Von Hagen, Jürgen and Michele Fratianni (1991), 'Policy Coordination in the EMU with Stochastic and Structural Asymmetries', in Clas Wihlborg, Michele Fratianni and Thomas D. Willett (eds) (1992), *Financial Regulation and Monetary Arrangements after 1992*, Amsterdam: North-Holland.

Von Hagen, Jürgen and George W. Hammond (1998), 'Regional Insurance Against Asymmetric Shocks: An Empirical Study for the European Community', *The Manchester School of Social and Economic Science*, **66** (3), 331–53.

Von Hagen, Jürgen and M.J.M. Neumann (1994), 'Real Exchange Rates Within and Between Currency Areas: How Far Away is EMU?', *Review of Business and Statistics*, **76** (2), 236–44.

Von Hagen, Jürgen and Ralph Süppel (1994), 'Central Bank Constitutions for Federal Monetary Unions', *European Economic Review*, **38** (3–4), 774–82.

Wagner, Richard E. (1986), 'Central Banking and the Fed: A Public Choice Perspective', *Cato Journal*, **6** (2), 519–38.

Wagner, Richard E. and James D. Gwartney (1988), 'Public Choice and Constitutional Order', in Richard E. Gwartney and Richard Wagner (eds) (1988), *Public Choice and Constitutional Economics*, Greenwich: JAI Press Inc., 29–56.

Wallace, William (1990), *The Transformation of Western Europe*, published for the Royal Institute of International Affairs, Chatham House Papers, William Wallace, Series editor, New York: Council on Foreign Relations Press.

Walters, Alan (1988), 'A Critical View of the EMS', *Cato Journal*, **8** (2), 503–56.

Weigall, David and Peter Stirk (eds) (1992), *The Origins and Development of the European Community*, Leicester: Leicester University Press.

Weingast, Barry R. (1981), 'Regulation, Reregulation, and Deregulation: The Political Foundations of Agency Clientele Relationships', *Law and Contemporary Problems*, **44** (1), 147–77.

Weingast, Barry R. and M.J. Moran (1983), 'Bureaucratic Discretion or Congressional Control: Regulatory Policy Making by the Federal Trade Commission', *Journal of Political Economy*, **91** (5), 765–800.

Westlake, Paul (1994), *A Modern Guide to the European Parliament*, London: Pinter Publishers.

Whiteley, Paul (1985), 'Perceptions of Economic Performance and Voting Behavior in the 1983 General Election in Britain', in Heinz Eulau and Michael S. Lewis-Beck (eds) (1985), *Economic Conditions and Electoral Outcomes: The United States and Western Europe*, New York: Agathon Press, 62–77.

Wildavsky, Aaron (1975), *Budgeting: A Comparative Theory of Budgeting Processes*, Boston: Little, Brown.

Willett, Thomas D. with Edward Keen (1990), 'Studying the Fed: Toward a Broader Public Choice Perspective', in Thomas Mayer (ed.) (1990), *The Political Economy of American Monetary Policy*, Cambridge: Cambridge University Press, 13–25.

Williams, David (1963), 'London and the 1931 Financial Crisis', in Mark Thomas (ed.) (1996), *The Disintegration of the World Economy Between the World Wars*, Vol. 2, Cheltenham, UK and Brookfield, VT: Elgar Reference Collection, Growth of the World Economy series, Vol. 4, 87–105.

Wilson, Thomas (1992a), 'The Scope of Monetary Policy', in Thomas Wilson (1992), *The Power 'To Coin' Money: The Exercise of Monetary Powers by the Congress*, Armonk: M.E. Sharpe, Inc., 13–38.

Wilson, Thomas (1992b), 'Creation and Control of the Federal Reserve System', in Thomas Wilson (1992), *The Power 'To Coin' Money: The Exercise of Monetary Power by the Congress*, Armonk: M.E. Sharpe, Inc., 179–206.

Wittman, Donald (1995), *The Myth of Democratic Failure: Why Political Institutions are Efficient*, Chicago: University of Chicago Press.

Wood, David M. and Birol A. Yesilada (1996), *The Emerging European Union*, New York: Longman Publishers.

Woolley, John T. (1984), *Monetary Politics: The Federal Reserve and the Politics of Monetary Policy*, Cambridge: Cambridge University Press.

Yellen, Janet L. (1984), 'Efficiency Wage Models of Unemployment', *American Economic Review*, **74** (2), 200–205.

Index